Gay Families and the Courts

Gay Families and the Courts

The Quest for Equal Rights

Susan Gluck Mezey

ROWMAN & LITTLEFIELD PUBLISHERS, INC.
Lanham • Boulder • New York • Toronto • Plymouth, UK

Published by Rowman & Littlefield Publishers, Inc.
A wholly owned subsidiary of The Rowman & Littlefield Publishing Group, Inc.
4501 Forbes Boulevard, Suite 200, Lanham, Maryland 20706
http://www.rowmanlittlefield.com

Estover Road, Plymouth PL6 7PY, United Kingdom

British Library Cataloguing in Publication Information Available

Library of Congress Cataloging-in-Publication Data

Mezey, Susan Gluck, 1944–
   Gay families and the courts : the quest for equal rights / Susan Gluck Mezey.
   p. cm.
   Includes bibliographical references and index.
   ISBN 978-0-7425-6218-9 (cloth : alk. paper) — ISBN 978-0-7425-6219-6
(pbk. : alk. paper) — ISBN 978-1-4422-0070-8 (electronic)
   1. Gay rights—United States. 2. Gays—Legal status, laws, etc.—United States.
I. Title.
   KF4754.5.M48 2009
   342.7308'7—dc22
   2009018024

∞ ™ The paper used in this publication meets the minimum requirements of
American National Standard for Information Sciences—Permanence of Paper for
Printed Library Materials, ANSI/NISO Z39.48-1992.

Printed in the United States of America

With love for Rebecca, Norah, Paul, and Benjamin

Contents

+

Acknowledgments

I was inspired to write this book when working on my previous book on gay rights litigation, *Queers in Court: Gay Rights Law and Public Policy*. Published in 2007, *Queers in Court* examined the effectiveness of litigation, primarily in the federal courts, in securing equality of rights for gay adults. As I was writing it, I became aware that there was another story to tell about equal rights—a story about gay families, that is, a family in which an adult or a child is gay. This realization, coupled with the knowledge that there is no book focusing on the litigation efforts of gay adults and gay children in the United States, propelled me to begin this project. *Gay Families and the Courts* thus builds on my earlier book by investigating the role of judicial decision making in gay rights policymaking affecting adults and children in gay families.

Sarah Skowronski, a Ph.D. student at Loyola University Chicago, provided me with able assistance in my work on this book. Sarah's excellent research skills in collecting judicial rulings; government documents, including state and federal statutes; and law review articles and tracking down myriad sources of information were critical to the timely completion of the book. Jay Barth made helpful suggestions after reading an earlier draft of the manuscript.

I want to thank Loyola University's Office of Research Services for its support in supplying research funds for this project. In particular, I want to recognize Tracy Foxworth for always being generous with her time in solving my grant-related problems and for her efficiency in processing the paperwork associated with the grant.

On a personal note, this book would not have been possible without my husband, Michael. In addition to helping me survive my first year as department chair by listening to my problems and offering sage advice, he stepped up to the plate by taking over most of the family responsibilities while I was engaged in the research and writing of this book. As always, I owe him more than these few words and this limited space can express. Finally, I want to thank my children: Jennifer Mezey and her husband, Jonathan Levy, and Jason Mezey and his wife, Deirdre McMahon. They make our lives worthwhile, fulfilling, and interesting—in no small measure by having given us four wonderful grandchildren: Rebecca, Norah, Paul, and Benjamin (listed in order of seniority).

In the short time since *Queers in Court* was published, public policy has shifted in a more positive direction for equality of rights for gays. I hope that these four little ones will grow up to a world in which sexual orientation no longer defines an individual's rights and opportunities.

+

Introduction

Despite their recent political and social advances, members of the lesbian, gay, bisexual, and transgender (LGBT) community in the United States continues to experience systematic discrimination in basic human rights, including choosing a marriage partner, adopting a child, and joining a private organization—solely because they are gay.[1] Borrowing from the tactics of earlier civil rights groups, the LGBT community turned to the courts to seek equal rights, adopting the familiar pattern of groups with little political clout at the ballot box. Lawsuits on behalf of gay plaintiffs date back to the early 1950s, but gay rights litigation began in earnest when public interest law groups, such as Lambda Legal Defense and Education Fund, the American Civil Liberties Union Lesbian and Gay Rights Project, the National Center for Lesbian Rights (previously known as the Lesbian Rights Project), and the Gay and Lesbian Advocates and Defenders, began to represent the gay community in the state and federal courts.

The suits were aimed at remedying the effects of discrimination in marriage and other legal family arrangements, laws criminalizing sodomy, and unequal opportunities in employment, especially in the military and government service. The litigation was often accompanied by the efforts of organizations, such as the Human Rights Campaign, Human Rights Watch, and the Gay Straight Alliances, that sought to further the aims of the litigation through other means, including assistance with preparation of amicus briefs as well as public education and lobbying, primarily at the state and local level.

Some of their legal challenges sought to achieve narrow goals for individual gay plaintiffs, such as relief from harassment in school; others

1

consisted of broad-based impact litigation, with plaintiffs seeking a declaration of rights under state or federal law, such as in marriage or adoption cases. No matter how broad or narrow the basis of the lawsuit, in requesting the courts to adjudicate their legal claims, gay rights litigants believed it likely that a victory in their case would further the goals of the movement by eliminating the role of sexual orientation in public policy decision making. In addition, they hoped that the litigation would focus society's attention on their unequal status and bring about equality of rights in other policy areas.

Gay rights have been litigated in almost every state in the union, chiefly as a result of lawsuits brought by gays as plaintiffs in civil cases in state and federal court. However, although much has been written about gay rights litigation in the United States, the scholarly literature has largely neglected to assess the role of courts in advancing equality for gay families, broadly defined as a family in which an adult or a child is gay. To remedy this gap in the literature, this study examines litigation in U.S. courts affecting the lives of such families over the past several decades. Specifically, the chapters in the book detail attempts by gay parents to formalize legal arrangements in the home with respect to custody, adoption, and marriage as well as litigation brought by or on behalf of gay youth to redress discriminatory treatment on the basis of sexual orientation in schools and private social organizations.[2] The primary aim of the analysis is to evaluate the role of judicial decision making in furthering the policy goals of the LGBT community and determine the degree to which the community's belief in litigation as a strategy to achieve social and political reform is justified.[3]

THE COURTS AS SOCIAL REFORMERS

In their efforts to combat the inequality that constrains their opportunities and choices, members of the LGBT community followed the example of the civil rights groups that preceded them by placing litigation in the front and center of their efforts to challenge laws and policies in which sexual orientation plays a significant role in structuring their legal, social, and political rights. By treading the same ground as racial minorities, women, and people with disabilities, the LGBT community demonstrated its belief that the courts are more effective venues in which to challenge inequality than popularly elected representative institutions (Andersen 2005; Pierceson 2005).

Cain (2000, 1) believes that gay rights groups are wise to pursue litigation, arguing that "courts understand and apply the notions of equality much more readily than legislatures or than members of society in general." She adds that "whether one believes that courts do in fact cause so-cial change, courts are nonetheless crucial in any battle over equal rights." Lewis and Edelson (2000, 198) agree, contending that "when Congress enters the debate and the forum grows more public, gay rights advocates generally lose."

This view of the courts is not universally shared—even among gay rights supporters. Some scholars argue, for example, that litigation is not only ineffective but also works to the detriment of the gay rights community by siphoning off vital resources or producing a backlash against efforts at achieving equality (see, for example, Klarman 2005; Rosenberg 2008). Brewer, Kaib, and O'Connor (2000) also criticize the courts for refusing to take cases brought by gay rights litigants, and Wald (2000) agrees that courts are likely not the best forum for gays to air their grievances.[4] But although the decision to rely on a rights-based litigation approach has had its detractors, for the most part, the gay community opted for the courts as the preferred arena for bringing about social and political change (for debates over the wisdom and efficacy of pursuing litigation to advance gay rights, see Button, Rienzo, and Wald 1997; Eskridge 2002; Feldblum 1997; Keck 2009; Rimmerman 2000; Stoddard 1997; Vaid 1995).[5] Ironically, as anti–gay rights activists have sought to halt or reverse the advance of equal rights, litigation has become a two-edged sword, with both sides adopting the rhetoric of rights in the judicial arena and claiming to occupy the moral high ground in the battle for support from the public.

The civil rights groups largely adopted a litigation strategy because of their assumptions that the courts would look more favorably on their attempts to bring about social reform; they hoped that the courts would champion their rights by playing a countermajoritarian role and overrid-ing policy decisions of the popularly elected institutions. The extent to which the courts have furthered the goals of social reform movements by adopting a countermajoritarian stance has been the subject of extensive debate—among a host of scholars and legal practitioners.

Some scholars argue—one of the earliest and most notable being Dahl (1957)—that the Supreme Court's rulings are not countermajoritarian but instead mirror society's prevailing views. Although Dahl's position has widespread support among scholars, others believe that the judi-ciary—especially the lower federal courts—have played a major role in protecting minority interests at the expense of the majority. For more than a half a century, scholars have debated the Dahl thesis—with the issue far from settled—and, not surprisingly, there is a voluminous literature on the subject (for some more recent examples of debate over judicial policymaking as an instrument of social reform, see Chermerinsky 2004; Friedman 1998; Hutchinson 2005; Kramer 2004; Mishler and Sheehan 1993; Tushnet 1999).

In a recent book on gay rights policymaking, Mucciaroni (2008) suggests the need for a more nuanced view of judicial decision making in gay rights policymaking, maintaining that the success of the gay community's litigation strategy is influenced by a number of factors, including, he argues, the type of issue and the type and level of court.[6]

EXPLAINING THE SUCCESS OF GAY RIGHTS LITIGATION

Although it is impossible to identify a single factor that accounts for the accomplishments of social movement litigation, this study focuses on three variables believed to be related to the success of gay rights litigation: the type of case, the type of court, and the court's role as a coordinate or subordinate policymaker (for discussion of the first two variables, see Mucciaroni 2008). Of the three, it is expected that the latter will be the most significant in explaining the outcome of the litigation on behalf of gay families.

The Type of Case

The cases are divided into four broad areas of litigation involving gay children and adults: parenting, same-sex relationships, schools, and exclusion from private organizations. Within these parameters, the analysis focuses on second-parent and joint adoptions, marriages and civil unions, harassment and freedom of expression in schools, and membership in the Boy Scouts of America. Because courts are more accustomed to and comfortable with adjudicating claims of civil and political equality than claims of social equality, it is expected that the gay rights litigants will be more successful in cases seeking to expand traditional political and civil rights (such as freedom from harassment and freedom of expression in schools) than in cases seeking to expand social rights (such as adoption, marriage, and participation in private organizations).

The Type of Court

The type of court variable is simply divided into state and federal courts. The conventional wisdom about rights-based litigation is that the federal court system, especially the U.S. Supreme Court, is the preferred arena for systemic reform efforts by litigants who feel themselves unable to influence policy in other policymaking institutions. Litigants chose the federal forum for their rights-based claims because the appointed-for-life judges were thought to be insulated from majoritarian political pressures.

Unlike the earlier civil rights struggles in which the federal judiciary played a leading role in expanding civil rights, more recently, perhaps because of the increasing conservatism of the federal courts, litigants have been turning to the state courts. Thus, subnational courts have become an increasingly significant locus of decision making for gay family members and recent evidence indicates that state court judges are more supportive of gay rights litigants than their federal counterparts (see Pinello 2003). Some possible reasons for this include the fact that many state supreme court judges, although not appointed for life, are appointed for long terms and therefore enjoy a good deal of the job security enjoyed by federal court judges.[7] Additionally, as Mucciaroni (2008, 40) notes, because the effects of the gay rights decisions—and the possible negative publicity that often follows—are limited to a narrower geographic scope, the state courts may be more receptive to the claims put forward by gay rights litigants. Thus, it is expected that gay rights litigation will be more successful in the state courts than in the federal courts.[8]

The Court as Policymaker

The third variable believed to play a role in the outcome of the litigation involving gay families is the extent to which courts act as coordinate or subordinate policymakers, that is, the degree to which they exert their influence over public policymaking by overriding laws and policies arising out of the legislative or the executive branches or through popular referenda. Because the success of gay rights litigation often turns on the court's willingness to protect minority rights at the expense of the majority, this variable exemplifies the debate over the court as a countermajoritarian decision maker. It is a measure of the court's exercise of its authority over representative institutions in the adjudication of rights-based demands and, of the three variables, is most likely to affect the outcome of the gay rights claims.

Whether engaged in constitutional or statutory review, courts often signal their position on policymaking by the method of analysis used to decide the case—before proceeding to the merits of the parties' arguments. In rights-based constitutional interpretation, the courts invariably begin by identifying the level of scrutiny with which they will review the challenged laws; the type of scrutiny in turn depends on their view of the nature of the litigants before them, that is, the class of people affected by the law. Applying a heightened level of scrutiny to such laws reflects the courts' concerns about the effects of majoritarian decision making on groups whose members are less able to challenge discriminatory policies through the electoral process.[9]

The U.S. Supreme Court initially formulated a two-tiered level of scrutiny for determining the constitutionality of laws challenged on equal protection and due process grounds. In cases involving a suspect classification (such as race and national origin) or a fundamental right (such as privacy), the Court created the concept of strict scrutiny, with the burden of proof on the state to show a compelling interest in the law and demonstrate that the means are necessarily related to the ends sought to be achieved and are narrowly tailored to those ends. Thus, it uses strict scrutiny for laws affecting a group (a "suspect class") that has a history of discrimination, possesses the immutable (innate) characteristics of a distinct group, and is politically powerless.

The use of strict scrutiny analysis stems in part from footnote 4 in *United States v. Carolene Products* (1938), in which Chief Justice Harlan Fiske Stone suggested the courts must look more closely at laws affecting "discrete and insular minorities" who lack adequate representation in the political branches to seek redress of their grievances. Since then, the scholarly literature has been replete with analyses of the Court's use of strict scrutiny; one of the earliest and perhaps the most famous is Gunther's (1972, 8) oft-quoted characterization of the Warren Court's "aggressive 'new' equal protection, as scrutiny that is 'strict' in theory and fatal in fact." Over the years, a mystique has surrounded the use of strict scrutiny, a mystique that springs up not only from the language and mind-set accompanying the Court's strict scrutiny analysis but also, and perhaps even more important, from a strong presumption against the constitutionality of the law under review.

Under the original two-tiered formulation, the Court applies minimal scrutiny to ordinary social or economic legislation, merely asking if there is a legitimate reason for the law and if the classification is rationally related to the goals the state seeks to achieve.[10] In *Craig v. Boren* (1976), the Court adopted an intermediate level of scrutiny in equal protection cases for laws involving sex-based classifications. To survive a constitutional challenge, a law reviewed under intermediate scrutiny, also known as heightened scrutiny, must further an important governmental objective and be substantially related to that objective. In 1996, in deciding the case of the Virginia Military Institute's exclusionary admissions policy (*United States v. Virginia* 1996), Justice Ruth Bader Ginsburg's majority opinion gave rise to speculation that the Court had moved to a higher level of scrutiny in sex-based classifications.[11]

Determining the appropriate level of scrutiny and the characterization of the class alleging discrimination is more than mere legal gymnastics; it precedes a decision on the merits of the case and is crucial to the outcome. A statute reviewed under minimal scrutiny almost always receives the Court's approval, and, conversely, statutes reviewed under strict scrutiny almost never do. Thus, in using strict or intermediate scrutiny, a reviewing court signals a greater willingness to substitute its view for the decision-making body that formulated the policy, in other words, act as a coordinate policymaker. Conversely, applying a lower level of scrutiny indicates the opposite, namely, that the court believes that principles of judicial restraint require it to defer to other policymaking institutions, typically, the legislative branch, in other words, act as a subordinate policymaker.

Most courts have refused to use any form of heightened scrutiny—either intermediate or strict—in cases involving gay rights claims.[12] Litigants in same-sex marriage cases, for example, variously argue that the right to marry is a fundamental right and that the classification based on sexual orientation deprives them of equal protection, each entitling them to heightened scrutiny. However, although courts recognize that the right to marry is a fundamental due process right, they stress that marrying someone of the same sex has never been recognized as fundamental.

Similarly, in determining the proper level of scrutiny in an equal protection claim, courts often treat gay litigants' claims of discrimination as illusory and question whether lesbians and gay men are sufficiently like existing protected classes to merit the same constitutional right of equal protection.[13] In declining to impose a higher level of scrutiny on laws affecting gays and lesbians, the courts specify any or all of the following reasons: that gays do not have inferior economic and political resources, they are not victims of historical discrimination, and sexual orientation is not immutable because it is a self-selected behavioral characteristic that can be altered at will. In the end, by declining to apply a higher level of scrutiny in cases brought by gay rights litigants, the courts invariably defer to the legislature and function as subordinate policymakers.

Although it has always attracted less attention than constitutional interpretation, over the past three decades, legal scholars have begun to look more closely at the role of the court in cases involving statutory construction. In his review of the history of statutory interpretation, Popkin (1999) identifies two perspectives of judicial decision making in statutory construction. The first is the outmoded "'airtight compartment' conception of legislating and judging [which] allocates the lawmaking function exclusively to the legislature, with judges accorded only a minimal role" (2). A more realistic—and more nuanced—view, which he calls "ordinary judging" enables and indeed expects judges to "play a discretionary lawmaking role" in which the courts "contribute to good government" (2).

When asked to construe the meaning of statutes, courts are always mindful of their constitutional duty to defer to the written statutory command in the legislation or be vulnerable to charges that they are interfering with democratic policymaking and usurping the legislature's prerogative to make policy. In practice, at one extreme, are the judges who follow the "airtight compartment" model of decision making and adhere strictly to the legislative intent as stated in the statutory text and perhaps evidenced by legislative history. At the other end of the continuum are the judges who follow the "discretionary lawmaker role" and attempt to effectuate the perceived purpose behind the legislation and adjudicate in the interstices of the statute, especially when they are faced with conflicting or insufficient evidence of legislative intent.

Thus, whether engaged in statutory interpretation or constitutional adjudication in the gay rights cases, judges must frequently decide the extent to which they view themselves as subordinate or coordinate policymakers and rule accordingly. It is expected that gay rights claims are less likely to succeed when judges believe that their judicial roles require that they adopt a subordinate policymaking role. Conversely, when judges are more willing to act as coordinate policymakers and construe laws and constitutional text more broadly, the gay rights claim is more likely to be successful.

NOTES

1. The terminology in the discourse of social reform movements is always important, and the gay rights movement is no exception; additionally, the significance of labels for the actors involved in the movement cannot be overestimated. More recently, the term "LGBT" has been expanded to "LGBTQ" to include the term "queer." Although "queer" has been and continues to be used by outsiders as a derogatory term, it has been incorporated by gay rights advocates to encompass the broadest reaches of the gay community. Whatever term is used, as with other social movements, its members often stress different priorities and urge different strategies for achieving social reform; it would be foolish to deny the diversity of interests, based on characteristics such as sex, race, education, and socioeconomic status, among members of the LGBTQ community. But no matter how divergent the interests of these individuals within the movement may be, outsiders generally perceive them as an undifferentiated whole, without recognizing distinctions among them in the policymaking process. Without intending to minimize these distinctions or oversimplify a complex set of attitudes and behaviors, this study refers to "lesbians" and "gay men" as well as bisexual and transsexual persons when appropriate to denote members of the gay community. At times, for stylistic reasons, it uses a shorthand approach and refers only to "gays" to encompasses both men and women. When referring to nonadults who identify themselves as gay, the favored terms are "gay teens," "gay youth," and "gay youngsters." Also, without meaning to suggest that the motives and tactics of the individuals within these broad groupings do not vary, the study refers to "gay rights advocates" or "gay rights activists" to signify the individuals and groups who favor equality for members of the gay community, broadly defined, and "anti–gay rights advocates" or "anti–gay rights activists" to depict those who, regardless of their motivations, oppose some or all of these goals. Finally, despite the fact that the term "homosexual" is disfavored today because of its clinical connotation and its earlier iden-

tification as a pathology, it is necessary to use it for historical accuracy, especially when discussing judicial opinions and legislation because of the frequency with which public policymakers still use it to refer to gays.

2. The opinions relating to gay families were collected through searches of Westlaw and Lexis-Nexis, the two primary legal databases. This method yielded all relevant opinions published in bound reporters as well as rulings reported only to Westlaw or Lexis-Nexis. Additional cases were incorporated into the analysis when cited in the principal opinions, thus helping to ensure that the study includes all relevant cases within each policy area.

3. Although the LGBT community is not a monolithic whole, and it places different priorities on specific policies, such as the importance of gay marriage, it is certainly plausible to assume that all gays and lesbians, no matter what their priorities, support policy outcomes that expand equal rights and opportunities for members of gay families.

4. As with all social movements, the LGBT community does not rely exclusively on litigation but combines a number of strategies, including grassroots organization, public education, lobbying, and political mobilization.

5. In reviewing the development of same-sex marriage policy, Keck (2009), for example, questions those who view litigation as ineffective. His analysis underscores the complexity of social policy reform and the difficulty of determining the influence of one policymaker, such as the courts, in the process.

6. Mucciaroni (2008) also identifies the extent to which "Americans perceive their demands as threatening" (30) as another variable that determines the success with which gay rights advocates achieve their policy goals. There has been extensive public opinion polling on the issues he writes about: the armed services' "don't ask, don't tell" policy, hate crimes legislation, privacy, marriage, and, to some extent, adoption (see also Mezey 2007). Except for marriage—and to a much lesser extent, adoption—the topics in this study are much less visible to the public, and consequently there are no public opinion polls to measure the extent to which equal rights in these areas are viewed as threats.

7. For information about the length of justices' terms in state supreme courts, see, for example, Alaska Judicial Appointment Process (2008), Hawaii State Judiciary (2008), Massachusetts Court System (2006), New Jersey Court System (2008), State of Connecticut (2006), Supreme Court of California (2007), and Vermont Supreme Court (2008).

8. By grounding their claims in state constitutional law, litigants are able to avoid review by the federal courts and escape the possibility of reversal by the U.S. Supreme Court, as the high court refrains from reviewing state court decisions made on the basis of state constitutional claims.

9. Although the state and federal courts may not always agree on the level of scrutiny they apply, they all seem to accept the concept of differential levels of review based on different classes of litigants.

10. However, even when applying minimal scrutiny, the Court may examine the purpose and effect of the law more carefully if it appears to be based on dislike of or a desire to harm a targeted group.

11. If so, there is no indication that the courts have demonstrated a willingness to extend it to classifications based on sexual orientation.

12. Although there are a number of concurring and dissenting opinions in which federal circuit court judges have argued for the use of strict scrutiny in classifications based on sexual orientation, their views did not prevail in the court as a whole. On the state level, the California Supreme Court's decision in *In re Marriage Cases* (2008) applied a higher level of scrutiny to the marriage restrictions, but most state courts have not done so in gay rights claims. If they have used heightened scrutiny, they have done so because they viewed the law as implicating a fundamental right or constituting a sex-based classification.

13. Gerstmann (2003, 9) accuses the Court of using the terms "suspect class" and "suspect classification" inconsistently in a way that disadvantages gays. On the one hand, it refuses to accord gays the status of a suspect class (and apply strict scrutiny to laws affecting them) on the grounds that they are not politically powerless. However, he maintains, when whites complain that they have been subjected to discrimination as a result of an affirmative action program, the Court applies strict scrutiny because race is a suspect classification.

1

Parenting

It is estimated that there are as many as 10 million children living in families with lesbian, gay, or bisexual single parents or couples; moreover, studies have found that one-third of lesbian households and one-fifth of gay male households have children living in them (Mallon 2006).

There are numerous legal obstacles placed in the path of gay parents. Together, disputes over custody, visitation, foster care, and adoption comprise the greatest single area of litigation for gays and lesbians or their domestic partners and are "the most important in terms of impact on the greatest number of gay litigants" (Pinello 2003, 17; Moss 2005, 618 n153).[1] However, as in most family law cases, these disputes are often resolved at the state trial or appellate court levels.[2] Thus, despite the importance of these issues, the litigation serves little or no precedential value (see Connolly 1996; Skidmore 2000–2001). Not surprisingly, with little controlling judicial authority to yield more uniform results, the rulings in such cases are inconsistent, with the rights of gay and lesbian parents varying from state to state—and even from county to county (Lambda Legal 2007a).[3] And because such matters are governed by state statute and decided in the state courts, they are largely outside the purview of the federal courts and federal constitutional principles, further diminishing the likelihood of uniform policies and practices.[4]

THE SUPREME COURT AND FAMILY RELATIONSHIPS

With family law issues almost entirely within the jurisdiction of the state courts and governed by state statute and state constitutional principles, the U.S. Supreme Court has played only a minor role in adjudicating matters of family relationships, confining itself primarily to recognizing a liberty interest in family autonomy that is protected by the Fourteenth Amendment's due process clause. But, although the cases show that the Court has broadened the reach of the due process clause beyond the confines of the traditional nuclear family, it has also been reluctant to offer full constitutional protection to nontraditional family arrangements.

Meyer v. Nebraska (1923) provided one of the first opportunities for the Court to extend constitutional protection to families by recognizing a right of family autonomy. The case arose out of an unlikely Nebraska law that prohibited teaching a foreign language to children below the eighth grade. Without precisely defining the parameters of the liberty protected by the Fourteenth Amendment, the Supreme Court broadly stated that the amendment's due process clause extends to "the right of the individual to contract, to engage in any of the common occupations of life, to acquire useful knowledge, to marry, establish a home and bring up children, to worship God according to the dictates of his own conscience, and generally to enjoy those privileges long recognized at common law as essential to the orderly pursuit of happiness by free men" (626). The Court reversed the conviction of the teacher found guilty of violating the law.

Moore v. City of East Cleveland (1977) broadened the definition of family by recognizing the right of a nontraditional family, consisting of a grandmother, a son, and her two grandsons, to live together despite a city zoning ordinance that restricted residents to a single family unit. The grandsons were first cousins; John had come to live with the family when his mother died. The city claimed that John's presence violated the ordinance and ordered Mrs. Moore to evict him. When she refused, she was criminally charged and convicted.

Underscoring the importance of the family in U.S. society, the Court stated that "ours is by no means a tradition limited to respect for the bonds uniting the members of the nuclear family. . . . Even if conditions of modern society have brought about a decline in extended family households, they have not erased the accumulated wisdom of civilization, gained over the centuries and honored throughout our history, that supports a larger conception of the family." It ended by saying that "recent census reports bear out the importance of family patterns other than the prototypical nuclear family" (504–5).[5]

In *Smith v. Organization of Foster Families for Equality and Reform* (1977), decided the same year as *Moore*, a unanimous Court made it clear that although it was prepared to extend the definition of family beyond the nuclear family, it drew the line at biological relationships, refusing to equate foster families with biological or "genetic" families.[6]

In *Smith*, foster parents challenged a New York law allowing the state to remove foster children from their homes prior to a hearing. They argued that the Fourteenth Amendment entitled them to a due process hearing before removal.

The high court acknowledged the problems associated with efforts to define a family, citing *Meyer* and *Moore*, among others. Although for the most part, it said, a family is defined by "biology," it is also linked by emotional ties and "biological relationships are not [the] exclusive determination of the existence of a family" (*Smith* 1977, 843). The Court recognized the deep family feelings between foster parents and children, especially those living in the foster home all their lives, saying that "no one would seriously dispute that a deeply loving and interdependent relationship between an adult and a child in his or her care may exist even in the absence of blood relationship" (844).[7] But, it noted, unlike a biological family, a foster family is entirely a creature of the state law and, as such, has limited expectations of permanency. Although foster parents may claim a degree of due process protection, it does not rise to the level of the natural family's. The Court concluded that the state's procedural safeguards in the law satisfy due process.

The Supreme Court again privileged the traditional family structure in *Michael H. v. Gerald D.* (1989) by upholding a challenged California law. In 1981, Carol D. gave birth to Victoria D. while she was married to Gerald D., who was listed as the child's father on her birth certificate. Michael H., claiming he was Victoria's natural father, provided a blood test showing a 98.07 percent probability that he was her father. For the first three years of her life, Victoria (and her mother) intermittently lived with Michael, Gerald, and another man. During the time Carol lived with Michael, she acknowledged that he was Victoria's father; Victoria called him "Daddy."

In 1982, when Carol refused to allow him to visit Victoria, Michael filed a paternity action in a California superior court, seeking visitation rights. The court appointed a guardian ad litem for Victoria who argued that the child should be able to maintain a relationship with both Gerald and Michael. The court, however, granted Gerald's motion for summary judgment, ruling that California law created a conclusive presumption that a child born to a married woman living with her husband, barring impotence or sterility, is the child of the marriage; the court also denied Michael visitation rights.[8]

The appellate court affirmed, ruling that the state's interest in the marital family and the child's welfare took precedence over Michael or Victoria's due process rights (*Michael H.* 1989). The court upheld the state's authority to determine that it would not be in Victoria's best interests to be declared Michael's child.

In a plurality opinion, four justices of the U.S. Supreme Court voted to uphold the lower courts, agreeing that the state law reflected the legislature's desire to preserve the family unit.[9] Although the Court seemed amenable to extending the definition of family to a "household of unmarried parents and their children," it was unwilling to extend it to include both a natural father and a stepfather (*Michael H.* 1989, 124 n3).

In this case, because Victoria lived in a two-parent household (Gerald and Carol had reunited), the Court was unwilling to disturb their family. The ruling also rejected the guardian ad litem's suggestion that Victoria maintain relationships with both men, citing the familiar argument against a substantive due process claim that such an approach did not derive from the history or traditions of the nation.[10] The Court did not explain under what conditions a biological father such as Michael would be able to rebut the presumption of paternity the law accorded to the woman's husband. But in this case, the plurality believed that Michael's liberty interest did not outweigh the state's aim of protecting the family unit. Although he concurred with the ruling, Justice John Paul Stevens wrote separately to express concern that the plurality opinion seemed to flatly deny constitutional protection to all "unconventional family settings" (133). He believed that there might be circumstances in which Michael's liberty interest might prevail over the state's interest. Four justices dissented, arguing that Michael's relationship with Victoria created a liberty interest the state must recognize.

More recently, in *Troxel v. Granville* (2000), the high court ruled on the constitutionality of a Washington State law that broadly permitted "'[a]ny person' to petition a superior court for visitation rights 'at any time,' and authorizes that court to grant such visitation rights whenever 'visitation may serve the best interest of the child'" (60).

The case arose when Tommie Granville sought to limit Jenifer and Gary Troxel's access to her two daughters; the Troxels were the parents of their deceased father, Brad.[11] The state supreme court struck the statute, finding that the U.S. Constitution prohibited the broad grant of visitation privileges to a third party without a showing of harm to the child.

In a fractured ruling, the high court affirmed the state court. Justice Sandra Day O'Connor delivered a plurality opinion in which she acknowledged that "demographic changes of the past century make it difficult to speak of an average American family," citing census data to show the increasing number of "single-parent households" in the nation. "Understandably," she added, "in these single-parent households, persons outside the nuclear family are called upon with increasing frequency to assist in the everyday tasks of child rearing" (63–4). Nevertheless, despite acknowledging the expanding definition of the family, the Court still maintained that parents retained a fundamental right to make crucial decisions regarding their children's welfare.

Because the law implicated a fundamental right, O'Connor applied heightened scrutiny and found the Washington statute unconstitutional because it gave judges total discretion over the grandparent's visitation, even allowing them to disregard the parent's wishes. Although the Court struck the Washington law because it gave insufficient consideration to the parent's interests, the ruling offered little guidance to lower courts on how to resolve custody and visitation disputes that may arise between lesbians and their ex-partners (see Polikoff 2001).[12]

LESBIAN AND GAY PARENTS

The U.S. Bureau of the Census (2003) reported that in 2000 there were 5.5 million unmarried couples living in the United States. Most, nearly 5 million (4.9) were opposite-sex couples, with 594,000 (about one in nine) consisting of same-sex partners; of the latter, there were 301,000 male partner households and 293,000 female partner households.

Although precise data do not exist, the National Center for Lesbian Rights (NCLR) (2004) estimated that by 2004, there were more than 6 million children being raised in families headed by same-sex parents in the United States. A later American Civil Liberties Union (ACLU) Foundation report (Cooper and Cates 2006), suggests that from 1 million to 9 million children (1 to 2 percent of all children) have at least one gay parent. Moreover, there is evidence that about one-third of lesbian couples and one-fifth of gay male couples are raising children (Rosato 2006, 74).

There is a virtual avalanche of writing on gay parenting, especially on lesbian mothers as singles or part of a couple. Some of it is sympathetic; largely based on personal accounts of gay parents raising children, they present positive images of the lives of the children and the adults (see, for example, Benkov 1994; Mallon 2006; Pollack and Vaughn 1987). These portrayals, frequently aimed at refuting the charges that children are harmed by growing up in gay households, typically characterize accounts of inappropriate gender identity, emotional turmoil, child molestation, and stigmatization as biased and stereotypical.

The scholarly research on the effects of lesbian and gay parenting on children is voluminous as well, appearing in a variety of disciplines, including, psychology, sociology, psychiatry, and medicine.[13] Although there is some dispute, the consensus among most scholars is that there are few if any differences among children raised by gay and non-gay parents (see Patterson 1995; for more recent data, see Bradley 2007; Connolly 2001; Hong 2003).

A number of scholars have aggregated data from diverse sources, examining the totality of research related to gay parenting (see Ball 2003). One such meta-analysis, released in a 2002 report by the Committee on Psychosocial Aspects of Child and Family Health of the America Academy of Pediatrics, reviewed dozens of studies of children living with gay and lesbian parents. The report found that despite problems with the samples, "the weight of evidence gathered during several decades using diverse samples and methodologies is persuasive in demonstrating that there is no systematic difference between gay and non-gay parents in emotional health, parenting skills, and attitudes toward parenting. No data have pointed to any risk to children as a result of growing up in a family with 1 or more gay parents" (Perrin 2002, 343).

Similarly, in their compilation of the extant research, Meezan and Rauch (2005) review more than fifty studies as well as literature reviews and conference papers spanning more than thirty years. After demonstrating the methodological deficiencies of earlier research on the subject, they conclude that the more recent—and more rigorous—analyses support the claim that children are not negatively affected by growing up with gay parents.

Largely as a result of this research, beginning in 1975, organizations such as the Child Welfare League of America, American Psychological Association, National Association of Social Workers, American Psychiatric Association, American Academy of Pediatrics, American Psychoanalytic Association, American Bar Association, American Medical Association, American Academy of Family Physicians, and American Academy of Child and Adolescent Psychiatry have issued policy statements stressing that sexual orientation should not be a variable in determining the best interests of the child in making adoption, custody, and foster care decisions (Mallon 2006; see Polikoff 1990).[14]

In a much-cited study, however, despite their claim of sympathy with gay and lesbian parenting, Stacey and Biblarz (2001, 176) contend that the sexual orientation of the parent should be considered in such decisions. Based on their meta-analysis, they maintain that "there is suggestive evidence and good reason to believe that contemporary children and young adults with lesbian or gay parents do differ in modest and interesting ways from children with heterosexual parents." In their view, "most of these differences, however, are not causal, but are indirect effects of parental gender or selection effects associated with heterosexist social conditions under which lesbigay-parent families currently live." However, they also find that "the evidence, while scanty and under-analyzed, hints that parental sexual orientation is positively associated with the possibility that children will be more likely to attain a similar orientation" (2001, 77–8).[15]

But, although Stacey and Biblarz's analysis of the effect of gay parenting is tentative and nuanced, it provided ammunition for antagonists of gay and lesbian adoption (see Ball 2003). Wardle (2003), for example, who has written extensively on the subject, asserts that "we do not know the full effects of homosexual parenting on children. The evidence," he warns, "is just beginning to be assembled, and it is far from reliable or complete. It may take another 20–25 years before substantial, reliable data about the effects of homosexual parenting on children is available" (376).[16] Specifically, citing Stacey and Biblarz, Wardle challenges the validity of data showing little or no effects on children raised by gay parents. He points to the inherent bias and faulty methodology in the "no difference" studies, their failure to ask the right questions about the risks involved and the longitudinal effects on the children, and their undervaluing the known beneficial effects of a two-gender household (Wardle 2004, 2005).

On the other hand, while conceding the validity of some of Wardle's criticisms, Bradley (2007, 139–40) charges that the studies cited by him suffer from the same deficiencies as the studies he criticizes. Rosato (2006, 74) sums up the argument cogently, saying that

> although it is undisputed that children deserve protection from harm, there is no evidence that raising them in this [with gay parents] environment actually negatively affects them. The optimistic "Pollyanna" version of this argument is that children are somehow better with married, heterosexual parents—even though this assumption has yet to be proven. In the end, neither the pessimistic nor optimistic reasons should prevail. The abstract possibility of harm or benefit simply cannot outweigh the realities of existing children who have the same emotional and economic needs as other children. These real needs should trump abstract ones, and the law should reflect such a prioritization of values.

CUSTODY AND VISITATION

The early legal battles over custody and visitation typically arose as divorced gay parents became entangled in disputes with their ex-spouses. Until fairly recently, most of the children involved in such disputes had been born into heterosexual relationships, with the courts typically entering the fray when the non-gay parent sought to deny custody or visitation to the gay parent (see Connolly 1996, 2001; see also Benkov 1994; Susoeff 1985).

In ruling on such matters, judges typically relied on a "per se" rule, denying custody or visitation to gays and lesbians for the following reasons: their "alleged mental instability," the "influence they allegedly assert[ed] on the sexual development of their children," or "the peer harassment and sexual exploitation which courts expect[ed] their children to experience."

And when they could not base their rulings on the "direct harm" that might befall them, they cited "'community standards' of morality" to justify the outcome (Susoeff 1985, 858–9; for the myriad reasons cited by judges in custody disputes involving gay parents, see Polikoff 1990).[17] In at least one case, the judge was so determined to prevent the lesbian mother from retaining custody of her child that he granted custody to the father, who had murdered a former wife over a visitation dispute (Connolly 2001, 113).

In part, because of the judge's belief that gay parents transmit their sexual orientation to their children, most gay parents did not do well in custody disputes. The reasons stem from factors such as "the presumed criminality of gay parents in sodomy law states, the stigma that the children of gay parents sometimes face, or simply a judge's distaste for gay sexuality" (Larsen 2004, 53–4; see Duran-Aydintug and Causey 2001; Robson 2001; see also Benkov 1994). Often, when considering the effect of a parent's homosexuality in a custody or visitation dispute, the court would simply rule that, as a matter of law, homosexuality rendered a parent unfit; at best, it would treat it as a rebuttable presumption of unfitness (see Robson 2001).[18]

Bottoms v. Bottoms (1995), a much-litigated case in the Virginia courts, demonstrates the use of the per se rule in a custody dispute where the mother's sexuality was the determining factor. This legal battle, initiated by the grandmother's suit for custody of two-year-old Tyler, drew national media attention, with both sides viewing it as a test case (Swisher and Cook 2001). The lower courts ruled for the grandmother, holding that she had demonstrated that the child's mother was unfit. The court of appeals, however, reversed, ruling that lesbianism was not per se proof of unfitness and that the plaintiff had not proved her case by clear and convincing evidence as required. The state supreme court reversed. Although it held that her lesbianism did not make Sharon Bottoms per se unfit, it did not make clear what legal effect it should play in a determination of her unfitness. At the same time, in discussing the child's relationship with his mother and the mother's fitness for child rearing, the court noted that it would not "overlook the mother's relationship with Wade [her partner], and the environment in which the child would be raised if custody is awarded the mother" (108).

THE NEXUS TEST

Adopting a more enlightened approach that gradually became the majority position, courts eventually began to apply a "nexus" standard in which a parent's conduct, including homosexuality, played a role in a custody determination only if evidence was presented that it adversely affected the child.

The nexus test, allowing a judge wide latitude in determining the best interests of the child, is now standard in most courts. The nexus standard is illustrated in *Doe v. Doe* (1983), an early Massachusetts case involving a dispute over custody of the couple's son, David, following his parents' divorce. The couple had decided on joint custody arrangements, but after the wife's lesbian partner moved in with her, the husband sued for divorce and for sole custody; the wife sought joint custody. The husband argued that joint custody was inappropriate and pointed to her "deviant lifestyle" as the reason he should get full custody (295). The court disagreed, citing Massachusetts case law that a parent's lifestyle alone is not dispositive in a custody determination. In this case, the judge determined there was no evidence that David was adversely affected by his mother's homosexuality or her lifestyle arrangements and awarded joint custody to the parents (for other cases applying the nexus test, see National Center for Lesbian Rights 2000).[19]

In contrast to this approach, Alabama Supreme Court Judge Roy Moore's "special" concurring opinion in *Ex parte H.H.* (2002), in which the court found insufficient changed circumstances to transfer custody to the children's lesbian mother, indicates that not all courts follow the nexus approach. He said, "I write specially to state that the homosexual conduct of a parent—conduct involving a sexual relationship between two persons of the same gender—creates a strong presumption of unfitness that alone is sufficient justification for denying that parent custody of his or her own children or prohibiting the adoption of the children of others." Continuing in this vein, he stated that

> homosexual conduct is, and has been, considered abhorrent, immoral, detestable, a crime against nature, and a violation of the laws of nature and of nature's God upon which this Nation and our laws are predicated. Such conduct violates both the criminal and civil laws of this State and is destructive to a basic building block of society—the family. The law of Alabama is not only clear in its condemning such conduct, but the courts of this State have consistently held that exposing a child to such behavior has a destructive and seriously detrimental effect on the children. It is an inherent evil against which children must be protected. (26)

More recently, in *McGriff v. McGriff* (2004), the Idaho Supreme Court explained that "sexual orientation, in and of itself, cannot be the basis for awarding or removing custody; only when the parent's sexual orientation is shown to cause harm to the child, such that the child's best interests are not served, should sexual orientation be a factor in determining custody" (117).[20]

The state supreme court upheld the lower court decision, satisfied that the magistrate judge's decision to modify custody in favor of the wife and award her primary physical and legal custody (instead of the shared custody they had since the divorce) was not based on the father's homosexuality. Instead, the court found that the decision had been appropriately based on the father's seemingly inordinate degree of anger at the children's mother as well as his refusal to communicate with her and attend counseling with her.

Moss (2005), however, argues that despite the court's disclaimer, the ruling "suggest[s] a continuing disfavor for gay and lesbian parents that will outlive facially discriminatory rulings. His [the father's] loss demonstrates that there are more steps to be taken, not only to rid the legal system of overt partiality to heterosexuals, but also to supply the legal system with tools to curb the pernicious bias that has been embedded in the law through years of socially acceptable denigration of gays and lesbians" (594). In her view, the supreme court should have been more skeptical of the judge's avowal that the ruling was not based on the father's homosexuality and subjected the court's analysis to stricter scrutiny. More generally, she argues that even the more enlightened approach exemplified in the nexus test presupposes that a parent's homosexuality is harmful to the child and requires the gay parent to rebut the presumption.

Infanti (2007, 205–7) agrees, citing cases in Utah, Missouri, and Alabama in which custody decisions are based not on the per se rule but rather on judicial animosity to gay parents and the assumptions that heterosexual parents are more fit.[21]

When Maxwell and Donner (2006) examined the application of the nexus test in recent cases more closely, they found that many rulings continue to reflect disapproval of gay parents. When courts decide custody or visitation cases in favor of a gay parent, they do so only when the parent is "discreet," that is, "does not share a bedroom with his or her partner, or the parent does not express affection toward his or her partner or hug or kiss the partner in the presence of the children. On the other hand," their study showed that "parents who explain their sexual orientation to their children, kiss or hug their partners in front of their children, or attend gay-related events or activities, have a difficult time maintaining custody or having unrestricted visitation with their children." They conclude that the more recent cases continue to reflect "the earlier cases' assumption that parents harm their children by being open about their sexual orientation" (307).

ADOPTION

"The definition of parentage—and with it the determination of which adults receive legal recognition in children's lives—has become the most contentious issue in family law. Not only are jurisdictions irreconcilably divided in their approach to parentage, decisions under settled law in a given county may not necessarily come out the same way" (Carbone 2005, 1295). In the 1970s, the most common legal dispute involving a gay parent was the battle over custody of the child following divorce. Since then, as increasing numbers of gays and lesbians have become more open about their sexuality and their desire to raise children, other issues have emerged, with perhaps the most important and far reaching involving adoption (Benkov 1994, 13; see Pollack and Vaughn 1987).

Although the facts of the adoption case may vary, often depending on whether the child has a biological relationship with at least one of the adults, the prospective parent's sexual orientation inevitably plays a role in the adoption process.[22] However, perhaps because adoption by gays has received less media attention than same-sex marriage, it sometimes results in more favorable outcomes for members of the gay and lesbian community and their children (see Schacter 2000).[23] Unlike same-sex marriage, which is explicitly forbidden in most states by law, constitutional amendment, or both, most state laws are silent on adoption by same-sex individuals or couples.

In the face of this silence, the courts have assumed the dominant role in structuring family relationships between gay men and women and the children they seek to adopt (Fairchild and Hayward 1998, ch. 6). Although many courts acknowledge that the world is changing and that the definition of family is not static, this recognition is not always apparent in their rulings. Holtzman (2006, 8) argues that there are "two notions of family [in today's society]: first, that which is traditionally recognized and typically still enshrined in our religious and legal institutions and second, that which is popularly recognized and based on the lived experiences of people." The complexity of the issues that have arisen over the legality of adoption by same-sex couples is exacerbated by this dual perception of the family.[24]

The first adoption law was enacted by the Massachusetts legislature in 1851 (Lauretta 2003, 180). Since then, all states have legislatively established adoption procedures, and as creatures of the legislature, adoption schemes are entirely governed by state statute. Thus, in ruling on adoption petitions, the courts are conscious of their duty to defer to the written statutory command. Over the past several decades, in the absence of specific provisions permitting gays to adopt, adoption cases have generally fallen into two categories, with the parent's qualification often the least important determinant of the success of the petition. The first approach is characterized by judges liberally construing the state adoption law to allow the adoption, arguing that they are merely effectuating the legislative intent of furthering the "best interests of the child." In the second, judges block the adoption, principally by applying narrow rules of statutory construction and adhering to the plain language of the text. Relying on strict principles of statutory interpretation, the judges in the latter cases proclaim their reluctance to overstep their judicial bounds and usurp the legislature's authority (see Connolly 2001).

When sympathetic judges favor a broad interpretation of adoption and custody laws, they are often assailed as "judicial activists" who trample on legislative prerogatives.[25] Some, such as Wardle (2005), decry this approach as "judicial legislation," arguing that the courts are "creating new policy initiatives and moving a body of law in a new policy direction entirely." In his view, those courts that have refused to read the law broadly "have declined to create new policy but have specifically deferred to the legislature, and that exemplifies proper judicial respect for the separation of powers as well as the appropriate judicial self-restraint" (533).

ADOPTION POLICIES AFFECTING GAY PARENTS

Eleven states (California, Colorado, Connecticut, Illinois, Indiana, Massachusetts, New Jersey, New Mexico, New York, Oregon, and Vermont), in addition to the District of Columbia, explicitly allow joint adoptions statewide. They have also been permitted in a few jurisdictions in Nevada and New Hampshire, but most states are silent on the legality of joint adoptions by same-sex couples (Human Rights Campaign 2007a).

A 1977 Florida law, the only law of its kind in the nation, flatly prohibits all adoptions by homosexuals, whether singly or in couples.[26] Most states allow qualified single or married adults to adopt, but, although they allow single gays to adopt, some states exclude gay and lesbian couples (Duncan 2003; National Center for Lesbian Rights 2004).

In 1987, New Hampshire enacted a law preventing gays from adopting or becoming foster parents; it also required applicants to sign a form stating that there were no gay adults in the house.[27] The bill's sponsor, Mildred Ingram, said that the law was "designed to protect children from an 'unnatural role model' and 'possible sexual abuse'" (*New York Times* October 4, 1987). Indeed, the debate over the bill revolved around charges that gays were child molesters and would transmit the AIDS virus (*Associated Press* December 31, 1998).

The legislature had enacted the law following the state supreme court's ruling earlier that year. Unlike the federal courts, state supreme courts are often permitted to issue advisory opinions about the constitutionality of proposed legislation. In this case, the state House of Representatives asked the court to render an opinion on the constitutionality of House Bill (HB) 70, as modified by HB 32, a bill that would bar gays from adopting, becoming foster parents, or operating licensed day care centers.[28] In *In re*

Opinion of the Justices (1987), the court assessed the impact of the law, first proposed in 1985, on state and federal constitutional guarantees of due process, equal protection, right to privacy, and freedom of association.

Speaking for the majority, with future U.S. Supreme Court Justice David Souter joining in the opinion, Justice David Brock noted that, according to House Resolution 32, the law was intended to provide "appropriate role models" and "positive nurturing" for adoptive children as well as "eliminate the 'social and psychological complexities' which living in a homosexual environment could produce in such children" (24).

Applying minimal scrutiny because homosexuality was neither a suspect classification nor a fundamental right, nor was there a fundamental right to adopt (or become a foster parent or day care operator), the court asked whether excluding all homosexuals from these three areas was rationally related to the state's purpose. It concluded that because parents are the primary socialization agents, it was reasonable for the legislature to believe that gay parents might influence the child's sexual orientation and thus the state could prevent them adopting or serving as foster parents. But because the relationship between day care operators and their charges was attenuated, the role model theory did not apply, and the law would deprive them of equal protection under both the state and the federal constitution.

The court also found no due process violations—under either the state or the federal constitution in the adoption and foster care provisions. Individuals are entitled to due process only when liberty or property interests are threatened, and clearly neither adoption nor foster care can be considered as liberty or property. Similarly, citing *Bowers v. Hardwick* (1986), it ruled that because the right to privacy did not extend to the right to engage in homosexual conduct, no (state or federal) privacy interests were at stake.[29] Finally, because freedom of association is dependent on the right to privacy, the court found that denying gays the right to adopt and serve as foster care parents does not deprive them of the right to associate freely.

Justice William Batchelder argued in dissent that the proposed law was discriminatory because it was based on a rebuttable presumption that all gays were unfit. He charged that according to the law, "financial stability is irrelevant; the strength to discipline a child firmly yet patiently is irrelevant; and the courage and love to be generous and loyal, the intelligence to provide proper education, and similar attributes are all irrelevant" (28). He criticized the legislature's reliance on stereotypes and bias in determining that gay parents have fewer parenting skills or will harm their children. Indeed, he noted, the available evidence shows that the opposite is true and that the law has sufficient safeguards to determine the qualifications of a prospective adoptive or foster parent regardless of sexual orientation.

In 1998, amid mounting opposition to the law, House Democratic Whip Raymond Buckley sponsored a bill to repeal it. He said that it had sprung up during "the height of the season of hate," adding that he perceived it not as a gay rights matter but as an opportunity to improve the lives of New Hampshire children in need of foster care and adoptive homes (*Associated Press* December 31, 1998). Buckley later said that the law "was enacted despite the lack of a single complaint, not one shred of evidence [nor] . . . a single incident of concern" (*Associated Press* January 20, 1999). In March 1999, the New Hampshire lower house voted 226 to 130 to repeal the ban on adoption and voted 233 to 123 to repeal the prohibition against gay foster parents (*Union Leader* March 19, 1999). A month later, the state senate voted 18 to 6 in favor, and the bill was signed into law by Democratic Governor Jeannne Shaheen on May 3, 1999; the repeal took effect two months later (*Associated Press* May 4, 1999).

At the time New Hampshire repealed its law, Florida was the only state to prohibit adoption by single gays. However, since then, more than a dozen states, including South Carolina in 1997, Alabama and Michigan in 1998, and Indiana, Texas, Oklahoma, and Arkansas in 1999, attempted measures to ban gay adoptions.[30] For a variety of reasons, a decade later, these have not succeeded (LeBlanc 2006, 99–100; see also Hong 2003).[31]

In 2000, Mississippi enacted a law prohibiting adoption by same-sex couples.[32] And a 2000 Utah law bars adoption by a person living in a relationship not recognized as legal in the state.[33] The Utah law did not affect single persons, that is, noncohabiting adults, whatever their sexual orientation, from adopting or serving as foster parents.[34]

A few years later, in September 2004, the attorney general of Michigan declared that the state would no longer allow adoptions by gays or recognize such adoptions legalized in other states (Chen 2005, 172).

In 2004, the Oklahoma legislature also enacted a law preventing recognition of an out-of-state adoption by a same-sex couple.[35] The impetus behind the Oklahoma law was a lawsuit by two gay men, residents of Washington, who adopted a child born in Oklahoma. They asked the state to issue a new birth certificate for her, but the Oklahoma State Department of Health (OSDH) produced a certificate that only listed one of them as the parent. When they challenged that decision, the state agency sought the state attorney general's opinion who responded that out-of-state adoptions are valid and must be recognized in Oklahoma. The OSDH issued a new birth certificate, listing both men as parents. One month later, the Oklahoma legislature enacted the adoption amendment (see Ball 2007).

The law did not survive a legal challenge, however. In *Finstuen v. Edmondson* (2006), an Oklahoma federal district court granted summary judgment to the plaintiffs, holding that by refusing to recognize a sister court's grant of a final adoption order, the Oklahoma adoption code amendment violated the full faith and credit clause of the U.S. Constitution as well as the families' equal protection and substantive due process rights (see Chen 2005; Spector 2005).[36] On appeal, the Tenth Circuit affirmed the lower court in *Finstuen v. Crutcher* (2007).[37]

Several years later, the Arkansas Family Council Action Committee, a conservative religious group, spearheaded an effort to place Initiative 1 on the 2008 ballot. Approved in a vote of 57 to 43 percent, it banned all unmarried couples from adopting or serving as foster parents (CNN.com January 12, 2009).[38] Although the ban—which took effect on January 1, 2009—is written in gender-neutral language, applying to both same-sex and opposite-sex couples, its primary goal was to prevent gay couples from serving in this capacity (*Chicago Tribune* December 3, 2008). Democratic Governor Mike Beebe and former President Bill Clinton publicly opposed the measure, citing the lack of available foster care families in the state. Also critical of the new law, which applies to state and private adoption agencies, the president of the Arkansas chapter of the National Association of Social Workers asked, "We don't have enough quality homes as it is, and now we're going to place more restrictions?" (*Chicago Tribune* December 3, 2008).

The Family Council was also largely responsible for the anti-gay marriage amendment passed earlier (*Seattle Post-Intelligencer* November 6, 2008; *Arkansas News Bureau* 2008). One of its leaders indicated that the group had led the drive to ban adoptions by gay parents in part because of its belief "that the best place for a child to grow up is in a stable home with a married mother and father." But, he said, more broadly, it was also aimed at "blunting a gay agenda that we see at work in other states with regard to marriage and adoption issues" (*New York Times* November 9, 2008).

FOSTER CARE

Recognizing the desperate need for foster parents, most states have not imposed restrictions on foster parenting in gay homes.[39] But despite their pressing needs, some states preclude gays from serving as foster parents by making heterosexuality a basis for eligibility; at times they do this through child welfare agency regulations and at other times by legislative decree. Indeed, despite Connecticut's laws against discrimination on the basis of sexual orientation, the law allows state adoption agencies to consider the sexual orientation of the prospective adoptive or foster care parent when placing a child.[40] Other states have considered but not enacted such restrictive legislation. But by 2005, only three states—California, New Jersey, and Massachusetts—had legislated against discrimination on the basis of sexual orientation in foster care placement (Berman and Leichter 2005, 676).[41]

For more than a decade, the courts have played an important role in reining in some of these restrictive policies and practices. Both Florida and New Hampshire once prohibited gays from becoming foster parents. A state court struck the Florida law in 1994, and the New Hampshire law was repealed by the legislature in 1999 (see Polikoff 1997).

In 1999, the Arkansas Child Welfare Agency Review Board promulgated a regulation prohibiting any person from becoming a "foster parent if any adult member of that person's household is a homosexual." As a result of litigation in *Howard v. Child Welfare Agency Review Board* (2004), an Arkansas circuit court struck the regulation as an unconstitutional violation of the separation of powers doctrine. Two years later, the Arkansas Supreme Court unanimously affirmed the lower court in *Department of Human Services and Child Welfare Agency Review Board v. Howard* (2006). The state high court held that the testimony presented at trial indicates "that the driving force behind adoption of the regulation was not to promote the health, safety, and welfare of foster children, but [was] rather based upon the Board's views of morality and its bias against homosexuals" (8). Republican Governor Mike Huckabee deplored the opinion. "I'm very disappointed," he said, "that the court seems more interested in what's good for gay couples than what's good for children needing foster care" (*Washington Post* July 1, 2006).

The next year, in March 2007, the Arkansas House Judiciary Committee rejected a bill that would have banned gay people and most unmarried heterosexual couples living together from adopting or serving as foster parents (*Stephens Media Group* March 13, 2007). But a year later, the anti-gay forces achieved their goal when state voters approved a law on the 2008 ballot barring all unmarried couples from adopting or fostering children.[42]

A few states—Nebraska, Utah, and Arkansas—also explicitly restrict gays from serving as foster parents.[43] In 1995, claiming that she was filling a gap in the regulations, the Nebraska director of social services instructed her agency to refrain from placing children "in the homes of persons who identify themselves as homosexuals" or "where unrelated, unmarried adults reside together" (*Omaha World-Herald* January 26, 1995). Utah's ban on adoption by nonmarried "cohabiting" persons extends to foster care as well, preventing an agency from placing a child "either temporarily or permanently, with any individual or individuals who do not qualify for adoptive placement pursuant" to state law.

Attempts to restrict gays from becoming foster parents have not always succeeded. In 2005, the Texas legislature considered a bill that had first been introduced in 1999. As originally proposed, it would have prevented the Department of Family and Protective Services from "placing a child in foster care" with a "homosexual or bisexual" person and required the state to remove children currently in such foster care homes. Because of opposition in the state senate, the bill was watered down to simply give married couples priority in placements and to remove the retroactivity provision (*Austin American-Statesman* May 27, 2005). As discussed in a Lambda Legal (2005) press release, "Proposed AntiGay Texas Law Is Unconstitutional," the sponsor of the bill, Republican Representative Robert Talton was quoted as saying that "we do not believe that homosexuals or bisexuals should be raising our children. Some of us believe they would be better off in orphanages than in a homosexual or bisexual household because that's a learned behavior." Had the bill passed in its original version, it would have made Texas the only state in the nation at the time to ban foster parenting by gay, lesbian, and bisexual adults by statute. Despite his efforts, however, the bill did not pass.

JOINT AND SECOND-PARENT ADOPTIONS

According to *Black's Law Dictionary* (2004), a second-parent adoption is "an adoption by an unmarried cohabiting partner of a child's legal parent, not involving the termination of a legal parent's rights; especially, an adoption in which a lesbian, gay man, or unmarried heterosexual person adopts his or her partner's biological or adoptive child."[44]

The NCLR formulated the model of the second-parent adoption in the early 1980s (National Center for Lesbian Rights 2003; see Croteau 2004).[45] Since then, there have been an increasing number of gays seeking second-parent adoptions.[46] Indeed, the majority of reported cases in which the adoption is approved arise in second-parent, also known as coparenting, situations (Gardner 2004, 24).[47] In most second-parent adoptions, the prospective adoptive parent must overcome the barrier presented by the termination, or cutoff, requirement in which the existing legal parent's rights must be terminated.[48]

All states allow an exception for adoption by a child's stepparent, waiving the termination requirement for the child's legal parent (see Starr 1998).[49] In case after case, gay petitioners analogized the second-parent adoption to the stepparent adoption, arguing that the courts should waive the statutory termination requirement; in legal terms, they asked the courts to judicially expand on the stepparent exception by applying it to the second parent.[50]

The plaintiffs contended that the legislature had created the stepparent exception because it recognized that changing patterns of family life (divorce, blended families, stepparents) required a new model. They argued that in a stepparent adoption, the legislature had properly envisioned that the custodial parent would remain part of the child's life and that to terminate that parent's relationship with the child would be absurd. Similarly, it would be absurd to terminate the legal parent's relationship with the child in a second-parent adoption. Moreover, they emphasized, expert testimony showed that it was in the child's best interests to formalize the coparenting relationship by a second-parent adoption.

In ruling in such second-parent adoption cases, courts asked whether strict statutory construction justifies denying a second-parent adoption petition, especially when the child will remain with at least one gay parent no matter what the outcome of the ruling. Persuaded by these arguments, some courts have determined that it is more sensible to allow the adoption than deny it. Others, citing their fealty to their judicial role, refused to deviate from the text of the statute that allowed the court to waive the cutoff provision in the case of stepparents only.[51]

The laws governing second-parent adoptions in the United States more resemble a patchwork quilt of statutes and case law; they vary by state and sometimes even within states in the absence of controlling appellate opinion. There are nine states (California, Connecticut, Illinois, Indiana, Massachusetts, New Jersey, New York, Pennsylvania, and Vermont), as well as the District of Columbia, that allow second-parent adoptions on a statewide basis—by appellate court ruling or statute.[52]

Second-parent adoptions have also been allowed in selected cities or counties in fifteen states (Alabama, Alaska, Delaware, Hawaii, Iowa, Louisiana, Maryland, Minnesota, Nevada, New Hampshire, New Mexico, Oregon, Rhode Island, Texas, and Washington). Four states (Colorado, Nebraska, Ohio, and Wisconsin) do not allow second-parent adoptions statewide because of appellate court rulings. Twenty-two states (Arizona, Arkansas, Florida, Georgia, Idaho, Kansas, Kentucky, Maine, Michigan, Mississippi, Missouri, Montana, North Carolina, North Dakota, Oklahoma, South Carolina, South Dakota, Tennessee, Utah, Virginia, West Virginia, and Wyoming) have no published rulings on same-sex second-parent adoptions. Some states (Florida, Mississippi, Utah, and, most recently, Arkansas) restrict adoptions by single gays or same-sex couples by statute (Human Rights Campaign 2007b; National Gay and Lesbian Task Force 2007; see Colorado 2005; Cooper and Cates 2006; Croteau 2004; National Center for Lesbian Rights 2004).[53]

The difficulty in second-parent adoptions arises from the termination requirement when the courts are reluctant to stray beyond the confines of the statutory text and apply the stepparent exception.[54] The second-parent adoption succeeds when courts analogize the second parent to a stepparent, reasoning that in both cases the child's existing legal parent would continue to live with the child and termination was unnecessary, unwise, and not in the child's best interests (see Storrow 2006).

State adoption codes, first appearing in the mid-nineteenth century, have been amended numerous times to reflect changing circumstances of single parent adoption, divorce, and open adoption. However, for the most part, laws have not reflected the growing trend of gay parenting. The litigants must often begin by convincing the courts of the underlying aim of adoption laws: to promote the best interests of the child. However, the bulk of the cases do not focus on the best interests of the child or even the controversy over homosexuality and the implications of gay adoption for same-sex marriage laws; rather, they revolve around the mundane rules of statutory interpretation, which, as even the courts concede, often thwarts the best interests of the child.[55]

In one of the earliest cases to construe a state statute arising out of a petition for second-parent adoption, *In re Adoption of B.L.V.B.* (1993), the Vermont Supreme Court focused its attention on the stepparent exception. The lower court, reading the law narrowly, refused to apply the exception and rejected the adoption petition filed by Jane and Deborah. Jane was the biological mother of the children; Deborah, her partner, sought to adopt them through a second-parent adoption. The adoption was endorsed by all the professionals implicated in the case, yet the judge did not reach the question of whether the adoption was in the children's best interests. He denied the petition on the grounds that it was inconsistent with Vermont's adoption law. Reading the relevant provisions of the law together, he held that a birth parent such as Jane could retain her parental rights to the children only if part of a married couple. Unable, of course, to marry, Jane and Deborah together were ineligible to become the children's legal parents.

The state high court noted that to carry out its role of effectuating the legislative intent of advancing the interests of the children, it must apply common sense and construe the law broadly. In creating the stepparent exception, the court held, the legislature had assumed that except in the case of a stepparent, an adopted child would no longer be living with the natural parent. It would be absurd for the legislature to seek to terminate the rights of a parent who continued to live with and be responsible for raising the child. To think otherwise "would," said the court, "produce the unreasonable and irrational result of defeating adoptions that are otherwise indisputably in the best interests of children" (1274). In 1995, the Vermont legislature enacted a law allowing second-parent adoptions without terminating the existing parent's rights.[56]

Shortly after *Adoption of B.L.V.B.* was decided, the Massachusetts Supreme Judicial Court (the state supreme court) ruled on another second-parent adoption in *Adoption of Tammy* (1993). Here, a lesbian couple, Susan and Helen, jointly filed to adopt Susan's biological daughter. The probate judge found that each was functioning well as Tammy's parent and that it was in her best interests to approve the petition. To secure the judgment, as permitted by state law, this judge reported the matter to the appellate court, and the supreme court promptly transferred the case to its docket on its own motion.

Reviewing the financial and legal benefits of the joint adoption (including the right to inherit from Helen's substantial trust fund), the court summarized the voluminous testimony about their flourishing family life, including a report from the state department of social services, and concluded that there was unanimous agreement that the joint adoption was clearly in Tammy's best interests. The court then looked to the issue of whether an adoption would run afoul of state law. The initial question was whether state law precluded adoption by an unmarried couple. Massachusetts law allows any person to petition the probate court to adopt a younger unrelated person.[57] It therefore does not permit or deny another from joining in the petition; moreover, there is a long-standing legislative rule that allows a plural to be substituted for a singular noun unless the outcome would be contrary to the legislative intent. In this case, according to the court, "where the legislative intent is to promote the best interests of the child . . . and the adoption of a child by two unmarried persons accomplishes that goal, construing the term 'person' as 'persons' clearly enhances, rather than defeats, the purpose of the statute" (319).[58]

In *Matter of Adoption of Evan* (1992), a New York trial court judge forthrightly discussed the sexual orientation of the prospective adoptive parents. The case arose when Diane F. sought to adopt Evan, her partner's six-year-old biological child; the child's mother, Valerie C., consented to the adoption but objected to the termination of her parental rights as the law required. Judge Eve Preminger appointed a number of professionals, including New York University law professor Sylvia Law as guardian ad litem, to investigate the family, and all testified that the adoption was in Evan's best interests. Preminger noted the well-functioning family structure in which Evan lived, emphasizing that being adopted by Diane would provide him with additional emotional stability and financial benefits as well as continued ties to Diane if the partners separated.

Questioning whether the state adoption law prevented the adoption, she analogized Diane and Valerie's relationship to marriage.[59] In her view, the two had "a marital relationship at its nurturing supportive best and they seek second-parent adoption for the same reasons of stability and recognition as any couple might" (847). The difficulty was the termination (or cutoff) provision, a required part of the adoption proceedings, but Preminger found that complying with the law would lead to the "absurd outcome" of terminating Valerie's rights (848). She believed that the state did not require adopted children to sever all ties with their natural parents or siblings and that it would be unjust to force the child to choose between her two parents. She concluded that the only sensible solution was to allow the second-parent adoption when it is in the child's best interests.

Preminger also took judicial notice that New York law prohibits discrimination in adoptions on the basis of sexual orientation; moreover, she cited the voluminous social science evidence on children growing up with gay parents as well as numerous trial court rulings allowing second-parent or joint adoptions by lesbian couples.[60] She ended by lauding the successful family life this couple had established for their children, saying that "there is no reason in law, logic or social philosophy to obstruct such a favorable situation" (852).

Three years later, *Matter of Adoption of Evan* became the law of the state when the New York State Court of Appeals (the state's highest court) ruled in *Matter of Jacob* (1995). In this consolidated case, one lesbian couple and one opposite-sex couple each sought to adopt a child. As in *Matter of Adoption of Evan*, the court was asked to determine whether the cutoff provision was mandatory. The lower court found that the adoption was likely in the children's best interests yet dismissed the petitions, holding that the law required an adopting couple to be married. On appeal, the high court interpreted the New York law, noting that although statutes must be strictly construed, the court must effectuate the legislature's intent and purpose. Thus, a court must be mindful that adoption is a means of furthering the child's best interests in finding a good home. Clearly, adoption would further these interests in allowing the individuals who already serve in that capacity to become their legal parents. The court also noted that it would promote their "emotional security" as well as allow them to gain access to rights of inheritance and their parents' life and health insurance as well as Social Security benefits (399).

Turning to the language and legislative history of the much-amended adoption law, originally enacted in 1873, the New York high court determined that the individuals (as "an adult unmarried person") in each of these cases were fully authorized to adopt under the statute; moreover, there was nothing in the law to prevent an unmarried person adopting a child in conjunction with another unmarried person. Over time, the legislature had expanded the types of individuals considered eligible to adopt; this was consistent, the court noted, with an ever-expanding definition of family. Therefore, the court concluded that "a reading of section 110 granting appellants, as unmarried second parents, standing to adopt is therefore consistent with the words of the statute as well as the spirit behind the modern-day amendments: encouraging the adoption of as many children as possible regardless of the sexual orientation or marital status of the individuals seeking to adopt them" (401).

The court also noted that §117, which freed the biological parent from responsibility for the child and precluded inheriting from the child, was concerned primarily with property rights and inheritance. However, later amendments, as well as other statutes regulating the adoption process, led to ambiguity about the necessity of terminating the natural parent's rights, which "should be resolved in the children's favor" (403). Therefore, the court refused to require the biological parent to relinquish her rights in the child in the second-parent adoption. This is not a situation, it emphasized, in which a child or the adoptive family must be protected from a natural parent; in this situation, as in so-called open adoptions, applying §117 strictly would have the unfortunate effect of negating a child's opportunity to live with two parents. And although the state may not have foreseen such family arrangements, the court should not use §117, which was designed to protect adoptive families from outside interference from birth parents and others, to prevent second-parent adoptions such as these.

This is particularly true, said the court, in the case of this couple, for no matter what the outcome of the legal action, Jacob's mother could simply evade the consequences of the law by marrying the prospective adoptive father. But because of the state's restrictions on same-sex marriage, Dana's mother would be unable to marry, and thus Dana would lose the legal advantages to be gained from the adoption solely on the grounds of her mother's sexual orientation. In a final note, the court added that there was no justification for disapproving the adoption on grounds of homosexuality or single-parent status, as there were no restrictions on adoptions by homosexuals or by single persons. Indeed, state law prohibited adoption agencies from disfavoring individuals solely on the basis of their homosexuality.[61]

Three justices dissented, arguing that the court exceeded its judicial authority in interpreting the state law so expansively. Basing their objections solely on grounds of statutory interpretation and denying that sexual orientation or discrimination played a role in their views, the justices stressed that the petitioners simply failed to conform to state adoption law. They emphasized that adoption was solely a matter of legislative design and that, unlike common law decision making, a court cannot circumvent the plain language of the law under the guise of judicial interpretation or effectuation of a beneficial purpose.

In re M.M.D. (1995), decided in the Court of Appeals of the District of Columbia, also illustrates another legal hurdle confronting a gay couple's effort to adopt. In 1991, after reaching agreement with the birth mother, Bruce M., a gay man living in the District of Columbia, adopted two-year-old Hillary. Two years later, with Bruce's consent, Mark, his partner of seven years, petitioned to adopt the child also. Despite her determination that both men singly or together were suitable parents for Hillary, the trial court judge denied the petition, citing the district's adoption law enacted by Congress in 1954. Reasoning that adoption was derived from a statute rather than common law, the judge emphasized that the law must be strictly construed according to the legislative intent and that there was no indication that Congress intended to allow more than one person to adopt at any one time.

Speaking for a divided appellate court, Judge John Ferren noted that the case raised two questions: first, whether more than one person can adopt, and, second, if so, whether that may include an unmarried couple.[62] He characterized the District of Columbia's adoption law, requiring a spouse to join in adopting the other's child but not specifying arrangements between unmarried couples, as ambiguous.[63] Ferren rejected the lower court's strict construction of the district's adoption law, pointing out that it was common practice in many jurisdictions to interpret adoption statutes liberally to effectuate their intended purpose. After a lengthy analysis of the rules of statutory construction, he concluded that the law permitted more than one adult to adopt a child. He then turned to the more difficult question of whether the two adults must be married to each other.[64]

The court noted that Congress had not limited adoptions to married couples as it easily could have done; moreover, there was sufficient uncertainty in the law to believe that Congress had not intended to do so. Indeed, an exhaustive review of the legislative history yielded no further indication of its intent. Thus, Ferren concluded that standard rules of statutory construction left the meaning of the law unclear and that the court must determine its intent and purpose, keeping its focus on the best interests of the child. The judge outlined the various advantages to Hillary if both men legally adopted her: joint financial responsibility; employment benefits, including health insurance, workers' compensation, and Social Security benefits; authority in medical situations, inheritance rights; and legal guardianship if Bruce died. Surveying these manifold benefits, the court concluded that it should concentrate on Hillary's well-being rather than on what "the particular family format shall look like" (859).

The final question to be resolved is whether the stepparent exception was applicable under these circumstances. Again, the lower court had interpreted the statute narrowly, giving the term "spouse" its literal meaning. The appellate court disagreed, citing case law from Massachusetts and Vermont. Applying a "commonsense interpretation," the court ruled that the stepparent exception should be extended to this same-sex couple, thus avoiding the need to terminate the existing parent's rights.

Judge John Steadman's brief dissent objected to the court's expansive reading of the statute. In his view, it expressly limited joint adoptions to married couples unless the husband or wife was the child's biological parent. "Where the legislature has concretely provided for a regimen for joint adoption," he said, "I think that an expansion of the regimen to other forms of joint adoption should only be made by the legislature" (866).

An Illinois case, *In re Petition of K.M.* (1995), decided shortly after the District of Columbia court handed down its ruling in *M.M.D.*, dealt with adoption under slightly different circumstances. In this consolidated case, two lesbian couples filed adoption petitions under the Illinois Adoption Act. In one, K.M. and D.M. jointly sought to adopt K.M.'s biological daughter. In the other, K.L. and M.M. petitioned jointly to adopt K.L.'s natural and adopted sons. Although each couple was awarded temporary custody of the children, the circuit court ruled that they lacked standing to file the adoption petitions.

Judge Gino DiVito, delivering the opinion of the appellate court, began by noting that the couple's sexual orientation was entirely irrelevant to the outcome of the case, with the decision resting entirely on the court's interpretation of the statute. He stressed that the court's only task was to divine and effectuate the legislature's intent; in this case, the legislature made it clear that Illinois law must be liberally construed to achieve the legislative purpose.[65] Conceding that there was no commonly accepted definition of liberal construction, he noted that it generally permitted a court to go beyond the text to give effect to the purpose of the law. Moreover, because the act also explicitly states that its primary concern is to further the best interests of the child, a court should not interpret it to limit opportunities for adoption. The court ended by noting that the Massachusetts and Vermont supreme courts as well as several lower state courts had reached the same conclusion. However, because the lower court judge had explicitly reserved the question of whether the adoption was in the children's best interests, the appellate court remanded the case to allow the court to determine the issue.

A New Jersey appellate court ruled on a similar issue in *Matter of Adoption of Two Children by H.N.R.* (1995), in which H.N.R. sought to adopt her partner's biological daughters with their mother's consent. The lower court judge, declaring that the law did not permit adoptions by same-sex partners, denied the petition. The appellate court confined itself to the question of whether the adoption, if approved, necessitated the termination of the mother's parental rights.

The appellate court reviewed the circumstances of the children's (twins) birth and their family life, noting that the adoption would not alter their emotional ties to the children, but would cement their legal responsibilities and afford the children access to health insurance and other benefits. It also quoted extensively from the adoption agency's enthusiastic endorsement of the adoption.

Because the law explicitly provided for liberal construction to achieve the children's best interests, the court noted that under New Jersey law, single people of any sexual orientation are eligible to adopt.[66] More difficult was the provision requiring that, except in the case of a stepparent, the right of the natural parent must be terminated following the adoption. The court concluded, however, that "the stepparent exception to the natural parent's termination of rights should not be read literally and restrictively when to do so would defeat the best interests of the children and would produce a wholly absurd and untenable result" (538).

The dissent simply stated that the majority view contravened the statute, which requires the natural parent's right to be terminated following an adoption. It argued that the majority's interpretation of the law exceeded its authority by usurping the legislature's responsibility to change the law.

More recently, the Pennsylvania Supreme Court ruled on second-parent adoptions in *In re Adoption of R.B.F and R.C.F.* (2002), a consolidated case based on the termination requirement in the state's adoption law.[67]

Supreme Court Justice Stephan Zappala delivered the unanimous opinion of the court. He began by noting that as a creature of the legislature, adoption law must be strictly interpreted; however, he was persuaded that a 1982 amendment permitted a court to circumvent the mandatory language of the act "for good cause shown" (1201). The couples had argued that the lower court judges should have allowed them to present evidence that would constitute "cause." The court agreed that they must be given an opportunity to explain why they could not conform to the act and that the court must be permitted to waive the termination requirement if a waiver is in the child's best interests. It hastened to add that it was "not creating a judicial exception to the requirements of the Adoption Act, but rather [was] applying the plain meaning of the terms employed by the Legislature" (1202).

Zappala ended by pointing out that the law does not prohibit unmarried partners from adopting. According to the lower court's interpretation of the law, adoptions would be permitted only in situations in which neither prospective adoptive parent was related to the child (and prohibited in situations in which one of the couple was legally related to the child). Such a result, the supreme court believed, was "absurd" (1202). He added that although the legal parents could have relinquished their parental rights and then filed a joint adoption petition with their partner, this "convoluted procedure," although legal, "would serve no valid purpose" (1203).[68]

A year later, in *In re Adoption of M.M.G.C.* (2003), a case of first impression in Indiana, the appellate court ruled on whether the law allowed a second-parent adoption without terminating the existing adoptive mother's parental rights. Shannon had adopted three children through international adoption agencies. With her consent and the endorsement of the county child welfare service agency, her partner, Amber, then sought to adopt them in a second-parent adoption.

The trial court judge had ruled that Amber could adopt the children only if she were Shannon's legal relative, and the only way to accomplish that was to marry her, an impossibility under Indiana law. Thus, because they were not related, Amber's motion could be granted only if the court terminated Shannon's rights, which was, of course, unacceptable to the couple.

Speaking for the appellate court, Judge Sanford Brook rejected the trial court judge's legal conclusions. First, he found that the law did not require Shannon and Amber to be married; it required only that Amber be a legal resident of the state.[69] Second, he held that the adoptive parent's rights do not have to be terminated in a second-parent adoption. The law mandated only termination of the biological parent's rights except in the case of a stepparent adoption.

Because the statute did not clearly permit two unmarried adults to adopt, the court looked to common law, emphasizing that the essence of common law decision making is flexibility, consistent with the goals of public policy. "We cannot close our eyes to the legal and social needs of our society, and this Court should not hesitate to alter, amend, or abrogate the common law when society's needs so dictate" (270). The state has an overriding interest in furthering the best interests of the child, and there was little doubt in the court's mind that "allowing a second parent to share legal responsibility for the financial, spiritual, educational, and emotional well-being of the child in a stable, supportive, and nurturing environment can only be in the best interest of that child" (270–1).

A year later, in *In re Adoption of K.S.P.* (2004), another Indiana appellate court ruling addressed the question left open in *Adoption of M.M.G.C.* In this case, a lesbian petitioned to adopt her partner's two biological children, in part to place them under her health insurance policy.[70] Although the child welfare agency approved the proposed adoption, the lower court denied the petition, citing the termination provision.

On appeal, Judge Ezra Friedlander cited *Adoption of M.M.C.G.*, acknowledging that the statute specifically required the biological parent's rights to be terminated in an adoption. However, he also noted the exceptions in the law, such as the biological parent retaining visitation rights or the stepparent adoption. Although he believed that the lower court was correct to conclude that a strict interpretation of the law required termination, "in light of the purpose and spirit of Indiana's adoption laws, we conclude that the legislature could not have intended such a destructive and absurd result" (*In re Adoption of K.S.P.* 2004, 1257). The state's adoption policy must always be guided by the best interests of the child, and courts must not construe the law so narrowly that they defeat its purpose. When, as here, both the biological parent and the prospective adoptive parent are fulfilling the role as parents, "Indiana law does not require a destructive choice between the two" (1260).

OPPOSITION TO SECOND-PARENT ADOPTIONS

Recognizing that state adoption laws often reflected a static view of family relationships, a number of courts were willing to go beyond the confines of the text to facilitate second-parent adoptions. However, several state courts declined to adopt this approach, refusing to waive the cutoff provision in second-parent adoptions by gays and lesbians on the grounds of judicial restraint.

In Interest of Angel Lace M. (1994), a Wisconsin Supreme Court ruling, addressed Annette G.'s petition to adopt Angel Lace M., her partner's six-year-old biological child. Georgina, Angel's mother, had been married to Terry, and when they divorced, he paid court-ordered child support but was not involved in the child's life. A few years later, after Georgina and Annette moved in together following a commitment ceremony, Annette petitioned the court to adopt Angel; Georgina petitioned to terminate Terry's parental rights and allow Annette to adopt. Terry raised no objections to the termination of his rights.

Although the county circuit court determined that it would be in Angel's best interests to be adopted by Annette, it rejected the adoption petition. Citing Wisconsin law, it held that Annette was not permitted to adopt Angel, nor was Angel permitted to be adopted by Annette.[71]

Speaking for a divided supreme court, Justice Donald Steinmetz began with the familiar nod to the rules of statutory construction, emphasizing that the adoption law was a creature of the legislature and must be strictly construed. In following this principle, he stressed, the court must be careful not to rewrite legislation. The couple pointed to the provision of the law stating that "the best interests of the child shall always be of paramount consideration" and contended that the lower court should have granted the petition on the basis of its finding that it would be in the child's best interest. The supreme court, however, held that the statute could not be interpreted so broadly because that would obviate all other parts, making every adoption mandatory as long as it was in the child's best interests.

The court found that as an unmarried adult resident of Wisconsin, Annette satisfied the statutory requirements for adoption. It devoted the bulk of its opinion to determining whether Angel was eligible for adoption despite the fact that her mother retained her parental rights and despite the requirement that in all but stepparent adoptions, both parents' rights had to be terminated. Interpreting the law according to the conventional rules of statutory construction, the court held that termination was mandatory; by specifically exempting stepparents, it held, the legislature had indicated its intent not to exempt other types of second-parent adoptions. Thus, the appellate court held, the lower court had correctly rejected the adoption petition.

In one of the few cases to address constitutional arguments, the court also considered whether the law abridged Angel's or Annette's constitutional rights. It quickly disposed of the child's due process claim, ruling that she had neither a liberty nor a property interest in having her best interests considered. With adoption a privilege—not a right—and a relatively recent one at that, there was no fundamental right to adopt. Moreover, he said, denying the adoption did not prevent her from associating with Annette, only from having the association legitimated by law.

The judge also rejected the argument, first offered by the ACLU as amicus curiae, that the state law was discriminatory because it classified children by whether they lived in a traditional or nontraditional family and considered the best interests of children only in the former.[72] He characterized it as differentiating between children with parents and children without parents whose parental rights had been terminated. Such a scheme, Steinmetz said, involved neither a fundamental right nor a suspect classification and therefore must be upheld as long as the state's interest is legitimate and the law is reasonably related to it. Citing *Michael H.* (1989), the court found that the state's interest in preserving the traditional family unit, exemplified by marriage, is legitimate and the law rationally related to it.

The court similarly declined to accept the ACLU's argument that the law discriminated against Annette on the basis of gender or sexual orientation because if she were a man, she would be able to adopt. Not so, said the court, Annette cannot adopt only because she is not married to the child's parent. The state's prohibition against same-sex marriage is arguably the culprit, not the adoption statute, and as the plaintiff had not raised that issue in this case, the court would not address it. The majority concluded that "the Wisconsin legislature has enacted a statutory scheme for adoption that balances society's interest in promoting stable, legally recognized families with its interest in promoting the best interests of the children involved. The adoption proposed in this case does not fall within the confines of this constitutionally valid legislative scheme" (686).

Justice Janine Geske's concurring opinion agreed that the law prohibited Annette from adopting without severing Georgina's parental rights but urged the legislature to reassess adoption law to fulfill its responsibility to promote the best interests of the child. She ended by emphasizing that adoption policymaking was a legislative, not a judicial, duty.

A vigorous dissent by Chief Justice Nathan Heffernan focused on his disagreement with the majority's application of the principles of statutory construction. He turned the majority's argument around by pointing out that the legislation itself directed the courts to liberally construe adoption laws, adding that the law specified that the best interests of the child should predominate but that the courts should also consider the interests of other parties involved as well as society's. Given this legislative mandate, he believed that the courts must interpret adoption laws liberally when such an interpretation furthers the child's best interests. And in this case, all the authorities agreed that granting Annette's petition advanced Angel's best interest as well as society's in producing stable, loving families.

The issue in the case, Heffernan said, was whether the statute required the termination of both parents' rights to make her eligible for adoption.[73] But, he reasoned, the statute cannot be interpreted in this way because that would eliminate stepparent adoptions as well. Based on a liberal interpretation of the statute, he believed that only one parent's rights had to be terminated as long as the other endorsed the adoption. After more discussion of the majority's faulty method of statutory construction, he noted that the only two state supreme courts, Vermont and Massachusetts, to rule on similar statutes came to the opposite conclusion. Those courts had held that the best interests of the child permitted a second-parent adoption and a joint petition for adoption, respectively. Moreover, in those cases, the courts did not even have the benefit of the legislature's directions on liberal construction of the laws. In this case, he charged, the majority is flouting the legislative will by interpreting the statute narrowly and ignoring Angel's best interests.

Justice William Bablitch also took issue with the majority's emphasis on judicial restraint, noting that "the legislature at times, as here, deliberately paints with a very broad and ambiguous brush. By design, it left the details to us, even the most controversial ones. We abdicate our responsibility by passing this back to the legislature, particularly when we know the likelihood of the legislature ever acting is minimal at best" (695).

Shortly after *Angel Lace M.*, a Colorado appellate court ruling, *Matter of Adoption of T.K.J.* (1996), also rejected a second-parent adoption. Here, a lesbian couple, G.K. and L.J., sought to adopt each other's biological child. The partners had done all they could to secure a legal relationship with the other's child by creating wills and broad-based powers of attorney. The only possibility for the couple and their children was a mutual (coparent) adoption. And, as the court noted, no matter what the outcome of the adoption petition, the family would endure.

The lower court judge, Michael Villano, noted that the law specifies that, except in the case of a stepparent, the biological parent's right is terminated on adoption.[74] He concluded that because these children were "not available for adoption," the court lacked the jurisdiction to grant the adoption petition and must dismiss it.

On appeal, Judge Karen Metzger of the Colorado Court of Appeals pointed to the crux of the plaintiffs' legal argument: the statute is silent on whether a person may adopt the child of another to whom that person is not married without terminating the parental rights of the natural parent. Noting that although it is well established that adoption laws are liberally interpreted, she stressed that a court cannot "rewrite the statute." Metzger cautioned that the liberal construction is appropriate only when the words of the statute are ambiguous and cannot be given "their commonly accepted and understood meaning" (492). In this case, because the relevant provisions were written in specific and mandatory language, it left no room for the court to interpret the statute beyond the plain text without exceeding its judicial authority and transgressing the boundaries of separation of powers.

She noted that there are only two adoption procedures permitted by law: first, the natural parent's rights being terminated (or relinquished), thus ending all rights and responsibilities between the child and the parent, and, second, the stepparent adoption, in which the adopting parent is married to the natural parent. Absent a marriage, this couple does not fit within the statutory exception of the latter, and the children were therefore clearly "not available for adoption."

The couple had argued that the lower court should not have dismissed their petition without holding an evidentiary hearing to determine if the adoptions were in the children's best interests. Metzger disagreed, ruling that it was unnecessary to determine whether the adoption was in the children's best interests, as they were not subject to adoption. Additionally, she rejected the constitutional arguments that the absence of a hearing was a denial of due process. A hearing was required, the court held, only if there were a liberty or property interest in the adoption, and there was neither—neither for the children nor for their prospective adoptive parents. Similarly, there was no equal protection violation because the statute was reasonably related to the state's legitimate goal of furthering the best interests of children and families. If the law was contrary to society's current values and norms, it was up to the people's representatives, the legislature, to change it.

Thus, this court construed the statute narrowly and, without basing its opinion on the sexual orientation of the couple, refused to allow the children the additional legal protection that would have been provided by a successful second-parent adoption. Judge Edwin Ruland, concurring specially, said that the statute failed to explain why the best interests of the child should be disregarded simply because the biological parent was not married to the prospective adoptive parent. He noted that although the equal protection claim was not raised properly in this case, there was something unsettling about a law that diminished an opportunity to parent a child simply because of the marital status of the prospective adopted parent, adding that this question should be raised and resolved in a proper legislative or judicial forum.

In 1998, an Ohio appellate court reviewed a lower court decision that dismissed an adoption petition from the lesbian partner of eight-year-old Jane Doe's biological mother in *In re Adoption of Doe* (1998). The issue was whether the law allowed the biological mother to retain her parental rights if her partner or she and her partner together adopted the child. Speaking for the appeals court, Judge Sheila Farmer held that the lower court correctly interpreted the Ohio adoption law in disallowing the adoption petition while the mother retained her parental rights.[75]

Farmer approvingly noted that the trial court's conclusion was properly based on a strict interpretation of the law. The governing principle, she explained, was that the judiciary must strictly construe laws concerning adoption because it was solely a legislative creation. Although the plaintiffs cited cases showing that trial court judges have discretionary power over adoption petitions and must be guided by the best interests of the child, she distinguished them because they involved eligibility to adopt, not termination of parental rights. Expressing sympathy for the plaintiffs' "dilemma," she emphasized that "it is not within the constitutional scope of judicial power to change the face and effect of the plain meaning of [the law]. This case is not about alternative lifestyles," she insisted, "but about statutory construction" (1073). Nor, she held, did the lower court err by not considering the best interests of the child. The issue in the case was not whether the adoption should go forward but whether the mother's rights would be terminated if it did.[76]

Judge John Wise concurred, underscoring the dilemma faced by the couple. He stated that the only solution was for the legislature to either allow same-sex couples to marry or amend the adoption law to permit their adoption. Failing that, the law as presently written, cannot be interpreted to sanction the legal arrangement the plaintiffs seek.[77]

Similarly, in *In re Adoption of Baby Z.* (1999), the Connecticut Supreme Court considered the question of second-parent adoption for the first time. The case began with an adoption application from Anne, Baby Z's natural mother, requesting that her partner, Malinda, be declared an adoptive parent of Baby Z without terminating Anne's parental rights. As in most states, an existing parent's rights were terminated except in the case of adoption by a stepparent.

The probate court dismissed the petition, ruling that it did not conform to the statutory requirements. After determining that the adoption was in the child's best interests, the superior court reversed and remanded the case to the lower court with instructions to submit a waiver of the statutory parent requirement to the Adoption Review Board, which could then allow the adoption to go forward without terminating Anne's parental rights. The board, however, determined that it did not have jurisdiction to consider or grant the waiver application and denied the petition. The plaintiffs went back to superior court, which again ruled in their favor and ordered the board to reconsider.

Both the plaintiffs and the Adoption Review Board appealed, and the case ultimately reached the Connecticut Supreme Court. Speaking for the majority in a complex ruling submerged in jurisdictional and procedural issues, Chief Justice Robert Callahan ruled that although the adoption was in the child's best interest, the judiciary cannot bend the law to achieve this result. After extensive analysis of the statute and stressing that it must show restraint in construing the adoption law, he noted that the adoption agreement (between Anne and Malinda) was not within the categories specified in the statute. Citing *Angel Lace M.*, he concluded that "the members of our legislature, as elected representatives of the people, have the power and responsibility to establish the requirements for adoption in this state. The courts simply cannot play that role" (1060).

In a lengthy dissent, Justice Robert Berdon countered with two main points. First, both women were currently acting as parents, and it was emphatically in the child's best interests that they formalize their legal status. Second, rather than strict construction, adoption laws should be liberally construed to protect the interests of the children involved. Unlike the majority, he addressed the issue of the plaintiffs' sexual orientation, remarking that courts in New Jersey, Illinois, Massachusetts, Vermont, and the District of Columbia had allowed adoptions by gay and lesbian couples and that there were only two states—Colorado and Wisconsin—in which the courts reached a contrary result. But in those cases, unlike this one, the courts had failed to address the question of whether the adoption was in the child's best interests. In refusing to extend the stepparent exception to these plaintiffs, the majority had defined the term "spouse" too narrowly. Today's family arrangements, he insisted, require a more expansive interpretation. Indeed, "In terms of the way in which people structure their lives and conduct their interpersonal relationships, he said, your spouse is the person with whom you vow to share your life and raise your family. Although Malinda," he continued, "does not technically qualify as Anne's spouse . . . it is clear that she is" (1076).

A year later, the legislature reversed *Baby Z.*, enacting a law to permit second-parent adoptions.[78]

In re Adoption of Luke (2002) more recently demonstrates the court's failure to give sufficient weight to evidence of the child's best interests. In this case, a lesbian couple, A.E. and B.P., sought to have A.E. adopt five-year-old Luke, B.P.'s biological child.[79] After a trial in which the testimony favored the adoption, the lower court dismissed the petition, ruling that the child was not eligible for adoption because Nebraska law required termination of the legal parent's rights except in the case of a stepparent.[80]

Because the lower court had not ruled on them, the state supreme court refused to consider state and federal constitutional issues. The plaintiffs had argued that B.P.'s consent was an adequate substitute for relinquishment and cited rulings in Massachusetts, Illinois, the District of Columbia, New York, New Jersey, and Vermont for support. The state simply pointed out that the language of the statute only allowed a parent to retain parental rights in the case of a stepparent adoption and cited rulings in Colorado, Connecticut, Ohio, and Wisconsin to bolster its argument.

In a per curiam opinion, the court limited its discussion to interpreting the adoption law. Without any reference to the petitioner's sexual orientation, the court noted that the law clearly stated that with the exception of stepparent adoptions, the legal parent's rights must be relinquished before a child is considered eligible for adoption. Thus, it held that the biological mother's consent was irrelevant. It ended with the usual reminder that adoption is governed by statute and that adoption petitions must satisfy the provisions of the law as enacted by the legislature.

Justice John Gerrard argued in dissent that the majority had erred in interpreting the lower court opinion; in his view, that decision was based solely on the plaintiffs' status as an unmarried couple, who may not adopt under Nebraska law, rather than on the requirement that the parent must relinquish parental rights before an adoption can take place. Surely, he argued, the legislature did not intend that parental rights be relinquished prior to adoption in all cases. In his view, neither the law nor case law supported the majority's conclusions about the indispensability of the step of relinquishment.

Gerrard criticized the majority for straying from the established principle of interpreting adoption laws liberally, focusing on whether the law specifically allowed the adoption rather than determining whether it specifically prohibited it. Following this principle does not usurp legislative authority, he argued, because judges are authorized to make individual determinations in adoption decisions and these decisions should be based on the best interests of the child. In his view, the majority ignored the most important tenet of adoption law: whether the adoption will advance the best interests of the child. And when the adoption is in the child's best interests and the biological parent has consented, it is incumbent on the court to allow the adoption to proceed and not to place obstacles in its path because it believes it must adhere to a policy of judicial restraint and legislative deference. He urged that the case be remanded to allow the lower court to make the crucial finding about whether the adoption is in Luke's best interests.

PARENTING POLICIES IN FLORIDA AND CALIFORNIA

This chapter ends with a closer examination of the protracted litigation in the Florida and California courts to illustrate the importance of the courts in determining parental rights and the role of sexual orientation in parenting policies.

In the Florida case, a single gay man challenged the state law that prevented him from adopting his "special needs" foster child who had lived with him since infancy. The California litigation arose when a lesbian couple's relationship dissolved and each tried to solidify her own legal status with the children—at the expense of the other. Thus, although the legal and factual elements in these cases are quite different, together they illustrate the central role the courts play in sorting out the complex legal arrangements and the dynamic interaction between courts and legislatures in formulating policies affecting gay families. These cases also exemplify opposing views on the proper role of the judiciary in family policymaking.

Florida's law, straightforwardly barring all gays—both singles and in couples—from adopting, was challenged in the case that captured the nation's attention, *Lofton v. Kearney* (2001). Although the lower federal court judges who decided the case stressed that they were not influenced by bias or stereotypical thinking about gay parenting, by upholding the state's discriminatory policies, they played a role in perpetuating the anti-gay sentiment that had been manifest in the state for almost three decades.

In the wake of Anita Bryant's anti-gay "Save the Children" Campaign in 1977, Florida amended its adoption law to prohibit all gays from adopting.[81] The law was the first of its kind in the nation.[82]

Steven Lofton challenged the 1977 Florida law; the defendants in this case were Kathleen Kearney, secretary of Florida's Department of Children and Families (DCF), and Charles Auslander, administrator of DCF's District XI, covering both Dade and Monroe counties.[83]

Lofton was a registered pediatric nurse and a certified long-term foster parent. He and Roger Croteau, his partner of twenty years, were foster parents to several special needs children, some of whom lived with them from infancy. Exemplary foster parents over a number of years to children with multiple health problems, including HIV and AIDS, Lofton and

Croteau had received the "Outstanding Foster Parenting" award from the child placement agency licensed by the state; numerous newspaper articles were written about them and their role in the lives of children in state care.[84] Their foster son, Bert (known as John Doe), born in 1991, had been living with them since he was nine weeks old; he became eligible for adoption in 1994 when he tested negative for HIV. Lofton's petition for adoption was rejected because of his homosexuality.[85]

Plaintiff Douglas Houghton was a clinical nurse specialist and had been legal guardian of the other child plaintiff, John Roe, since the boy was four years old. When the boy's biological father terminated his parental rights, Houghton filed an adoption petition in state court. During the requisite home study interview, he was told that his application would have been approved if he were not a homosexual.

Two other plaintiffs, Wayne Larue Smith and Daniel Skahen—licensed foster parents who submitted an at-large adoption application—were also denied because they were gay. Other plaintiffs included a couple who claimed they wanted to specify a homosexual relative as legal guardian and eventual adoptive parent of their children and a lesbian who charged that the law automatically disqualified her from becoming an adoptive parent.[86] Florida Federal Court Judge James King initially dismissed all the plaintiffs but Lofton and Doe on grounds of standing (*Lofton v. Butterworth* 2000) but reinstated some after they showed that the statute had prevented them from adopting.[87]

Lofton, Houghton, and the two children based their challenge on their federal constitutional "right to familial privacy, intimate association and family integrity" protected by the First Amendment and the Fourteenth Amendment's due process clause (*Lofton v. Kearney* 2001, 1377). All the plaintiffs also argued that the Florida law unconstitutionally infringed on their right to equal protection under the Fourteenth Amendment.

The four plaintiffs, Lofton and Houghton and the two children, relied on *Troxel* to support their due process claim, citing the high court's declaration that "'the interest of a parent in the care, custody, and control of their children [to be] perhaps the oldest of the fundamental liberty interests'" (65). They argued that this interest should be extended to foster parents and legal guardians because of the "emotional bond that develops between family members as a result of shared daily life irrespective of the existence of a blood relationship" and that only the permanence of adoption will allow them to secure these ties (*Lofton v. Kearney* 2001, 1378).[88]

In granting the state's motion for summary judgment, King acknowledged that the Supreme Court had not restricted families to biological units only and recognized that the relationships between Lofton and Houghton and their foster children are on a par with those in biologically related families.[89] However, citing *Smith*, King said that despite the emotional bonds, "foster parents do not have justifiable expectations of an enduring companionship because the emotional ties originate under state law . . . and it is this justified expectation of enduring companionship that has become the benchmark for protected liberty interest in the family."[90]

He acknowledged that "the concept of family embraces relationships other than the archetypical nuclear family, [but emphasized that] the Constitution protects only those social units that share an expectation of continuity justified by the presence of certain basic elements traditionally recognized as characteristic of the family" (*Lofton v. Kearney* 2001, 1379). The most basic of these elements, he stressed, was the existence of a biological relationship, although that fact alone would not inescapably create a liberty interest.

In Lofton and Houghton's case, he found that their status as foster parents and legal guardians did not entitle them to claim the kind of permanent relationships that trigger due process protection, as both were aware that the relationships were intended to be impermanent and subject to the state's control. Finally, the judge emphatically rejected the plaintiffs' argument that they must be allowed to adopt to achieve the permanent relationship they sought, saying "it is undisputed there is no fundamental right to adopt . . . nor is there a fundamental right to be adopted" (1380). Consequently, there is no fundamental right to apply for adoption. King concluded the due process analysis by repeating the Supreme Court's warning in *Washington v. Glucksberg* (1997) that courts must be wary of engaging in substantive due process analysis to extend fundamental rights because such action excludes legislative decision making and implicates the courts in public policymaking.

Turning to the equal protection claim, King rejected their argument that he apply a higher level of scrutiny to the Florida law because it implicates their fundamental right to adopt, simply repeating that foster parents and legal guardians cannot claim a fundamental right to familial privacy and intimate association or a fundamental right to adopt or be adopted. A more difficult question, he noted, was whether he should apply heightened scrutiny because gays and lesbians were a suspect or semisuspect class. Here, he was guided by the U.S. Supreme Court's opinion in *Romer v. Evans* (1996), in which the high court had applied minimal scrutiny in striking Colorado's Amendment 2 on equal protection grounds.[91] Moreover, he affirmed, no other circuit had used heightened scrutiny when adjudicating challenges to laws affecting the rights of homosexuals.

Applying minimal scrutiny, the judge assessed the state's claim that the law "reflects the State's moral disapproval of homosexuality consistent with the legislatures [sic] right to legislate public morality." Such antipathy to homosexuality, it argued, was "based on beliefs firmly rooted in Judeo-Christian moral and ethical standards for a millennia" (1382). Citing *Romer*, the court held that public morality does not suffice as a reason for a law and that states may not legislate against a group of which it disapproves.[92]

King accepted the state's second argument that excluding gays advances the children's best interests, which are "to be raised in a home stabilized by marriage, in a family consisting of both a mother and a father" (*Lofton v. Kearney* 2001, 1383).[93] Although the plaintiffs admitted that excluding homosexuals from adoption in the best interests of a child might be legitimate, they argued for an opportunity to demonstrate that this was merely a pretext for the state's animosity toward homosexuals. The court ignored this argument, saying that under minimal scrutiny, a court does not delve into the motives behind the state's asserted reasons if they are plausible and reasonable; indeed, under minimal scrutiny, the state has no obligation even to prove its assertions.[94] The plaintiffs bear the burden of showing that the state's reasons are untrue in all circumstances, that is, that homosexual families are as stable, provide gender-appropriate role models, and are less stigmatizing for children. The court held that the plaintiffs had not met their burden.

The ruling ended with the familiar caution that courts must refrain from setting public policy under the guise of constitutional adjudication. Using code language for minimal scrutiny, the court stressed that "the Equal Protection Clause of the Fourteenth Amendment is not a license for courts to judge the wisdom, fairness, or logic of legislative choices. . . . Where there is a plausible reason for the State's action, this Court's inquiry must end" (1384).

On appeal, the three-judge panel of the Eleventh Circuit unanimously affirmed, characterizing the matter as a "states' rights issue" (*Lofton v. Secretary of Department of Children and Family Services* 2004a, 806). The court began by noting that there had been several legislative attempts to repeal the law and that it had also been unsuccessfully challenged in the courts as well.[95]

In addition to appealing the lower court's holding on their due process and equal protection claims, Lofton and the other plaintiffs cited the Supreme Court's recent decision in *Lawrence v. Texas* (2003), in which the Court struck a Texas antisodomy law and recognized a fundamental right to engage in homosexual conduct; they argued that the Florida law unconstitutionally infringed on this right.

Speaking for the three-judge appellate panel, Judge Stanley Birch agreed with the lower court that emotional ties between an adult and a foster child do not give rise to a constitutional right. Citing the recognition that the U.S. Supreme Court accorded foster parents in *Smith*, the plaintiffs had contended that foster parents and legal guardians had a liberty interest that arises not from "biological ties or official legal recognition, but the emotional bond that develops between and among individuals as a result of shared daily life" (*Lofton v. Secretary of Department of Children and Family Services* 2004a, 813). *Smith*, however, Birch noted, differentiated between natural families and foster families and accorded a narrower liberty interest to the latter, an interest limited by state law. The court hypothesized that although a state may, if it chooses to, create an expectation of permanency in a foster or legal guardian relationship, Florida had not done so.[96]

The plaintiffs also challenged the lower court ruling on substantive due process grounds, arguing (for the first time on appeal) that the Florida law burdened their "fundamental right to private sexual intimacy," derived from *Lawrence* (*Lofton v. Secretary of Department of Children and Family Services* 2004a, 815), and therefore merited strict scrutiny in keeping with the Supreme Court's traditional fundamental rights analysis.[97] Birch disagreed, holding that *Lawrence* had been decided on the basis of a confluence of rights rather than on a single fundamental right. He relied most heavily on the fact that the high court had used minimal scrutiny in deciding the case, not strict, as it would have done if adjudicating a law threatening a fundamental right.[98] The appeals court concluded that "it is a strained and ultimately incorrect reading of *Lawrence* to interpret it to announce a new fundamental right" (*Lofton v. Secretary of Department of Children and Family Services* 2004a, 817). It noted that the facts are sufficiently different in the two cases that the ruling in *Lawrence* does not govern the decision in *Lofton*, citing differences between the Texas law, which burdened the constitutional rights of adults to engage in consensual sex in which the state is precluded from interfering, and the Florida law, which involves minors and the privilege of adoption created by statute and controlled by the state.

Turning to the equal protection challenge, the court quickly dismissed the plaintiffs' argument that it must apply heightened scrutiny, citing the U.S. Supreme Court's opinion in *Romer* and noting that no other circuit has applied a heightened level of scrutiny to laws affecting sexual orientation. With neither a fundamental right nor a suspect class involved, the court assessed the state's justifications for the statute under minimal scrutiny, namely, that its goal of promoting the best interests of the child is most advanced by placing them in families with married couples to maximize family stability. Birch cited the state's claim that the law "emphasizes a vital role that dual-gender parenting plays in shaping sexual and gender identity and in providing heterosexual role modeling" (*Lofton v. Secretary of Department of Children and Family Services* 2004a, 818). He credited the state's contention that by denying homosexuals the right to adopt, it was furthering its aim of providing children a stable adoptive home with two heterosexual married parents.[99]

Although the court also surveyed the plaintiffs' argument that the state's asserted reason is not the actual reason and merely a pretext for discrimination, Birch emphasized that under minimal scrutiny, a state does not have to be motivated by the asserted reason; it suffices if it "*could have reasonably believed*" that it was serving the best interests of Florida's children by enacting the challenged law (820, emphasis in the original). Thus, it was irrelevant that Florida allowed adoptions by unmarried heterosexuals because it could believe that there was at least a chance that they, unlike homosexuals, might be married someday and thus provide the stability that the state sought for adoptive children as well as provide more suitable sexual role models.[100] Setting the bar for passing minimal scrutiny very low, the court concluded that "for our present purposes, it is sufficient that these considerations provide a reasonably conceivable rationale for Florida to preclude all homosexuals, but not all heterosexual singles, from adoption" (822).

The plaintiffs also contended that the law reflected anti-gay bias because permitting gays to become foster parents and legal guardians indicates that the state does not believe that children are harmed by living in gay households. The court also deflected this argument, saying that such placement decisions are made by the executive branch (the Department of Children and Family Services) and thus irrelevant to the legislature's motives in proscribing homosexual adoption. Moreover, even if the legislature did intend such a distinction, it could rationally believe that such placements are sufficiently different from adoption to draw the line at adoption.

The court also distinguished the Florida statute from the one struck by the high court in *Romer*. Unlike Colorado's expansive Amendment 2, it held, the Florida law applies to adoption, is limited to homosexual conduct only (as opposed to status and conduct), and is credibly related to the state's declared interest in promoting the welfare of adoptive children.

Finally, the court rejected the plaintiffs' contention that the law does not further the state's interest in placing 3,000 children with married couples because excluding homosexuals does not increase the pool of available married couples. The state's interest is not in placing children quickly but in placing them well. And by excluding homosexuals, the court believed that the state could reasonably believe that the children would eventually be adopted by heterosexual couples. Similarly, the court dismissed the plaintiffs' argument that excluding gays was irrational because of social scientific evidence showing that children are not harmed by living in gay families. Again, defending the legislature's judgment, the court noted that legislators might have been persuaded by opposing evidence, that is, that children are harmed, or, if it did credit the studies cited by the plaintiffs, it might have believed that the findings were too recent to be reliable. In any event, the court believed that the legislature acted rationally.

Ending with the familiar battle cry of judicial restraint, the court stressed its unwillingness to become involved in the debate over homosexuality and adoption. "The State of Florida has made the determination that it is not in the best interests of its displaced children to be adopted by [homosexuals] . . . and we have found nothing in the Constitution that forbids this policy judgment. Thus, any argument that the Florida legislature was misguided in its decision is one of legislative policy, not constitutional law. The legislature is the proper forum for this debate," it stressed, not the courts (*Lofton v. Secretary of Department of Children and Family Services* 2004a, 828).[101]

Expressing support for the ruling, Republic Governor Jeb Bush said that it affirmed the state's belief that children are better off when "placed in a home anchored both by a father and a mother" (*New York Times* January 29, 2004).

Subsequently, in a vote of 6 to 6, the circuit court denied Lofton's petition for a rehearing en banc (*Lofton v. Secretary of Department of Children and Family Services* 2004b).[102] Two separate opinions by Birch and Judge Rosemary Barkett offer opposing views of the proper role of the courts in deciding such rights-based conflicts.[103]

Concurring specially in the denial of the rehearing, Birch, one of the judges on the original panel, reviewed the methodology in minimal scrutiny analysis, reiterating that the court must uphold a law whenever there is a plausibly rational basis for it, regardless whether the state was actually motivated by the proffered reason. Thus, in his view, under minimal scrutiny, a court is precluded from even inquiring into possible motivation, a position, he argued, that was consistent with *Romer*. In that case, he contended, the Supreme Court did not actually inquire into the legislature's motive and conclude that it was based on animosity toward gays; rather, it merely inferred it from the nature of the proposed amendment.

Birch warned against the dangers of courts imposing their views on the results of democratic decision making; at the same time, however, he thoughtfully conveyed the difficulty he faced in fulfilling this judicial role while disagreeing with the legislature's policy choice:

> I will conclude on a purely personal note. If I were a legislator, rather than a judge, I would vote in favor of considering otherwise eligible homosexuals for adoptive parenthood. In reviewing the record in this case one can only be impressed by the courage, tenacity and devotion of Messrs. Lofton and Houghton for the children placed in their care. For these children, these men are the only parents they have ever known. Thus, I consider the policy decision of the Florida legislature to be misguided and trust that over time attitudes will change and it will see the best interest of these children in a different light. Nevertheless, as compelling as this perspective is to me, I will

not allow my personal views to conflict with my judicial duty. (*Lofton v. Secretary of Department of Children and Family Services* 2004b, 1289)

Dissenting from the denial of en banc review, Barkett argued that the law is clearly unconstitutional, as there is no evidence that it rationally relates to a legitimate government interest. In a footnote, she explained that Birch had distorted her position, for, in her view, *Romer* stood for the proposition that when a court believes that a classification has no possible connection to a legitimate government interest, it may infer that the law is motivated by dislike of the group in question.[104] And in such circumstances, the court should strike the law because animus toward a group cannot be a legitimate government interest. She recognized that if there were "some conceivable legitimate government interest that can plausibly account for Florida's law," it might be constitutional despite some evidence that it was actually motivated by dislike of gays (*Lofton v. Secretary of Department of Children and Family Services* 2004b, 1296 n13).

Barkett systematically discredited the rationales behind the state's blanket exclusions of gay adoption, pointing to examples of inconsistencies and illogical reasoning. For example, she argued that although the state claimed that it promoted the best interests of the child with a placement in a family with a mother and father, it freely allowed adoptions by unmarried (heterosexual) persons. She also ridiculed the state's contention that heterosexuals provide role models for (presumably heterosexual) children because of their own experiences. "Is the panel suggesting," she asked sarcastically, "that heterosexual parents are necessary in order to tell children about their own dating experiences after puberty? For anyone who has been a parent, this will no doubt seem a very strange, even faintly comical, claim. There is certainly no evidence that the ability to share one's adolescent dating experiences (or lack thereof) is an important, much less essential, facet of parenting" (1299).

Finally, Barkett examined the legislative history of the exclusion that was spurred by Bryant's campaign to repeal Dade County's antidiscrimination ordinance and believed that it was clear that far from furthering the best interests of the child, the sole purpose of the law was to discriminate against gays.[105] Thus, she concluded that "Florida's proffered justifications for the categorical ban here are false, do not rationally relate to the best interests of children, and are simply pretexts for impermissible animus and prejudice against homosexuals" (1296).

In an unpublished opinion, on November 25, 2008, Judge Cindy Lederman of the Miami-Dade County Circuit Court declared the 1977 law unconstitutional.[106] The petitioner, Frank Gill, sought to adopt two half brothers, four-year-old John and eight-year-old James Doe, who had been living with him and his partner for four years. Lederman held that the

Florida law infringed on Gill's and the children's state equal protection rights and the federal Adoption and Safe Families Act of 1997.

Almost immediately after the decision was announced, Florida's attorney general, Bill McCollum, promised to appeal her ruling to the Third District Court of Appeals (MiamiHerald.com November 25, 2008). If the case ultimately goes to the state supreme court and the court strikes it solely on state constitutional grounds, it would foreclose review by the U.S. Supreme Court.

In contrast to Florida—where the courts deferred to the legislature in allowing sexual orientation to be the determinative factor in parenting policy, California's legislative and judicial policymaking institutions together helped minimize the role of sexual orientation in family policy, including adoption. Although the complex and protracted litigation between the biological mother and her ex-partner would seem to be a poor vehicle for policymaking, in adjudicating the legal battles between Sharon S. and her former partner, Annette F., to decide the fate of the two children at the heart of the controversy, the courts helped sort out the rights and obligations of prospective gay parents throughout the state.[107]

On October 14, 2001, California's governor, Democrat Gray Davis, issued a signing statement for Assembly Bill (AB) 25, which, among other things, he said, would allow partners to "adopt their partner's child."[108] On January 1, 2002, the California Domestic Partner Act took effect, amending the existing family law to allow the partner of a legal or biological parent to adopt the latter's child as long as he or she is a registered domestic partner.[109] Although most members of the gay community heralded the new law, it did not bring about full equality for gay couples with children.[110] Among other things, under California law, a child born to a married couple is presumed to be the legal child of both spouses; AB 25 did not entitle registered domestic partners to the same presumption, requiring the nonbiological parent to formally adopt the child.[111] Six months after AB 25 took effect, a San Francisco attorney noted that although the state now had "the most favorable laws ever . . . even in California there are limitations on what can be done and who can do it" (Scaparotti 2002).

Before it became law, however, the seemingly never-ending litigation between Sharon S. and Annette F. rocked the gay community, raising questions about the future of second-parent adoptions in California as well as causing apprehension about the thousands of existing second-parent adoptions that had become finalized prior to January 1, 2002.

For more than a decade, the California courts had sanctioned hundreds of second-parent adoptions without explicit statutory authority. In approving these adoptions, most courts cited *Marshall v. Marshall* (1925) and analogized them to stepparent adoptions, which did not require relinquishment of parental rights. In *Marshall,* the California Supreme Court was asked to rule on the validity of an adoption in which a woman retained her parental rights when her second husband adopted her children after they married. At the time, California law contained no express stepparent exception, specifying that all parents of adoptive children surrender their parental rights and responsibilities.

Marshall revolved around an appeal from a lower court decision that absolved the plaintiff's ex-husband from paying child support for her two children despite his agreement to provide $100 a month.[112] A series of complex legal actions followed, and the ex-husband returned to superior court, seeking to modify the decree, arguing that the court lacked jurisdiction to order child support because when she adopted the children after the marriage ended, their status changed so that they were no longer the children of the parties in the divorce action. The court agreed and terminated the arrangement. The mother appealed.

Rejecting the jurisdictional argument, the state supreme court determined that Mrs. Marshall's adoption of her children had no legal meaning, as her parental rights had not been terminated when her (now) exhusband had adopted the children at the start of the marriage, despite the provisions in Civil Code §229 that severed the ties between the child and the natural (or legal) parent following an adoption. The court held that the parties had clearly not intended this result, and indeed his adoption petition had specified that they would have joint custody and control of the children; her written consent to the adoption echoed this view, and the court's adoption order confirmed the arrangement. Despite the code's silence on the subject, the court reasoned that a husband and wife may adopt a child jointly and that the child becomes the child of both spouses. "We are not prepared," the court concluded, "to hold that section 229 of the Civil Code was intended to apply to a situation such as this, and to effect a result so plainly opposite to that which was intended" (38).

The case that rocked the gay community, *Sharon S. v. the Superior Court of San Diego County* (2001a), was a California appellate court ruling that questioned the precedent set by *Marshall* in authorizing second-parent adoptions to gay couples, dismissing it as dicta.[113]

The dispute in the case arose over a breakdown in the relationship between Sharon and Annette, former students at Harvard Business School, who became involved in a serious relationship in 1989 and moved to San Diego in 1990. As was common with lesbian couples who wanted a child, they agreed that Sharon would conceive a child through artificial insemination and that they would raise the child together as coparents. In 1996, when Sharon gave birth to Zachary, Annette, with Sharon's consent, successfully petitioned the superior court to adopt him, with Sharon retaining her parental rights. Three years later, in June 1999, after another artificial insemination from the same sperm donor, Sharon gave birth to Joshua and consented to allow Annette to adopt him as a coparent. The two signed an "Independent Adoption Placement Agreement," in which Sharon acknowledged that she could not revoke her consent after ninety days and that she was relinquishing her parental rights to Joshua.

As was customary in California at the time, she also signed a written addendum to the agreement in which she stated that despite the language of the agreement, she intended to retain her parental rights and that she understood that when the adoption was finalized, Annette would share equal parenting rights and responsibilities with her. Annette filed a separate statement, noting that Sharon had consented to the adoption and acknowledging that she was aware that Sharon intended to retain her parental rights. Although there was no statutory provision for this method of adoption, it was used by lesbian couples since the NCLR devised it in 1987. Indeed, the state department of social services provided the form on which the addendum was written (Scaparotti 2002).[114]

The county department of health and human services completed its routine investigation of Annette in April 2000 and recommended that the superior court grant her petition. But before the adoption was finalized, the relationship between the two became strained, and Sharon continually postponed the hearing on the petition. In August 2000, amid allegations of domestic violence, Sharon asked Annette to leave the couple's home. They entered into mediation and agreed to let Annette spend time with both children but were unable to agree on permanent custody or visitation. Two months later, Annette petitioned the court for sole physical custody of the two boys and to establish a legal relationship with Joshua.[115] Soon after, she filed a motion to adopt, arguing that Sharon's consent was irrevocable and that the time to withdraw it had elapsed. Both Sharon and Annette maintained they were acting in the children's best interests.

In November 2000, following a family court recommendation that the two share legal custody and that Annette have visitation with both boys, Sharon sought to withdraw her consent to the adoption, claiming that it had been obtained by "fraud, undue influence, and duress," resulting from Annette's domestic violence against her (*Sharon S. v. the Superior Court of San Diego County* 2001a, 110). At the same time, the county agency again recommended the adoption as in Joshua's best interests.

Soon after, both Sharon and Joshua's appointed counsel moved to dismiss Annette's petition. On March 19, 2001, San Diego Superior Court Judge Susan Hugenor denied the motions without specifically ruling on the motion to withdraw consent, simply pointing out that it was beyond the legal time limit. She permitted Annette to continue her attempt to adopt Joshua. Sharon, joined by Joshua's court-appointed counsel, appealed.

On appeal, the appellate court noted that California law permits only three types of adoptions: agency adoptions, independent adoptions, and stepparent adoptions. In a vote of 2 to 1 announced by James McIntyre, the court stressed strict adherence to the law and found that Annette's attempt to adopt Joshua did not fall within these three types.[116] Annette characterized her adoption as a modified independent adoption and urged the court to go beyond the narrow confines of the statute to allow it; she (and the numerous amici who filed briefs on her behalf) argued that the state had been permitting such adoptions for more than a decade. The agency supported this view, stating that in its efforts to seek the best interests of the child, it recommended adoptions on a case-by-case basis, without considering the applicant's marital status. It further explained that it has expedited second-parent adoptions over a number of years through two procedures: first, a modified independent adoption, such as Annette's and Sharon's, in which a parent consents to the adoption yet retains her parental rights and, second, an agency adoption in which the legal parent yields her parental rights to an agency and explicitly designates herself and her partner as the adoptive parents. McIntyre stated that the court's task was to determine whether a second-parent adoption can be accomplished through the independent adoption procedure as urged by Annette.

Citing *Marshall*, Annette and the amici argued that the court should construe the law liberally and follow *Marshall* by allowing the adoption despite the absence of explicit statutory authorization. The appeals court, however, "decline[d] to read *Marshall* as an open invitation to disregard the express language of the statutes governing independent adoptions" (*Sharon S. v. the Superior Court of San Diego County* 2001a, 113). Courts, McIntyre insisted, must adhere to the explicit text of the statute and not stray beyond it. The only legal adoption in which a parent retains parental rights is in the stepparent adoption. He pointed out that since *Marshall*, the legislature had amended the adoption code to legitimate stepparent adoptions by not requiring the termination of parental rights in such cases. In doing so, he stressed, the legislature had on at least two separate occasions considered and rejected a bill that would have permitted two unmarried adults to adopt a child. Indeed, he cited the recent passage of the domestic partnership bill (AB 25) as "a clear indication that the Legislature did not previously authorize the accomplishment of second-parent adoptions through the use of a modified independent adoption procedure" (*Sharon S. v. the Superior Court of San Diego County* 2001a, 115).

Annette alternatively argued that even if *Marshall* were not persuasive, the court should follow the lead of the other California courts that had been approving second-parent adoptions for more than a decade. Rejecting this view, the court emphasized that adoption procedures are properly left to the legislative branch and that a court may not interpret a legislature's silence on a subject as a signal to plunge into social policymaking. It granted Sharon the writ of mandamus she sought, ordering the trial court to permit her to withdraw her consent and terminate the adoption.

Judge Daniel Kremer, dissenting, argued that the majority opinion had wrongly interpreted *Marshall*, emphasizing that the state high court had refused to construe the language in the law strictly in that case and declare that the mother's rights had been terminated. "In effect," he contended, "the Supreme Court in *Marshall* read second parent-adoption into the statute and did not require full relinquishment or termination of the birth parent's parental rights. Further nothing in *Marshall* limited its reasoning about second-parent adoption to a stepparent context" (*Sharon S. v. the Superior Court of San Diego County* 2001a, 118). Moreover, he added, when a couple had intended a second-parent adoption, it would be "absurd" to terminate the biological mother's parental rights to allow her partner's adoption to take effect. He ended, quoting *Marshall*, that he would not interpret the law "to effect a result so plainly opposite" from the one intended by Sharon and Annette (*Sharon S. v. the Superior Court of San Diego County* 2001a, 118–9, quoting *Marshall*, 767).

On November 21, 2001, the court denied Annette's motion for a rehearing and, at the same time, modified its October 25, 2001 ruling (*Sharon S. v. the Superior Court of San Diego County* 2001b). The modified opinion attempted to assuage the fears of adoptive parents by declaring that its ruling did not speak to the legality of existing second-parent adoptions that had been authorized by courts through the modified independent adoption procedure such as the one Annette and Sharon had begun (and had been used in Zachary's adoption). The court refuted Annette's contention that its narrow view of the adoption laws will "jeopardize the validity and/or finality of thousands of adoptions that were undertaking [*sic*] under these laws," pointing to her own documents that suggested the likelihood "that at least most of these adoptions are no longer subject to viable challenge." It concluded that "the issue of the validity of such adoptions is not presented in this case and . . . we don't address it here" (*Sharon S. v. the Superior Court of San Diego County* 2001a, 115).[117]

Unconvinced, almost a dozen California bar associations, bar association sections, and public interest law firms, such as the Los Angeles County Bar Association and its Family Law Section, the Lesbian and Gay Bar Association, the Women Lawyers' Association of Los Angeles, and the Bay Area Lawyers for Individual Freedom, to name just a few, submitted a letter to the state supreme court on December 20, 2001, urging the court to accept the case for review or, in the alternative, to "depublish" it. The November modification had done nothing to allay their fears, they indicated. Indeed, they criticized it for "exacerbat[ing] the confusion and uncertainty" of the opinion (*Letter Supporting Review* 2002). They expressed concern that the decision could jeopardize the security of the thousands of children and parents in gay- and lesbian-headed families, charging that it "destabilizes California families by casting grave doubt on the legality of perhaps thousands of parent/child relationships affirmed through the practice of second-parent adoptions." In addition to the emotional trauma it could create, they warned that by raising questions about the legality of parent–child relationships in a number of areas such as inheritance, health insurance coverage, income tax dependency, pensions, and consent for emergency medical care, the opinion could lead to "contentious litigation." Their letter raised the specter of parents attempting to adopt their children again, perhaps unsuccessfully now or, by failing to do so, having to live with their apprehension (*Letter Supporting Review* 2002).

Contending that the appellate court's modified opinion had left important questions about completed second-parent adoptions unanswered, the National Center for Youth Law, the Alliance for Children's Rights, and Legal Services for Children also urged the supreme court to review the appellate opinion. When the high court agreed, many of these organizations as well as numerous others, including gay rights groups, filed amicus curiae briefs. Most took no position for Sharon or Annette, noting that their main concern was the legitimacy of the second-parent adoption procedure (see Ancar 2003).

The state supreme court agreed to review the case on January 28, 2002, limiting itself chiefly to deciding "whether the birth and adoptive parent in agency and independent adoptions can agree section 8617 [of the California Family Code] shall not apply" (Sungalia 2002, 401).[118] In her opinion for the court, Justice Kathryn Werdegar addressed two questions: whether a legal parent may waive the termination provision (§8617) in an adoption proceeding and whether a second-parent adoption in which a birth parent retains her parental rights is valid.[119]

Sharon had argued that the adoption Annette sought is not legal because the law specifies that all independent adoptions require the termination of parental rights. Citing *Marshall*, the court announced the familiar principle that adoption statutes must be liberally interpreted and that the legislation was not meant to prevent an adoption in which the parties clearly had not intended to terminate these rights.[120] Announcing the well-established rule that statutory rights may be waived absent specific prohibitions to the contrary, the court found no express or implied prohibitions in the law to negate a waiver.

The court agreed with the dissenting appellate court judge that *Marshall* controlled, rejecting Sharon's argument that because *Marshall* involved a stepparent rather than an unmarried couple, much less a same-sex couple, it was irrelevant. There was no evidence that *Marshall* was based on the parties' marital status or, more generally, Werdegar said, that the court intended it to be limited to the facts of the case. Moreover, in amending the adoption laws over time, the legislature explicitly stated that it was incorporating existing judicial case law. The court pointed to the state agency's similar interpretation of the law permitting waiver of the termination rule and, more broadly, allowing second-parent adoptions as a type of independent adoption. A ruling to the contrary, the court emphasized, would contravene a policy of allowing a type of adoption that had become familiar to the residents of the state and, indeed, was allowed in almost half the states.[121]

Clearly aware of the magnitude of its ruling, the court emphasized that a decision to affirm the lower court "not only would cast a shadow of uncertainty over the legal relationships between thousands of children and their adoptive parents . . . , but potentially could prompt some adoptive parents to disclaim their established responsibilities" (*Sharon S. v. the Superior Court of San Diego County* 2003, 571). It dismissed Sharon's contention that domestic partners could avail themselves of the new domestic partnership law to ratify earlier adoptions. For a variety of reasons, the court stressed, adoptive parents may find themselves beyond the reach of the law or be unwilling to place themselves under it.

Finally, the court addressed Sharon's constitutional argument. In opposing review of the case, Sharon had also argued that upholding the adoption would violate her due process rights, citing *Troxel*, the grandparent visitation case. The court easily distinguished *Troxel*, however, declaring that visitation was governed by different laws and that the Washington State law had been extremely broad in allowing any party to seek visitation.

Thus, in a vote of 6 to 1, the supreme court reversed the lower court decision and remanded the case to allow the court to determine whether the consent was obtained by fraud or duress as Sharon had claimed.[122]

The U.S. Supreme Court denied certiorari in March 2004 (*Sharon S. v. Superior Court of California, San Diego County* 2004).

Sharon's attorney expressed his "disappoint[ment] that the court has gone down the road of 'best interests' adoption [meaning that] a single judge in a private, sealed courtroom can allow anyone to adopt anybody as long as he or she thinks it's in [that child's] best interests" (*Metropolitan News Enterprise* [Los Angeles] August 5, 2003).

Numerous motions, petitions, and court rulings followed, with each side claiming the right to parent Joshua and arguing over visitation, amid myriad other issues, such as attorney conflict of interest, the court's jurisdiction to declare Annette a "presumed parent," and the effect of Sharon's domestic violence orders.[123]

The issue came to a head when, on June 15, 2004, the trial court rejected another of Sharon's motions to dismiss and ordered a bifurcated trial to determine the legitimacy of Sharon's claim that her consent was improperly obtained and to decide whether it would be in Joshua's best interests to approve Annette's adoption petition.

After conducting a trial on the merits in November 2004, the judge orally rejected Sharon's November 2000 motion to withdraw her consent to the adoption. Shortly thereafter, he ruled as well that it would be in Joshua's best interests to be adopted by Annette and, also orally, granted Annette's motion to mandate the adoption. Sharon appealed both rulings, and the court followed the order with a written opinion in early 2005. Many appeals followed, with rulings on Sharon's claim that the trial judge had abused his discretion in determining that Joshua's best interests would be served by Annette's adoption. The appeals courts further rejected Sharon's numerous constitutional and statutory claims, focusing primarily on the fact that her attempt to withdraw her consent to the adoption exceeded the ninety-day time limit specified in the statute. The battle between them continued with numerous ancillary rulings on charges of libel, award of attorneys' fees, the alleged bias of the trial court judge, child support payments, and Zachary's visitation schedule and religious affiliation.[124]

The litigation between Sharon and Annette, described as "one of the most litigated cases in the history of San Diego County" (*Annette F. v. Sharon S.* 2006, at 1), continued until it finally ground to a halt in 2007. Over its long history, the litigants, chiefly Sharon, unsuccessfully sought review by the state supreme court as well as the U.S. Supreme Court.

SUMMARY

In the 1980s and 1990s, gays who sought to adopt children were often forced to resort to litigation to seek judicial interpretation of their state's adoption laws. Thus, the courts played a crucial role in interpreting the legal boundaries of the rights of such prospective adoptive parents.

Ironically, despite the legislative commitment to further the child's welfare, the success of the litigation did not necessarily depend on the court's determination of whether the adoption was in the "best interests" of the child, on the worthiness of the prospective adoptive parent, or, even, surprisingly perhaps, on the fitness of gay parents as a whole. Instead, the court focused primarily on whether the adoption was consistent with the language and intent of the existing state adoption law.

The legal controversy over prospective adoptions by gay parents was sparked largely by two types of adoptions: joint and second-parent adoptions.[125] Because most state laws do not specify the legality of gay adoptions, the judges' rulings on these adoption petitions clearly illustrate the significant role the courts have played in determining the success of gay rights litigants in this policymaking arena. In case after case, the judges deciding in favor of the gay claimants stressed that they had a duty to effectuate the adoption laws and further the best interests of the child. In contrast, the judges ruling against the prospective adoptive parents emphasized that they were obligated to apply traditional rules of statutory construction and defer to the legislature.

These two perspectives were most evident in the rulings in the Florida and California litigation. The judicial restraint in the Florida federal courts stands in sharp contrast to the willingness of the California courts to assume a more expansive role in interpreting state law to facilitate adoption by gay parents.

Thus, the outcome of the adoption cases was most heavily influenced by the court's view of its policymaking role: judges who viewed themselves as coordinate policymakers and believed that they could exercise their authority to implement the legislature's intent were more likely to approve adoption petitions from gay parents than judges who refused to exceed the narrow bounds of the statutory text.

NOTES

1. The NCLR (2006) furnishes a state-by-state list of cases involving custody claims by same-sex partners; see Human Rights Campaign (2006) for another state-by-state examination of the role of sexual orientation in custody and visitation laws. The center is "a national legal organization committed to advancing the civil and human rights of lesbian, gay, bisexual, and transgender people and their families through litigation, public policy advocacy, and public education" (National Center for Lesbian Rights 2004). The Human Rights Campaign, today the single largest gay, lesbian, bisexual, and transgender advocacy group in the nation, is primarily engaged in political action, but also it indirectly aids litigation by public education and raising awareness of gay rights issues (Human Rights Campaign 2009a).

2. Mucciaroni (2008) suggests that such decentralized decision making is advantageous for gay rights litigants because it dampens the public's interest in (and opposition to) their claims. However, it also has the negative consequences of requiring battles to be fought repeatedly with the rulings confined to the state or even the county in which the claims are brought.

3. Lambda Legal is a national advocacy group "committed to achieving full recognition of the civil rights of lesbians, gay men, bisexuals, transgender people and those with HIV through impact litigation, education and public policy work" (Lambda Legal 2007a).

4. Federal constitutional claims are seldom raised in such cases; in the few instances that due process and equal protection arguments have been made, the

courts have uniformly rejected them; see, for example, *Matter of Adoption of T.K.J.* (1997). In his study of successful adoptions by gays and lesbians, Connolly (2002) found that none of the petitioners raised state or federal constitutional issues or argued gay rights claims. Instead, they grounded their arguments in the children's best interests.

5. The Court distinguished *Moore* from *Village of Belle Terre v. Boraas* (1974), in which it had upheld an ordinance banning more than two unrelated individuals from living together, allowing only those related by "blood, adoption, or marriage" to share the residence (9).

6. Although the Supreme Court and many other courts use the terms "biological families" and "biological parents," the Uniform Parentage Act (UPA)—the law adopted by almost half the states—refers to two types of parents: natural and adoptive. Substituting "natural" for "biological" indicates the UPA's view that parenthood involves more than just a genetic relationship (Black 2006, 239).

7. In a footnote, the Court added that "adoption, for example, is recognized as the legal equivalent of biological parenthood" (*Smith* 1977, 844 n51).

8. Under the statute, the presumption was rebuttable within two years if the putative father filed a paternity action.

9. In *Santosky v. Kramer* (1982), a New York case involving the standard of proof necessary to terminate a parent's rights in cases of child neglect, the Court reaffirmed "the fundamental liberty interest [protected by the Fourteenth Amendment] of natural parents in the care, custody, and management of their child" (753).

10. Substantive due process analysis requires the court to determine if an asserted right is an essential part of the due process clause such that the government must protect it as a fundamental right. Although often derided as judicial activism, substantive due process decision making plays an important role in protecting fundamental rights of autonomy and privacy (see Meyer 2004; Niemczyk 2005). The Supreme Court has stressed that federal courts must be cautious about expanding the substantive reach of the due process clause and must do so only if a right is "deeply rooted in this Nation's history and tradition" or "implicit in the concept of ordered liberty" (*Bowers* 1986, 192).

In *Glucksberg* (1997), the Court had articulated a new two-part test for determining whether to declare unspecified rights as fundamental. First, they must be "so rooted in the traditions and conscience of our people as to be ranked as fundamental" as well as "implicit in the concept of ordered liberty" so that "neither liberty nor justice would exist if they were sacrificed." Second, there must be a "careful description" of the claimed liberty interest at stake (721). This approach, it stressed, lessens the likelihood that judges will allow their own values to affect the decision-making process, a habitual concern in substantive due process decision making.

11. The issue of allowing third parties, that is, nonparents, access to children is a complex one with implications for gay parents. In the decades preceding the 1980s, advocates for lesbian mothers had argued for expanded constitutional rights of parents to raise their children protected by the Fourteenth Amendment. They contended that courts should not privilege third parties, such as their ex-husbands' parents or the second wives, over them in custody disputes without

showing that they were unfit. Thus, they maintained that "the best interests of the child" model was insufficient to protect their constitutional rights. By the mid-1980s, however, when disputes arose between lesbian mothers and their former partners over a child who was biologically related to one of them, some advocates for lesbian mothers began to change their stance, insisting that courts use "the best interests" standard. *Troxel* raised the unpleasant specter that gay parents might be more vulnerable if the courts were permitted to grant visitation (or possibly custody) of a child to a grandparent or another third party. Once again, this led members of the gay community to argue against the use of the "best interests" standard (Polikoff 2001).

12. Although *Troxel* protected gay parents from hostile grandparents, it might leave the former partners of gay parents in precarious situations, possibly foreclosing their rights to a child they had been raising together.

13. The gender-specific research most often focuses on the children of lesbians (Eisold 2001); see Erera and Fredriksen's (2001) citations to such studies.

14. Although it is well recognized that the child's best interests should be paramount in adoption cases, states also use adoption laws to exercise their authority over public morality, which is often expressed as disapproval of homosexuality. Whether articulated or not, judges often disfavor adoption by gays because of religious objections to homosexuality and the belief that the best way to raise children is in a household with a mother and father married to each other (see Krasnoo 2006; see also Susoeff 1985).

15. Ball's (2003, 702–3) thoughtful discussion of the Stacey and Biblarz study warns that it is too soon to be persuaded by their finding that gay parents shape their children's sexual orientation for two reasons. First, he argues, they base their findings on only one study with a sample size of twenty-five children and ignore the many studies that found precisely the opposite. Second, he believes that their finding is problematic because they do not account for the fact that most gays and lesbians came out of heterosexual households.

16. The Family Research Institute (2008), a nonprofit organization dedicated to "preserving America's historic moral framework and the traditional family," sponsors research that has reported negative outcomes for children of gay and lesbian parents. Not surprisingly, this work has been criticized by gay rights advocates (Infanti 2007).

17. More recently, clashes have arisen over visitation and custody when same-sex relationships end (see Delaney 1991; Polikoff 1990). In such cases, when the biological parent is the only legal parent, the courts are asked to determine the rights of the psychological (that is, the de facto) parent who claims to have had significant parenting responsibility for the child with close emotional ties. Along with a number of other scholars, Bartlett (1984) believes courts should accord greater legitimacy to de facto parenting and recognize that it may not always be in the children's best interests to have exclusive ties to their biological parents. The courts have been slow to accept the legitimacy of the nonbiological parent's claim (see Connolly 1996; see also, for example, two California appellate court decisions, *Curiale v. Reagan* [1990] and *Nancy S. v. Michele* [1991], in which the child's nonbiological parent was not accorded the status of a legal parent for purposes of custody or visitation).

18. In *Palmore v. Sidoti* (1984), the Supreme Court reversed a lower court decision awarding a father custody of his child because his ex-wife was married to an African American, stating that "private biases may be outside the reach of the law, but the law cannot, directly or indirectly, give them effect" (433). This principle has not been fully accepted in the case of gay parents.

19. A Michigan appellate court case, *Michigan v. Brown* (1973), demonstrates a similar approach, as does *D.H. v. J.H.* (1981), in which the court stated that homosexuality alone does not render a parent unfit. More recently, in *S.N.E. v. R.L.B.* (1985) and *In re Adoption of Charles B.* (1990), state supreme courts also applied the nexus test.

20. The Idaho high court cited the following of cases as authority for the use of the "nexus" test, indicating that this principle had become established in state courts around the nation: *T.C.H. v. K.M.H.* (1989), *In re Marriage of Birdsall* (1988), *Pryor v. Pryor* (1999), and *Scott v. Scott* (1995).

21. Such assumptions play a similar role in visitation decisions.

22. As Pollack and Vaughn (1987, 14–15) note in the introduction to their edited anthology about lesbian mothers, the term "parent" is "more inclusive" than "mother" (or "father"), which is usually reserved for the biological mother (or father). It seems clear that "parent" is preferable because it includes adult men and women with biological as well as nonbiological relationships to the children in their households.

23. Although it is well recognized that the child's best interests are paramount in adoption proceedings, courts have also been reluctant to prevent states from exercising their authority over public morality, which is often expressed as disapproval of homosexuality. Whether articulated or not, states disfavor adoption by gays because of religious objections to homosexuality and the belief that the best way to raise children is in a household with a mother and father married to each other (see Krasnoo 2006; see also Susoeff 1985). Milligan (2002) argues that adoption statutes are meant to be construed liberally and, in failing to do so when gays seek to adopt, judges are improperly reflecting their religious and moral beliefs; see also Lauretta (2003).

24. The law has not been entirely static as the departure from the common law principle of unconditional parental authority demonstrates. In a number of states, nonparents, most notably grandparents, have been able to pursue legal claims, primarily in the context of visitation. Undoubtedly reflecting the voting strength of this constituency, many state legislatures established grandparent rights to visitation under a variety of circumstances. In adjudicating the Washington State law, *Troxel* implicitly endorsed grandparent rights though subordinating them to the rights of fit parents. However, the plurality opinion in *Troxel* can also be interpreted as paving the way for a decline in parental rights (see Harvard Law Review Association 2003).

25. Some state legislatures have enacted overtly anti-gay policies to enshrine traditional views of the family, characterizing gays who seek to adopt as outside the mainstream of family life.

26. Fla. Stat. ch. 63.042(3) provides, "No person eligible to adopt under this statute may adopt if that person is a homosexual."

27. As a result of the 1987 law, N.H. Rev. Stat. Ann. §170-B:4 provided, "Any individual not a minor and not a homosexual may adopt." In 1999, the state

legislature amended the statute to remove the phrase "and not a homosexual" (Duncan 2003, 790).

28. As the court's opinion explained, the proposed House Bill 70 would amend a number of existing laws forbidding gays from serving as foster parents, adoptive parents, or child care agency operators, specifically, RSA 170-B:4, RSA 170-F:6, I, RSA 161:2, IV, and RSA 170-E:4 (*In re Opinion of the Justices* 1987, 23).

29. In *Bowers*, the U.S. Supreme Court upheld a Georgia law criminalizing sodomy.

30. The annotation to Ala. Code §26-10A-6 cites House Joint Resolution 35 (Acts 1998, No. 98-439), which states, "[The legislature] hereby express our intent to prohibit child adoption by homosexual couples" (Duncan 2003, 791).

31. Hong (2003, 39–40) cites press accounts indicating that such laws were a reaction to events in Hawaii and Vermont that threatened to recognize same-sex marriage and that the Utah and Mississippi legislatures wanted to forestall attempts to legalize same-sex marriage in their states.

32. Miss. Code Ann. §93-17-3(5) provides, "Adoption by couples of the same gender is prohibited."

33. Utah Code Ann. §78-30-1(3)(b) provides, "A child may not be adopted by a person who is cohabiting in a relationship that is not a legally valid and binding marriage under the laws of this state."

34. Wardle drafted the Utah state regulations restricting adoption and foster care placements to related adults (Stacey and Biblarz 2001, 160).

35. Okla. Stat. tit. 10, §7502-1.4(A) provides, "This state, any of its agencies, or any court of this state shall not recognize an adoption by more than one individual of the same sex from any other state or foreign jurisdiction."

36. The full faith and credit clause of article IV of the U.S. Constitution provides, "Full Faith and Credit shall be given in each State to the public Acts, Records, and judicial Proceedings of every other State. And the Congress may by general Laws prescribe the Manner in which such Acts, Records and Proceedings shall be proved, and the Effect thereof."

37. Three families challenged the Oklahoma law. The lower court denied standing to one couple on the grounds that the claimed injury—that the men were afraid to bring the child back to Oklahoma as their open adoption agreement required because the state might interfere with their family status—was too speculative. When the court ruled that the statute was unconstitutional, the state agency (neither the governor nor the attorney general joined in the appeal) appealed, as did the couple denied standing. The appellate court found that two couples lacked standing, but because one couple satisfied the standing requirement, the appeals court ruled on this couple's constitutional challenge and agreed with the lower court that the amendment was unconstitutional under the full faith and credit clause. The court found it unnecessary to decide the equal protection and due process claims.

38. Arkansas Initiative 1 provides, "An individual who is cohabitating outside of a valid marriage may not adopt or be a foster parent of a child less than eighteen years (ArkansasVotersGuide.com 2008).

39. Polikoff (1997) argues that it is helpful to gay youngsters to have openly gay foster parents; see Gesing (2004).

40. Conn. Gen. Stat. §45a-726a provides, "The Commissioner of Children and Families or a child-placing agency may consider the sexual orientation of the prospective adoptive or foster parent or parents when placing a child for adoption or in foster care. Nothing in this section shall be deemed to require the Commissioner of Children and Families or a child-placing agency to place a child for adoption or in foster care with a prospective adoptive or foster parent or parents who are homosexual or bisexual." It seems likely that this law violates the state constitution's guarantee of equal protection.

41. In 1986, the Massachusetts Department of Social Services issued a regulation preventing gays and lesbians from becoming foster parents. The policy was reversed during the settlement of a lawsuit (Hong 2003, 38).

42. In Missouri, a regulation prohibited gays from becoming foster parents until it was struck by a Jackson County, Missouri, circuit court in a case brought by the ACLU to challenge it.

43. Foster care expenses are much higher when children are kept in institutional settings as indicated in a recent report by the Evan B. Donaldson Adoption Institute (2008). The report cited a study by Gates et al. (2007) that estimated that a nationwide ban on members of the lesbian, gay, bisexual, and transgender community serving as foster parents would raise the cost of providing foster care from $87 million to $130 million a year.

44. Most second-parent adoptions involve lesbian couples in which one of the women is the child's biological mother (Schacter 2000, 933).

45. Shapiro (1999) presents a critical view of second-parent adoptions from the perspective of lesbian legal theory.

46. Parental status is necessary to make emergency medical decisions for a child, acquire private medical insurance, or even live in dwellings requiring family units (see *Matter of Jacob* 1995). It allows children to benefit from the parent's death through inheritance, Social Security, or workers' compensation. In the absence of second-parent adoption, gay and lesbian parents attempt to formalize relationships with their children with legal instruments such as wills, guardianship agreements, and powers of attorney for health care. Subject to interpretation, such documents are inferior to and do not provide the same security as adoption (see Croteau 2004).

47. Many courts were forced to be inventive, approving second-parent adoptions by applying doctrines such as "in loco parentis, de facto parenthood and intended parentage" (Lauretta 2003, 187, citations omitted).

48. In lesbian families, one of the partners is usually the biological mother of the child, typically through some form of donor insemination, and the coparenting partner seeks to adopt the child with the mother's consent. When the family consists of gay men, one partner has already adopted as a single parent or has become the legal father of the child through a surrogate mother, and his partner seeks to adopt or become a coparent.

49. See Connolly's (2002) report of interviews with twenty parents who succeeded in second-parent adoptions.

50. The American Academy of Pediatrics, American Psychiatric Association, and American Medical Association have specifically endorsed second-parent adoptions by gays and lesbians (see Mallon 2006).

51. Croteau (2004) discusses the tragedy that can follow with the death of the child's only legal parent. Instead of allowing the partner to adopt the child, the state may place the child in foster care or with relatives the child has never met; the only recourse may be protracted litigation.

52. Although the California legislature initially provided for second-parent adoptions for registered domestic partners only, the courts expanded eligibility. In enacting a law to allow second-parent adoptions, Connecticut reversed a ruling by the state supreme court; Vermont codified a 1993 judicial decision that permitted second-parent adoptions (see Croteau 2004).

53. See Connolly's (2002) study of interviews with twenty parents who succeeded in second-parent adoptions.

54. In some states, termination is required prior to approval of the adoption; in some states, it is simultaneous or occurs after the petition is approved.

55. This standard has evolved over time from the "tender years doctrine," in which the mother was almost automatically awarded custody of the children. Under the Uniform Marriage and Divorce Act, adopted by many states, judges take a number of factors into account, including the parents' wishes, the child's wishes, and the mental and physical health of the proposed custodians. Most courts also consider homosexuality a pertinent factor in determining custody, most often as a negative factor (see Connolly 1996).

56. Vt. Stat. Ann. tit. 15A, §1-102b provides, "If a family unit consists of a parent and the parent's partner, and adoption is in the best interest of the child, the partner of a parent may adopt a child of the parent. Termination of the parent's parental rights is unnecessary in an adoption under this subsection."

57. Mass. Gen. Laws, ch. 210 §1 provides, "A person of full age may petition the probate court in the county where he resides for leave to adopt as his child another person younger than himself."

58. In *In re Infant Girl W.* (2006), an Indiana appellate court decided the legality of a joint petition for adoption by a lesbian couple, assessing the law's requirement that adoption is limited to married couples and single individuals.

Interpreting the Indiana law allowing a "resident of Indiana" to adopt, the court cited the well-accepted rule of statutory construction that words used in the singular may include the plural. Thus, the court continued, the law applies to "residents" of the state, and there is no indication that the legislature intended that these residents be married. The court pointed out that the case was about the broader issue of unmarried couples, regardless of their sexual orientation.

Additionally, the court noted that unlike other states, such as Florida, the statute is also silent on the effect of sexual orientation on adoption. And although the legislature likely had not contemplated adoption by same-sex couples, the law does not preclude it if the best interests of the child are furthered in such an adoption. Again, the court recited the various benefits to the child if adopted by both women and, just as important, cited numerous instances in which the child would be harmed in the event of the couple's separation or the death of one when only one of them had a legal relationship to that child. Finally, although the law required the natural parent's rights to be terminated as part of an adoption proceeding, clearly, the court stressed, the legislature did not intend such a result when the natural parent was one of the petitioners in the adoption proceeding.

Judge Edward Najam, dissenting, hastened to make clear that the opinion was based not on antipathy toward the petitioners' sexual orientation. Rather, the objection was based on the court's interpretation of the law, which did not conform to the statutory text and could not be justified by the desire to further the best interests of the child. In the dissent's view, the court could have accomplished the same end simply by allowing Helen to adopt the child while permitting her biological mother to retain her parental rights, as it ultimately did in the second part of its opinion.

59. N.Y. Dom. Rel. Law §110 provides, "An adult unmarried person or an adult husband and his adult wife together may adopt another person."

60. In the mid-1980s, a number of trial courts in the District of Columbia, California, Washington, and Alaska permitted a nonbiological mother to adopt the child born to her lesbian partner without terminating the parental rights of the latter and granted the lesbian couples their joint petition to adopt a child to whom neither was related.

61. In 2004, New York courts were asked to decide whether two unmarried individuals could jointly adopt a child who was related to neither, a question left open in *Matter of Jacob*. Despite the enthusiastic approval of the adoption agency, the lower court had denied the applicants' joint adoption petition because the law did not expressly permit joint petitions for adoption by unmarried persons. Acknowledging that adoption law must be strictly construed, the court emphasized that it must also assess the legislative purpose of the law and apply it "in harmony with the humanitarian principle that adoption is a means of securing the best possible home for a child" (*In re Adoption of Carolyn B.* 2004, 69). With this in mind, the court found the joint petition permissible, ruling that no purpose would be served by forcing the couple to file two successive petitions to accomplish their ends.

Dissenting on procedural grounds, Judges James Lawton and Eugene Pigott Jr. said that it had been settled in *Matter of Jacob* that a same-sex couple could adopt but that the statute as written permits only married couples to file jointly. Any exceptions, they emphasized, must emanate from the legislature, not the court.

62. In a footnote, the court added that it would use the phrase "unmarried couple" to describe the plaintiffs, for the law made no distinction between opposite-sex and same-sex couples (*In re M.M.D.* 1995, 843 n2).

63. D.C. Code Ann. §16-302 provides, "Any person may petition the court for a decree of adoption."

64. The court cited a 1901 provision of the law that specified that words in the singular should include the plural unless it led to an "unreasonable" interpretation.

65. 750 Ill. Comp. Stat. 50/2 provides, "Any of the following persons, who is under no legal disability . . . and who has resided in the State of Illinois continuously for a period of at least 6 months immediately preceding the commencement of an adoption proceeding . . . may institute such proceeding." Similarly, in *In re Hart* (2001), a Delaware Family Court ruling pointed out that a 1992 amendment to the Delaware Adoption Law specified that the statute must be liberally interpreted, with the best interests of the child the predominant consideration in an adoption petition.

66. N.J. Stat. Ann. §9:3-43 provides, "Any person may institute an action for adoption except that a married person may do so only with the written consent of his spouse or jointly with his spouse in the same action or if living separate and apart from his spouse."

67. 23 Pa. Cons. Stat. Ann. §2901 provides, "Unless the court for cause shown determines otherwise, no decree of adoption shall be entered unless the natural parent or parents' rights have been terminated." The children in the case, R.B.F. and R.C.F., were the biological twin sons of a woman who had been artificially inseminated by an anonymous sperm donor. In *In re Adoption of R.B.F.* (2000), a Pennsylvania superior court affirmed the dismissal of her partner's adoption petition because the law required the mother to relinquish her parental rights. Similarly, in *In re Adoption of C.C.G and Z.C.G.* (2000), after one of the men adopted C.C.G. and Z.C.G., his partner also petitioned to adopt. The court also held that the adoption was invalid unless the adoptive father first relinquished his parental rights.

68. Shortly before the Pennsylvania Supreme Court decided *Adoption of R.B.F.* (2002) on August 20, 2002, the Nebraska Supreme Court had decided *Russell v. Bridgens* (2002) on June 28, 2002. This case began in 1996 when Bridgens, one of a same-sex couple, adopted a child in Pennsylvania. A year later, she and her partner, Russell, adopted the child jointly. After two years of living together, they separated, and in 2000, Russell sought custody of the child in a Nebraska court. Bridgens filed a motion for summary judgment, arguing that because she never terminated her parental rights in the child as required by Pennsylvania law, the adoption was invalid and that the court had lacked subject matter jurisdiction to grant it. A Nebraska trial court agreed that, under the circumstances, Nebraska was not required to recognize the adoption.

The case was quickly resolved when the state supreme court held that Bridgens had not met her burden of proof for summary judgment because she failed to show that the lower court lacked subject matter jurisdiction to grant the adoption. Although the adoption decree was in the record, there were no other documents to show that Bridgens had not relinquished her parental rights before the joint adoption proceeding. The supreme court remanded the case, noting that a decision on the issue of a court's subject matter jurisdiction in granting an adoption was forthcoming in the Pennsylvania Supreme Court.

69. Ind. Code §31-19-15-1 provides, "If the biological parents of an adopted person are alive, the biological parents are: (1) relieved of all legal duties and obligations to the adopted child; and (2) divested of all rights with respect to the child."

70. As part of this proceeding, the father agreed to relinquish his rights to the children.

71. Wis. Stat. §48.82 provides, "The following persons are eligible to adopt a minor if they are residents of this state: (a) A husband and wife jointly, or either the husband or wife if the other spouse is a parent of the minor (b) An unmarried adult."

72. The ACLU Lesbian and Gay Rights Project was established in the mid-1980s, adding its name to the roster of public interest litigation firms advocating for gay and lesbian rights.

73. Everyone involved, including the father, agreed that his parental rights should be terminated.

74. Colo. Rev. Stat. §19-5-211(2) provides, "The parents shall be divested of all legal rights and obligations with respect to the child, and the adopted child shall be free from all legal obligations of obedience and maintenance with respect to the parents." In 2007, the state amended its adoption law: Colo. Rev. Stat. §19-5-203(1)(d.5)(I) allows adoption with "written and verified consent in a second-parent adoption that the child has a sole legal parent, and the sole legal parent wishes the child to be adopted by a specified second adult."

75. Ohio Rev. Code Ann. §3107.15(A)(1) provides, "A final decree of adoption . . . except with respect to a spouse of the petitioner and relatives of the spouse, [shall] . . . relieve the biological or other legal parents of the adopted person of all parental rights and responsibilities."

76. The Ohio Supreme Court denied review in *In re Adoption of Doe* (1999).

77. Ironically, an earlier Ohio Supreme Court case approved an adoption by a single gay man in *In re Adoption of Charles B.* (1990). Here, Mr. B.'s petition to adopt eight-year-old Charles B. was opposed by the county department of social services although supported by the guardian ad litem appointed to represent the child. The trial court found that adoption was in Charles's best interests and granted an interlocutory order of adoption.

When the agency appealed, a divided appellate court reversed the trial court on the grounds "that, as a matter of law, homosexuals are not eligible to adopt" in Ohio (884) and that such an adoption would never be in a child's best interests. In a per curiam opinion, the supreme court quickly disposed of the case, emphasizing that under Ohio law, unmarried individuals are eligible to adopt and that in determining whether to allow adoption or custody, the court must be guided by the best interests of the child, with such decisions made on a case-by-case basis.

Moreover, the court held, evidence of sexual misconduct is admissible only if it adversely affects the child, and such evidence must be presented at the adoption hearing. Here, the only adverse witness was an agency administrator (who had spent barely an hour with the boy and had not seen the two together) who testified against the adoption on the grounds that Mr. B. did not fit "'the characteristic profile of preferred adoptive placement'" (888). Numerous witnesses testified in favor of the adoption, and on the basis of these factors, the supreme court held that the trial court judge did not abuse his discretion in approving it.

Justice Alice Robie Resnick contended that the parent's homosexuality "should not, in and of itself, be determinative . . . [but] neither," she said, "can it be ignored" (890). She argued that because the boy had a fragile physical and mental medical condition, with his immune system already compromised by leukemia, exposing him to an environment in which he ran an increased risk of contracting HIV or AIDS was not in his best interests. Acknowledging that Mr. B. had tested negatively for HIV, she stressed that because of his high-risk lifestyle, the long-term future was uncertain. In her view, therefore, the lower court judge had abused his discretion in consenting to the adoption.

78. Conn. Gen. Stat. §45a-724(a)(3) provides, "Any parent of a minor child may agree in writing with one other person who shares parental responsibility for the child with such parent that the other person shall adopt or join in the adoption

of the child, if the parental rights, if any, of any other person other than the parties to such agreement have been terminated."

79. Although a joint petition, this is a second-parent adoption because the parent, B.P., consented to the adoption but refused to relinquish her right to the child, Luke.

80. Neb. Rev. Stat. §43-101 provides, "Any minor child may be adopted by any adult person or persons and any adult child may be adopted by the spouse of such child's parent in the cases."

81. In 1977, a Dade County ordinance banned discrimination against gays in employment and housing. Bryant began her "Save the Children" campaign a few weeks after it passed, collecting 65,000 signatures to challenge the law and force its inclusion on a referendum ballot. Emphasizing the negative effects that gays and lesbians have on children and traditional families, its supporters succeeded in repealing the ordinance. The day after Bryant's ballot measure passed, the Democratic governor, Reuben Askew, signed a law banning same-sex marriage and gay adoption (Benkov 1994, ch. 4; see Mezey 2007, ch. 1, for more information on Bryant and the Save the Children campaign.)

82. Fla. Stat. ch. 63.042(3) provides, "No person eligible to adopt under this statute may adopt if that person is a homosexual." The law defines a homosexual as a person who is "known to engage in current, voluntary homosexual activity" (*Florida, Department of Health and Rehabilitative Services v. Cox* 1993, 1215).

See Cohen (2003, 239 n123) for citations to statutes in the forty-seven states plus the District of Columbia that allow homosexual adoption; excluded are Florida, Utah, and Mississippi, and, since November 2008, Arkansas.

83. Because the Eleventh Amendment bars suits against states under most circumstances, the defendants were sued in their official capacity under 42 U.S.C. §1983.

84. Gays were permitted to serve as foster parents or legal guardians. In *Matthews v. Weinberg* (1994), the Florida District Court of Appeal held that because the Florida Department of Health and Rehabilitative Services had not followed the rulemaking requirements, its policy of barring homosexuals as foster parents was invalid. The Florida Supreme Court denied review in *Matthews* (1995). In early 2000, between 3,000 and 4,000 children were in foster care in Florida (*New York Times* January 21, 2005; for a discussion of the inconsistency in the state's foster care and adoption policy with respect to adoption by gays, see Turbe 2003; see also Polikoff 1997).

85. The state argued for the first time in its motion for summary judgment that Lofton's application was rejected because it was incomplete on the grounds that it had not indicated his homosexuality. The court documents provided ample evidence that he was rejected because he was gay. Meanwhile, Lofton and Croteau and the children had moved to Oregon, but the children were still subject to Florida's supervision (Cohen 2003, 227–8).

86. The district court denied the plaintiffs' attempts to certify a class of foster parents and foster children as plaintiffs.

87. Robert Butterworth was the state attorney general.

88. In *Glucksberg*, the Court reiterated its oft-stated principle that fundamental rights must be "deeply rooted in this Nation's history and tradition" (720–1). In

this challenge to a Washington State ban on physician-assisted suicide, the Court upheld the law, rejecting the plaintiff's claims that they had a fundamental right to die.

89. Summary judgment is proper when "there is no genuine issue as to any material fact and . . . the moving party is entitled to a judgment as a matter of law" (Federal Rules of Civil Procedure §56[c]).

90. Crowley (2002, 264) argues that the court misapplied *Smith* since that case was about the process required to remove children from a foster home and Florida had no intention of removing the children from Lofton's home. Additionally, he argues that the court should have used *Smith* to explore the inconsistency of the Florida law allowing gays to be foster parents but not adoptive parents.

91. See Mezey (2007, ch. 2).

92. Florida has a long history of discriminating against gays, beginning well before the 1977 adoption exclusion amendment was enacted (see Turbe 2003).

93. In 2003, the state removed the preference for married couples, and since then one-quarter of Florida adoptions are by individuals (*Lofton v. Secretary of Department of Children and Family Services* 2004a, 820).

94. Ironically, the state had offered to make Lofton Doe's legal guardian, suggesting that it would be in the boy's best interests to remain with him. Strasser (2004; see Maurer 2006) argues that the state did not appear to be greatly interested in the child's welfare since it was surely not in his best interests to ignore his wish that Lofton adopt him and to remove him from the only home he had ever known and away from the only father he had ever known.

95. The appeals court was referring to the case brought by James Cox in the early 1990s. Cox was a gay man whose application to adopt a special needs child was denied on the basis of his sexual orientation. The lower court granted Cox's motion for summary judgment, relying on an earlier unpublished Florida lower court opinion, *Seebol v. Farie* (1991), in which the trial judge found the statute unconstitutional on the grounds of vagueness and violation of the rights of privacy and equal protection. The state did not appeal *Seebol*.

When the state appealed the ruling for Cox, the appellate court reversed. Citing judicial restraint, the court proclaimed that "the debate over the nature of homosexuality and the wisdom of the strictures that our society has historically placed upon homosexual activity cannot and should not be resolved today in this court. For purposes of governance, the legislature is the proper forum in which to conduct this debate so long as its decisions are permitted by the state and federal constitutions" (*Florida, Department of Health and Rehabilitative Services v. Cox* 1993, 1212).

The state supreme court affirmed the appellate court's decision upholding the statute but remanded the case to allow the lower court to obtain a more complete record on whether the law violated equal protection (*Cox v. Florida Department of Health and Rehabilitative Services* 1995). Cox dropped his suit before a retrial (Reding 2003, 1298; Turbe 2003, 378 n74).

96. The court added that even if the plaintiffs had a legitimate expectation of permanency and a constitutionally protected relationship, it would entitle them only to a right of procedural due process, not a substantive right to be beyond the state's control.

97. Because *Lawrence* had been decided after the plaintiffs lost their case in the district court and filed their appeals, they filed supplemental briefs in the appellate court.

98. The appeals court cited Justice Antonin Scalia's dissenting opinion twice to justify its conclusion that *Lawrence* did not identify a fundamental right. The Supreme Court never specifically declared the nature of the right at issue in *Lawrence*, nor did it announce that it was using minimal scrutiny to decide the case. Thus, there is a controversy over the precise nature of the right recognized in *Lawrence*. Some argue that the sentence near the end of the opinion, "The Texas statute furthers no legitimate state interest which can justify its intrusion into the personal and private life of the individual," indicates that the Court used minimal scrutiny, which it would not have done if it had considered the right in question a fundamental right.

Others contend that comparing the right in *Lawrence* to the rights implicated in other privacy cases indicates that the Court implicitly considered it a fundamental right. Still others claim that *Lawrence* is based on a liberty interest, triggering a higher form of scrutiny than traditionally accorded liberty interests by placing the burden on the state to justify the law rather than forcing the litigant to prove that the law burdens a fundamental right. Moreover, by overturning *Bowers*, which was about homosexual sodomy, they argue that *Lawrence* involved privacy of sexual relations among adults (Backer 2006).

99. The court did not rule on the state's claim that the statute furthered its interest in public morality beyond noting that advancing public morality was a legitimate state interest.

100. In a footnote, the court dismissed Lofton's argument that the state did not automatically exclude applicants with a history of drug abuse or domestic violence but instead evaluated them on a case-by-case basis. There was no evidence, however, said the court, that such persons were allowed to adopt if an investigation reveals that they committed such acts.

101. The *Lofton* rulings were extensively criticized for their cavalier treatment of the precedent set by *Lawrence*; see, for example, Jozwiak (2005) and Strasser (2005). For a discussion approving the decision, see Armstrong (2004).

102. The U.S. Supreme Court denied certiorari in *Lofton v. Secretary, Florida, Department of Children and Families* (2005).

103. A rehearing requires a majority vote.

104. In addition to *Romer*, Birch and Barkett each cited the following cases to prove their points: *City of Cleburne v. Cleburne Living Center, Inc.* (1985), *United States Department of Agriculture v. Moreno* (1973), and *Eisenstadt v. Baird* (1972). Barkett argued that because the Court found the purported motives implausible in these four cases, it determined that prejudice was the basis for the laws in question. Birch contended that the Court only inferred the motives rather than actually investigating them. In his view, these cases indicate that a reviewing court does not investigate a legislature's motivation.

105. Although Barkett thought equal protection sufficient to decide the case, she also believed that the law violated due process, citing *Lawrence*'s recognition of a right to sexual privacy.

106. Earlier in the year, Judge David Audlin Jr. of the Monroe County Circuit Court had also declared the 1977 law unconstitutional on state and federal

grounds. In a case involving a teenager who had been living with the gay petitioner, his legal guardian for five years, Audlin characterized the law as "bigotry." The state child welfare agency played no role in the case because the man was already the boy's permanent guardian. The ruling applied only to Monroe County and was not appealed to a higher court, thus limiting its use as precedent (Keysnews.com September 11, 2008; MiamiHerald.com September 24, 2008).

107. There are numerous cases dealing with parenthood, such as determination of legal parental status and support obligations; many are decided under the provisions of California's version of the UPA (see Steely 2007).

108. AB 26, passed in 1999 as Cal. Fam. Code §297, permitted same-sex couples to register as domestic partners and granted some rights, such as hospital visitation and health care benefits.

109. AB 25 was passed in 2001, amending four provisions of California law (Cal. Fam. Code §§9000, 9002, 9004, and 9005). It added the right to make medical decisions for partners, to inherit when a partner dies intestate, and to use sick leave to care for a domestic partner. Section 3 of the bill "authorize[d] the employment of the procedures applicable to stepparent adoption to the adoption by a domestic partner, as defined [in Section 297 of the California Family Code], of the child of his or her domestic partner." The law obviated the need for most second-parent adoptions by allowing a domestic partner to adopt the other's legal child without revoking the latter's parental rights, essentially equating the procedure to a stepparent adoption. AB 205, passed in 2003 and made effective on January 1, 2005, accorded all rights and responsibilities of marriage to domestic partners (Nelson 2008).

110. In *Koebke v. Bernardo Heights Country Club* (2005), the plaintiffs sued the country club for discrimination under the state civil rights act, which prohibited discrimination on the basis of marital status, gender, or sexual orientation. The plaintiffs charged that the club refused to extend club benefits to domestic partners on the same basis as spouses. In a landmark ruling, the court held that the legislative intent and the language of the Domestic Partner Rights and Responsibilities Act of 2003, made effective on January 1, 2005, must be broadly interpreted to mean that "there shall be no discrimination in the treatment of registered domestic partners and spouses" (1223) and that businesses are not permitted to treat registered domestic partners differently from spouses under the civil rights act. The court remanded the case for fact-finding on a number of issues, such as whether the club was a place of public accommodation as defined by the civil rights law.

111. California is one of almost two dozen states that have adopted the UPA in full, the UPA therefore governing all aspects of the state's family law. The "presumed father" provision of the UPA allows a man to claim paternity over a child fathered by another man under certain conditions; the most relevant of the UPA requirements for lesbian partners is the one in which the child must live in his home and he publicly declares the child as his own. In *Kristine Renee H. v. Lisa Ann R.* (2004), the appellate court allowed a nonbiological lesbian mother to claim "paternity" under the UPA by applying the "presumed father" provision to a nonbiological lesbian mother who lived with the child and held him out as her own. A few months earlier, in *Maria B. v. Superior Court* (2004), another California

appellate court refused to consider the nonbiological mother the children's parent and to order her to provide child support (see Manternach 2005). In August 2005, the California Supreme Court resolved this conflict in the lower courts in *Kristine H. v. Lisa R.* (2005), along with two other rulings affecting lesbian parents, *Elisa B. v. Superior Court of El Dorado County* (2005) and *K.M. v. E.G.* (2005). In these cases, the court broadly interpreted the UPA to encompass lesbian coparents (see Black 2006). The supreme court held that under the UPA, children born to gay and lesbian (or other nontraditional) parents were entitled to the same rights as other children. These rulings are important because "they represent the first reported decisions to hold that parental rights can be established by parents of the same gender without an adoption and without proof of a biological relationship to the child" (Wald 2005, 139; see Richmond 2005).

112. In the divorce agreement, he had committed to paying child support (called alimony at the time) and to "surrender" his adoptive rights to the children on the condition that she begin formal legal proceedings to adopt them.

113. The court issued its original opinion in *Sharon S. v. the Superior Court of San Diego County* (2001a) on October 25, 2001. On November 21, 2001, in denying a rehearing, the appellate court released a modified ruling to alleviate concerns about the validity of existing second-parent adoptions (*Sharon S. v. the Superior Court of San Diego County* 2001b). The October 25 opinion, superseded by the supreme court's grant of review, incorporated the items specified in the court in its November 21 ruling.

114. Lesbian couples also fell within the UPA, but for a number of reasons, this was not considered as advantageous as the method that Sharon and Annette used (see Scaparotti 2002).

115. Annette filed an order to show cause for custody and a petition to establish a parental relationship with Joshua (Lauretta 2003, 176).

116. Agency adoptions are situations in which the parents of the child surrender their parental rights to an adoption agency. An independent adoption is one in which the parents cede their parental rights directly to adoptive parents; they must consent to the adoption, at which point their parental rights are terminated, and are permitted ninety days in which to revoke their consent. An adoption by a stepparent, as in all states, does not require termination of parental rights.

117. In their letter to the state supreme court dated December 20, 2001, the amici emphasize that despite the court's attempt to reassure couples with second-parent adoptions, its opinion can offer support to those challenging a second-parent adoption at the outset and also raises concerns about couples who completed a second-parent adoption only within the past year. Moreover, they pointed out that the court's seeming reliance on the new domestic partnership law overestimated the degree to which it would resolve all adoption issues for same-sex couples (*Letter Supporting Review* 2002).

118. Cal. Civ. Code §229 became Cal. Fam. Code §8617.

119. The supreme court defined a "second-parent adoption" as an independent adoption in which a child is adopted by a legal parent's partner with the consent of the parent so that the child has two legal parents of equal legal status.

120. The court said that "in *Marshall*, we thus effectively read second parent adoption into the statutory scheme by approving a type of second parent adoption, step-

parent adoption, which at the time, the statutes did not expressly authorize. . . . In so doing, we necessarily determined that relinquishment of the birth parent's rights was not essential to adoption and that section 8617's predecessor was not mandatory" (*Sharon S. v. the Superior Court of San Diego County* 2003, 564).

121. The concurring justices also noted that at least twenty other jurisdictions permitted second-parent adoptions.

122. The superior court had not determined how Sharon's consent was obtained, so the appellate court remanded to the lower court for evidentiary findings on this matter (*Sharon S. v. the Superior Court of San Diego County* 2004). The appeals court addressed Sharon's arguments that Annette's discovery of her therapy records should have been limited and that her consent was invalid because the attorney had not strictly complied with the requirements of California adoption law.

123. The appeals court reversed the trial judge's declaration of Annette as the "presumed parent."

124. See, for example, *Annette F. v. Sharon S.* (2005), *In re Adoption of Joshua S.* (2005a), and *In re Adoption of Joshua S.* (2005b).

125. Although courts must approve all adoptions, adoptions involving gays are typically more complicated because courts do not merely approve an adoption petition but also must interpret the state adoption law before determining whether to place a child in a prospective adoptive parent's home.

2

✝

The Right to Marry: Part 1

Relationship recognition policies are traditionally within the purview of the states. Aside from rulings on marriage within the broad parameters of constitutional rights, the U.S. Supreme Court has been reluctant to interfere with the state government's prerogative to define civil marriage. When gay rights litigants turned to the state courts to adjudicate their constitutional claims, they discovered that the state judiciary was also largely unwilling to invade the legislature's authority over marriage.

In *Loving v. Virginia* (1967)—one of the U.S. Supreme Court's first rulings on marriage—the Court considered the constitutionality of Virginia's miscegenation policy. Although limited to interracial marriages, *Loving* "remains the most important, most coherent, clearest, most frequently cited case explaining the constitutional right to marry" (Wardle 1998, 347). This issue was new to the federal courts, but almost twenty years earlier, in *Perez v. Sharp* (1948), the California Supreme Court struck a state law prohibiting marriages between whites and nonwhites, ruling that it violated the equal protection clause of the U.S. Constitution; it also declared marriage a fundamental right.

Speaking for a unanimous Court in *Loving*, Chief Justice Earl Warren rejected the state's theory that the law did not involve a racial classification because it affected both races equally. Indeed, he found that it had no purpose beyond "invidious racial discrimination" (*Loving* 1967, 11) and, applying strict scrutiny, declared it unconstitutional on equal protection and due process grounds. "The freedom to marry," Warren observed, "has long been recognized as one of the vital personal rights essential to the orderly pursuit of happiness by free men" (*Loving* 1967, 12, quoting *Skinner v. Oklahoma* 1942, 541).[1]

More than a decade later, the Supreme Court returned to the subject in *Zablocki v. Redhail* (1978) and proclaimed marriage a fundamental right, declaring that laws that "significantly interefere[d] with decisions to enter into the marital relationship" must be reviewed with heightened scrutiny (386).[2] Because the Wisconsin law impinged on the right to marry, the Court ruled that it violated the equal protection clause. In *Safley v. Turner* (1987), the Court reaffirmed the importance of marriage. Citing *Zablocki*, it held that a Missouri prison regulation that prevented inmates from marrying without the prison superintendent's permission infringed on the constitutional right of marriage.

Loving's affirmation of freedom of choice in marriage became a rallying cry for same-sex couples in part because it set aside "the long-established emphasis on the ultimate responsibility of the states to regulate marriage in our federal system" (Wardle 1998, 306). Despite its sweeping rhetoric, however, most courts declined to interpret *Loving* to override legislative restrictions on same-sex marriages, refusing to analogize restrictions on sexual partners to restrictions on racial partners (see Nolan 1998). Throughout the 1970s and 1980s, in cases such as *Baker v. Nelson* (1971), *Jones v. Hallahan* (1973), *Singer v. Hara* (1974a), *Adams v. Howerton* (1982), *De Santo v. Barnsley* (1984), and *Dean v. District of Columbia* (1995), the courts signaled their unwillingness to interfere with the state legislature's authority to define marriage, justifying their rulings on principles of judicial restraint, deference to democratic decision making, and traditional views of marriage and even citing standard dictionary definitions of marriage.[3]

A FLEETING VICTORY FOR SAME-SEX MARRIAGE SUPPORTERS

As the cases show, "until the mid-1990s, same-sex marriage litigation was always something of a long shot" (Duncan 2004, 624). But plaintiffs began to gain ground when the Hawaii courts appeared open to a new approach to relationship policies.[4] In *Baehr v. Lewin* (1993), with Justice Steven Levinson announcing the opinion for a divided court, the Hawaii Supreme Court reversed the lower court's dismissal of a complaint from same-sex couples who sought marriage licenses. However, ruling that same-sex marriage was not an essential part of the nation's traditions and values, the court refused to accept the couples' claim that they had a fundamental right to marry. The majority proved sympathetic to their argument, however, that they were victims of sex discrimination, explicitly prohibited in the state constitution.[5] It remanded the case, ordering the state to show that the law furthered a compelling interest and was narrowly tailored to further that interest, in other words, to survive strict scrutiny.[6]

Judge Walter Heen dissented, distinguishing *Loving* and *Zablocki* because neither involved a right to marry a partner of the same sex. Echoing the "equal application" theory unsuccessfully propounded by Virginia in *Loving*, Heen contended that because the law applied equally to both sexes, it was not a sex-based classification and therefore did not merit strict scrutiny. He said he was satisfied with the legislature's purpose of "fostering and protecting the propagation of the human race through heterosexual marriages." And if the plaintiffs believed that they were being deprived of the benefits of marriage, their only recourse was to seek relief from the legislature whose task it is "to express the will of the populace" (*Baehr v. Lewin* 1993, 74).

Following a trial, in a decision announced on December 3, 1996, Circuit Court Judge Kevin Chang found that the state failed to meet its burden of justifying the discriminatory treatment toward same-sex couples and held that the Hawaii marriage law violated the state constitution; he barred the state from denying marriage licenses solely because the applicants were of the same sex (*Baehr v. Miike* 1996). Chang stayed his order pending the state's appeal, and in April 1997, the state legislature approved a constitutional amendment granting the legislature the power to restrict marriage to opposite-sex couples; following a referendum on November 3, 1998, it was adopted as part of the Hawaii Constitution.[7]

In a later unpublished opinion, the state high court affirmed Chang's ruling against the state (*Baehr v. Miike* 1997), but the decision had no effect because it was superseded by the constitutional amendment. Then, on December 9, 1999, the Hawaii Supreme Court reversed Chang's judgment, ruling that the marriage amendment obviated the equal protection challenge and mooted the case (*Baehr v. Miike* 1999).

Simply dismissing the case did not satisfy Justice Mario Ramil. He admonished the court for involving itself in the debate over same-sex marriage, an issue, he said, that "involves a question of pure public policy that should have been left to the people of this state or their elected representatives" (at 10).

CIVIL UNIONS

Just before the turn of the twenty-first century, the Vermont Supreme Court added a new dimension to the same-sex marriage debate. In July 1997, three gay couples sued the state, claiming that denying them marriage licenses violated the state constitution. Shortly after the Hawaii court acknowledged that its decision was usurped by the state constitutional amendment, the Vermont Supreme Court handed down its ruling in *Baker v. Vermont* (1999).

Speaking for the court, Chief Justice Jeffrey Amestoy ruled that there was ample evidence that the legislature intended to limit marriage to a man and a woman and that because both sexes are treated equally, the marriage law does not discriminate on the basis of sex. Relying on the common benefits clause of the Vermont Constitution, he stressed that the court did not base its ruling on the U.S. Constitution, in large part to justify applying more rigorous review of the law than would be used by the U.S. Supreme Court.[8] By exclusively relying on the state constitution rather than the federal charter, the state high court was able to insulate its decision from review by the U.S. Supreme Court.[9]

To survive under the common benefits clause, the state must show that the law "is reasonably necessary" to achieve its stated goals (878).[10] The state argued that the marriage law was reasonably related to its aim of strengthening ties between marriage and children, but the court found that same-sex couples were already engaged in child rearing, aided by artificial reproductive technology and legalized adoption. Indeed, it noted, the state had encouraged same-sex couples to adopt.[11]

In assessing the marriage–procreation–child rearing link, Amestoy noted that the law extended the benefits and protections of marriage to many persons with no logical connection to children. Opposite-sex couples marry for reasons unrelated to procreation; some never intend to have children, and others are incapable of doing so. "If anything," he said, "the exclusion of same-sex couples from the legal protections incident to marriage exposes their children to the precise risks that the State argues the marriage laws are designed to secure against. In short, the marital exclusion treats persons who are similarly situated for purposes of the law, differently" (882). The court was also not persuaded that the state's traditional opposition to same-sex marriage justified the ban, largely because it believed that it was motivated by animosity toward same-sex couples.

Accordingly, the Vermont high court held that the state had not met its burden of offering "a reasonable and just basis" to preclude same-sex couples from enjoying the benefits of a Vermont civil marriage (886). However, rather than fashioning a remedy, the court identified a range of constitutionally permissible options. Justice Denise Johnson objected, charging the court with abdicating its responsibility; in her view, it should have simply directed the state to issue marriage licenses to the plaintiffs.

Amestoy ended by eloquently proclaiming that "the extension of the Common Benefits Clause to acknowledge plaintiffs as Vermonters who seek nothing more, nor less, than legal protection and security for their avowed commitment to an intimate and lasting human relationship is simply, when all is said and done, a recognition of our common humanity" (889).

Despite this broad statement of principle, the relief provided was limited. The court ordered the state to extend the benefits and protections of marriage under Vermont law to same-sex couples, leaving it to the legislature to craft the appropriate means of addressing the constitutional mandate. Thus, the legislature could choose to allow same-sex couples to marry but was not required to do so as long as it made the benefits of marriage available to all.

In early February 2000, the legislature began work on a comprehensive domestic partnership law. The final bill that emerged retained the institution of marriage for opposite-sex couples but created a new status for same-sex partners known as civil unions. Couples entering into civil unions were granted many of the benefits and rights of marriage under state law, including inheritance rights, access to insurance policies, the right to use sick leave to care for a partner, and state tax benefits (Nelson 2008). The couples, however, remained ineligible for federal benefits and entitlements. Both houses of the legislature approved the civil unions bill, and on April 26, 2000, Democratic Governor Howard Dean signed the law guaranteeing parties to civil unions equality with spouses in a marriage (*Burlington Free Press* May 1, 2000).[12]

CIVIL MARRIAGE

Two years after civil unions became a reality in Vermont, seven couples who were denied marriage licenses sued the state of Massachusetts, asking the court to declare that forbidding same-sex marriage violated the state constitution.[13] As in Vermont, the lower court dismissed the complaint and ruled in favor of the state, linking its regulation of marriage to its interest in procreation and child rearing (*Goodridge v. Department of Public Health* 2002).

On appeal, in a vote of 4 to 3, the state supreme court compared the state constitution with the federal document, noting that the state charter demands a higher standard of liberty and equality than the federal Constitution. Speaking for the court, Chief Justice Margaret Marshall framed the question as "whether, consistent with the Massachusetts Constitution, the Commonwealth may deny the protections, benefits, and obligations conferred by civil marriage to two individuals of the same sex who wish to marry" (*Goodridge* 2003, 948).

She began by confirming the legislature's intent to restrict marriages to opposite-sex couples. Citing *Lawrence* four times, Marshall stressed the importance of marriage, characterizing it as "among life's momentous acts of self-definition" (955) and highlighting the financial and emotional benefits accompanying it.

The plaintiffs claimed that their inability to marry deprived them of equal protection and due process rights.[14] Marshall noted that when dealing with such matters as family and marriage, these two principles often converged and that the court would jointly consider the effect of the law on state constitutional guarantees of liberty and equality.

Not surprisingly, the parties differed on the proper level of scrutiny to apply. The court avoided the issue by subjecting the law to its version of rationality review, less than strict but more rigorous than the minimal scrutiny used by the U.S. Supreme Court. The state argued that the law furthered its interest in procreation and child rearing as well as conserving financial resources. The court rejected the first two arguments because the law did not refer to fertility as a condition of marriage, nor did the policy of restricting marriage to opposite-sex couples promote the state's interest in the welfare of children. Indeed, in the twenty-year-old opinion of *Doe v. Doe* (1983), the court held that the parents' sexual orientation or marital status was unrelated to the best interests of the child.

Marshall also rejected the state's argument that allowing plaintiffs to wed would "undermine the institution of civil marriage," saying that this was far from what the plaintiffs intended (*Goodridge* 2003, 965). Emphasizing its reliance on *Loving*, the court concluded that "recognizing the right of an individual to marry a person of the same sex will not diminish the validity or dignity of opposite-sex marriage, any more than recognizing the right of an individual to marry a person of a different race devalues the marriage of a person who marries someone of her own race" (*Goodridge* 2003, 965). Although the court never resolved the debate over scrutiny, because the law failed to satisfy even the minimal scrutiny test, there was no reason to subject it to a higher level of scrutiny.

Addressing the dissent's claim that its ruling usurped the legislature's authority over marriage policy, Marshall said, on the contrary, that the court was duty bound to adjudicate constitutional challenges, especially to laws involving marriage, reproduction, and child rearing. "We owe great deference to the Legislature to decide social and policy issues," she said, "but it is the traditional and settled role of courts to decide constitutional issues" (966). The court was also unpersuaded by the arguments of several amici that it should modify its opinion for the sake of comity among the states.

In the end, the court preserved the marriage license statute but redefined marriage as "the voluntary union of two persons as spouses, to the exclusion of all others" (969). It stayed its judgment until May 2004, giving the legislature six months to respond to the decision. Unclear whether it would be constitutionally acceptable to adopt the Vermont model of civil union, within a month of the decision, the Massachusetts senate proposed a bill barring same-sex couples from obtaining marriage licenses but allowing them to enter into civil unions. Unlike the federal system, Massachusetts law permits the legislature to seek an advisory opinion from the state supreme court. Thus, in January 2004, the senate brought the matter to the court, asking whether a law "which prohibits same-sex couples from entering into marriage but allows them to form civil unions with all 'benefits, protections, rights and responsibilities' of marriage, compl[ies] with the equal protection and due process requirements of the Constitution of the Commonwealth and . . . the Declaration of Rights?" (*In re Opinions of the Justices to the Senate* 2004, 566).

A month later, the same four justices who made up the majority in *Goodridge* held that the legislature's attempt to suggest that there was equivalency in the terms "civil union" and "civil marriage," while reserving the latter for opposite-sex couples, failed to satisfy the dictates of *Goodridge*. The court found that the state's interests in procreation and protecting children's welfare, although legitimate, were not rationally related to the separate legal status for same-sex couples; it ruled that the state violated the equal protection and due process clauses of the state constitution. It concluded by saying that "the bill maintains an unconstitutional, inferior, and discriminatory status for same-sex couples, and . . . the answer to the question is 'No'" (*Opinions of the Justices* 2004, 572).[15]

On May 17, 2004 (the fifty-year anniversary of *Brown v. Board of Education* 1954), Massachusetts became the first state in the nation to recognize same-sex marriage.[16]

An early attempt to derail *Goodridge* emerged from a federal lawsuit by a private citizen and eleven state representatives to enjoin enforcement of the state court's decision (*Largess v. Supreme Judicial Court for Massachusetts* 2004a). The plaintiffs argued that because the power to define marriage resided in the legislature, by redefining marriage, the Massachusetts high court had violated the separation of powers principles in the state constitution. They also alleged that in violating the state constitution, the court had simultaneously infringed on their right to a republican form of government, the guarantee clause of the U.S. Constitution.

District Court Judge Joseph Tauro dismissed their complaint, holding that the state court ruling "was a legitimate exercise of that court's authority and responsibility to decide with finality all issues arising under the Massachusetts Constitution" (84). In a per curiam opinion, the First Circuit Court affirmed (*Largess* 2004b).[17]

Shortly after the state supreme court issued its advisory opinion, the 200-person state legislature, known as the Massachusetts General Court, debated a number of constitutional amendments intended to bar same-sex marriage and allow civil unions instead. On March 29, it approved an amendment to "ban gay marriage and create same-sex civil unions instead," which passed in a vote of 105 to 92 (Crane 2003–2004, 471–3; *Boston Globe* February 13, 2004).

Overturning a Massachusetts Supreme Court decision requires a constitutional amendment, which under state law must be approved by a majority of the legislature sitting in joint session as a constitutional convention in two successive legislative sessions, followed by approval by a majority of the electorate in the next general election.[18] Thus, the state legislature was required to pass the amendment of March 29 again in the 2005 session, and if it succeeded, supporters of the amendment would be required to win approval from a majority of voters in the November 2006 election (*New York Times* March 30, 2004; see Miller 2005).

In September 2005, however, the Massachusetts legislature voted 157 to 39 to reject the proposed constitutional amendment to ban same-sex marriage and allow civil unions—the same amendment it had approved in March 2004. The overwhelming defeat of the amendment came about in part because fifty-five legislators who had supported it in 2004 voted "no" in 2005; moreover, seventeen of the eighteen new legislators voted with the majority against the amendment. One of the "no" votes from a newly elected representative explained his vote this way: "It is evident that the sky has not fallen [since May 17, 2004]" (*Boston Globe* September 15, 2005). Another said that "gay marriage has begun and life has not changed for the citizens of the commonwealth, with the exception of those who can now marry who could not before" (*New York Times* September 15, 2005; *Boston Globe* September 15, 2005). Some opponents of same-sex marriage also voted down the amendment, wanting simply to ban it—without allowing civil unions as an alternative (*Boston Globe* September 15, 2005).

On July 10, 2006, the Massachusetts Supreme Judicial Court ruled in *Schulman v. Attorney General* (2006) that an initiative petition that sought to overrule *Goodridge* and limit marriage to opposite-sex couples could be considered by the legislature. However, at the state constitutional convention on July 12, 2006, the legislature postponed the vote on the measure by adjourning before it was considered. In June 2007, both houses of the Massachusetts legislature again voted against placing a referendum on same-sex marriage on the 2008 ballot. Democratic Governor Deval Patrick warned that a referendum on the subject would not be in the state's best interests because it would deflect attention from more significant matters (*New York Times* June 15, 2007).

FEDERAL MARRIAGE POLICYMAKING

The success in Hawaii—fleeting as it was—proved to be a pyrrhic victory for same-sex marriage advocates; to their dismay, *Baehr* "provoked the biggest antigay backlash since the McCarthy era" (Eskridge 2002, 26). Fearing a domino effect as a consequence of the Hawaii litigation, Congress enacted the Defense of Marriage Act (DOMA) in 1996 to prevent couples from marrying in Hawaii and returning to their home states to demand that their marriage be recognized under the full faith and credit clause of the U.S. Constitution (see Koppelman 1996).[19] Senate Majority Leader Trent Lott, Mississippi Republican, claimed that DOMA was necessary as "a pre-emptive measure to make sure that a handful of judges, in a single state, cannot impose a radical social agenda upon the entire nation" (*New York Times* September 11, 1996).

DOMA authorizes states to decline to recognize same-sex marriages performed in other states and denies federal benefits (such as Social Security, veterans' benefits, and immigrant rights) to same-sex couples.[20] Although the law is unsettled, a number of scholars believe that DOMA was superfluous, as states were already equipped to defend their traditional marriage policies by citing the judicially derived "public policy exception" to the full faith and credit clause, permitting them to refuse to accept acts or decisions of other states that are inconsistent with their own. Thus, states could likely have denied recognition to same-sex marriages performed in other jurisdictions because they conflicted with their own state's public policy (see Holland 1998). The committee report accompanying DOMA acknowledged that Congress was aware that the "public policy exception" was a potent weapon against the possible spread of Hawaii's same-sex marriages to the rest of the nation but was unwilling to leave it to chance (Bossin 2005, 387).[21]

DOMA was overwhelmingly approved in the House in a vote of 342 to 67 on July 12, 1996, and a vote of 85 to 14 in the Senate on September 10, 1996 (*Congressional Record* 1996, H7506; S10129); it was signed by President Bill Clinton on September 21, 1996.[22]

Several years after the passage of DOMA, Congress once again sought to preclude recognition of same-sex marriages performed in Massachusetts with the Marriage Protection Act. This law would have denied jurisdiction to the federal courts, including the Supreme Court, in cases involving challenges to DOMA's nonrecognition provision. It was approved in the House in a vote of 233 to 194 (U.S. House of Representatives, July 22, 2004) and sent to the Senate, where it was referred to the Judiciary Committee in September, but no further action was taken on it.

Notwithstanding its inability to enact the Marriage Protection Act, Congress turned its efforts to passing a constitutional amendment to forestall actions by couples who were legally married in one state and sought recognition in their home states. Known as the Federal Marriage Amendment (FMA), it stated that "marriage in the United States shall consist only of the union of a man and a woman. Neither this Constitution, nor the Constitution of any State, shall be construed to require that marriage or the legal incidents thereof be conferred upon any union other than the union of a man and a woman" (*Congressional Quarterly Weekly* February 28, 2004; March 27, 2004; July 17, 2004; see Glidden 2004).[23]

President George W. Bush entered the debate over marriage protection by referring to the FMA in his State of the Union Address. He warned that the nation must "take a principled stand for one of the most fundamental, enduring institutions of our civilization" and criticized "activist judges [who] insist on forcing their arbitrary will upon the people" (Bush 2004a). Throughout 2004, Bush kept up the attacks; once he specifically referred to *Goodridge*, calling it "deeply troubling" (Bush 2004d). Later, he again assailed "activist judges and local officials [who] have made an aggressive attempt to redefine marriage" and warned that "on a matter of such importance, the voice of the people must be heard." He called on Congress to pass the amendment "defining and protecting marriage as a union between a man and a woman as husband and wife" (Bush 2004b).

As the year progressed and the presidential election grew nearer, Bush returned to the issue almost every month, renewing his support for the constitutional amendment, including a statement on May 17, 2004, the day the Massachusetts same-sex weddings became legal. After reiterating his criticism of "activist judges," he stressed his continued support for the FMA, saying that "the need for that amendment is still urgent, and I repeat that call today" (Bush 2004c).

On July 14, 2004, FMA supporters lost a Senate vote of 48 to 50 to invoke cloture; on September 30, it lost in the House 227 to 186, almost fifty votes short of the required two-thirds vote needed to approve a constitutional amendment (*Congressional Quarterly Weekly* October 1, 2004; January 17, 2005).

In February 2006, Senate Majority Leader Bill Frist, Republican from Tennessee, announced that he would bring a vote on the constitutional amendment, renamed the Marriage Protection Amendment (MPA) in 2005, to ban same-sex marriage to the Senate floor in early June. The proposed amendment provided, "Marriage in the United States shall consist only of the union of a man and a woman. Neither this Constitution, nor the Constitution of any State, shall be construed to require that marriage or the legal incidents thereof be conferred upon any union other than the union of a man and a woman." The majority leader said that it was necessary "to protect the majority of Americans," whom he said oppose same-sex marriage, "from the 'whims of a few activist judges' who seek 'to override the commonsense of the American people.'" He continued, "When America's values are under attack, we need to act" (*Washington Post* February 11, 2006).

In May, amid heated debate, the Senate Judiciary Committee voted 10 to 8 along party lines to send the proposed amendment to the Senate floor.

Although most observers agreed that it was unlikely to receive the sixty votes necessary to invoke cloture (and end the debate) and certainly not the requisite two-thirds vote needed for a constitutional amendment, Frist scheduled a vote in the Senate during the week of June 5 (*Washington Post* May 19, 2006; CNN.com May 19, 2006).

No state had legalized same-sex marriage since *Goodridge*, and no court of last resort upheld challenges to the state or federal bans on it. Nevertheless, amendment supporters sought to alarm the public by implying that such action was imminent. On the weekend before the vote was taken, Bush devoted his Saturday radio address to urge support for it. Speaking on the subject for the first time since his reelection, he repeated his criticism of "activist judges and some local officials [who] have made an aggressive attempt to redefine marriage in recent years." He warned that if DOMA "is overturned by activist courts, then marriages recognized in one city or state might have to be recognized as marriages everywhere else. That would mean that every state would have to recognize marriages redefined by judges in Massachusetts or local officials in San Francisco, no matter what their own laws or state constitutions say. This national question," he added, "requires a national solution, and on an issue of such profound importance, that solution should come from the people, not the courts" (Bush 2006a).

In his address at the Eisenhower Executive Office Building on June 5, 2006, amid frequent applause, Bush again urged Congress to pass the amendment and reiterated the need to "take this issue out of the hands of over-reaching judges and put it back where it belongs—in the hands of the American people" (Bush 2006b). As anticipated, amendment proponents were eleven votes short, able to garner only forty-nine of the sixty votes needed for cloture. Senator Sam Brownback, Republican from Kansas, promised supporters, "We're not going to stop until marriage between a man and a woman is protected" (*New York Times* June 7, 2006). House action on the amendment, largely symbolic and obviously futile, was promised for July; it also fell far short of the two-thirds majority needed for a constitutional amendment.

SAME-SEX MARRIAGE AROUND THE NATION

Although their attempt to establish a federal ban on same-sex marriage failed, opponents were more successful at the state level, enacting state DOMA's and ratifying constitutional amendments to achieve their ends and prevailing in the resulting litigation that challenged those policies. At the same time, however, in 2004, local government officials in Oregon, New York, New Jersey, California, and New Mexico issued marriage licenses to thousands of same-sex couples, ignoring the questionable legality of their actions.[24] They were soon reined in by state and local government authorities, including the courts, with the legality of the marriages performed by them frequently unresolved.[25]

Although the California marriages captured most of the nation's attention, weddings were taking place in other parts of the country as well. On February 20, 2004, New Mexico's Sandoval County began to grant marriage licenses to dozens of same-sex couples. The state attorney general, Patricia Madrid, called the issuance of the licenses illegal under New Mexico law, which limited marriage to a man and woman (*New York Times* February 21, 2004; *Albuquerque Journal* February 28, 2004). Responding to Madrid's petition, a state district court judge issued a restraining order on March 23, 2004, ordering the town clerk to stop issuing licenses to same-sex couples. Shortly thereafter, Madrid filed a writ with the state supreme court, seeking to prevent the restraining order from expiring.

In a unanimous opinion, the court denied the request for a writ but continued the restraining order against the issuance of licenses, putting the matter back in the lower court. Just before that court's decision, however, the clerk had begun to revise the marriage license application forms, changing them from "Male Applicant" and "Female Applicant" to "Applicant 1" and "Applicant 2" (*Albuquerque Journal* February 28, 2004; April 1, 2004). The case was eventually dismissed after the clerk left office and the attorney general reached an accord with his successor. The courts never ruled on the legality of the licenses (*Albuquerque Journal* March 10, 2005).[26]

About a week after the events in New Mexico were in the news, the nation's attention was drawn to the East Coast when, on February 27, 2004, the twenty-six-year-old Green Party mayor of New Paltz, New York, married twenty-five same-sex couples after the town clerk refused to issue licenses to them. Mayor Jason West's actions started a series of legal maneuvers involving numerous state and local government officials. Shortly after the weddings, New York Attorney General Eliot Spitzer issued a legal opinion that although state law did not specifically forbid same-sex marriage, the legislature had not intended to allow them. But, he added, he believed that New York must recognize marriages or civil unions performed outside the state. Spitzer said that his opinion was not binding on West (or on other mayors closely watching the events who had announced their intention to perform same-sex marriages) and urged the issue to be resolved in the courts.

On March 5, 2004, after a civil suit was filed against him, a state court judge ordered West to stop performing the weddings (*Poughkeepsie Journal* February 28, 2004; March 6, 2004; *Buffalo News* March 4, 2004; March 6, 2004). At the same time, the Ulster County district attorney charged West criminally with nineteen counts of violating the state's domestic relations law by "solemnizing a marriage without a license." After the court had issued the injunction against West, two Unitarian ministers took over the job of marrying unlicensed same-sex couples. The ministers were criminally charged as well, but the charges were subsequently dismissed (*Poughkeepsie Journal* March 7, 2004; July 10, 2005).

When asked whether he was surprised by the criminal charges—for which he could have been fined and sentenced up to a year in jail—West said, "No matter what happens, it would have been worth it. I don't have any regrets at all. Just seeing the looks on these couple's faces was worth any punishment any district attorney and judges could give me" (*Post-Standard* [Syracuse] July 10, 2005). On July 12, 2005, the prosecutor announced that he was dropping the criminal charges against West, saying that a "trial would be unnecessary and divisive" (*Times Union* [Albany] July 13, 2005).

In the meantime, while attention was focused on New Paltz, same-sex weddings were again taking place on the West Coast. On March 3, 2004, officials in Multnomah County, Oregon, began to issue marriage licenses to same-sex couples after the county attorney, responding to a question from the county board, stated that he believed that refusing to grant marriage licenses to same-sex couples was a probable constitutional violation. However, when asked by Governor Ted Kulongoski to analyze the applicable Oregon law, Attorney General Hardy Myers took a contrary position, explaining that he interpreted Oregon marriage law as prohibiting county clerks from issuing marriage licenses to same-sex couples. He added, however, that even though the courts would likely find the law unconstitutional, it must be enforced (*The Oregonian* March 3, 2004; March 13, 2004; March 14, 2004).

Despite the governor's request to stop, officials in Multnomah County continued to issue licenses throughout March and April; they soon numbered more than 1,000 (*The Oregonian* March 15, 2004). Eventually, all sides to the dispute agreed to have the matter settled in court (*The Oregonian* March 16, 2004; March 20, 2004). The American Civil Liberties Union (ACLU), several same-sex couples (including four who were married in Multnomah County), and numerous intervenors filed suit in the state circuit court, charging that the state's refusal to accept the marriages violated the privileges and immunities of the state constitution.[27] The judge agreed and ordered the state to register the marriages already performed but barred the county from continuing to issue licenses (*Li v. Oregon* 2004). On appeal, the state supreme court reversed, holding that Oregon law limited marriage to opposite-sex couples and that, because the county had lacked the authority to issue the marriage licenses, they were "void at the time they were issued." Thus ended the Multnomah County weddings (*Li* 2005, 398).[28]

STATE NONRECOGNITION POLICIES

One of the earliest attempts to enshrine the traditional role of marriage in a state constitution occurred in Alaska. The same month that Hawaii voters ratified its proposed constitutional amendment, Alaska voters approved an amendment restricting marriage to opposite-sex couples.[29] The circumstances surrounding this vote closely resembled those in Hawaii. In *Brause v. Bureau of Vital Statistics* (1998), Alaska Superior Court Judge Peter Michalski upheld the plaintiffs' challenge to the Alaska law that refused to recognize a same-sex marriage performed in another jurisdiction and denied same-sex partners the benefits of marriage. Michalski noted, "It is the duty of the court to do more than merely assume that marriage is only, and must only be, what most are familiar with. In some parts of our nation mere acceptance of the familiar would have left segregation in place"; he added that "in light of . . . [the plaintiffs'] challenge to the constitutionality of the relevant statutes, this court cannot defer to the legislature or familiar notions when addressing this issue" (at 2).

Michalski disagreed with the Hawaii Supreme Court's refusal to characterize same-sex marriage as a fundamental right. "The relevant question," he said, "is not whether same-sex marriage is so rooted in our traditions that it is a fundamental right, but whether the freedom to choose one's own life partner is so rooted in our traditions" (at 4). Finding that it was, he ruled that under the state constitution's right to privacy, marriage was a fundamental right and that the state must show a compelling reason to infringe on it.[30]

The judge stayed his ruling, pending the state's appeal. In the interim, the legislature proposed—and the voters ratified—a constitutional amendment, made effective on January 3, 1999, to limit marriage to a man and a woman. As in Hawaii, when the amendment was adopted, the case became moot (*Brause v. Department of Health & Social Services* 2001).[31]

Alarmed by *Baker* and *Goodridge* and the rising tide of same-sex marriages around the nation, over the next several years, numerous states restricted marriage to opposite-sex couples and precluded recognition of same-sex relationships solemnized outside their borders; the bans often extended to civil unions and domestic partnerships as well as to marriage. Additionally, fearing that the courts would declare state DOMAs unconstitutional and perhaps even the federal DOMA, states sought further insurance by inserting prohibitions against same-sex marriage in their constitutions (Bossin 2005, 414). A good number of these amendments merely duplicated the existing state DOMAs that were already in place (Evans 2004, 14).

Given the opportunity, most voters supported the bans on same-sex marriage. A few states, such as Alaska, adopted nonrecognition policies before 2004, but the citizens in most states registered their opposition to same-sex marriage in the 2004 election. Across the nation, voters in eleven states—Arkansas, Georgia, Kentucky, Michigan, Mississippi, Montana, North Dakota, Ohio, Oklahoma, Oregon, and Utah—approved policies banning same-sex marriage by substantial majorities: from 86 percent in Mississippi (by a margin of 6 to 1) to 57 percent in Oregon. Indeed, in all but two states—Oregon and Michigan—the approval ratings were more than 60 percent.[32]

Although most states put their nonrecognition policies in place by 2004, the trend continued over the next few years, albeit at a slower pace. In April 2005, in a vote of 71 to 29 percent, Kansas voters overwhelmingly approved a constitutional amendment to ban same-sex marriage, becoming the eighteenth state to do so; the amendment also barred domestic partnerships, and civil unions (*Topeka Capital-Journal* April 6, 2005). In November 2005, Texas voters approved Proposition 2 to amend the Texas Constitution by a majority of 76 to 24 percent (*Associated Press State and Local Wire* November 9, 2005; see *Austin American Statesman* November 6, 2005; *Dallas Morning News* November 9, 2005). And there was overwhelming support for an Alabama marriage amendment in the June 2006 election.[33] Later in the year, voters in South Dakota, South Carolina, Virginia, Wisconsin, Tennessee, Colorado, and Idaho also approved constitutional amendments restricting marriage to a man and a woman only. At that time, Arizona was the only state that rejected a proposed constitutional amendment (National Conference of State Legislatures 2008).

By the time the flood of constitutional bans on same-sex marriage had subsided, a total of twenty-six states had constitutional amendments restricting marriage to one man and one woman, with a few other state legislatures still considering whether to propose banning same-sex marriage in their constitutions (Human Rights Campaign 2008c).[34]

In November 2008, voters in three more states (Arizona [again], Florida, and California) went to the polls to decide whether their state constitutions should be amended to bar same-sex marriage (Human Rights Campaign 2008a). This time, Arizona opponents of same-sex marriage scored a victory when the voters approved Proposition 102, a constitutional amendment banning same-sex marriage, in a vote of 56 to 44 percent (CNN.com January 12, 2009). Florida's Amendment 2 also won in a vote of 62 to 38 percent (CNN.com January 12, 2009).[35] Both amendments appeared superfluous, as those states had already banned same-sex marriage by statute.[36]

CHALLENGING STATE NONRECOGNITION POLICIES

Most challenges to state nonrecognition policies were heard in the state courts, and a few such cases were heard in the federal courts; the cases adjudicated by the federal courts frequently combined challenges to the federal DOMA as well as to the state DOMAs.

In a number of states, the plaintiffs asked the courts to declare state non-recognition policies unconstitutional on procedural grounds, namely, that they violated the rule that constitutional or legislative enactments must be confined to a single subject. Although some of the plaintiffs succeeded at the lower court level, all these rulings were reversed on appeal. Plaintiffs filed suit in Louisiana after voters approved an amendment that restricted marriage to a man and a woman and precluded recognition of domestic partnerships and civil unions (see Peterson 2004). The lower court ruled in their favor, and when the state appealed, the court of appeals transferred the case to the state supreme court (*Forum for Equality PAC v. McKeithen* 2004). The Louisiana Supreme Court overturned the lower court, rejecting the challengers' argument that the amendment violated the "single-object requirement," in which a proposed constitutional amendment must "be confined to one object" (*Forum for Equality* 2005, 729).

On November 4, 2005, Joseph Guimond, a Marion County, Oregon, circuit court judge, ruled that a 2004 ballot initiative banning same-sex marriage, among other things, did not violate the "separate-vote require-ment" for amending the state constitution as the plaintiffs charged (*Martinez v. Kulongoski* 2005).[37]

Similarly, in 2006, the Georgia Supreme Court overruled a lower court decision that struck the same-sex marriage amendment defining marriage as the union of a man and a woman, banning civil unions, and denying recognition to marriages performed in other states; it had been approved in the November 2004 election. The Georgia Supreme Court held that the amendment did not violate the state's "single-subject rule" and restored it to the state constitution (*Perdue v. O'Kelley* 2006, 3).

Finally, in *Arizona Together v. Meadows* (2007), plaintiffs argued that placing a voter-initiated proposition to amend the constitution to define marriage violated the state constitution's "separate-amendment rule." The measure defined marriage and broadly prevented recognition of same-sex relationships (including marriage, civil unions, and domestic partnerships). The Arizona Supreme Court found the provisions were sufficiently related, with "the purpose of both . . . to preserve and protect marriage" (746).

CHALLENGING FEDERAL AND STATE DOMAs

In courtrooms around the country, same-sex couples argued that the federal DOMA (as well as, in some cases, a state nonrecognition policy) infringed on a wide array of federal and state constitutional rights, including the full faith and credit and the privileges and immunities clauses. Most plaintiffs were unable to survive the government's motions to dismiss, the courts ruling chiefly that they lacked standing to challenge DOMA.

In *Wilson v. Ake* (2005), the first case in which the litigants directly challenged DOMA, Florida Federal Court Judge James Moody granted the defendant's (the U.S. government) motion to dismiss the complaint brought by a lesbian couple who had been legally married in Massachusetts and sought to have their marriage recognized in Florida. The couple, Nancy Wilson and Paula Schoenwether, argued that DOMA and Florida's marriage law infringed on their fundamental right to marry, violating numerous constitutional protections, including the full faith and credit clause and the equal protection and due process clauses of the Fourteenth Amendment.[38]

The court disagreed. Limiting its ruling to DOMA, Moody ruled that Congress had proper authority to enact the law under the full faith and credit clause to regulate conflicts among the states over the legality of same-sex marriages. To rule otherwise, he held, would allow a single state to make policy for the entire nation. Moreover, the court added, the "public policy exception" clearly protects Florida's right to determine its own policy toward same-sex marriage.

The judge acknowledged that the U.S. Supreme Court has recognized that marriage is a fundamental right but emphasized that no federal court has ever held that this right encompassed the right to marry a person of the same sex, and he declined to be the first to create such a fundamental right. He was also not persuaded that strict scrutiny should be applied to laws affecting sexual orientation because it is not a suspect classification. Applying minimal scrutiny, Moody found that DOMA rationally furthered the federal government's interest in "the development of relationships that are optimal for procreation" and "encourage[d] the creation of stable relationships that facilitate the rearing of children by both of their biological parents" (1308).[39]

Around the same time, in Orange County, California, a gay couple brought suit after they were denied a marriage license on the basis of their sex. They claimed that DOMA, as well as California's marriage acts, infringed on the federal equal protection and due process clauses as well as the full faith and credit clause. Because the matter of the constitutionality of the California law was pending in the state court, the federal court abstained from deciding on the state law issue. It held that the plaintiffs lacked standing to challenge DOMA's §2; although it allowed them to challenge §3, in the end, the court upheld the law as constitutional (*Smelt v. County of Orange* 2005).[40]

The Ninth Circuit agreed that, because the matter was pending in state court, the federal court had properly abstained from ruling on the

California statutes. It also affirmed the lower court's decision that the plaintiffs lacked standing to challenge §2 but reversed the court's ruling granting them standing to object to §3. The appeals court held that because the plaintiffs had not been married in any state, they could not claim to be injured by either section of the federal law (*Smelt v. County of Orange* 2006).[41]

Another set of plaintiffs on the West Coast attempted to challenge DOMA on constitutional grounds in a federal bankruptcy proceeding. A lesbian couple had married in British Columbia in 2003 and filed a joint petition for Chapter 7 bankruptcy in Tacoma, Washington, two months later. The federal government opposed the petition, contending that only spouses may file jointly and that DOMA precluded this couple from declaring themselves spouses. The plaintiffs argued that DOMA was unconstitutional under the Fourth, Fifth, and Tenth Amendments.

In a case of first impression in a bankruptcy court, Judge Paul Snyder applied minimal scrutiny and found DOMA rationally related to the federal government's interest in advancing the welfare of children in an opposite-sex marriage (*In re Kandu* 2004). He added that although he may not agree with Congress's view of same-sex marriage, "it is within the province of Congress, not the courts, to weigh the evidence and legislate on such issues . . . [and he] cannot say that DOMA's limitation of marriage to one man and one woman is not wholly irrelevant to the achievement of the government's interest" (146).

Similarly, in *Bishop v. Oklahoma* (2006), the plaintiffs were two lesbian couples. One couple, Mary Bishop and Sharon Baldwin, wanted to be married in Oklahoma; the other, Susan Barton and Gay Phillips, who had entered into a civil union in Vermont and then were legally married in Vancouver, Canada, wanted their marriage recognized in Oklahoma. The couples argued that DOMA and article 2 of the Oklahoma Constitution violated the equal protection, due process, and privileges and immunities clauses of the Fourteenth Amendment as well as the full faith and credit clause.[42] As in other DOMA challenges, their case floundered on their inability to persuade the court that they had standing to sue because they were harmed by DOMA.

Addressing the standing issue separately for each couple, Oklahoma Federal Court Judge Terence Kern agreed with the government that Bishop and Baldwin lacked standing to sue because §2 did not affect them, as they had never married in another state.

Barton and Phillips might be able to challenge §2, for it arguably prevented Oklahoma from giving "effect" to their civil union as well as their Canadian marriage. Interpreting DOMA narrowly, Kern held that the Vermont civil union was not "treated as a marriage under the laws" of Vermont (1244) and concluded that DOMA did not apply to civil unions.

Similarly, although he acknowledged that the Vancouver wedding re-sulted in a marriage, it also did not fall within DOMA because Canada was not a "state." Thus, he found that these plaintiffs also had no legally cognizable marriage in a "state." Consequently, because §2 had not pre-vented Oklahoma from recognizing their marriage, they were not injured by it and had no standing to challenge it.

Kern also rejected Bishop and Baldwin's claim that DOMA deprived them of federal benefits. Because their relationship did not entitle them to such benefits, DOMA was not responsible for any deprivation, and there-fore Bishop and Baldwin also lacked standing to challenge §3. However, distinguishing between the California domestic partnership at issue in *Smelt* and a Vermont civil union, with the latter more like a marriage than the former, Kern declined to dismiss Barton and Phillip's challenge to §3 at this stage of the litigation. Instead, the court preserved their claim until the parties presented a factual record and legal arguments to support their allegations.

The court concluded as well that because no marriage had been per-formed in another state, the plaintiffs lacked standing to challenge the nonrecognition provision of the Oklahoma marriage amendment. But as all of them had proclaimed their desire to be wed in Oklahoma and were prevented in doing so by the opposite-sex marriage requirement, the court granted the couples standing to challenge the Oklahoma policy and denied the state's motion to dismiss.[43]

With these challenges to DOMA dismissed on grounds of standing, the only plaintiffs who could mount challenges to DOMA were those who could claim injury under the law by showing that they were legally married under state law and denied federal benefits as a result of §3 of DOMA.

The hurdle posed by the standing doctrine appeared to be overcome when, on March 3, 2009, eight married couples and three surviving spouses, all Massachusetts citizens, filed suit in a Massachusetts federal district court in *Gill v. Office of Personnel Management* (2009). They found support in two recent orders issued by Ninth Circuit Judges Stephen Re-inhardt and Alex Kozinski, jurists generally considered at opposite ends of the ideological spectrum (*New York Times* March 13, 2009).

Because federal judicial employees are barred from litigating claims in federal court, their employment discrimination complaints are heard by federal judges as part of an internal dispute resolution process. In Febru-ary 2009, Reinhardt responded to a complaint brought by an employee in the federal public defender's office that his same-sex spouse was denied health care benefits because of DOMA. (The couple was one of the 18,000 couples who had married during the months when gay marriage was legal in California.) Reinhardt upheld the challenge, writing that "the denial of federal benefits cannot be justified simply by a distaste for or disapproval of same-sex marriage or a desire to deprive same-sex spouses of benefits available to other spouses in order to discourage them from exercising a legal right afforded them by the state." He found no rational basis, he said, for denying health benefits to same-sex spouses while granting them to opposite-sex spouses. He concluded that DOMA unconstitutionally discriminated against the employee and his spouse on the basis of sex and sexual orientation (*Los Angeles Times* February 6, 2009; February 5, 2009).

The previous month, Kozinski had granted benefits to another judicial employee on the grounds that DOMA was vague about whether benefits were available to someone outside the family; he said that the federal government was not barred from providing such benefits to same-sex spouses. Following these decisions, a spokesperson for President Barack Obama reiterated the president's view that he opposed gay marriage, supported repealing DOMA, and favored providing health care benefits to same-sex partners of federal employees (*New York Times* March 13, 2009). Obama made good on the latter in part on June 17, 2009 (*Washington Post* June 17, 2009).

The *Gill* plaintiffs sought an injunction (and money damages for a few) and a declaration that §3 is unconstitutional as applied to them; they were represented by lawyers from the Gay and Lesbian Advocates and Defenders, the same group that successfully argued *Goodridge* before the state high court. The defendants, sued in their official capacity, included the postmaster general, the Social Security commissioner, the secretary of state, and the attorney general.

The plaintiffs claimed that by denying them benefits to which other married couples were entitled, the federal government abridged their right of equal protection guaranteed in the due process clause of the Fifth Amendment. The federal government does not issue marriage licenses but relies on state law to determine eligibility for federal programs. The plaintiffs, consisting of federal employees and retirees, taxpayers, Social Security recipients, and passport holders, cited the 2004 Government Accounting Office report on the more than 1,100 federal laws pertaining to marital status. They focused their claims on only a few of these, for which they had applied and had been denied: Social Security survivor and death benefits, federal income tax, passports, and federal employment and retirement benefits. On July 8, 2009, Massachusetts Attorney General Martha Coakley filed suit against the federal government, challenging §3 of DOMA (*New York Times* July 8, 2009).

Although Obama has indicated that he favors the repeal of DOMA, he has not taken meaningful steps to do so. The attorneys in the *Gill* case expressed the hope that a court victory would hasten it (see Gay and Lesbian Advocates and Defenders 2009).

In a statement in *The Voice*, a Christian magazine, the legal counsel for the Alliance Defense Fund criticized the lawsuit, saying that "public policy should be decided by the public, not by one judge and a very small number of radical activists." This nation, he went on to say, "continues to overwhelmingly reaffirm that marriage is one man and one woman. Does the democratic process mean anything anymore" (*The Voice* 2009)?

The outcome of the case will depend in large part on the court's determination of the proper level of scrutiny to apply to the equal protection challenge, that is, the court's view of its role as a subordinate or coordinate policymaker.

THE LEGAL CHALLENGES CONTINUE

After Nebraska voters approved a sweeping nonrecognition policy by constitutional amendment in 2000, a number of public interest groups filed suit in federal district court, arguing that the provision violated the federal constitution.[44] In a rare victory for same-sex couples, the judge denied the state's motion to dismiss the plaintiffs' action for lack of standing (*Citizens for Equal Protection v. Bruning* 2003). In ruling on the merits, Nebraska District Court Judge Joseph Bataillon cited *Romer* and declared the Nebraska amendment unconstitutional, finding it "indistinguishable" from Colorado's Amendment 2 (*Bruning* 2005, 1002). Following the example of the Colorado high court, Bataillon applied strict scrutiny because the amendment infringed on "the fundamental right to participate equally in the political process" (1003, quoting *Evans v. Romer* 1993, 1282).[45]

On appeal, a unanimous Eighth Circuit panel reversed the district court, rejecting the challenge to Nebraska's constitutional amendment against same-sex marriage (*Bruning* 2006). Speaking for the panel, Judge James Loken agreed that the plaintiffs had standing to challenge the amendment but criticized Bataillon for emulating the Colorado Supreme Court and applying strict scrutiny to the Nebraska amendment rather than following U.S. Supreme Court precedent and applying minimal scrutiny to laws affecting sexual orientation.[46] Emphasizing that policies regulating marriage must be accorded great deference, Loken said that he believed that the state's reason for barring same-sex unions—to promote procreation by married heterosexual couples—was legitimate and that the amendment did not deny same-sex couples equal protection of the law.[47]

On July 7, 2003, a few days after the U.S. Supreme Court decided *Lawrence*, Donald Standhardt and Tod Alan Keltner applied for a marriage license in a Maricopa County, Arizona, courthouse. When they were denied, they petitioned the appellate court to compel the clerk to issue a license, claiming that the denial violated their state and federal constitutional rights.[48]

In one of the first suits to challenge a state DOMA alone, the plaintiffs argued that they had a fundamental liberty interest in marriage and that the court must use strict scrutiny to determine the constitutionality of the laws involved.[49] Acknowledging that marriage is a fundamental right, the state appellate court held that "neither the United States Supreme Court nor any Arizona court has explicitly recognized that the fundamental right to marry includes the freedom to choose a same-sex spouse." Speaking for the court, Judge Ann Scott Timmer was not persuaded that *Lawrence* or any other case, including *Loving*, had "recognized such a right" (*Standhardt v. Superior Court* 2003, 456).

Applying minimal scrutiny, Timmer conceded that "children raised in families headed by a same-sex couple deserve and benefit from bilateral parenting within long-term committed relationships just as much as children with married parents" but nevertheless believed that the state may limit marriage to opposite-sex couples (463). Because only opposite-sex couples are able to procreate, she found that the state could rationally believe that it could encourage such couples to assume the legal obligations of marriage and increase the likelihood that children would be raised by parents in committed stable relationships. And because same-sex partners could not procreate, legislators might reasonably believe that marriage between them would not further the state's aim of "ensuring responsible procreation within committed long-term relationships" (463).[50]

A short time later, three Indiana same-sex couples who had entered into civil unions in Vermont were denied marriage licenses in Indiana on the basis of that state's DOMA.[51] They filed suit, charging that the law violated, among other things, the equal privileges and immunities clause of the Indiana Constitution.[52]

The trial court dismissed their complaint. On appeal, in *Morrison v. Sadler* (2005), the court avoided the question of whether same-sex marriages would harm the institution of marriage, emphasizing that the issue was whether recognizing same-sex marriages would further the state's interest in "responsible procreation" (42).[53] The plaintiffs contended that since many same-sex couples were raising children (through either adoption or assisted reproductive technology), they were entitled to all the benefits available to married heterosexual couples. However, Judge Michael Barnes rejected that argument, ironically by extolling the virtues of same-sex partners wishing to have children, saying that they "are, by necessity, heavily invested financially and emotionally, in those processes [which] require a great deal of foresight and planning" (24). And because of their forethought and care, he believed that the state can assume that they will provide a stable environment for their children even without marriage. In contrast, because opposite-sex couples can have children naturally without such "foresight" or "planning," the state can rationally decide that the institution of marriage is a necessary measure to ensure that their children will enjoy the same degree of stability as those of same-sex couples. Thus, the court concluded, the state can rationally extend the benefits of marriage to opposite-sex couples while denying them to same-sex couples.

Despite these losses, same-sex couples continued to challenge state laws that prevented them from fulfilling their wishes to marry. For the most part, the courts refused to agree that the challenged state policies infringed on their constitutional rights. The major obstacle the litigants faced was their inability to persuade the courts to apply a higher level of scrutiny to the laws under review. In applying minimal scrutiny, the courts simply accepted the government's explanations that restrictions on same-sex marriage were justified by its concern for procreation (when demonstrating no concern about the procreative capabilities or intentions of other couples), its solicitude for children's well-being (in the absence of evidence that the children of same-sex couples were at greater risk), and its beliefs that marriage will offset the impulsiveness and thoughtlessness in which heterosexual couples produce children (based on a view that opposite-sex couples haphazardly produce children). The outcomes of these cases demonstrate the judiciary's willingness to accept almost any explanation proffered by the state, however implausible, for prohibiting same-sex marriage.

Meanwhile, all eyes were on New York as same-sex couples eagerly awaited a ruling on their suits challenging the constitutionality of the state's domestic relations law banning same-sex marriage.[54] The case arose when forty-four gay and lesbian couples from around the state—in Albany, New York City, and Ithaca—contested the state authorities' refusal to issue them marriage licenses. Filing four separate lawsuits, they alleged violations of their state due process and equal protection guarantees.[55] Although one group had initially succeeded in the trial court, all had lost on appeal and took their cases to the state supreme court.[56]

The cases were consolidated on appeal, and on July 6, 2006, in the much-awaited ruling in *Hernandez v. Robles* (2006), a majority of 4 to 2 in the New York Court of Appeals upheld the New York domestic relations law against all constitutional challenges.

Writing for a divided court, Justice Robert Smith began by underscoring the importance of marriage as an economic and social institution.[57] He assessed the state's two justifications for banning same-sex marriage. Noting the positive effect of a stable home life on children's welfare, Smith found that the state could reasonably believe that extending the benefits of marriage to couples who are more likely to unwittingly and unthinkingly produce children would encourage them to form a stable relationship and thus promote greater stability in the home. And because same-sex couples must necessarily be more methodical and thoughtful when having children, the government could credibly suppose that it would advance its goal of a stable home environment by restricting the benefits of marriage to opposite-sex partners only.

Second, Smith noted that the legislature could rationally decide that children fare better when growing up in a household with a mother and a father. Although he conceded that this belief might be mistaken, Smith nevertheless held that it would be reasonable for the legislature to rely on this "commonsense premise." In the end, holding the plaintiffs to a high burden of proof, the court ruled that the state's insistence on withholding marriage licenses from same-sex couples was not a "wholly irrational one, based solely on ignorance and prejudice against homosexuals" (8).

In closing, Smith took pains to point out that a ban on same-sex marriage was not comparable to the prohibition on interracial marriage that the U.S. Supreme Court struck in *Loving*. The injustices committed against gays were indeed serious, he acknowledged, but they were not comparable to the history of racism in the nation. In rapid succession, he rejected the plaintiffs' arguments to strike the law because it infringed on their fundamental right to marry, to apply a heightened level of scrutiny because it involved a sex-based classification, or to find that it stemmed from animosity toward gays. Thus, in the end, the court held that the legislature had not contravened the state's equal protection and due process guarantees. Emphasizing that he was expressing no opinion on the wisdom of the policy, the justice urged both sides to take their arguments to the legislature and seek resolution of the controversy there.

Similar events were taking place on the West Coast as two groups of plaintiffs (nineteen gay and lesbian couples in all) challenged Washington State's 1998 DOMA on several state constitutional grounds after they were denied marriage licenses.[58] They won summary judgments in the lower courts in *Castle v. Washington* (2004) and *Andersen v. King County* (2004), successfully arguing that the law violated their privileges and immunities and due process rights under the state constitution.[59] They did not succeed in convincing either trial court judge that the law infringed on their rights under the state Equal Rights Amendment.[60] Because the lower courts stayed their decisions pending review by the state supreme court, the plaintiffs were not issued marriage licenses despite their victory.

The Washington Supreme Court consolidated the cases and decided *Andersen* (2006) in a divided ruling.[61] Stressing the limited nature of its role in deciding the constitutionality of the law, Justice Barbara Madsen, speaking for the three-justice plurality, took pains to point out that the court was not being asked to give its personal views and would refrain from doing so. Citing numerous cases that reached the same conclusion, she applied minimal scrutiny because the plaintiffs failed to show that sexual orientation was a suspect classification or that they had a fundamental right to marry a same-sex partner.[62]

Prior to assessing whether the legislature's goal was legitimate (a feature of rational basis review), the court rejected the plaintiffs' contention that, as with Colorado's Amendment 2, the law was motivated by animus toward the gay population. To support its rationale that the legislature was not acting out of anti-gay sentiment, the court pointed to fifteen state legislators who had voted for DOMA while at the same time approving the addition of sexual orientation as a protected classification in the state law against discrimination.

Reiterating a number of times that it was expressing no views on the law, the court applied the "highly deferential standard" (983) of minimal scrutiny and found no privileges and immunities violation. It held that the legislature could reasonably believe that marriage between persons of the opposite sex promotes "procreation" and "the well-being of children" and that permitting marriage between a same-sex couple would have the opposite effect (969). Moreover, because there is a rational relationship between DOMA and these interests, there is no due process violation, nor is there a violation of the plaintiffs' right to privacy. Finally, accepting the "equal application" theory that Virginia unsuccessfully advanced in *Loving*, the court held that the law did not implicate the state Equal Rights Amendment because it treated members of both sexes equally.[63]

The Maryland Court of Appeals (the state supreme court) dealt another blow to same-sex marriage advocates in *Conaway v. Deane* (2007), once again reversing a lower court finding in the gay litigants' favor. At the lower court level, Baltimore City Circuit Court Judge M. Brooke Murdock had granted summary judgment to the plaintiffs: nine couples and a single gay man.[64] Relying on *Loving*, she held that the Maryland law that recognized marriage only between a man and a woman violated the state constitution's Equal Rights Amendment.[65] Following Murdock's ruling, Republicans in the state House of Delegates unsuccessfully attempted to gather enough votes to place a constitutional amendment outlawing same-sex marriage on the November 2008 ballot (*Washington Post* February 3, 2006).

In the Court of Appeals, Justice Glenn Harrell Jr. reversed the lower court. Speaking for a majority of 4 to 3, he upheld the state law defining marriage as the union of a man and a woman.[66] Harrell ruled that there was no equal rights violation because the state constitution's Equal Rights Amendment was intended to prevent impermissible distinctions between men and women as a class, not classifications based on sexual orientation. Engaging in a lengthy analysis to determine the proper level of scrutiny, the majority acknowledged that although gays may be victims of discrimination, they were not without political power to correct the inequities.

It refused to consider the plaintiffs a suspect class and apply heightened scrutiny under due process or equal protection analysis.

Using minimal scrutiny, the court found that the government has a legitimate interest in fostering procreation and that that interest is rationally related to a preference for heterosexual marriage. Harrell ended by emphasizing that its "opinion should by no means be read to imply that the General Assembly may not grant and recognize for homosexual persons civil unions or the right to marry a person of the same sex" (635).

There was predictable reaction from both sides of the debate in Maryland. Gay rights advocates vowed to continue their fight for equality in the Maryland General Assembly, while opponents praised the court for deferring to the legislature on marriage policy and promised to enshrine traditional marriage by launching a drive for a constitutional amendment (*Washington Post* September 19, 2007).

The battle over recognition of same-sex marriage did not end as a result of these defeats in courts or on ballot initiatives. And while there continued to be setbacks for advocates of same-sex marriage throughout the decade, events occurring in 2005 and beyond suggest that this year may have marked the beginning of a new phase of policymaking for same-sex marriage.

NOTES

1. For more than two decades, *Loving* was cited as recognizing the right to marry as a fundamental right (Wardle 1998, 308–9).

2. Courts often use the term "heightened scrutiny" when they mean "strict scrutiny," ignoring the fact that there is a distinct level of scrutiny called "heightened" or "intermediate scrutiny."

3. The Washington Supreme Court denied review in *Singer* (1974b). The U.S. Supreme Court summarily dismissed the appeal in *Nelson* (1971) "for want of a substantial federal question" (*Nelson* 1972), which a number of courts interpret as a denial of the fundamental right to marry a person of the same sex (see Bossin 2005; Duncan 2004). Most courts cite *Hicks v. Miranda* (1975) for this interpretation of a summary dismissal (see *Morrison v. Sadler* 2005; *Wilson v. Ake* 2005).

4. Article 1, §5, of the Hawaii Constitution provides, "No person shall be deprived of life, liberty or property without due process of law, nor be denied the equal protection of the laws, nor be denied the enjoyment of the person's civil rights or be discriminated against in the exercise thereof because of race, religion, sex or ancestry." Article I, §6, provides, "The right of the people to privacy is recognized and shall not be infringed without the showing of a compelling state interest."

5. Article 1, §3, of the Hawaii Constitution provides, "Equality of rights under the law shall not be denied or abridged by the State on account of sex."

6. Coolidge (1998, 204–5) believes that the "*Loving* Analogy" was the primary impetus for the court's ruling; "as *Loving* [was] about broadening marriage to

include interracial couples, so *Baehr* [was] about broadening marriage to include same sex couples."

7. Article 1, §23, of the Hawaii Constitution provides, "The legislature shall have the power to reserve marriage to opposite-sex couples."

8. Known as the Common Benefits Clause, chapter I, article 7, of the Vermont Constitution provides, "That government is, or ought to be, instituted for the common benefit, protection, and security of the people, nation, or community."

9. The U.S. Supreme Court held in *Michigan v. Long* (1983) that a state court decision is insulated from high court review when the state court unambiguously declares that the ruling is exclusively grounded in the state constitution.

10. The principle by which state courts interpret their state constitutions more expansively than the U.S. Constitution, known as judicial federalism, has been in evidence for a number of decades. Justice William Brennan, one of its foremost proponents of judicial federalism on the Supreme Court, urged state courts to be more protective of civil liberties and civil rights in the face of retrenchment by the high court (Brennan 1986; see Fitzpatrick 2004).

11. As discussed in chapter 1, the state legislature authorized adoption by same-sex couples after the Vermont Supreme Court held that the statute barring such adoptions was unconstitutional in *In re B.L.V.B.* (1993).

12. Vt. Stat. Ann. tit. 15, §1204(a) provides, "Parties to a civil union shall have all the same benefits, protections and responsibilities under law, whether they derive from statute, administrative or court rule, policy, common law or any other source of civil law, as are granted to spouses in a marriage."

13. Massachusetts law was silent on the legality of same-sex marriage. The court addressed the question of whether the legislature intended to prevent same-sex couples from marrying.

14. Among other things, the plaintiffs claimed that the state violated their rights under articles 1, 6, 7, and 10 of the Massachusetts Declaration of Rights. Article 1 provides, "All people are born free and equal and have certain natural, essential and unalienable rights. . . . Equality under the law shall not be denied or abridged because of sex, race, color, creed or national origin."

Article 6 provides, "No man, nor corporation, or association of men, have any other title to obtain advantages, or particular and exclusive privileges, distinct from those of the community, than what arises from the consideration of services rendered to the public."

Article 7 provides, "Government is instituted for the common good; for the protection, safety, prosperity, and happiness of the people. . . . Therefore the people alone have an incontestable, unalienable, and indefeasible right to institute government; and to reform, alter, or totally change the same, when their protection, safety, prosperity and happiness require it."

Article 10 provides, "Each individual of the society has a right to be protected by it in the enjoyment of his life, liberty and property."

15. In April 2004, state lawmakers unsuccessfully attempted to have the four justices in the *Goodridge* majority removed from the court.

16. Before *Goodridge* was decided in November 2003, same-sex marriages were permitted in Belgium, the Netherlands, and the Canadian province of Ontario (Duncan 2005, 114). Following *Goodridge*, courts in eight provinces and one terri-

tory as well as the Supreme Court of Canada upheld the legality of same-sex marriage. In July 2004, the Canadian Parliament enacted legislation legalizing same-sex marriage in the entire nation. In 2005, South Africa, the United Kingdom, and Spain also allowed same-sex marriage (Miller 2006, 296–7).

17. The U.S. Supreme Court denied certiorari in *Largess* (2004c).

18. Constitutional amendments may also be placed on the ballot by initiative if supporters gather 65,000 voters' signatures and fifty legislators vote to approve it in two successive sessions. Same-sex marriage opponents attempted to force the legislature to vote for a constitutional ban on same-sex marriage and place it on the ballot in the November 2008 election (Miller 2006, 297–8). By December 2005, they had collected 170,000 signatures and defeated an effort to stop them in the courts. In January 2007, they secured sixty-two votes in the legislature to place it on the ballot, but in June, the legislature voted 151 to 45 against it; the vote ensured that the measure could not be placed on the ballot until 2012 at the earliest (National Conference of State Legislatures 2008; *New York Times* June 15, 2007).

19. Article IV of the U.S. Constitution, the full faith and credit clause, provides, "Full Faith and Credit shall be given in each State to the public Acts, Records, and judicial Proceedings of every other State. And the Congress may by general Laws prescribe the Manner in which such Acts, Records and Proceedings shall be proved, and the Effect thereof."

20. Section 2 of DOMA, codified at 28 U.S.C. §1738C, provides, "No State, territory, or possession of the United States, or Indian tribe, shall be required to give effect to any public act, record, or judicial proceeding of any other State, territory, possession, or tribe respecting a relationship between persons of the same-sex that is treated as a marriage under the laws of such other State, territory, possession, or tribe, or a right or claim arising from such relationship." Section 3, codified at 1 U.S.C. §7, provides, "In determining the meaning of any Act of Congress, or of any ruling, regulation, or interpretation of the various administrative bureaus and agencies of the United States, the word 'marriage' means only a legal union between one man and one woman as husband and wife, and the word 'spouse' refers only to a person of the opposite sex who is a husband or a wife." There are numerous financial and legal benefits that accrue from being legally wed. A 1997 General Accounting Office study reported 1,049 "federal rights, responsibilities, and privileges" adhering to marriage. These included taxation, survivor benefits, family law, health care, real estate, and bankruptcy. A subsequent analysis in 2004 showed the number had risen to 1,138 (American Bar Association Section Family Law Working Group on Same Sex Marriages and Non-Marital Unions 2004, 16).

21. DOMA was passed while the legality of same-sex marriage was being adjudicated in the Hawaii courts.

22. Public Law 104-199.

23. Presumably, this language would have permitted states to recognize civil unions.

24. California's experience with same-sex marriage is discussed in chapter 3.

25. Koppelman (2005) discusses judicial responses to cases involving recognition of same-sex marriages performed outside the state that conflict with the state's public policy.

26. The New Mexico Senate soon approved a bill limiting marriage to opposite-sex couples.

27. Article I, §20, of the Oregon Constitution provides, "No law shall be passed granting to any citizen or class of citizens privileges, or immunities, which, upon the same terms, shall not equally belong to all citizens."

28. In November 2004, Oregon voters approved an amendment to the state constitution banning same-sex marriage. The Oregon Supreme Court heard oral arguments shortly after the ban went into effect and dismissed the plaintiffs' appeal in its April 2005 ruling.

29. Article I, §25, of the Alaska Constitution provides, "To be valid or recognized in this State, a marriage may exist only between one man and one woman."

30. Article I, §22, of the Alaska Constitution provides, "The right of the people to privacy is recognized and shall not be infringed."

31. The plaintiffs' complaint was based on three counts. The first two, claiming that the state's refusal to grant them a marriage license violated the Alaska Constitution, was mooted by the adoption of the constitutional amendment against same-sex marriage. Count 3 challenged the Alaska marriage law on state and federal constitutional grounds. The superior court ruled that the complaint did not sufficiently allege that the plaintiffs were denied any specific benefits but merely claimed that the Alaska marriage law violated the state and federal constitutions; it dismissed this count on the grounds that the matter was not ripe for controversy, and the Alaska Supreme Court affirmed (*Brause v. Department of Health & Social Services* 2001).

32. Although same-sex marriage loomed large in the 2004 election, there is disagreement over the extent to which it influenced the outcome of the presidential race. After the election, the media characterized it as one of the deciding factors, especially in Ohio, because it increased turnout among "social conservatives" (see *San Francisco Chronicle* November 4, 2004; *New York Times* November 4, 2004; *Washington Post* November 4, 2004; *Chicago Tribune* November 4, 2004). The weight of scholarly opinion rejects this view (see, for example, Egan, Persily, and Wallsten 2006; Hillygus and Shields 2005; Lewis 2005; Menand 2004).

33. In *American Civil Liberties Union of Tennessee v. Darnell* (2006), the Tennessee Supreme Court upheld a lower court ruling, dismissing the ACLU's suit on the grounds that it lacked standing to sue. The organization claimed that the state's failure to publish the proposed amendment as required hindered its ability to lobby against its passage in the 2004 election.

34. Alabama (2006), Alaska (1998), Arkansas (2004), Colorado (2004), Georgia (2004), Kansas (2005), Idaho (2006), Kentucky (2004), Louisiana (2004), Michigan (2004), Mississippi (2004), Missouri (2004), Montana (2004), Nebraska (2000), Nevada (2002), North Dakota (2004), Ohio (2004), Oklahoma (2004), Oregon (2004), South Carolina (2006), South Dakota (2006), Tennessee (2006), Texas (2005), Utah (2004), Virginia (2006), and Wisconsin (2006) (Human Rights Campaign 2008c).

35. Florida's Amendment 2—"Inasmuch as marriage is the legal union of only one man and one woman as husband as wife, no other legal union that is treated as marriage or the substantial equivalent thereof shall be valid or recognized"—is one of the broadest in the nation, extending to civil unions and likely domestic partnerships as well.

36. California voters also approved a constitutional amendment banning same-sex marriage; see chapter 3.

37. The court rejected the plaintiffs' argument that the amendment would revise, not amend, the state constitution, and that because it affected multiple parts of the constitution, it required separate votes. Three years later, the state court of appeals affirmed the lower court (*Kulongoski* 2008).

38. Fla. Stat. ch. 741.212 (1) provides, "Marriages between persons of the same sex entered into in any jurisdiction . . . are not recognized for any purpose in this state."

39. There is no recorded appellate court ruling in *Wilson*.

40. See *Valley Forge Christian College v. Americans United for Separation of Church & State, Inc.* (1982) and *Lujan v. Defenders of Wildlife* (1992) for discussion of the rules of standing.

41. The U.S. Supreme Court denied certiorari in *Smelt v. Orange County* (2006).

42. Adopted in the 2004 general election, Article 2, §35, of the Oklahoma Constitution provides, "A. Marriage in this state shall consist only of the union of one man and one woman. Neither this Constitution nor any other provision of law shall be construed to require that marital status or the legal incidents thereof be conferred upon unmarried couples or groups. B. A marriage between persons of the same gender performed in another state shall not be recognized as valid and binding in this state as of the date of the marriage."

43. Kern rejected the plaintiffs' challenges to §3 on full faith and credit clause and privileges and immunities grounds but believed that the record should be more fully developed with respect to the equal protection and due process claims; he allowed the case to proceed to the summary judgment stage. There is no recorded appellate opinion in *Bishop*.

44. Article 1, §29, of the Nebraska Constitution provides, "Only marriage between a man and a woman shall be valid or recognized in Nebraska. The uniting of two persons of the same sex in a civil union, domestic partnership, or other similar same-sex relationship shall not be valid or recognized in Nebraska."

45. Colorado's proposed Amendment 2 would have prevented the state and municipalities from "enact[ing] . . . any . . . policy whereby homosexual, lesbian or bisexual orientation, conduct, practices or relationships shall constitute or otherwise be the basis of or entitle any person or class of persons to have or claim any minority status, quota preferences, protected status or claim of discrimination."

46. Although the U.S. Supreme Court upheld the Colorado Supreme Court's ruling in *Romer*, it rejected the state court's strict scrutiny analysis and applied the lower level of scrutiny more common in equal protection cases involving claims of discrimination based on sexual orientation.

47. The Eighth Circuit also reversed the lower court's ruling that the amendment was an unconstitutional bill of attainder and violated the plaintiffs' right to associational freedom under the First Amendment.

48. Over the state's objections, the appellate court accepted jurisdiction of the action, without requiring the couple to have their claims heard in the lower court first.

49. There are two Arizona statutes barring same-sex marriage: (1) Ariz. Rev. Stat. §25-101(C) provides, "Marriage between persons of the same sex is void and

prohibited," and (2) Ariz. Rev. Stat. §25-125(A) provides, "A valid marriage is contracted by a male person and a female person."

50. In *Standhardt v. MCSC* (2004), the state supreme court denied the plaintiffs' petition for review without comment.

51. Ind. Code §31-11-1-1(a) provides, "Only a female may marry a male. Only a male may marry a female." In 2004, the Indiana senate approved a measure to amend the state constitution to bar same-sex marriage; it failed to pass the state house of representatives.

52. Article 1, §23, of the Indiana Constitution provides, "The General Assembly shall not grant to any citizen, or class of citizens, privileges or immunities, which, upon the same terms, shall not be equally belong to all citizens." The plaintiffs originally claimed the state law violated the federal constitution's full faith and credit clause but did not pursue this argument on appeal.

53. There is no recorded appellate opinion in *Morrison*.

54. Although articles 2 and 3, the two sections of the New York domestic relations law governing marriage, do not explicitly restrict marriage to persons of the opposite sex, various portions of the statute support this interpretation by referring to "husband and wife" and "bride and groom."

55. The New York Constitution's article I, §6, the due process clause, provides, "No person shall be deprived of life, liberty or property without due process of law"; article I, §11, of the state constitution, the equal protection clause, provides, "No person shall be denied the equal protection of the laws of this state or any subdivision thereof."

56. One set of plaintiffs succeeded in the trial court but lost on appeal. New York Mayor Michael Bloomberg, who claimed that he was in favor of same-sex marriage, said that he appealed the lower court's ruling to allow the appellate court to determine the constitutionality of the restriction (*New York Times* July 6, 2006). Another group of plaintiffs sued the city department of health, claiming that the state domestic relations law restricting marriage to opposite-sex couples was unconstitutional. The department was granted summary judgment, and the appellate division affirmed. In the third case, other same-sex couples lost at trial as well as on appeal. And in the fourth case, the department was granted summary judgment the appellate court affirmed.

57. There was a split of 3 to 1 among the majority, with one justice writing a concurring opinion.

58. Wash. Rev. Code §26.04.010(1) provides, "Marriage is a civil contract between a male and a female"; §26.04.020(1)c prohibits marriage "when the parties are persons other than a male and a female."

59. Article I, §12, provides, "No law shall be passed granting to any citizen [or] class of citizens, . . . privileges or immunities which upon the same terms shall not equally belong to all citizens, or corporations."

Article I, §3, provides, "No person shall be deprived of life, liberty, or property, without due process of law."

60. Article XXXI, §1, provides, "Equality of rights and responsibility under the law shall not be denied or abridged on account of sex."

61. *Andersen* (2006), a ruling of 5 to 4, was decided by a plurality of three justices, with two concurring and three dissenting opinions. The dissents argued that

the law lacked a rational basis and charged that the ruling endorsed discrimination.

62. Madsen explained that under the circumstances, analysis of the state privileges and immunities guarantee is identical to the analysis used in the Fourteenth Amendment's equal protection clause.

63. Ironically, about a month before the state supreme court handed down its ruling in *Andersen,* the Washington Law Against Discrimination (Wash. Rev. Code §49.60.030 [1] [a-f]) went into effect, prohibiting discrimination on the basis of sexual orientation in employment and public accommodations as well as real estate, credit, and insurance transactions. Section 49.60.040(15) broadly defined "sexual orientation" to include "heterosexuality, homosexuality, bisexuality, and gender expression or identity."

64. The nine couples had been denied marriage licenses; the single man indicated that he wished to apply for one in the future.

65. Article 46 of the Maryland Declaration of Rights provides, "Equality of rights under the law shall not be abridged or denied because of sex."

66. The state supreme court had issued a writ of certiorari to the intermediate appellate court before the latter court ruled on the appeal.

3

The Right to Marry: Part 2

Before 2005, notwithstanding the short-lived victory in Hawaii in 1996, same-sex marriage supporters had suffered significant defeats in the legislative arena, beginning with the passage of Defense of Marriage Act (DOMA) in 1996 and continuing with the widespread adoption of state laws and constitutional amendments that barred same-sex couples from marrying. And although Congress rejected the proposed constitutional amendment against same-sex marriage, the measure had numerous supporters, including the president and the Senate and House leadership. In the executive branch, although some local public officials attempted to sanctify same-sex relationships by performing weddings for gay couples, their efforts were also largely annulled. In the judicial branch, despite their important triumphs in the Vermont and Massachusetts supreme courts, the trend was against marriage equality, and although some gay rights litigants prevailed in the lower courts, these rulings were largely reversed on appeal.

By 2005, although a significant number of states denied legal recognition to gay relationships, same-sex couples began to score some victories in securing equality of rights (see Human Rights Campaign 2008b). Connecticut, New Jersey, and New Hampshire joined Vermont in allowing same-sex couples to enter into civil unions. Other jurisdictions, such as the District of Columbia, Oregon, Hawaii, Maine, Maryland, New York, Washington, California, and, more recently, Nevada, granted an assortment of domestic partner benefits to same-sex couples, such as power of attorney, the right of inheritance, hospital visitation, explicit protection under domestic violence laws, the ability to make funeral arrangements, the ability to sue for the wrongful death of a partner, and the power to make at least some health care decisions (see Nelson 2008).

In 2008, the Connecticut and California supreme courts joined the Massachusetts high court in striking the bans on same-sex marriage. And although the California decision was subsequently negated by the voters, thousands of same-sex couples were able to be wed in that state as a result of the court ruling, and their marriages remain valid. Events in the spring of 2009 signaled further changes for marriage equality, and media reports indicate that other states, such as Illinois, New Jersey, and Minnesota, to name a few, may adopt marriage equality laws in the near future.

National public opinion polls, reporting declining opposition to same-sex marriage among the American people, also suggest that 2005 may have been the start of a new approach to gay marriage in the United States. The results of these surveys indicate that the public's acceptance of it has gradually grown since 2003 and 2004, when resistance to it was at an all-time high following *Goodridge* and *Lawrence*.

Surveys conducted by the Pew Research Center for the People and the Press (2006) have tracked views on same-sex marriage since 1996. When Pew first began asking questions about legalizing same-sex marriage in June 1996, 65 percent were opposed. In March 2001, 57 percent of the respondents declared themselves against same-sex marriage. Then, according to Pew, the public became more familiar with *Lawrence* and *Goodridge*, and the issue began to play an increasingly important role in the 2004 election campaign. With the talk of a constitutional amendment to make it illegal, opposition mounted, and by February 2004, it had climbed to 63 percent.

The Pew data show that resistance began decreasing in 2005, with 53 percent opposed in a July 2005 poll and 51 percent opposed in a March 2006 survey. Similarly, 42 percent of the respondents said that they were "strongly opposed" in February 2004, and only 28 percent indicated strong opposition in March 2006. The 2006 survey concluded that "the atmosphere surrounding the issue of gay marriage has cooled off, and public intensity has dissipated compared with two years ago" (Pew Research Center for the People and the Press 2006).

The trend continued, with Gallup reporting in May 2007 that "there is still considerable public opposition to complete equality for gays, particularly with respect to marriage. However, after several years of lower support for gay rights, support is now springing back to the relatively high levels seen in 2003" (Gallup News Service 2007). And in a July 2008 national poll, conducted by *Time* magazine, there was an even split between those who responded positively and negatively to the question "Should gay and lesbian couples be allowed to marry, giving them full legal rights of married couples, or not?" Moreover, there was a 5 percent rise in agreement with the statement—from 42 to 47 percent—between June and July 2008 (PollingReport.com 2008). Finally, a poll released by the Roper Center in January 2009 shows that 46 percent of the respondents agreed that it was discriminatory to deny same-sex couples the right to marry, with only 37 percent completely disagreeing with the statement. And in the same poll, only 20 percent believed that "there should be no legal recognition of a relationship between gay or lesbian couples" (Roper Center for Public Opinion Research 2009).

Additionally, there is a likelihood that support for same-sex marriage will increase over time, as polls also show that younger people are more likely to believe that it is discriminatory to prevent gays from marrying. A Quinnipiac University poll conducted on April 30, 2009, shows that 60 percent of people ages eighteen to thirty-four agreed "that not allowing same-sex couples to get married is discrimination"; among people over fifty-five, only 38 percent viewed it as discrimination (Quinnipiac University Polling Institute 2009; *New York Times* May 23, 2009).

Thus, the future for same-sex couples who sought to marry began to look brighter, as an increasing number of states adopted more egalitarian marriage policies in the latter part of the decade.

MASSACHUSETTS AND ITS NEIGHBORS

On May 17, 2004, the day that same-sex marriage became legal in Massachusetts, couples from New York, Rhode Island, Connecticut, New Hampshire, Vermont, and Maine traveled to Massachusetts to secure marriage licenses. Their plans were initially thwarted by Republican Governor Mitt Romney, who announced that only Massachusetts residents would be permitted to marry in the state.[1] He cited a forty-eight-word law, enacted in 1913, that prohibited nonresidents from marrying in Massachusetts if the marriage would be "void" in their home state unless they intended to reside in Massachusetts. In an interview, Romney said that he was interpreting the law as broadly as possible, even extending it to states that did not explicitly ban same-sex marriage. Gay rights advocates called the 1913 law, which had been enacted to bar interracial couples from marrying in the state, "archaic and discriminatory" (*New York Times* April 25, 2004).

The next day, Romney demanded copies of license applications from officials in four cities and towns that he claimed were defying his order not to marry out-of-state couples. His legal counsel called offices in Somerville, Worcester, Springfield, and Provincetown, ordering the applications to be sent to the state capitol (*New York Times* May 19, 2004). As a result, eight couples from the neighboring states filed suit in a Massachusetts state court, seeking a preliminary injunction to block enforcement of the 1913 statute, claiming that it was discriminatory. Judge Carol Ball of the superior court denied the injunction, noting that although she was disturbed that the state began to enforce this law only after *Goodridge*, she believed that it satisfied constitutional standards because it was applied evenhandedly to both same-sex and opposite-sex couples (*Cote-Whitacre v. Department of Public Health* 2004).

On March 30, 2006, the state supreme court upheld Ball's position on the law (*Cote-Whitacre* 2006a). Although there was no majority opinion, there was sufficient agreement among the justices that the 1913 law prohibited couples from Connecticut, Maine, New Hampshire, and Vermont from marrying in Massachusetts because those states explicitly outlawed same-sex marriage. The court ordered the lower court to enter judgment for the state with respect to those couples. But because same-sex marriages were not explicitly banned in Rhode Island or New York, the fate of the couples in those states was unclear, and the court ordered the lower court to determine the status of same-sex marriage in those states. The sole dissenter in *Cote-Whitacre* (2006a), Justice Roderick Ireland, charged that "the Commonwealth's resurrection and selective enforcement of a moribund statute, dormant for almost one hundred years, not only violates the 'spirit' of *Goodridge*, . . . but also offends notions of equal protection. It is, at its core, fundamentally unfair" (660–1).

When the case returned to the trial court, Suffolk County Superior Court Judge Thomas Connolly found that Rhode Island did not forbid same-sex marriage by statute, constitutional amendment, or controlling court decision, thus clearing the path for a Rhode Island lesbian couple to wed in Massachusetts (*Cote-Whitacre* 2006b).[2] But since the New York Court of Appeals had upheld the ban on same-sex marriage in July 2006—before Connolly handed down his decision—he held that New York couples were unable to be legally married in Massachusetts.

When the New York couples challenged this interpretation of the law, they found an unexpected ally in Massachusetts Attorney General Martha Coakley. She agreed that the couples who had wed in Massachusetts between May 17, 2004, and July 6, 2006, were legally married, as it had not been established during that time that New York law forbids same-sex marriages. Connolly signed off on this agreement on May 10, 2007 (*Cote-Whitacre* 2007).

The next year, events in New York led to an announcement that the state would recognize same-sex marriages legally performed in other states. On February 1, 2008, a New York appellate court held that a gay employee's valid Canadian marriage was entitled to recognition in New York for the purpose of eligibility for spousal health care benefits (*Martinez v. County of Monroe* 2008a). Relying on this ruling, the New York attorney general's office declared that henceforth as a matter of state policy, New York would recognize marriages legally performed elsewhere (*New York Times* May 16, 2007).[3]

On May 14, 2008, Democratic Governor David Paterson issued a directive ordering all same-sex marriages legally performed in other jurisdictions to be recognized in New York. The directive required the state to revise more than 1,300 state regulations, ranging from obtaining fishing licenses to filing joint tax returns (*New York Times* May 29, 2008). Spearheaded by the Alliance Defense Fund, a group of taxpayers and state legislators challenged the governor's directive, arguing that he did not have the authority to recognize marriages performed outside the state; Attorney General Andrew Cuomo moved to dismiss the case. On September 2, 2008, in *Golden v. Paterson* (2008), Bronx Civil Supreme Court Judge Lucy Billings granted the state's motion to dismiss the complaint, noting that New York law has had a long tradition of recognizing marriages legally performed elsewhere even if they could not legally be performed in the state. Billings stressed that "the Governor's Directive is an incremental but important step toward equality long denied, even if, according to the New York Court of Appeals, full equality is not constitutionally mandated" (at 3). Addressing the policy issues involved, she continued, "when partners manifest the commitment to their relationship and family . . . by solemnizing that commitment elsewhere, through one of life's most significant events, and come to New York, whether returning home or setting down roots, to carry on that commitment, nothing is more antithetical to family stability than requiring them to abandon that solemnized commitment. It is both a personal expression of emotional devotion, support, and interdependence and a public commitment" (at 19–20). The Alliance Defense Fund promised to appeal (*New York Sun* September 3, 2008).

In July 2008, the Massachusetts legislature voted to repeal the 1913 law, thus ending the last vestige of legal opposition to same-sex marriage in the state by its opponents.

CIVIL UNIONS

Some gay rights advocates view civil union laws as significant victories, for despite their limitations, they grant most of the rights and benefits of marriages. Others argue that civil unions are demeaning, a form of second-class citizenship that denies the rights and privileges of civil marriage (see Eskridge 2002; Evans 2004; Kubasek, Frondorf, and Minnick 2004).

In 2007, New Hampshire joined the ranks of states to enact legislation to allow gays to enter into civil unions, the fourth in the nation to do so.

The state had initially reacted to *Goodridge* by denying recognition to same-sex marriages performed there and by establishing a commission to study civil unions.[4] On December 1, 2005, the commission, staffed primarily by gay marriage opponents, recommended the state adopt a constitutional ban on same-sex marriage.

In April 2007, following a sweep by Democratic majorities in the state legislature, the state house voted 243 to 129 to establish civil unions, and later in the month, the state senate agreed in a party-line vote of 14 to 10; the law also permitted recognition of civil unions and marriages validly entered into in other states as civil unions in New Hampshire.[5] The governor signed the bill into law on May 31, 2007, and it took effect on January 1, 2008, making New Hampshire the last state in the region to permit same-sex couples a measure of partnership equality.[6]

In New Jersey, seven same-sex couples, each of whom had been in committed relationships for more than ten years (most with children), filed suit in June 2002 after being denied marriage licenses under the New Jersey law restricting marriage to heterosexual couples.[7] They claimed that the denials violated their procedural and substantive due process and equal protection guarantees of the state constitution found in article 1, paragraph 1.[8] In an unpublished opinion issued in November 2003, Superior Court Judge Linda Feinberg granted summary judgment to the state, and the plaintiffs appealed. She determined that even absent a specific prohibition against same-sex marriage, she had no doubt that the framers of the state's 1912 marriage law would have been opposed to it and found no constitutional violations in preventing same-sex couples from marrying (*Lewis v. Harris* 2006, 203).

While the case was awaiting a ruling from the appellate division, the state legislature enacted the Domestic Partnership Act (DPA) on January 12, 2004.[9] It took effect six months later on July 10, 2004, conferring significant legal rights on same-sex partners by entitling them to certain health care, tax, insurance, and pension rights on the same basis as married couples. It also extended the state Law Against Discrimination (LAD) to include a prohibition on discrimination on the basis of domestic partnership status.[10] Ironically, while the law conferred quasi-marital rights on same-sex couples, it specified that they were not entitled to marry.

In June 2005, the appellate division had upheld the lower court, in a vote of 2 to 1, rejecting the plaintiffs' argument that marriage is a fundamental right (*Lewis* 2005). Writing for the majority in assessing the due process claim, Judge Stephen Skillman held that although marriage is a fundamental right, the state supreme court has never extended that right to same-sex partners. Indeed, he added, because of their view of the relationship between marriage and procreation and the benefits afforded children raised by married couples, no jurisdiction other than Massachusetts had upheld a constitutional challenge to a state law restricting same-sex marriage.

Skillman determined that the framers of the 1947 state constitution would have been loathe to approve of same-sex marriage and did not intend article I to be interpreted to support it, nor would the voters who had approved article I have been willing to do so. Over time, he added, although the public has become more tolerant of gay rights, it has not accepted same-sex marriage. In the end, the court rejected the plaintiffs' plea that the state recognize their relationships as marriages, saying that "our society and laws view marriage as something more than just State recognition of a committed relationship between two adults. Our leading religions view marriage as a union of men and women recognized by God . . . and our society considers marriage between a man and woman to play a vital role in propagating the species and in providing the ideal environment for raising children" (268–9). Thus, he concluded, denying the plaintiffs marriage licenses does not abridge their due process rights.

Addressing the equal protection violation, the court applied the three-part balancing test for determining equal protection violations under the state constitution: "the nature of the affected right, the extent to which the governmental restriction intrudes upon it, and the public need for the restriction" (271, quoting *Greenberg v. Kimmelman* 1985, 302).[11] Because the court had concluded that same-sex couples lacked a fundamental right to marry, he held that they failed to meet their burden of identifying the recognized constitutional right to which they were entitled, thus ending the inquiry. *Loving*, he added, did not apply because it said nothing about impermissible state restrictions on same-sex marriages. Nor did *Lawrence* aid the plaintiffs, he said, quoting from the majority and concurring opinions that stressed that the decision did not apply to the institution of marriage.

Skillman cited the DPA as further evidence that the legislature did not sanction marital rights for same-sex couples while granting them a panoply of rights and benefits short of marriage. He cited innumerable cases indicating the limited nature of the court's constitutional authority to oversee legislative action; "a constitution," he said, "is not simply an empty receptacle into which judges may pour their own conceptions of evolving social mores" (*Lewis* 2005, 265). He ended by expressing confidence that when the public became more accepting of civil marriage for same-sex partners, lawmakers would enact legislation to allow it. While denying their claim, however, the court held out the hope that same-sex couples may have valid constitutional arguments that they were entitled to additional benefits arising from marriage.

The split opinion in the appellate court created an automatic right of appeal to the state supreme court, which heard oral arguments in the case in February 2006. In announcing its decision in *Lewis* (2006), the state high court posed the central question as to whether same-sex couples were entitled to the "legal benefits and privileges" afforded to married heterosexual couples (200). In doing so, the court was able to avoid the thornier question of whether the constitution guaranteed same-sex partners a fundamental right to marry, a right that must be "deeply rooted in the traditions, history, and conscience of the people" (200). In legal terms, this would mean that the court would base its decision on the state constitution's equal protection guarantee rather than on a substantive due process right.

The supreme court divided in a vote of 4 to 3. The ruling, announced by Justice Barry Albin, began by painting a very sympathetic picture of the couples in the case, describing their work, their children, and their long-standing commitments to their relationships. He also observed that the state's position against same-sex marriage no longer arose from the view that marital status, procreation, and child rearing were inextricably linked; instead, it derived from respect for tradition and history, and a belief that any policy changes may come only from the legislature. The outcome of the case seemed likely when the court avoided the "all or nothing approach" of a vote for or against the right of same-sex couples to marry but instead framed the issue as "whether committed same-sex couples have a constitutional right to the benefits and privileges afforded to married heterosexual couples, and, if so, whether they have the constitutional right to have their 'permanent committed relationship' recognized by the name of marriage" (206).

The supreme court revisited the plaintiffs' argument that they have a fundamental right to marry. Applying traditional due process analysis, the court found that they failed to show that the right they claimed is "deeply rooted in this State's history and its people's collective conscience" (208). Indeed, the opposite was true, as the state's marriage statutes, although not prohibiting same-sex marriage explicitly, included numerous references to both sexes. Moreover, in establishing domestic partnerships, Albin said, the legislature explicitly rejected same-sex marriage, and he agreed with the lower courts that the plaintiffs failed to demonstrate the existence of such a fundamental right.

Turning to the equal protection analysis, Albin noted the growing concern among state officials about discrimination on the basis of sexual orientation, most recently manifested by including sexual orientation within LAD. Acknowledging that the DPA was aimed at redressing some of the gay community's grievances, he stressed that gays were still deprived of significant rights and benefits accorded to heterosexual couples, especially in the area of family law—leaving aside the issue of the right to marry.

In assessing the state's justifications for treating same-sex couples differently from opposite-sex couples, he said that he believed that it was irrational for the state to commit itself to furthering the "basic human dignity and autonomy" of same-sex couples through the DPA but granting them only "an incomplete set of rights when they follow the inclination of their sexual orientation and enter into committed same-sex relationships" (217). He also rejected the state's contention that it was concerned about maintaining consistency with the laws of other states. For unlike other states, New Jersey does not discriminate on the basis of sexual orientation and has not enacted antirecognition laws. In this regard, he stressed that New Jersey's profile is more like its northeast neighbors (Massachusetts, Connecticut, and Vermont) than any other states.

In the end, the court found that the disparity between same-sex and opposite-sex couples represented an unconstitutional denial of equal protection and offered the state two options: within 180 days, either amend the marriage law or establish a separate legal structure such as a civil union. In presenting this choice to the legislature, the court implicitly rejected the plaintiffs' position that true equality requires marriage and that anything less than marriage relegates them to inferiority. In an explicit reference to its obligation to defer to majoritarian decision making, the court stressed that the final decision is and must be in legislative hands and committed to the democratic process.

Although the court had stopped short of ordering the state to allow gays to marry, gay rights opponents reacted to the ruling with cries of judicial activism and threats of impeachment. Democratic Governor Jon Corzine applauded the decision, saying that he looked forward to legislative resolution of the matter (*New York Times* October 26, 2006; *Washington Post* October 26, 2006). On December 14, 2006, the New Jersey legislature voted 56 to 19 in the general assembly and 23 to 12 in the senate to create civil unions. Signed by Corzine on December 21, 2006, the law went into effect two months later.[12] In June 2009, Corzine expressed support for marriage equality (*Philadelphia Inquirer* June 21, 2009).

MARRIAGE LITIGATION SUCCEEDS

On August 24, 2004, seven same-sex couples, most of whom were raising children, filed suit in a Connecticut state court after they were denied marriage licenses in the town of Madison (*Kerrigan v. Connecticut* 2006). They sought a court order to grant them marriage licenses, complaining that the state's refusal to recognize their relationships led to inequities in policies relating to hospital visitation, taxation, and insurance benefits. The couples claimed that denying them the right to marry infringed on their constitutional rights of equal protection, due process, and freedom of association.[13]

Shortly before the suit was filed, Connecticut Attorney General Richard Blumenthal issued an opinion in a letter to two town officials who asked for his comments on whether town officials could issue marriage licenses or perform weddings for same-sex couples. Reminding them that the decision must be left to the state legislature, he said, "I have concluded that the Connecticut Legislature has not authorized the issuance of a Connecticut marriage license to a same-sex couple, or the performance of a marriage ceremony for a same-sex couple, in Connecticut. I can reach no conclusion on whether a Connecticut court would hold that limiting the status of 'marriage' to opposite-sex couples violates constitutional standards. Ultimately, the courts will have the final say in interpreting our laws, and more particularly in determining whether those laws conform to constitutional principles. Unless and until such time as they are declared unconstitutional, however, our marriage statutes enjoy a presumption of constitutionality" (Connecticut Attorney General May 17, 2004).

On April 20, 2005, before the trial court handed down its decision in the *Kerrigan* litigation, Republican Governor M. Jodi Rell of Connecticut signed a law authorizing civil unions for same-sex couples. The bill was first approved in the lower house in a vote of 85 to 63 and in the upper chamber in a vote of 26 to 8. Rell was on record as opposing same-sex marriages but favoring civil unions. Although the law had originally been proposed to allow same-sex marriage, because of insufficient support, the legislators compromised on a civil union bill. And in an attempt to mollify conservatives, the law also defined marriage as a "union of one man and one woman" (*Boston Globe* April 21, 2005).

The statute, which went into effect on October 1, 2005, was the first in the nation to establish civil unions without a court order and equated civil unions with marriage (*Washington Post* April 13, 2005; April 14, 2005).[14] As in other states, although Connecticut same-sex couples became eligible for the benefits of marriage under state law, their unions were not recognized under federal law or acknowledged in most other states (*Connecticut Post* September 29, 2005; *New York Times* October 1, 2005).[15]

A few months after the state legalized civil unions, the plaintiffs filed a brief, attacking civil unions as discriminatory. Their amended complaint focused on the constitutionality of the civil union law and, more specifically, on its restriction on same-sex marriage. On July 12, 2006, Connecticut Superior Court Judge Patty Jenkins Pittman ruled on the parties' motions for summary judgment. The outcome of the case seemed clear when she began by characterizing the legislature's action in establishing civil unions as "courageous and historic" (*Kerrigan v. Connecticut* 2006, 90). The plaintiffs, now eight couples, maintained that they were entitled to the security of marriage and that establishing civil unions did not redress the harm done to them.

The opinion began by enumerating the state's efforts to prohibit discrimination on the basis of sexual orientation by repealing the law against consensual sodomy in 1969; prohibiting discrimination in employment, housing, public accommodations, credit, and education in 1991; allowing second-parent adoptions in 2000; and establishing civil unions in 2005. Despite these advances, the same-sex couples had expressed concern that their relationships were seen as "less worthy" than marriage and that they were perceived as "not good enough for marriage" and "second-class citizen[s]." They argued that the idea of the civil union "feels inferior and demeaning" (94). The state did not attempt to deny the legitimacy of their feelings of inferiority but contended that, however sincere, they were insufficient to rebut the presumption of constitutionality in the Connecticut civil union law.

Pittman said that were it not for the civil union bill, she would have applied *Loving* and engaged in a traditional constitutional analysis to assess the state's justifications for the policy. However, because gay couples were permitted to enter into civil unions, she gave little credence to their charge that they were considered inferior and relegated to second-class citizenship. By denying their unequal status, she was able to avoid addressing their equal protection arguments.

She was skeptical that the law denigrated their relationships by implicitly characterizing marriage as superior to civil unions. In her view, same-sex couples were equal to opposite-sex couples in the eyes of the law. "Indeed," she said, "the broad sweep of the statute indicates a legislative intent to confer not only equal but identical rights on same sex couples. Though the plaintiffs may feel themselves to be relegated to a second class status, there is nothing in the text of the Connecticut statutes that can be read to place the plaintiffs there."[16]

In the end, although she conceded that the plaintiffs were harmed by federal and state nonrecognition laws, she stressed that the injury was not attributable to Connecticut's decision to adopt the term "civil union" for same-sex couples. Rather, the harm was caused by the other jurisdictions' refusal to grant equal rights to same-sex partners, and neither the court nor the state legislature could affect those decisions.

Emphasizing its duty to refrain from exceeding its constitutional bounds and intruding on the legislative and executive prerogatives, Pittman stressed that legislation duly enacted by the legislature and signed by the executive is entitled to a presumption of constitutionality. In a classic statement of judicial deference, she warned that a court must "tread carefully in this area [as] it is the legislature that is the arbiter of public policy . . . [and] the judicial branch has very limited authority to interfere with the determination by the General Assembly as to those provisions of law that are intended to further the welfare of the citizens of Connecticut" (101).

She ended by reiterating that, notwithstanding the nomenclature, the plaintiffs had acquired the equal rights and benefits of marriage, consistent with their equal protection and due process rights. Reducing the controversy to one over semantics, she concluded that "the Connecticut constitution requires that there be equal protection and due process of law, not that there be equivalent *nomenclature* for such protection and process" (102, emphasis added). Based on this, she granted the state's motion for summary judgment.

The court's ruling was only a stopgap in the struggle over same-sex marriage, and the debate was far from over. In April 2007, the Connecticut General Assembly's Judiciary Committee voted 27 to 15 to legalize same-sex marriage, but the leadership declined to bring the measure to the house floor for a vote, and Rell promised a veto if it passed. On May 14, 2007, the lawyers for both sides squared off against each other in oral arguments before the state supreme court as the debate over the symbolic importance of the word "marriage" took on new life. Advocates of same-sex marriage were torn over their support for the civil union compromise, vowing to continue the fight to obtain their ultimate goal of marriage. Even the *Kerrigan* plaintiffs were divided over whether to enter into civil unions or hold out for marriage (*New York Times* May 13, 2007; October 11, 2008).

More than a year later—on October 10, 2008—the Connecticut Supreme Court ruled, with Supreme Court Justice Richard Palmer announcing the opinion for a majority of 4 to 3; the decision, *Kerrigan v. Commissioner of Public Health* (2008), was published on October 28, 2008.[17]

Palmer began by evaluating the plaintiffs' constitutional claims, namely, that denying them the right to marry and restricting marriage to a man and woman violated their fundamental right to marry and constituted sex discrimination, violating article first, §20, of the state constitution.[18] In response to these claims, the state contended that the plaintiffs were not harmed because the civil union law granted them equality of rights and there was no fundamental right to marry an individual of the same sex. It also insisted that the law did not discriminate on the basis of sex or sexual orientation because it allowed both heterosexuals and gays to marry a person of the opposite sex. Finally, the state maintained that even if the law were discriminatory, it was rationally related to a state objective, and laws affecting gays are not entitled to a higher level of scrutiny.

Palmer disagreed with the lower court's conclusion that there was no constitutional distinction between civil unions and marriages, accepting the plaintiffs' view that legal equality was insufficient given the backdrop of historical discrimination against gays. Quoting *Loving* and other cases proclaiming marriage as a sacred and basic right, he observed that "the civil union law entitles same sex couples to all of the same rights as married couples except one, that is, the freedom to marry, a right that 'has long been recognized as one of the vital personal rights essential to the orderly pursuit of happiness by free men [and women]' and 'fundamental to our very existence and survival'" (*Kerrigan v. Commissioner of Public Health* 2008, 416–7, quoting *Loving* 1967, 12).

Acknowledging that the intent of the civil unions law was undoubtedly benign, the court refused to accept the state's argument that in creating legal equality between civil unions and marriages, it had satisfied its constitutional mandate not to discriminate.

The state argued that it was inappropriate to apply equal protection principles to the law because the state is obliged to treat only "similarly situated" groups alike—and same-sex couples were different from opposite-sex couples. Citing similar reactions from the New Jersey, Vermont, and California supreme courts, the Connecticut high court found that both sets of couples were alike in seeking the goals of having a family and raising children in a loving atmosphere. It also rejected the state's claim that the state charter specified eight classifications meriting strict scrutiny, adding that even if it were true, it did not rule out the use of intermediate scrutiny for other, nonlisted classifications.

Modeling itself after the high court in determining the criteria for meriting heightened scrutiny—the group has historically been a victim of discrimination, the classification bears no relationship to ability, the immutability of the characteristic, and political powerlessness—the court held that classifications based on sexual orientation are quasi suspect and require heightened scrutiny. Although Palmer conceded that gays were not totally devoid of political power, he viewed the term misleading. The more appropriate inquiry, he said, was "whether the group lacks sufficient political strength to bring a prompt end to the prejudice and discrimination through traditional political means," that is, through "the democratic process" (*Kerrigan v. Commissioner of Public Health* 2008, 444).[19]

Palmer saw no reason for the court to refrain from injecting itself into this public policy debate and defer to the legislature's authority to define marriage. Because society's antipathy toward gays was so extreme and enduring, he said that he doubted that they would succeed in redressing their grievances through the legislative process. As with women and racial minorities, he believed that judicial intervention, in other words, an activist court, was needed to secure their equality. To accomplish this task, the judiciary must apply a heightened scrutiny standard to the law. After conducting an exhaustive survey of contrary federal and state rulings denying the use of heightened scrutiny for classifications involving sexual orientation, he was persuaded that those analyses and conclusions were incorrect and should not alter his view of the propriety of using heightened scrutiny in this case.

Applying the heightened scrutiny standard, the court assessed the state's two justifications for banning same-sex marriage: "to promote uniformity and consistency with the laws of other jurisdictions; and (2) to preserve the traditional definition of marriage as a union between one man and one woman" (476). Conceding that the first reason may be rational, the court held that it did not pass the heightened scrutiny standard, especially as the state merely asserted it as a justification without citing any precedent for support.

The state refrained from arguing that the law promoted its interest in children's welfare or in procreation. Instead, it maintained that its view of heterosexual marriage was traditional and that, with so many legislators adhering to this view, it was necessary to include the opposite-sex marriage provision to garner sufficient legislative support to pass the civil union bill. Parsing the word "tradition," the court found that it simply meant that the discrimination was long standing and deep seated, neither of which constituted the "exceedingly persuasive justification" the state was required to offer.[20]

Palmer ended by noting that just as the barriers to interracial marriage and full equality for women and racial minorities had fallen, the barrier to same-sex marriage must fall—at least in Connecticut. Because the state failed to meet its heavy burden of justifying its ban on same-sex marriage, the court declared it unconstitutional and remanded the case to the lower court with an order to grant the plaintiffs summary judgment and issue orders to the town clerks. The ruling did not affect the status of existing or future civil unions.

Blumenthal announced that the marriages could begin as early as the week of November 10 and that Connecticut would recognize marriages and civil unions from beyond its borders (*State Line News* October 28, 2008). Expressing her reaction to the decision, Rell declared, "The Supreme Court has spoken [but] I do not believe their voice reflects the majority of the people of Connecticut" (*New York Times* October 11, 2008). Other opponents of same-sex marriage, including the state's Roman Catholic bishops who declared themselves "extremely disappointed" with the ruling, immediately called for a constitutional convention to reverse the decision. The exact path to achieve this goal is unclear, as there would be a number of steps that would have to be taken, including a vote by the legislature and ultimate approval by the electorate (*Boston Globe* November 3, 2008; *Hartford Courant* October 11, 2008).

On the night of the election, it was clear that the electorate would overwhelmingly reject the proposed constitutional convention that would have permitted direct voter initiatives to be placed on the ballot (*Hartford*

Courant November 5, 2008). On November 12, 2008, Judge Jonathan Silbert, a New Haven Superior Court judge, entered a final judgment in the *Kerrigan* litigation, allowing marriage licenses to be distributed by municipal clerks throughout the state. And on the same day, the first same-sex couples were married in Connecticut (CNN.com November 12, 2008; *New York Times* November 13, 2008).[21]

Perhaps the most interesting developments in same-sex marriage policymaking took place in California, beginning as early as 2000. On March 7, 2000, California voters reaffirmed the state's commitment against same-sex marriage by approving Proposition 22, which provided that "only marriage between a man and a woman is valid or recognized in California" (Gavin 2004). Also known as the Limit on Marriages, or Knight, Initiative after its principal sponsor, William Knight, Proposition 22 won by an overwhelming vote of 61 to 39 percent and became section 308.5 of the California Family Code (*Sacramento Bee* September 9, 2005).

Notwithstanding these legal constraints, on February 12, 2004, at the direction of newly elected mayor of the city and county of San Francisco, Democrat Gavin Newsom, county clerks began to issue marriage licenses to same-sex couples.[22] A week later, more than 2,600 couples applied (*New York Times* February 18, 2004).[23] Newsom said that he was duty bound to follow the constitution rather than obey the law. When questioned about his motives in flouting the law, Newsom said, "I did it because I thought it was right" (*New York Times* February 19, 2004).[24]

On February 13, 2004, the state attorney general, Democrat William Lockyer, and the Arizona-based religious group Alliance Defense Fund filed suit in superior court to halt the issuance of the marriage licenses. In separate rulings on the plaintiffs' motions to halt the weddings, two superior court judges declined to issue temporary restraining orders against the city to halt the marriages (*New York Times* February 18, 2004).[25]

The next month, however, on March 11, 2004, the state supreme court ordered city and county officials to obey the ban and cease issuing marriage licenses.[26] The court indicated, however, that the plaintiffs might seek a judicial determination on the constitutionality of the state's marriage laws by filing a separate action in superior court (*Lockyer v. City & County of San Francisco* 2004a).[27] Notwithstanding the limitations of the court's ruling, Knight applauded the decision, saying that "finally, the courts have taken action to put an end to the anarchy in San Francisco" (*New York Times* March 12, 2004).

The case solely revolved around the question of whether the mayor abused his power by refusing to enforce California's law banning same-sex marriage because he believed it unconstitutional. In May 2004, the court held its first public hearing on the matter, but although lawyers for the city, the state, and the Alliance Defense Fund were present to argue on the ability of a local official to interpret state law, there were no lawyers representing the gay couples whose rights would be most affected by the ruling (*New York Times* May 26, 2004).

Emphasizing that the issue was separation of powers, not marriage, and that it was not ruling on the merits of the debate over same-sex marriage, the supreme court handed down its decision in *Lockyer* (2004b) on August 12, 2004. In a unanimous vote, the court held that Newsom had exceeded his authority in deciding that the law was unconstitutional and that local government officials must enforce all duly enacted laws. Continuing to emphasize that it was taking no position on the constitutionality of the state marriage restrictions, the court also held in a vote of 5 to 2 that the city must take all necessary steps to undo its past actions, including informing the almost 4,000 couples who believed themselves married because of the ceremonies performed between February 12 and March 11, that their marriages were "void and of no legal effect" (464).

As the court noted a number of times, its decision turned solely on the city's authority to issue the licenses, not on the constitutionality of the state law against same-sex marriage or on the constitutional issues the city raised. Chief Justice Ronald George stressed that "the substantive question of the constitutional validity of California's statutory provisions limiting marriage to a union between a man and a woman is not before our court in this proceeding, and our decision in this case is not intended, and should not be interpreted, to reflect any view on that issue" (464). Justice Joyce Kennard dissented from the decision to void the existing marriages, saying that the supreme court should wait until the superior court ruled in the case challenging the marriage limitations on constitutional grounds.

With the supreme court's decision in Lockyer pending, the Judicial Council coordinated the three existing cases challenging the marriage laws (City and County of San Francisco v. State of California, Tyler v. State of California, and Woo v. Lockyer), along with a fourth (Clinton v. State of California) filed later in the year, and directed them to Judge Richard Kramer of the Superior Court of San Francisco County for resolution.28 The state supreme court assigned the two cases (*Proposition 22 Legal Defense and Education Fund v. City and County of San Francisco* [2004] and *Campaign for California Families v. Newsom* [2004]) that had been stayed pending the court's ruling in Lockyer to Kramer as well.

Kramer handed down his ruling in the six consolidated cases on March 14, 2005.[29] It marked the first time that a court explicitly considered the constitutionality of the restrictions on same-sex marriage in the California marriage laws (§§300 and 308.5).[30]

He determined that the court must use strict scrutiny in assessing the constitutionality of the marriage laws because they reflected an express gender-based classification.[31] However, emphasizing that there would be no difference in the outcome of the case no matter which standard was used, Kramer applied both minimal and strict scrutiny. He began by reviewing the state's claim that the marriage code "embodies California's traditional understanding that a marriage is a union between a male and a female" (*Marriage Cases* 2005, at 3).[32] But, he noted, in both *Perez* and *Lawrence*, the states had cited tradition in attempting to justify their laws. Similarly, he was not persuaded by the state's contention that because it had granted same-sex partners equal rights in its domestic partner law, it could rationally reserve the term "marriage" for opposite-sex partners. If the state's decision to deny marriage to same-sex couples was unreasonable, he insisted, it had not cured the inequity by providing some rights to improve their situation.

Kramer compared the state's grant of marriage rights to gays without allowing them to marry to the "separate but equal status" that the U.S. Supreme Court had rejected in *Brown* because it "generates a feeling of inferiority as to their status in the community that may affect their hearts and minds in a way unlikely ever to be undone" (*Marriage Cases* 2005, at 5, quoting *Brown* 1954, 494).

In the end, Kramer concluded that there was no rational basis for distinguishing between same-sex and opposite-sex couples, including the state's purported interest in procreation—an argument raised by the interest groups intervening in the case. Citing *Loving* and *Perez*, he held that the laws involved a gender-based classification and rejected the state's argument that they did not discriminate on the basis of gender because they applied equally to men and women. He said, "It is the gender of the intended spouse that is the sole determining factor. To say that all men and all women are treated the same in that each may not marry someone of the same gender misses the point. The marriage laws establish classifications (same gender vs. opposite gender) and discriminate based on those gender-based classifications. As such, for the purpose of an equal protection analysis, the legislative scheme creates a gender-based classification" (*Marriage Cases* 2005, at 9).

He also refused to accept the state's contention that there is no fundamental right to marry a person of the same sex. Again citing *Perez*, he stressed that individuals have the right to marry a person of their choosing absent a legitimate state interest in withholding the right. This law denies citizens that basic right without a legitimate justification.

Like the U.S. Supreme Court, the California courts apply strict scrutiny when the law implicates a fundamental right; but unlike the high court, the California courts subject sex-based classifications to strict scrutiny. Kramer's conclusion was therefore anticlimactic, for if a law is unable to pass the rational basis test, it must obviously fall under strict scrutiny as well. Thus, absent a rational basis—much less a compelling one—for the law, he held that both sections of the California civil code violated the equal protection guarantee of the state constitution. He stayed his ruling, however, pending a meeting with the parties (*San Francisco Chronicle* March 15, 2005; *New York Times* March 15, 2005).[33]

As is common in same-sex marriage cases in which plaintiffs are victorious, Kramer was attacked for being a liberal activist judge; the irony is that he had been appointed to the California bench by Republican Governor Pete Wilson. Reacting to his ruling, an attorney for gay marriage opponents promised that "the people of California will move forward, just as in other states, to amend their constitutions in order to take judges out of the marriage-management business." Another opponent also attacked the decision and the man, calling it "a crazy ruling by an arrogant San Francisco judge who apparently hates marriage and hates the voters" (*San Francisco Chronicle* March 15, 2004).

Thereafter, events moved quickly. In 2005, San Francisco Assemblyman Democrat Mark Leno introduced legislation, Assembly Bill 849, called the Civil Marriage and Religious Freedom Protection Act, which would have removed gender-specific language from the state marriage laws. It was approved by the California legislature in September (*New York Times* September 7, 2005; CNN.com September 7, 2005).[34]

Less than twenty-four hours after the bill's passage, Republican Governor Arnold Schwarzenegger announced his intention to veto it. Citing Proposition 22, the governor said that the people had spoken on the issue and that the matter should be resolved either by the courts or by the electorate (*Daily News of Los Angeles* September 8, 2005).

A few weeks later, on September 29, 2005, Schwarzenegger fulfilled his promise to veto, although his veto message insisted that he still believed in "full protection under the law" for gay couples. He also reiterated his support for domestic partnerships and signed other legislation to expand laws prohibiting discrimination on the basis of sexual orientation. Leno was not mollified, charging the governor with "hiding behind the fig leaf of Proposition 22," adding that "he cannot claim to support fair and equal legal protections for same-sex couples and veto the very bill that would have provided it for them" (*Los Angeles Times* September 30, 2005; *San Francisco Chronicle* September 30, 2005).

Meanwhile, the attorney general and two anti–gay marriage groups returned to court, appealing Kramer's ruling to the state appellate court. Oral arguments, lasting six hours, took place on July 10, 2006, and, on October 5, 2006, the First District Court of Appeal announced its decision of 2 to 1 in *In re Marriage Cases* (2006a).[35] Speaking for a divided court, Judge William McGuiness began by noting that resolution of the case "requires us to venture into the storm of a fierce national debate" (685). Outlining each side's position, he emphasized the centrality of the court's role in the controversy: "one side argues the time has come for lesbian and gay relationships to enjoy full social equality, and it is fundamentally unfair for the state to continue to reserve marriage as an institution for heterosexual couples only. The other side stresses the need for judicial restraint and the importance of preserving the traditional understanding of marriage—which is very important to many Californians, who fear such a fundamental change will destroy or seriously weaken the institution at the heart of family life." The court's "task," he continued, "is not to decide who has the most compelling vision of what marriage is, or what it should be," but is solely to determine whether the state's restrictions on marriage run afoul of the state constitution (685).[36]

McGuiness signaled the outcome of the case when he noted that the chief obstacle that same-sex marriage advocates must overcome is that their success depends on the court's willingness to override the legislature's authority and democratic decision making to make social policy by defining marriage, a barrier that he was clearly reluctant to surmount. He chided the dissent, Judge Anthony Kline, for disregarding this canon of judicial oversight.

As in most equal protection cases, the key to the plaintiff's success is the court's decision about the proper level of scrutiny to use. Reviewing the state's history with same-sex marriage policymaking, including the DPA and the ill-fated Religious Freedom and Civil Marriage Protection Act vetoed by Schwarzenegger, the court turned to the marriage advocates' constitutional challenges under article I of the state constitution.[37] Taking his cues from the U.S. Supreme Court, McGuiness observed that although the high court had recognized a fundamental right to marry, the right had always been restricted to marriage with opposite-sex partners. Noting that principles of judicial restraint are intended to constrain courts from expanding existing fundamental rights, he rejected the plaintiffs' plea to define the right to marry broadly to include same-sex partners.

McGuiness declared that *Perez* and *Loving* were not helpful to the plaintiffs either, as the rulings in those cases were premised on racial discrimination. He ended his discussion of the fundamental rights analysis by attempting to reassure same-sex marriage advocates that rights evolve over time but, at the same time, insisted that courts cannot take a leading position in formulating social policy to hasten their appearance.

Acknowledging that the state constitution accords a higher level of review to gender-based classifications than the federal charter, McGuiness disagreed with Kramer's assessment that the marriage law is a gender-based classification. On the contrary, he said, "the laws treat men and women exactly the same, in that neither group is permitted to marry a person of the same gender. We fail to see how a law that merely mentions gender can be labeled 'discriminatory' when it does not disadvantage either group" (706).

The key is unequal treatment, he emphasized, not merely mention of a classification. And unlike the laws in *Perez* and *Loving*, which stemmed from inequality of the races, the marriage laws do not have the purpose or effect of treating either men or women unequally. Although the court agreed that the state marriage laws classify on the basis of sexual orientation, it declined to apply strict scrutiny. Combing through federal and state case law, McGuiness simply stated that "there is no precedent for doing so" (710).[38]

Stressing its obligation to defer to the legislature, the court used minimal scrutiny and found the state had a legitimate interest in preserving and promoting a traditional definition of marriage as a union between a man and a woman. The passage of the DPA does not undermine this interest; on the contrary, he said, "it is rational for the Legislature to preserve the opposite-sex definition of marriage, which has existed throughout history and which continues to represent the common understanding of marriage in most other countries and states of our union, while at the same time providing equal rights and benefits to same-sex partners through a comprehensive domestic partnership system. The state may legitimately support these parallel institutions while also acknowledging their differences" (720–1).

McGuiness was also persuaded by the state's argument that it had a legitimate interest in enforcing the people's will as expressed in the passage of Proposition 22. Granting that the people's will cannot justify an unconstitutional policy, he again reiterated that under minimal scrutiny, it must defer to the state's estimation of how to strike a proper balance between competing rights. At the end of the day, he concluded, the judiciary cannot rewrite the marriage laws, for "the Legislature has control of the subject of marriage, subject only to initiatives passed by the voters and constitutional restrictions." Paradoxically, in light of the governor's reason for vetoing the bill allowing same-sex marriages, McGuiness added that "change must come from the people—either directly, through a voter initiative, or through their elected representatives in the Legislature" (726).

At the end of the year—on December 20, 2006—the state supreme court unanimously granted review to the six petitions, representing fifteen same-sex couples (*In re Marriage Cases* 2006b). It heard oral arguments on March 4, 2008, and announced its decision a few months later on May 15, 2008.

During arguments, the stage was set when Justice Carlos Moreno asked, "Doesn't this just boil down to the use of the m-word—marriage?" Both sides to the dispute agreed that this was the fundamental question and stressed the importance of marriage and the family in their arguments to the court. The litigants for same-sex marriage, including the City and County of San Francisco, contended that calling their relationships anything less than marriages constituted discrimination; the opponents argued that calling their relationships marriages would threaten the institution of marriage. The attorney for the governor told the court that the decision to call the union of same-sex couples a marriage should be decided by the people of the state of California through their legislative representatives, not by the courts (*New York Times* March 5, 2008).[39]

Speaking for the court in a ruling of 4 to 3, the chief justice began by emphasizing that this case differs from those in other states in which the courts assessed the constitutionality of laws restricting marriage to opposite-sex couples. In this case, George said, because both opposite-sex and same-sex couples have identical "legal rights and obligations" under the state's 1999 domestic partnership law, the question is whether the state may reserve the term "marriage" for opposite-sex couples only. In other words, does "the failure to designate the official relationship of same-sex couples as marriage violate . . . the California Constitution" (*In re Marriage Cases* 2008, 398)? Repeatedly citing *Perez* as well as more recent California case law, George emphasized that the right to marry is not restricted to heterosexuals and that despite the state's attempt to treat both sets of couples equally, the possibility remains that the state law might still infringe on the constitutional rights of same-sex couples. In turning to the constitutional inquiry, he likely signaled the outcome of the case by announcing that the court would apply strict scrutiny.

Noting that *Perez* had not merely established a limited right to interracial marriage, he cited numerous cases broadly recognizing the ties between marriage and children and family, all protected by the state constitution's due process clause. Citing both state and federal case law for support, the court held that "the right to marry represents the right of an individual to establish a legally recognized family with the person of one's choice" and must be guaranteed to all Californians regardless of sexual orientation (*In re Marriage Cases* 2008, 423).

Assessing the plaintiffs' equal protection claim, George was not persuaded by the plaintiffs' argument that the law differentiated on the basis of sex and thus merited strict scrutiny. However, he acknowledged that it was based on sexual orientation and applied the traditional test for determining whether a classification is suspect: if it is based on an immutable characteristic, if it is unrelated to ability, and if there is a history of discrimination against the group. The last two criteria were easily satisfied, he said, but he lingered on the question of immutability, which the lower court had determined did not apply to gays. George concluded, however, that either the characteristic was immutable or the cost of change was too high. Thus, the court held that laws distinguishing on the basis of sexual orientation are suspect and, like race and sex, must be subject to strict scrutiny.

Scrutinizing the "differential treatment" inherent in the law's dichot-
omy between same-sex and opposite-sex couples, the court held that
preserving the traditional view of marriage is not a compelling reason,
nor is the treatment a necessary means to achieve the state's goal. The
court reached this conclusion by reasoning that, contrary to the opponents' assertions, allowing same-sex couples to marry will not change the
institution of marriage. Moreover, by excluding same-sex couples from
the privilege of marriage, the state sends a message that such couples are
disfavored, creating an image that the state attempted to dispel by enacting the domestic partnership law.

Finding that the law unconstitutionally deprives same-sex couples of
the right to designate themselves as married, the judge offered two possible remedies: allow gay couples to use the term "marriage" or deny
opposite-sex couples the right to apply it to themselves; he believed the
former was clearly preferable.

> In the present case, it is readily apparent that extending the designation of
> marriage to same-sex couples clearly is more consistent with the probable
> legislative intent than withholding that designation from both opposite-sex
> couples and same-sex couples in favor of some other, uniform designation.
> In view of the lengthy history of the use of the term "marriage" to describe
> the family relationship here at issue, and the importance that both the sup-
> porters of the 1977 amendment to the marriage statutes and the electors who
> voted in favor of Proposition 22 unquestionably attached to the designation
> of marriage, there can be no doubt that extending the designation of mar-
> riage to same-sex couples, rather than denying it to all couples, is the equal
> protection remedy that is most consistent with our state's general legislative
> policy and preference. (453)

The majority opinion ended by striking both sections of the civil code
restricting same-sex partners from the lawful status of marriage. The opponents had thirty days, until June 16, 2008, to seek a rehearing, and the
couples would be able to procure marriage licenses the day after.

Justice Marvin Baxter, concurring and dissenting, stated that although
he believed that the state should allow same-sex partners to marry, the
court had exceeded its authority in mandating this position, for such a
decision must be left to the people in a democratic process. "A bare majority of this court," he charged, "not satisfied with the pace of democratic
change, now abruptly forestalls that process and substitutes, by judicial
fiat, its own social policy views for those expressed by the People themselves. Undeterred by the strong weight of state and federal law and
authority, the majority invents a new constitutional right, immune from
the ordinary process of legislative consideration [and] . . . regardless of
the popular will" (457–8).

Justice Carol Corrigan, also concurring and dissenting, expressed a similar view. Pointing to the "the significant achievements embodied in the domestic partnership statutes," she urged that "if there is to be a new understanding of the meaning of marriage in California, it should develop among the people of our state and find its expression at the ballot box" (471).

Kennard objected to her colleagues' characterizing the opinion as judicial legislation. "The architects of our federal and state Constitutions," she said, "understood that widespread and deeply rooted prejudices may lead majoritarian institutions to deny fundamental freedoms to unpopular minority groups, and that the most effective remedy for this form of oppression is an independent judiciary charged with the solemn responsibility to interpret and enforce the constitutional provisions guaranteeing fundamental freedoms and equal protection" (455).

Gay rights advocates "rejoiced" over the ruling; the legal director for the National Center for Lesbian Rights (NCLR), who argued the case before the court, applauded it, stating that "with today's ruling, the California Supreme Court declared that lesbians and gay men have an equal right to make that cherished commitment [of marriage]" (*New York Times* May 16, 2008). But the struggle was far from over. The next weapon in the opponents' arsenal was an effort to seek a stay of the court's ruling (declined by the court early in June).[40] Failing that, they turned to the voters through an initiative to amend the state constitution in the November 2008 election. On the day the court's decision was announced, the head of National Organization for Marriage California promised that "these out-of-touch judges will not have the last word on marriage." The chief counsel for Liberty Legal Institute charged that "this is outrageous judicial activism and should be a wake-up call to the country." Schwarzenegger pledged to "uphold" the court's decision and refrain from supporting the ballot initiative that would amend the constitution to prohibit same-sex marriages (*Washington Post* May 16, 2008).

Even before the ruling was announced, the opponents of same-sex marriage had obtained the necessary signatures to put the amendment on the ballot.[41] In the midst of gearing up for the fight, hundreds of gay and lesbian couples took time out to celebrate the court's ruling—which had become official on Monday, June 16, 2008, at 5:01 P.M.—by marrying. One of the first couples to do so in Newsom's office was Del Martin, eighty-seven years old, and Phyllis Lyon, eighty-four years old. They had been together for more than fifty years.

The opponents put their energies behind the California Marriage Protection Act, known as Proposition (Prop) 8; it would add §7.5 to article I of the state constitution to provide "Only marriage between a man and a woman is valid or recognized in California." The effort was spearheaded by two groups: Protect Marriage and National Organization for Marriage California. One of the first skirmishes between supporters and opponents of the measure was over the legal definition of Prop 8. If judged to be a constitutional revision, it could not be adopted simply through the initiative process; if an amendment, it could be proposed by the requisite number of citizens of the state and passed by a majority vote at the polls (*Los Angeles Times* July 17, 2008; see Grodin 2009).

The difference lay in the significance of the change involved: a "revision" consists of a fundamental change to the constitutional structure and must be proposed by a constitutional convention or two-thirds of the legislature, followed by a popular vote (see Lee 1991). The "No on 8" side argued that the measure was a revision because it would reverse a supreme court ruling that the right to marry was fundamental. The court dismissed their petition without discussion of the merits. This issue would resurface after the vote.

At the end of July, marriage equality opponents attempted to block the attorney general's proposed change to the title and summary. The title would now read, "Proposition 8 eliminates right of same-sex couples to marry. Initiative Constitutional Amendment." The new summary consisted of two bulleted points: "Changes the California Constitution to eliminate the right of same-sex couples to marry in California" and "provides that only marriage between a man and a woman is valid or recognized in California." California Attorney General Edmund "Jerry" Brown, Jr., defended the alteration by saying that circumstances had changed since the original text was formulated; California same-sex partners were now able to marry, and voters should be told that a "yes" vote would take away their right. Both sides agreed that the language change would make a "yes" vote more unlikely, as voters would be more reluctant to destroy an established right (*Los Angeles Times* July 29, 2008). After losing twice in the lower courts, the "Yes on 8" campaign admitted defeat and accepted Brown's language, declining to appeal the matter to the state supreme court (SFGate.com August 12, 2008).

By the end of August, polls indicated that Prop 8 was likely to lose, with a majority (54 percent) of the people saying they opposed it, while only 40 percent said they favored it (*Los Angeles Times* August 27, 2008).

As with most California ballot initiatives, Prop 8's success depended largely on the amount of money collected for media advertising. Reversing an earlier trend, about a month before the election, the "Yes on 8" side reported that it had raised $25 million to fund its operation; the "No on 8" side was almost $10 million behind. The money flowed from conservative religious groups, with a good portion of the contributions reportedly coming from members of the Mormon Church (*Los Angeles Times* October 8, 2008). By that time, it was estimated that more than 11,000 couples had wed since May (*New York Times* October 8, 2008). The legality of these weddings would be uncertain if Prop 8 were passed.

Exit polls on Election Day indicated that the measure would likely be defeated by a vote of 53 to 47 percent (CNN.com November 4, 2008). However, when the results were in, California voters had approved Prop 8 by a vote of 52 to 48 percent.[42] It is believed that polls typically undercount opposition to marriage equality; California had a similar experience in 2000 when Proposition 22 was put to a vote. Then a preelection poll showed that 53 percent were in favor, and the final result was 61 percent in favor (*New York Times* November 4, 2008).

Although an amendment is supposed to take effect the day after its approval by the voters, lawyers for the American Civil Liberties Union (ACLU), the NCLR, and Lambda Legal immediately sought a stay by filing suit on behalf of Equality California and six unmarried same-sex couples. Other plaintiffs joined them, including a couple that had married before Prop 8 took effect. They argued that a ballot measure, such as Prop 8, cannot be used to override a court's declaration of a group fundamental right. The senior counsel for Lambda Legal charged that the measure was "too big a change in the principles of our constitution to be made just by a bare majority of voters."

On November 19, 2008, the state supreme court denied the request for a stay but agreed to rule on the validity of Prop 8; it also allowed Prop 8 proponents to intervene in the action. The court ordered the parties to brief the following issues: "(1) Is Proposition 8 invalid because it constitutes a revision of, rather than an amendment to, the California Constitution? (See Cal. Const., art. XVIII, §§1–4.) (2) Does Proposition 8 violate the separation of powers doctrine under the California Constitution? (3) If Proposition 8 is not unconstitutional, what is its effect, if any, on the marriages of same-sex couples performed before the adoption of Proposition 8?" (Judicial Council of California 2008; Supreme Court of California 2008).

Attempting to calm the fears of the married couples, the attorney general said that the state would honor the 18,000 marriages that had taken place between June 17, the day that same-sex marriage became legal, and November 5, the day that Prop 8 took effect. The California courts are generally unwilling to apply an initiative retroactively unless it is specified in the text, but until the state supreme court ruled at the end of May 2009, the outcome for the couples was uncertain (Lambda Legal 2008; *Washington Post* November 11, 2008; *Los Angeles Times* May 26, 2009; see Choper 2009).

The postmortems following the vote centered largely on the Mormon Church's overwhelming support for the measure. Protestors took to the streets in San Francisco, Los Angeles, as well as in Salt Lake City, home of the Mormon Church, which had purportedly donated most of the funding of the "Yes on 8" campaign. In some cities, demonstrators specifically targeted Mormon temples and businesses.[43] Another blow for same-sex marriage advocates was the discovery that 70 percent of African American voters and 53 percent of Latino voters voted "yes" on Prop 8, thus splintering the image of solidarity among minority groups in support of civil rights (*Washington Post* November 7, 2008).

On December 19, 2008, California's attorney general filed a 111-page brief with the state supreme court, urging it to invalidate Prop 8 (Answer Brief in Response to Petition for Extraordinary Relief, *Tyler v. State of California* 2008). A press release issued by Brown's office that day stated that "Proposition 8 must be invalidated because the amendment process cannot be used to extinguish fundamental constitutional rights without compelling justification" (Office of the Attorney General 2008).

In early February, the supreme court announced that it would hear oral arguments on the validity of Prop 8 in March. On March 5, 2009, amid widespread interest in California and the rest of the nation, the arguments were streamed live on the California Channel, a public affairs cable network (Judicial Council of California 2009; Supreme Court of California 2009).[44] The court announced it would issue its ruling at the end of May.

As the California courts struggled over same-sex marriage policy, the seven justices of the Iowa Supreme Court ruled on the constitutionality of the Iowa law limiting marriage to opposite-sex couples.

The case arose when six same-sex couples filed suit in the Polk County District Court after being denied marriage licenses by the county clerk. They claimed that the 1998 law restricting marriage to opposite-sex couples violated the Iowa Constitution. After reviewing the voluminous record, based largely on affidavits and depositions, the state trial court judge, Robert Hanson, granted summary judgment to the plaintiffs in August 2007; he ruled that the limitation on same-sex marriage violated the state constitution's due process and equal protection guarantees. However, although he ordered the state to begin to issue marriage licenses, no weddings took place, as he stayed his ruling to allow the county to appeal to the state supreme court.

In December 2008, the Iowa Supreme Court had heard oral arguments in *Varnum v. Brien* (*Omaha World-Herald* December 10, 2008; *The Gazette* [Cedar Rapids] December 10, 2008).

In a unanimous opinion announced by Justice Mark Cady, the supreme court ruled on April 3, 2009, that the marriage law, as amended in 1998, violated the state's equal protection guarantee.[45] The outcome of the case seemed clear at the outset when the court stated that "the idea that courts, free from the political influences in the other two branches of government, are better suited to protect individual rights was recognized at the time our Iowa Constitution was formed" (at 4).

The court first addressed the threshold test that the equal protection clause does not apply because the plaintiffs as same-sex couples are not similarly situated to opposite-sex couples in being unable to procreate. Cady concluded that apart from their sexual orientation, the couples are also in committed, loving relationships, many raising children, and that, just like opposite-sex couples, they would benefit from societal recognition of their marital status.

Again rejecting the county's argument that the statute as written does not discriminate on the basis of sexual orientation, the court declared that the law defined them by their sexual orientation by precluding their right to marry a person of the same sex. Cady emphasized the court's traditional obligation to defer to the legislative judgment, typically by applying minimal scrutiny to the challenged legislation. But after reviewing the four standard indicia of a suspect class (a history of discrimination, relationship to ability to make societal contributions, immutability of sexual orientation, and political powerlessness), he concluded that classifications based on sexual orientation must be subject to a heightened level of scrutiny because gays require a higher degree of protection from the operation of majority rule.[46]

Applying intermediate scrutiny analysis, Cady asked whether the law preventing gays and lesbians from marrying is substantially related to an important government objective. The court concluded that the state's primary justifications for the law—maintaining the integrity of traditional marriage, creating an optimal child-rearing environment, and promoting procreation—fail on a number of grounds, primarily overinclusiveness and underinclusiveness. Although he conceded that at least some of the state's objectives are important, Cady found that excluding same-sex couples from civil marriage did not substantially advance those goals. Rejecting the possibility of allowing the state to offer civil unions as an alternative to marriage, the court flatly ordered it to allow gays and lesbians "full access to the institution of civil marriage" (at 30).[47]

The plaintiffs were predictably ecstatic at their victory and at their opportunity to marry when the ruling became final at the end of April. Although opponents vowed to continue their fight to oppose gay marriage, their options are rather limited, as overturning a supreme court ruling requires two successive votes in the state legislature followed by approval by voters in a statewide ballot. The Democratic-controlled houses of the state legislature manifested no interest in undertaking these measures.

Both sides sought to identify the opinion with Iowa traditions. Senior counsel for Lambda Legal characterized the court's ruling as "vindicating quintessential Iowa values." A spokesperson for National Organization for Marriage charged that "the gay marriage movement has once again used the power of the courts to push an untruth on unwilling Iowans" (*New York Times* April 4, 2009).The suit was clearly a result of careful planning by marriage equality strategists. One of the lead attorneys for Lambda Legal commented that "people who know Iowa have been saying for some time that it is different from its neighbors. There's a tradition of independence and willingness to stand up on issues of fairness" (*New York Times* April 5, 2009).

The ruling took effect on April 27, 2009, permitting same-sex couples to apply for marriage licenses. Because there are no residency requirements in Iowa, the decision opened the door for non-Iowa citizens to be wed there also; couples traveled from Illinois, Wisconsin, Missouri, and even North Carolina, for this purpose (*Telegraph Herald* [Dubuque] April 28, 2009; *The Gazette* [Cedar Rapids] May 2, 2009).

The ongoing battles over marriage equality soon moved to the East Coast. On April 7, a few days after the Iowa decision, Vermont became the next state to allow gays to marry when the legislature voted to override Republican Governor Jim Douglas's veto. His veto message said that the law would not give gays access to federal benefits or to rights in any other state, and he expressed disappointment that the issue distracted the legislature from dealing with more important issues, such as jobs and the economy. The next day, the Senate voted 23 to 5 and the House voted 100 to 49 to override the veto; the vote in the House was the minimum number needed for an override (CNN.com April 7, 2009; *New York Times* April 8, 2009). When the law took effect on September, 1, 2009, Vermont became the first state in the nation to enact marriage equality without a judicial directive.

On May 5, 2009, in a vote of 12 to 1, the Council of the District of Columbia approved a plan to allow recognition of same-sex marriages performed in other jurisdictions. A few days later, Mayor Adrian Fenty signed the bill, sending it to Congress for review. Under D.C. home rule provisions, if Congress took no action by July 6, it would automatically become law (*Washington Post* May 6, 2009; May 10, 2009). On May 21, two members of the House, Democrat Dan Boren of Oklahoma and Republican Jim Jordan of Ohio, introduced legislation to define marriage in the district as a union of a man and a woman. Known as the D.C. Defense of Marriage Act, the bill was cosponsored by a bipartisan group of thirty representatives (*Washington Post* May 22, 2009).[48]

The day after the D.C. Council vote, Democratic Governor John Baldacci of Maine signed a bill legalizing gay marriage after it was approved in the state senate in a vote of 21 to 13 and in the state house in a vote of 89 to 57. Baldacci's action made him the first governor to sign a marriage equality bill without a court order. Although he had opposed gay marriage previously, he noted that he "did not come to this decision lightly or in haste," adding, "I have come to believe that this is a question of fairness and of equal protection under the law and that a civil union is not equal to civil marriage." Scheduled to take effect three months later, gay marriage opponents promised to challenge the law by collecting the requisite 55,000 signatures to bring it to the voters in a November referendum (*Portland Press Herald* May 6, 2009; *Boston Globe* May 7, 2009; *New York Times* May 7, 2009).

Events did not go as smoothly for marriage equality legislation in Maine's neighboring state—New Hampshire. On March 26, 2009, the state house rejected a proposed bill to eliminate the restriction on same-sex marriage in a vote of 183 to 182; the same day, however, on reconsideration, it voted 186 to 179 in favor of the bill. About a month later, on April 29, in a vote of 13 to 11, the senate approved a slightly different version that differentiated between civil and religious marriages. When the measure was returned to the house for its approval, it passed in a vote of 178 to 167.

The bill was sent to New Hampshire Democratic Governor John Lynch, who released a statement on May 14, saying that he understood "the very real feelings of same-sex couples that a separate system is not an equal system [and] that a civil law that differentiates between their committed relationships and those of heterosexual couples undermines both their dignity and the legitimacy of their feelings." At the same time, he added, he appreciated the "equally deep feelings and genuine religious beliefs . . . [of citizens who] fear that this legislation would interfere with the ability of religious groups to freely practice their faiths." He concluded by declaring that despite his earlier opposition to gay marriage, he would sign the bill when it reached his desk if the legislature adopted his proposed language that permitted members of religious organizations and churches to refuse to participate in gay marriage ceremonies or provide services, facilities, or goods to gay weddings; without this language, he warned, he would veto the bill (Lynch 2009).

The senate approved Lynch's changes in a party-line vote of 14 to 10 on May 20. That same day, in a surprise move, the house voted 188 to 186 against incorporating the text that Lynch sought, continuing the uncertainty about the bill's final passage. In a second vote of 173 to 202, the house rejected a measure that would have killed the bill; it then voted 207 to 168 to send the bill to conference committee. Gay marriage supporters, some of whom voted against the Lynch version, expressed their frustration with it, saying that constitutional and statutory guarantees protecting religious liberties were already in place. Gay marriage opponents complained that the additional language did not go far enough because it did not exempt private business owners, like florists or photographers, from being forced to provide goods or services to gay couples.

On Friday, May 29, conference committee members unanimously agreed to insert the following preamble into the bill: "Each religious organization, association, or society has exclusive control over its own religious doctrine, policy, teachings and beliefs regarding who may marry within their faith." Adopting Lynch's language, it also insulates religious groups and their employees from civil suits as well as allows organizations affiliated with religious groups that operate "for charitable or educational purposes" to deny marriage services individuals who violate the group's religious tenets (*Boston Globe* May 7, 2009; May 15, 2009; May 17, 2009; May 21, 2009; May 30, 2009; *Concord Monitor* May 17, 2009; May 21, 2009; *Union Leader* May 30, 2009).

On the morning of June 3, 2009, the senate again voted 14 to 10 in favor of the bill; later in the day, the house also passed it in a vote of 198 to 176. The governor, who had indicated that this new version was acceptable to him, signed it the same day, making New Hampshire the fifth state in New England and the sixth state in the nation to legalize gay marriage. The law, taking effect on January 1, 2010, also recognizes out-of-state gay marriages and civil unions; New Hampshire residents already in civil unions will automatically be considered married on January 1, 2011. In signing the bill into law, Lynch said that "today, we are standing up for the liberties of same-sex couples by making clear that they will receive the same rights, responsibilities, and respect under New Hampshire law" (BayWindows.com June 3, 2009; *Reuters* June 3, 2009; *New York Times* June 4, 2009; *Boston Globe* June 4, 2009).

Further to the south, in New York, the state assembly approved a marriage equality bill on May 12, 2009. The bill, sponsored by the governor, won in a vote of 89 to 52. Senate passage of the bill before the state legislature adjourned for the year was by no means certain, and same-sex marriage supporters did not anticipate an easy victory in the upper chamber, where it needed 32 (of 62) votes to pass. No Republican announced support for the bill, and, although the Democrats had a majority of 32 to 30 in the upper chamber, some members of the party indicated that they did not support it either. The party leaders said that they would not bring the bill to the floor for a vote unless they had enough votes for passage (*Newsday* May 13, 2009; *Daily News* May 18, 2009; *New York Times* May 13, 2009; May 18, 2009; *Buffalo News* June 2, 2009).[49]

The month of May ended with a major setback for marriage equality advocates. On May 26, the California Supreme Court announced its decision on the validity of Prop 8 in the consolidated cases of *Strauss v. Horton* (S168047), *Tyler v. State of California* (S168066), and *City and County of San Francisco v. Horton* (S168078), declaring that California voters had properly amended the state constitution to bar same-sex marriages. The ruling was decided 6 to 1, with the chief justice announcing the opinion; Kennard and Werdegar concurred, and Moreno dissented.

Speaking for the majority, George noted that this was the third time the court has been asked to rule on same-sex marriage policy. Being careful to explain the parameters of judicial authority, he cautioned that the court was not being asked to decide on the wisdom of adding Prop 8 to the constitution. Emphasizing the court's subordinate policymaking role, George stressed that justices are "limited to interpreting and applying the principles and rules embedded in the California Constitution, setting aside our own personal beliefs and values" (*Strauss* 2009, at 24).

The outcome of the case, he explained, turned on the limitations of the initiative process in altering the state constitution. Because of the importance of this question, the chief justice devoted most of the opinion to assessing whether Prop 8 was an amendment or revision; if the latter, it must emanate from the state legislature or constitutional convention, not from the citizenry as Prop 8 did. To determine its status as an amendment or a revision, he said, the court must base its decision on "(1) the meaning and scope of the constitutional change at issue, and (2) the effect—both quantitative and qualitative—that the constitutional change will have on the basic governmental plan or framework embodied in the preexisting provisions of the California Constitution" (at 30).

The court initially held that Prop 8 was less sweeping than its proponents claimed. It did not, George emphasized, fundamentally contravene the constitutional guarantees proclaimed in *In Re Marriage Cases* (2008), in which the court upheld due process and privacy rights of same-sex couples and established equality of rights between same-sex and opposite-sex couples. The sole effect of Prop 8, he declared, although not insignificant, was to reserve the term "marriage" for relationships between opposite-sex couples. "In all other respects," he observed, aside from the marriage label, the constitution still protects the right of same-sex partners "'to establish—with the person with whom the individual has chosen to share his or her life—an officially recognized and protected family possessing mutual rights and responsibilities and entitled to the same respect and dignity accorded a union traditionally designated as marriage'" (*Strauss* 2009, at 89–90, quoting *In Re Marriage Cases* 2008, 399).

Following a lengthy analysis, the court concluded that Prop 8 did not qualify as a revision, as it had no impact on the state's governmental structure, nor did it violate separation of powers by restricting the court's power of judicial review as the attorney general had argued. Conceding that it did not alter the "governmental plan or framework," the challengers claimed that Prop 8 diminished fundamental constitutional rights and that such changes can be realized only through the revision process. George rejected these contentions, saying that the Prop 8 opponents could cite no authority to support their claim and that, over time, there were numerous constitutional amendments with important effects on judicial rulings that had arisen through the initiative process.

The crucial element, he emphasized, was the "scope" of the change, not its "importance" (*Strauss* 2009, at 180). To qualify as a revision, he reiterated, "a constitutional measure must make a far reaching change in the fundamental governmental structure or the foundational power of its branches as set forth in the Constitution" (at 172). This could not be said of Prop 8. George pointed out that the Prop 8 opponents were really complaining of the ease with which voters could alter the constitution, but he carefully explained that the court lacked the authority to restrict the procedures for amending the constitution through ballot initiatives.

The next question the court addressed was the validity of the approximately 18,000 marriages that had taken place in the few months when same-sex marriage was legal. George began by referring to the commonly accepted principle that legislative and constitutional provisions are applied prospectively absent specific indications to the contrary. Because the brief text of Prop 8 did not provide clear evidence of the voters' intent in either direction, the court was forced to discern it from extrinsic sources, not an easy task in the absence of documents discussing the issue in the months leading up to the election. Commenting on this silence, the court speculated that if the electorate had been told that a positive vote on Prop 8 would annul thousands of marriages, the outcome might have been different. Thus, seeing no reason to deviate from the customary practice of applying the amendment going forward, George added that the failure to do so would violate state due process guarantees of the couples that had relied on the supreme court's ruling in 2008 and entered into valid marriages. The court voted unanimously to sustain the validity of the existing marriages.

In an apparent concession to the dissenting justices in the 2008 ruling who had urged that changes in marriage policy should be left to the popular will, George ended by saying that "if there is to be a change to the state constitutional rule embodied in that [Prop 8] measure, it must 'find its expression at the ballot box'" (*Strauss* 2009, at 254–5, quoting *In re Marriage Cases* 2008, 471).

In her concurring opinion (for herself, Werdegar, and Moreno [in part]), Kennard observed that she had signed onto the majority opinion in *In re Marriage Cases* and had even written a separate opinion in that case to rebut the dissent's argument that the judicial branch should refrain from attempting to resolve social policy issues such as same-sex marriage. She insisted that she did not waiver in her belief that courts were obliged to adjudicate such constitutional rights claims; "what has changed, however," she stressed, "is the state Constitution that this court interpreted and enforced in the *Marriage Cases"* (*Strauss* 2009, at 257). She pointed out that although an initiative cannot change the judiciary's interpretation of the constitution, it may alter the text to expand or contract a constitutional right as Prop 8 had.

Werdegar's concurrence agreed with the majority's characterization of Prop 8 as an amendment; however, she wrote separately because she believed that the majority erred in defining a revision too narrowly. In her view, the majority was wrong to hold that a significant change to constitutional principles could not qualify as a revision, absent a structural alteration of the government. She compared the California law at issue in *In re Marriage Cases* (2008) with Prop 8. Acknowledging that both measures infringed on the right of gay couples to have "'their family relationship accorded respect and dignity equal to that accorded the family relationship of opposite-sex couples,'" she believed that Prop 8 did not bring "about such a broad change in the principle of equal protection as to amount to a constitutional revision" (*Strauss* 2009, at 273–4, quoting from *In re Marriage Cases* 2008, 445).

Echoing the majority, she concluded that Prop 8 did not affect equality of rights between same-sex and opposite-sex couples; it only barred the state from designating their relationships as marriages. She ended by reiterating the state's obligation to protect the equal rights guarantees it had promised to uphold in 2008.

Moreno dissented, warning that the decision jeopardized the guarantee of equality for all minorities by "weaken[ing] the status of our state Constitution as a bulwark of fundamental rights for minorities protected from the will of the majority" (*Strauss* 2009, at 279). In protecting minority rights and restraining majority impulses, he pointed out, the equal protection clause is inherently countermajoritarian, especially when strict scrutiny is involved. He seemed particularly troubled by the ruling because he believed that the court had rightfully curbed the majority will in *In re Marriage Cases* by declaring sexual orientation a suspect classification and requiring courts to view laws affecting it through a strict scrutiny lens.

He rejected the majority's interpretation that Prop 8 represented only a rhetorical shift. Quoting from *In re Marriage Cases*, Moreno stressed that the court had proclaimed the right to marry as a fundamental right and declared legal parity between same-sex and opposite-sex couples. Like the others, Moreno focused on the distinction between an amendment and a revision, concluding that the majority had misinterpreted California case law. He maintained that an alteration of a fundamental constitutional principle must also be considered a revision, adding that the court has never "held that the Constitution properly may be amended to deprive a minority group of a fundamental right." In his view, "withholding a fundamental right from a minority group on the basis of a suspect classification is inherently antithetical to the core principle of equal protection that minorities are to be protected against the prejudice of majorities" (*Strauss* 2009, at 304–5).

Returning to his main thesis, Moreno declared that the court's holding placed no constraints on a majority that seeks to discriminate against an unpopular minority on the basis of race, religion, gender, national origin, or any other characteristic. He expressed dismay that the court seemed prepared to abdicate its role as protector of minority rights and subject the fundamental rights of gays and lesbians to majoritarian decision making.

Concluding, he dissented from the majority's view that Prop 8 simply amended the constitution, saying that because it encroached on the essence of a minority's constitutional right to equal protection, Prop 8 was a revision and could not be adopted through the initiative process.

Predictably, the reaction to *Strauss* was swift. Even before the court decision was announced, both sides promised to renew their fight in other arenas if they lost (*Christian Science Monitor* May 26, 2009). Immediately following the decision, marriage equality advocates mounted protests, demonstrating in front of the supreme court building in San Francisco; the rainbow flag in Harvey Milk Plaza was lowered to half-mast. A small number of Prop 8 supporters also showed up at the court building to indicate their support for the ruling. The governor issued a statement that he would abide by the decision but "believe[d] that one day either the people or courts would recognize gay marriage" (*Los Angeles Times* May 26, 2009).

Numerous leaders of gay rights groups, such as Equality California, NCLR, Lambda Legal, and the ACLU, announced their intention to submit the issue to the electorate again as another initiative, possibly as early as 2010, and asked supporters to contribute to the effort. Human Rights Campaign president Joe Solmonese expressed disappointment with the decision but predicted "a groundswell to restore marriage equality in our nation's largest state" (Human Rights Campaign 2009b). Gay rights litigator Evan Wolfson, executive director of Freedom to Marry, likened the incrementalism of the gay rights movement to other social movements. "The classic pattern of civil rights advance in the United States is patchwork [and] the gay rights movement is going to follow the classic pattern," he said. On the other side, Prop 8 supporters expressed pleasure with the ruling, calling it appropriate that the court allowed the people to amend the constitution (*Washington Post* May 27, 2009; *New York Times* May 27, 2009).

In a surprising move, the day after the decision was announced, attorneys Theodore Olson and David Boies, chief lawyers on opposing sides of the *Bush v. Gore* (2000) litigation, filed suit in federal court on behalf of two Los Angeles gay and lesbian couples to enjoin the enforcement of

Prop 8. Their motion for an injunction in *Perry v. Schwarzenegger* (2009) alleged that Prop 8 infringed on the equal protection and due process guarantees of the federal Constitution as well as §1983. More specifically, they charged that Prop 8 violated their fundamental right to marry and discriminated against them on the basis of sex and sexual orientation.

The complaint quoted extensively from *Brown, Loving, Romer,* and *Lawrence* as well as *In re Marriage Cases* (2008). The plaintiffs' due process argument was based on the premise that when fundamental rights are at issue, courts must use strict scrutiny; they added, however, that Prop 8 would not even pass muster under minimal scrutiny because the state had no rational basis for depriving same-sex couples of the right to marry. The only plausible grounds for the denial, they insisted, stemmed from moral disapprobation, which, as the U.S. Supreme Court made clear in *Lawrence,* was not a legitimate reason and could not survive even minimal scrutiny.

On equal protection grounds, they contended that the classification was irrational because it deprived gays and lesbians of a right they had previously possessed under the state constitution to which all other citizens are still entitled. Even though they believed that Prop 8 could not pass minimal scrutiny, they advanced reasons why classifications based on sexual orientation meet the standard for heightened scrutiny. They also argued that they were discriminated against on the basis of sex and cited ample authority for using heightened scrutiny to review classifications based on sex.

The case was assigned to Chief Judge Vaughn Walker. Some gay rights movement leaders were not pleased with the Olson–Boies initiative, expressing concern that if the case reached the U.S. Supreme Court, the conservatives on the bench could set the gay rights movement back many years by enshrining inequality in the U.S. Constitution (*New York Times* May 28, 2009). At the end of June, a number of key groups announced their support for the lawsuit (*Washington Post* June 26, 2009).

SUMMARY

Relationships between same-sex partners are regulated by myriad laws and policies ranging from marriages in Massachusetts, Connecticut, Iowa, Vermont, Maine, and New Hampshire; civil unions in New Jersey; and domestic partner arrangements in numerous states, including California, Oregon, Hawaii, Nevada, and New York. With the exception of DOMA, restrictions on same-sex couples vary by state, leading to an assortment of rights and prohibitions governing the intimate lives of same-sex partners. Marriage equality litigation has been confined largely to the state courts, with litigants arguing most frequently over interpretations of state constitutional law principles.

This chapter and the previous one discussed the hotly litigated areas of law reflecting society's battles over legal recognition of gay relationships, with the status of the law constantly changing as states imposed new restrictions on same-sex relationships and litigation over such restrictions became more common. As gay rights advocates pursued a litigation strategy to achieve marriage equality, the courts became key players in the same-sex marriage debate; the outcome of these cases most often depended on the court's willingness to adopt a countermajoritarian stance by subjecting laws to higher levels of scrutiny. As in other areas of rights-based litigation, gay rights advocates were more successful when judges believed that they had the authority to interpret constitutional guarantees of due process and equal protection to override policies made in other branches of government or through the popular will. When judges believed that they lacked such authority and viewed their roles predominantly as subordinate policymakers, marriage equality claims were less successful.

The first phase of same-sex marriage policymaking (from 1996 to approximately 2005) was characterized primarily by the successful efforts of the states and the federal government to bar same-sex couples from legally marrying. Despite the ephemeral triumph in Hawaii and the more lasting victories in Vermont and Massachusetts during these years, the gay rights movement clearly lost ground in the struggle to secure marriage equality.

It is difficult to pinpoint the exact date when same-sex marriage policymaking entered into a new phase, but beginning around 2005, marriage equality advocates began to accomplish some of their goals in the courts and state legislatures. Moreover, although it is too early to determine whether same-sex relationships will ever achieve legal status throughout the nation, after 2005, public opinion became more accepting of gay couples, especially among the younger generation.

NOTES

1. An opponent of same-sex marriage, Romney asked the supreme court to stay its ruling in *Goodridge* to provide an opportunity for the legislature to vote on the constitutional amendment. The state attorney general, Democrat Thomas Reilly, did not permit him to approach the court with this request, saying that it can come only from the attorney general; Reilly refused to seek the court's intervention (for discussion of the interactions among Massachusetts state officials in the same-sex marriage debate, see Miller 2006).

2. Mass. G.L. c.207 §§11 and 12 was first enacted by St. 1913, c.360 as part of the Uniform Marriage Evasion Act (*Cote-Whitacre* 2006b).

3. The state supreme court dismissed the motion for leave to appeal in *Martinez* (2008b).

4. On February 21, 2007, Attorney General Patrick Lynch issued a nonbinding opinion that Rhode Island would recognize same-sex marriages performed in Massachusetts. Responding to a request from a state higher education agency about whether to treat employees who were wed in Massachusetts as married, Lynch said, "This is about Rhode Island citizens who entered into a valid, legally recognized same-sex marriage and returned here to live and work. There is no way, no law, no constitutional provision and, in my estimation, no right to allow the denial of basic human rights" (*New York Times* February 22, 2007). Despite Lynch's stance, gay marriage supporters believe that there is little likelihood that the state will enact a marriage equality law during Republican Governor Donald Carcieri's tenure in office; his term ends in 2011 (*Providence Journal Bulletin* May 9, 2009; May 14, 2009; *Boston Globe* May 11, 2009).

Rhode Island had banned discrimination on the basis of sexual orientation in employment, housing, public accommodations, and credit in 1995 (*New York Times* May 20, 1995).

5. N.H. Rev. Stat. Ann. §457-A:6 provides, "Notwithstanding any other law to the contrary, the parties who enter into a civil union pursuant to this chapter shall be entitled to all the rights and subject to all the obligations and responsibilities provided for in state law that apply to parties who are joined together pursuant to RSA §457 [the law relating to marriage]." Section 457-A:8 provides, "A civil union or a marriage between a man and another man or a woman and another woman legally contracted outside of New Hampshire shall be recognized as a civil union in this state."

6. In contrast to the civil union laws in the other states, the New Hampshire law is vague and provides no enforcement mechanism or penalties for noncompliance. See Levchuk (2008) for analysis of the effect of state and federal law, including DOMA and the Family and Medical Leave Act, on persons united in New Hampshire civil unions.

7. New Jersey marriage laws were first enacted in 1912.

8. Article I, paragraph 1, of the New Jersey Constitution provides, "All persons are by nature free and independent, and have certain natural and unalienable rights, among which are those of enjoying and defending life and liberty, of acquiring, possessing, and protecting property, and of pursuing and obtaining safety and happiness." The New Jersey Supreme Court has interpreted this passage to encompass a right to equal protection and due process (Stauss 2004, 318).

9. At the time that New Jersey enacted the DPA, there were three other states providing benefits to same-sex couples: Hawaii, California, and Vermont. Ironically, in light of its initial position on same-sex marriage, Hawaii's is the least expansive, with Vermont and California offering benefits closely resembling marriage. Although it included many of the traditional rights of marriage, in excluding parental and property rights, the New Jersey law was not as far reaching as the latter two (Stauss 2004, 306–7).

10. The New Jersey DPA (N.J.S.A. §26:8A-2) was passed by the New Jersey assembly on December 15, 2003, in a vote of 41 to 29, with nine abstentions, and by the state senate on January 8, 2004, in a vote of 23 to 9. It was signed into law

on January 12, 2004, by Democratic Governor James E. McGreevey and became effective on July 10, 2004 (see Stauss 2004). Section 8A-2(d) provides, "All persons in domestic partnerships should be entitled to certain rights and benefits that are accorded to married couples under the laws of New Jersey, including: statutory protection through the 'Law Against Discrimination' . . . against various forms of discrimination based on domestic partnership status . . . ; visitation rights for a hospitalized domestic partner and the right to make medical or legal decisions for an incapacitated partner; and an additional exemption from the personal income tax and the transfer inheritance tax on the same basis as a spouse." Opposite-sex couples are permitted to register as domestic partners after they turn sixty-two (Nelson 2008).

11. Unlike the U.S. Supreme Court, which assigns levels of scrutiny to classifications in determining constitutional violations, the New Jersey Supreme Court applies a three-part test.

12. N.J.S.A. §37:1-28(d) provides, "Those rights and benefits afforded to same-sex couples under the 'Domestic Partnership Act' should be expanded by the legal recognition of civil unions between same-sex couples in order to provide these couples with all the rights and benefits that married heterosexual couples enjoy."

13. The judge never addressed these claims because she concluded that the plaintiffs had not suffered harm.

14. Conn. Gen. Stat. § 46b-38nn provides, "Parties to a civil union shall have all the same benefits, protections and responsibilities under law, whether derived from the general statutes, administrative regulations or court rules, policy, common law or any other source of civil law, as are granted to spouses in a marriage, which is defined as the union of one man and one woman."

15. In 2000, Connecticut began offering domestic partner benefits to state employees.

16. Pittman's position was reminiscent of the U.S. Supreme Court's ruling in *Plessy v. Ferguson* (1896, 551), in which it rejected the plaintiff's contention "that the enforced separation of the two races stamps the colored race with a badge of inferiority. If this be so," said the Court, "it is not by reason of anything found in the act, but solely because the colored race chooses to put that construction upon it."

17. One justice recused herself.

18. Article first, §20, of the Connecticut Constitution provides, "No person shall be denied the equal protection of the law nor be subjected to segregation or discrimination in the exercise or enjoyment of his or her civil or political rights because of religion, race, color, ancestry, national origin, sex or physical or mental disability." The term "sex" was added in 1974.

19. Justice David Borden's dissent argued that the majority got it wrong, that gays were not politically powerless.

20. In *Mississippi University for Women v. Hogan* (1982), the U.S. Supreme Court inserted the "extremely persuasive justification" language into the heightened scrutiny test; see also *United States v. Virginia* (1996).

21. In March 2009, the Connecticut legislature considered a bill to transform civil unions into marriages (*Associated Press State & Local Wire* March 7, 2009).

22. Two days earlier, on February 10, 2004, Newsom had directed the county clerk to change the marriage license forms in order to issue them to couples regardless of their gender or sexual orientation.

23. By March 5, 2004, more than 4,000 licenses were issued, and more than 4,000 marriages were performed (*Lockyer* 2004b, 465).

24. Ironically, Newsom had been considered the conservative candidate in the San Francisco mayoral election in which he defeated his opposition in a nonpartisan runoff election. At the time, he was best known for his position of being tough on the homeless (*New York Times* February 19, 2004).

25. The superior court judges, James Warren and Ronald Quidachay, ruled in cases brought, respectively, by the Proposition 22 Legal Defense and Education Fund (*Proposition 22*) and the Campaign for California Families and the Alliance Defense Fund (*Campaign for California Families*). After the judges denied the stays, the state attorney general and several taxpayers filed two separate petitions, seeking writs of mandamus, with the state supreme court.

26. On March 11, 2004, in addition to ordering the city to cease issuing marriage licenses, the supreme court issued a "show cause" order in the original writ proceedings and stayed the actions in the two cases.

27. Following the court's prompting, the city and twenty same-sex couples from Los Angeles and San Francisco filed suit to challenge the state law in *City and County of San Francisco, Tyler v. State of California* (2004), and *Woo v. Lockyer* (2004).

28. Plaintiffs' ages ranged from thirty to eighty, with varying occupations and diversity in race and ethnicity; most had been together for more than a decade, and many were raising children (*In re Marriage Cases* 2008, 403–4).

29. The six cases were: *Clinton; City and County of San Francisco; Tyler; Woo; Proposition 22; Campaign for California Families.*

30. Cal. Civ. Code §300(a) provides, "Marriage is a personal relation arising out of a civil contract between a man and a woman"; §308.5 provides, "Only marriage between a man and a woman is valid or recognized in California." Section 300 was enacted in 1992, replacing §4100, which did not contain any reference to a man and a woman prior to 1977. Then, in 1977, §4100 was amended to include the sex-specific language. Section 308.5 was added on March 8, 2000, as a result of the voter-approved initiative, Proposition 22. See *Knight v. Superior Court* (2005) and *Armijo v. Miles* (2005) for judicial interpretations of Proposition 22.

Two other provisions of the California marriage code specify gender: §301 provides, "An unmarried male of the age of 18 years or older, and an unmarried female of the age of 18 years or older, and not otherwise disqualified, are capable of consenting to and consummating marriage"; §302(a) provides, "An unmarried male or female under the age of 18 years is capable of consenting to and consummating marriage upon obtaining a court order granting permission to the underage person or persons to marry."

31. In *Sail'er Inn, Inc. v. Kirby* (1971), the California Supreme Court declared that gender-based classifications are subject to strict scrutiny.

32. On appeal, the case was known as *In re Marriage Cases.*

33. The California First District Court of Appeal heard arguments in the case in July 2006.

34. An earlier Leno bill had failed to pass the assembly.

35. This case consolidated the several lawsuits revolving around the same-sex marriage issue. Same-sex marriage opponents had filed petitions in court seeking writs to prohibit Newsom from issuing marriage licenses to lesbian and gay couples. The state attorney general also filed an original writ petition with the state high court. The court ordered city officials to enforce the state law restricting marriage to a man and a woman but did not rule on its constitutionality. Meanwhile, the city and several groups of same-sex couples sought a declaratory judgment that the state marriage law was unconstitutional, and the court coordinated these actions with the opponents' actions into a single proceeding (*In re Marriage Cases* 2006a, 675).

36. The court initially determined that the two groups, Campaign for California Families and Proposition 22 Legal Defense and Education Fund, lacked standing to pursue their claims for a declaratory judgment. But since it was required to weigh any reasonable justification offered by the state, it noted that it would take their arguments into consideration anyway.

37. Article I, §1, provides, "All people are by nature free and independent and have inalienable rights. Among these are enjoying and defending life and liberty, acquiring, possessing, and protecting property, and pursuing and obtaining safety, happiness, and privacy"; §2 (a) provides, "Every person may freely speak, write and publish his or her sentiments on all subjects, being responsible for the abuse of this right. A law may not restrain or abridge liberty of speech or press"; §7(a) provides, "A person may not be deprived of life, liberty, or property without due process of law or denied equal protection of the laws."

38. The court also rejected the arguments on the basis of privacy and freedom of association.

39. The state was represented by a lawyer in the office of the attorney general, but Schwarzenegger sent his own lawyer because of a disagreement over the issue with Brown (*New York Times* March 5, 2008).

40. Warning that gay couples would marry in California and return home to challenge state restrictions on marriage in their home states, ten Republican attorneys general joined in asking the court to stay its decision (*New York Times* May 31, 2008).

41. An initiative measure requires the signatures of 8 percent of those who voted in the last gubernatorial election. Same-sex marriage opponents submitted more than 1 million (1,120,801) signatures to place the initiative on the ballot, far exceeding the 694,354 signatures needed (California Secretary of State News Release June 2, 2008).

42. With 100 percent of precincts reporting, CNN reported that the vote was 7,001,084 to 6,401,482 (CNN.com January 12, 2009).

43. Prop 8 opponents believe that Mormons contributed over 50 percent of the $40 million spent to support the initiative (*Washington Post* May 29, 2009).

44. Although it is difficult to predict the outcome of a case from the oral arguments, it appeared to some observers that the court did not wish to overturn the vote on Prop 8. George and Kennard, who were in the original majority that upheld the constitutional right of same-sex couples to marry, seemed skeptical that the court should assert itself into the policymaking process at this point—after the

people had spoken. Kennard, however, took pains to point out that she did not believe that the 18,000 marriages that had taken place before Prop 8 was passed were now illegal (*New York Times* March 6, 2009).

45. Article I, section 6, of the Iowa Constitution provides, "All laws of a general nature shall have a uniform operation; the general assembly shall not grant to any citizen or class of citizens, privileges or immunities, which, upon the same terms shall not equally belong to all citizens."

46. Ironically, although the outcome was different, in determining the proper level of scrutiny to use, the Iowa Supreme Court applied the principles articulated in U.S. Supreme Court rulings.

47. Because the law did not pass under intermediate scrutiny analysis, it was unnecessary to apply strict scrutiny.

48. Before the deadline for Congress to act had ended, a group of D.C. residents tried (and failed) to persuade a superior court to order the D.C. Board of Elections to conduct a referendum on the measure. Their suit was in response to the board's ruling that a vote on the matter would violate a D.C. law that bars votes on issues covered by the 1977 Human Rights Act, in this case, discrimination on the basis of sexual orientation (*Washington Post* June 18, 2009). At 12:01 A.M. on Tuesday, July 7, 2009, with no action by Congress, the District of Columbia began to recognize same-sex marriages legally performed in other jurisdictions (*Washington Post* July 7, 2009).

49. Over the next several weeks in June 2009, the focus on same-sex marriage was lost, as the parties battled for control of the senate. In the week before the session was scheduled to end, two Democrats joined the Republican Party; one returned in short order, leaving a tie between the parties. There was an impasse for more than a month until the Democrats finally regained their slim majority in early July. The senate worked on legislation that had languished during this time, but the same-sex marriage bill was not considered. Although he had vowed to bring it to the body for a vote, on July 11, 2009, Paterson announced that the chamber was too "unsettled" to vote on the matter and he was delaying the vote until sometime in September (*New York Times* June 25, 2009; July 11, 2009).

4

The School Setting

Because children spend most of their waking hours in a school setting, it is vitally important that school policies are cognizant of and
sensitive to the needs of America's gay youth. Studies indicate that 5 to 6
percent of U.S. high school and middle school students are lesbian, gay,
bisexual, and transgender (LGBT);[1] extrapolating from recent census data,
Human Rights Watch estimates that there are approximately 2 million
gay, lesbian, and bisexual children.[2] Moreover, as the American Academy
of Pediatrics reports, adolescents are becoming aware of their sexual
orientation at an earlier age (Frankowski 2004).[3] In their book on gay children and their families, Fairchild and Hayward (1998, ch. 2) describe the
pain and turmoil many children experience in learning about and deciding whether, when, and to whom to reveal their sexual orientation (see
Newman and Muzzonigro 2001; Oswald 2001). Infanti's (2007) firsthand
account confirms the difficulties of life as a gay youth; remaining in the
"closet" for safety, he internalized his classmates' and society's attacks on
gays, "coming out" only after entering law school.

As increasing numbers of children make their sexual orientations and
gender identities known (or at least are more open about them), there is a
corresponding increase in the number of legal issues school districts must
grapple with, issues that they were able to ignore not too long ago. Beginning in the late 1990s, school districts learned that it can be quite costly
to ignore complaints from students who claim they are being harassed
because they are gay—or because their classmates think they are (see
American Civil Liberties Union 2007; Gay, Lesbian and Straight Education Network 2005).[4] Moreover, in addition to claims against the district

and its school board members, students may also sue school officials individually for failing to protect them from harassment, subjecting them to potential liability for damages if the courts deny them immunity (see Bedell 2003).

Although such suits revolved primarily around issues related to harassment and bullying, there are also controversies over dress codes, curriculum, and student organizations arising from both gay and anti-gay activists. To avoid litigation, school officials must accommodate myriad conflicting demands from students, parents, teachers, community members, and state lawmakers. Their attempts to maintain peace among the disputing parties is complicated by the glare of media attention on them. And because both sides invoke legal arguments, the courts must resolve the disputes, having to balance competing First and Fourteenth Amendment rights as well as the dictates of federal and state law. And in adjudicating these claims, the courts must decide the degree to which they must adopt a subordinate policymaking role by strictly adhering to the rules of statutory construction and judicial restraint. As in the parenting policy cases, their inclination in this regard often determines the outcome of the case.[5]

HARASSMENT IN SCHOOL

Sexual harassment in schools is a common experience for many children, according to surveys commissioned by the American Association of University Women (AAUW). In a 1993 survey—the first systematic study of sexual harassment—researchers asked 1,632 public school students in grades 8 through 11 in seventy-nine junior and senior high schools nationwide whether they had ever experienced sexual harassment. An overwhelming number of them—85 percent of the girls and 76 percent of the boys—said they had.

When replicated in 2001, the results were strikingly similar. This survey of 2,064 public school children in grades 8 through 11 found that 83 percent of girls and 79 percent of boys reported experiencing harassment. The study showed that the practice begins in elementary school and that teachers often witness the harassing behavior (American Association of University Women 2001). Although most students reported incidents of verbal harassment, more than half claimed that they were physically harassed by their schoolmates. Ironically, most students in the survey indicated they were aware of their school's policy against sexual harassment.

The findings of the AAUW study are confirmed in more recent national surveys conducted for the Gay, Lesbian and Straight Education Network (GLSEN) in 2005 and 2007 (see Harris Interactive and Gay, Lesbian, and

Straight Education Network 2005; Kosciw and Diaz 2006; Kosciw, Diaz, and Greytak 2008; see also Human Rights Watch 2001). The results of these surveys, which include both LGBT and non-LGBT students, indicate that harassment in school is a frequent occurrence, explained by a number of different factors. A majority of teenagers report being subjected to verbal and physical harassment as well as assault on the basis of gender, sexual orientation, gender expression, race, ethnicity, disability, and religion.

ANTI-GAY HARASSMENT IN SCHOOLS

"It's always open season on gay kids" (Sedgwick 1993, 69). In 2007, six students threw a can of Lysol at a fifteen-year-old gay student on his way home from school (Gay, Lesbian and Straight Education Network 2007a). More recently, in 2008, another fifteen-year-old student who had recently disclosed that he was gay was fatally shot in the head at an Oxnard, California, junior high school (*Los Angeles Times* February 17, 2008). In preparing a defense, the defendant's lawyer charged the school with failing to defuse the tension created by the victim's open display of his sexuality (*Los Angeles Times* May 8, 2008).[6]

Thus, although many children are victimized by harassment to varying degrees, gay children are often special targets. As Pearson, Muller, and Wilkinson (2006) note, adolescents with nonheterosexual feelings are often confronted with "a system of social norms that silences them and labels them as different" (524). In internalizing these negative reactions, young people attracted to members of their sex, especially boys, are more likely to withdraw from classroom activity, suffer emotional stress, and underperform in school. Moreover, LGBT youth often engage in risky behavior and are more likely to abuse drugs, alcohol, and tobacco at an earlier age than non-LGBT youth (see Frankowski 2004).

Given the problems of obtaining accurate information, it is difficult to determine the extent to which gay teens are subject to harassment on the basis of their sexual orientation. This difficulty is enhanced because heterosexual youths are harassed on the basis of perceived sexual orientation, and slurs relating to sexual orientation or gender identity are now part of the derogatory vernacular of teenage life.

Lovell (1998, 623) describes an indirect method of determining the extent to which sexual orientation harassment exists in junior high and high schools. Her method consists of evaluating studies of students to determine the percentage of gay youth in these grade levels and then ascertaining the percentage of those who report being harassed. On the basis of this analysis, she concludes "that a substantial percentage of queer youth are harassed in regard to their sexual orientation. This fact,

combined with the finding that numerous youths are lesbian, gay, or bisexual, suggests that student-to-student sexual orientation harassment is
a frequent occurrence in American schools" (see Bedell 2003; Eisemann
2000; Mayes 2001).

A more direct method of investigating harassment is demonstrated
in the biennial National School Climate Surveys, the latest conducted
by GLSEN in 2007 (Kosciw et al. 2008; see Harris Interactive and Gay,
Lesbian, and Straight Education Network 2005; Kosciw and Diaz 2006).[7]
To ensure a representative national sample of LGBT youth, respondents
were surveyed in two ways. First, fifty community-based groups were
randomly selected from a list of more than 300 groups nationwide, and
their members were asked to answer the survey on paper. Second, notices
were posted on LGBT-youth oriented listservs and websites and were
emailed to GLSEN chapters and youth advocacy organizations. Adver-
tisements were posted on MySpace to reach youth between thirteen and
eighteen years of age who identified themselves in their user profiles as
gay, lesbian, or bisexual. The sample consisted of a total of 6,209 LGBT
students between ages thirteen and twenty-one from the fifty states and
the District of Columbia. About two-thirds of the sample (64.4 percent)
was white, over half (57.7 percent) was female, and over half identified
as gay or lesbian (53.6 percent). Students were in grades 6 to 12, with the
greatest number in tenth and eleventh grades.

The survey examined a large number of indicators of a negative school
climate, including whether students experienced incidences of harassment and assault in school; whether they felt unsafe because of personal
characteristics, including sexual orientation; and whether they reported
experiences of victimization to school officials and the consequences of
such reports. The results showed that 90 percent of the students heard
biased language at school, most often homophobic comments; nearly
75 percent heard such comments often or frequently. The survey also
showed that nearly 61 percent of students in the survey reported feeling
unsafe at school because of their sexual orientation. These feelings reflected the fact that almost 90 percent of students reported being verbally
harassed at school because of their sexual orientation; almost 45 percent
were physically harassed, and, even more alarming, almost 25 percent
reported physical assaults because of their sexual orientation. Most students who were harassed or assaulted did not report it to school authorities, not trusting that action would be taken. Indeed, almost 33 percent of
the students who filed reports said that nothing was done in response.
Not surprisingly, LGBT students reported missing school at least one day
in the past month because they felt unsafe.

Ironically, to make matters worse, as gays have become more open
about their sexual orientation, words such as "gay" and "fag" have be-

come part of the parlance of children, even at the elementary school level, synonymous with "stupid or unusual or strange" (*Washington Post* June 19, 2001).

LEGAL RECOURSE FOR HARASSMENT

The equal protection clause of the Fourteenth Amendment prohibits public schools from treating students differently on the basis of sex.[8] The major hurdle for litigants in seeking legal recourse for anti-gay harassment was the difficulty of convincing the courts of the similarities between harassment based on sexual orientation (uncharted territory) and harassment based on sex. Some courts recognized the similarities between the two types of discrimination and applied the Fourteenth Amendment to anti-gay conduct in public schools.

Nabozny v. Podlesny (1996) illustrates a Fourteenth Amendment claim against a school board for harassment.[9] The plaintiff, Jamie Nabozny, charged that the school violated his federal constitutional rights of equal protection and due process as well as his right to be free from discrimination under Wisconsin law. Moreover, he asserted, despite his complaints to school officials, he had been subjected to verbal and physical harassment by his classmates throughout his middle school and high school years.[10]

The federal district court judge, John Shabaz, granted the school's motion for summary judgment without addressing his claim of discrimination on the basis of sexual orientation; he simply held that Nabozny did not show the defendants discriminated against him because of his sex. He also denied his due process claims, ruling that he had failed to provide the necessary evidence to substantiate his charges that he was deprived of due process.

On appeal, speaking for a unanimous three-judge panel of the Seventh Circuit, Judge Jesse Eschbach graphically described the years of abuse that began with Nabozny's discovery that he was gay when he entered middle school in seventh grade.[11] His fellow students reacted badly to his decision to "come out," calling him names, hitting him, spitting on him, and tormenting him in a variety of ways. When he first complained to his school guidance counselor, she successfully shielded him from the abuse for a period of time until she was replaced by another counselor. When Nabozny reported the continuing abuse to her replacement, he forwarded the complaint to the principal without taking any action on his own.

After a meeting in which Nabozny revealed he was gay, the principal promised to protect him from the bullies. It was soon apparent this was an empty promise as the harassment grew more severe, including a "mock rape" in a science class by two students with almost two dozen others observing and ridiculing him. When he managed to break loose and run to the principal's office, she exclaimed, "Boys will be boys" and told him "that if he was 'going to be so openly gay,' he should 'expect' such behavior from his fellow students" (451). He fled her office and was later reprimanded for leaving school without permission. No disciplinary action was taken against the other students involved.

The harassment persisted for four years, throughout his middle and high school years (from seventh grade through most of eleventh grade). Despite his parents' constant efforts to seek help from school officials, they either ignored the attacks on him or responded with meaningless gestures: transferring him to a special education class, notwithstanding the fact that his chief tormentors were in the class, and allowing him to attempt to evade the abuse by changing his seat on the school bus. Various school authorities indicated that they believed that he deserved his treatment and essentially left him to fend for himself despite the physical abuse to which he was subjected and three suicide attempts. He had charged that school officials ignored his pleas for help, and, indeed, there were some indications, according to the court, that some of them even "mocked Nabozny's predicament" (449).

After leaving the school and moving away, he filed a civil rights action against the school district and a number of officials, including the principals of both schools.

Eschbach noted that Wisconsin students were protected from discrimination on the basis of sex and sexual orientation: in 1988, the school district adopted a policy to protect students against physical assault as well as verbal harassment.[12] To prevail under equal protection principles, Nabozny had to show that the school intentionally discriminated against him, that is, treated him differently from other students by failing to protect him because of his sex and sexual orientation.[13] The school district argued that it vigorously punished all violators of its antiharassment policy, including those who tormented Nabozny. It contended that school officials had been responsive to his complaints and punished the guilty students when possible.

The appeals court disagreed, finding that the school authorities did not adhere to the policy when Nabozny complained of harassment and that their failure to do so was evidence of discriminatory intent on the basis of sex.[14] Citing the principal's "boys will be boys" comment, the court believed that this reaction would have been unthinkable had a female student complained of being victimized by a "mock rape."

Persuaded that he was a victim of discrimination, the appellate court next considered whether the suit must be dismissed because the district was entitled to immunity from liability because its officials acted in good faith. Citing *Owen v. City of Independence* (1980), in which the U.S. Supreme

Court held that municipalities are not entitled to immunity in Section 1983 suits, Eschbach rejected the district's argument.[15]

The next step was to determine if the school officials were entitled to qualified, that is, good faith, immunity. Borrowing from *Harlow v. Fitzgerald* (1982), in which the high court held that "government officials performing discretionary functions generally are shielded from liability from civil damages insofar as their conduct does not violate clearly established statutory or constitutional rights of which a reasonable person would have known," the *Nabozny* court applied an objective test (*Nabozny* 1996, 455, quoting *Harlow*, 818). Thus, it held, the key to determining immunity was whether the law against sex discrimination had been "clearly established" in 1988, when the harassment began. Applying intermediate scrutiny, the court concluded that, absent an important governmental interest, school officials were required to treat harassment complaints from male and female students alike and that the law had been clear on this before Nabozny started middle school in 1988.

Although the district court had failed to specify why it dismissed Nabozny's complaint of discrimination on the basis of sexual orientation, the appeals court easily found that school officials had discriminated against him on these grounds. The court credited Nabozny's evidence that they had ignored or minimized his complaints and that some had even appeared amused at his plight, apparently believing that he merited abuse because he was gay.

In deciding whether to grant the officials immunity, the court had to determine whether they knew (or should have known) that they acted illegally under the law at that time—before 1988. Applying minimal scrutiny, the court emphasized that "the Constitution prohibits intentional invidious discrimination between otherwise similarly situated persons based on one's membership in a definable minority, absent at least a rational basis for the discrimination" (457). Gays are clearly such a minority group, said the court, and had been in 1988. Moreover, there was a state law against discrimination on the basis of sexual orientation, providing ample evidence that gays were a recognized minority group in need of protection. The judge stressed that there was no rational basis to justify the discrimination against Nabozny, that is, the school's failure to respond to the attacks on him because of his sexual orientation.

The court gave short shrift to the district's argument that there was no clear understanding of the state of the law before 1988. It concluded that although the law on sexual orientation discrimination was not as clearcut as the law on sex discrimination, school authorities could reasonably know that discriminating against Nabozny on the basis of his sexual orientation was unconstitutional—at least as far back as 1988.

The circuit court, however, rejected Nabozny's due process arguments, holding that he had not presented sufficient evidence that the school officials' inaction had increased the likelihood that he would be harmed.[16] When it remanded the case to the district court to rule on his discrimination claims, a jury found in Nabozny's favor. The case was ultimately settled, with Nabozny receiving $962,000 in damages and medical expenses (Broz 1998, 757 n52; Gay, Lesbian and Straight Education Network 2005).

Nabozny was a landmark ruling, for it represented the first case in which a federal appellate court held a school district and its employees accountable for harassment of a gay student (Broz 1998, 752; So 2002, 366).

Nabozny also demonstrated that school officials may escape liability if they can successfully argue that they were unaware that their actions or inactions violated students' known constitutional rights. The principle of immunity played an important role in a complaint brought by six former students who were or were believed to be gay, lesbian, or bisexual. They filed suit in federal court against the Morgan Hill, California, school district, charging that from 1991 to 1998, school officials refused to respond to their complaints of anti-gay harassment by their peers. They claimed that the school authorities—principals and assistant principals in the district's middle and high schools—as well as school board members violated their rights by failing to halt and punish the discrimination and verbal and physical harassment to which they were subjected.[17]

The defendants argued that they were entitled to qualified immunity because it had not been clearly established at the time that their actions infringed on the students' constitutional rights. Quoting *Nabozny*, the district court reaffirmed the unconstitutionality of discriminating on the basis of "one's membership in a definable minority, absent at least a rational basis for the discrimination," adding that "there can be little doubt that homosexuals are an identifiable minority" (*Flores v. Morgan Hill Unified* 2000, at 2–3, quoting *Nabozny* 1996, 457). The lower court denied the defendants' motion for summary judgment on the grounds of qualified immunity, holding that "it must be determined whether under the clearly established law, a reasonable school district administrator in Defendants' position could have believed his or her conduct was lawful" (*Flores v. Morgan Hill Unified* 2000, at 3).

When the defendants appealed to the Ninth Circuit, it remanded the case to the lower court to reconsider and apply the newly established test of *Saucier v. Katz* (2001), in which the Supreme Court held that in assessing a defendant's claim of qualified immunity, the court must first inquire whether there are sufficient facts that the defendant committed a constitutional violation. On remand, the district court held that the plaintiffs produced evidence that school officials treated them differently on the basis of their sexual orientation. Judge James Ware found that a jury could find that the defendants failed to take action to protect them despite their awareness of the harassment and that their failure was motivated by the students' perceived or actual sexual orientation.[18] Also citing the defendants' failure to establish antiharassment policies, the court concluded that the facts could lead to an inference that they were deliberately indifferent to their equal protection rights.

In assessing whether the right was "clearly established," the court pointed out that the right at issue was not "the students' right to protection from peer sexual orientation harassment" but "the more general right against sexual orientation discrimination"; this right, said the court, had been "clearly established by the Ninth Circuit since at least 1990—one year prior to the date the alleged violations commenced" (*Flores v. Morgan Hill Unified School District* 2001, at 11). The court concluded that "a reasonable administrator would have been on notice during the period 1991–1998 that intentional discrimination against or deliberate indifference towards students on the basis of their actual or perceived sexual orientation was unlawful if lacking a rational basis" (at 12). Applying the *Saucier* test, the district court again denied the defendants' motion for summary judgment.

The Ninth Circuit affirmed (*Flores v. Morgan Hill Unified School District* 2003). Speaking for a unanimous three-judge panel, Judge Mary Schroeder rejected the district's argument that there was no evidence of intentional discrimination. She believed that the plaintiffs would be able to demonstrate that district officials were guilty of either intentional discrimination or deliberate indifference. In her view, a jury could infer that each of the defendant officials was deliberately indifferent to the students' rights by failing to enforce their harassment policies.

She also dismissed the defendants' argument that no specific Supreme Court or Ninth Circuit ruling had established the right to be protected against peer sexual orientation harassment. Citing its holding in *High Tech Gays v. Defense Industry Security Clearance Office* (1990), which held that the equal protection clause applies to sexual orientation, the court ruled that the administrators had "fair warning that they could not accord homosexual and bisexual students less protection on account of such students' sexual orientation" (*Flores v. Morgan Hill Unified School District* 2003, 1137). The court was also not persuaded by the school officials' argument that their responses, albeit ineffective, negated a finding of deliberate indifference because it believed a jury could infer that the defendants "took no more than the minimal amount of action in response to the complaints of harassment" (1138).[19]

TITLE IX LITIGATION

Title IX of the Education Amendments of 1972 prohibits sex discrimination in educational institutions receiving federal aid; as written, the law specifies that the penalty for noncompliance is termination of federal funding.[20] Title IX was the brainchild of House Democrat Edith Green of Oregon and Senator Birch Bayh, Democrat from Indiana. Green, as chair of the Special Education Subcommittee, included provisions barring sex discrimination in a higher education bill; hearings were held during June and July 1970, but the bill never cleared the subcommittee. In 1971, similar bills were introduced in the House, and a committee-approved bill was sent to the full House and approved late in 1971. During that summer, when the Senate was considering a higher education bill without a sex discrimination provision, Bayh unsuccessfully introduced an amendment to prohibit sex discrimination in higher education. The House-approved bill, which included the sex discrimination provisions, was sent to the Senate Committee, and the version that passed out of committee, similar to the earlier Senate version, did not contain a sex discrimination provision.

In 1972, Bayh's amendment was approved by the Senate in part because he had exempted separate admissions policies in private undergraduate colleges. During conference, the conferees were forced to conciliate 250 differences between the two versions of the bill, eleven of which concerned sex discrimination. Because conference debate was centered primarily on court-ordered busing, little attention was paid to the sex discrimination provisions, which were approved with minimal discussion. The conference version passed both houses, and the bill was signed by President Richard Nixon on June 23, 1972 (see Fishel and Pottker 1977).

Title IX bans discrimination on the basis of sex in admission to all vocational, professional, and graduate schools and most public undergraduate schools. It allows a single-sex admissions policy in most elementary and secondary schools, private undergraduate schools, and public undergraduate institutions "that traditionally and continually" from their inception admitted only students of one sex. The law also excluded two classes of institutions from the reach of Title IX: schools with a "primary purpose" of training students for the military services or merchant marine and religious schools "to the extent that the provisions of Title IX would be inconsistent with the basic religious tenets of the school." Two years later, Congress amended Title IX to exempt single-sex groups such as sororities and fraternities, YMCA and YWCAs, and the Boy Scouts, Girl Scouts, and Campfire Girls. In 1976, further amendments shielded father–son and mother–daughter activities from Title IX's ban on sex discrimination as well as scholarships awarded to beauty contest winners.[21]

Over time, the U.S. Supreme Court has expanded its interpretation of the law to include sexual harassment as a form of sex discrimination, applying the ban on harassment to students as well as teachers and setting standards for Title IX liability. The state of the law is unclear, however, when the harassment is based on sexual orientation. Despite the similarities, the courts are often unwilling to equate claims of harassment on the basis of sexual orientation to claims of harassment based on sex.

ANTI-GAY HARASSMENT LAWS

On July 23, 2007, Representative Linda Sanchez, Democrat from California, with sixty-three cosponsors, introduced the Safe School Improvement Act (HR 3132) as an amendment to the Safe and Drug-Free Schools and Communities Act (Title IV of the No Child Left Behind Act). The bill had two major purposes: to require schools to prevent and respond to incidences of bullying and harassment and to collect and report data on this behavior. Although it is unclear where the line between harassment and bullying should be drawn, it seems that certain children become targets for a variety of reasons or no reason at all (see *New York Times* March 24, 2008). Because school authorities have a great deal of discretion in reacting to such incidents, lawsuits often arise because victims and their parents believe that the responses are insufficient, especially if the behavior continues unabated.

The proposed law would have required schools to disseminate this information as part of their annual reports on disciplinary violations and to adopt a mechanism for student and parents' complaints (Gay, Lesbian and Straight Education Network 2007d). It defined harassment as "conduct that is based on a student's actual or perceived race, color, national origin, sex, disability, sexual orientation, gender identity, religion, or any other distinguishing characteristics that may be defined by a State or local educational agency." It specified that illegal harassment "deprives students of access to educational opportunities or benefits provided by the school; and . . . adversely affects the ability of a student to participate in or benefit from the school's educational programs or activities because the conduct as reasonably perceived by the student is so severe, pervasive, and objectively offensive conduct." The bill was referred to the Healthy Families and Communities Subcommittee of the House Education and Labor Committee in September 2007, but no further action was taken on it.[22]

More than half the states have laws or policies against harassment and discrimination on the basis of sexual orientation in schools.[23] Although modeled on Title IX, most explicitly prohibit harassment and intimidation on the basis of sexual orientation, and some include gender identity as well. In her survey of state laws, Feiock (2002) expresses concern that Title IX and the equal protection clause are ineffective in protecting children from harassment; in her view, state laws may be more effective.

Some laws, such as the California Student Safety and Violence Prevention Act of 2000, prohibit discrimination in educational institutions receiving state financial aid on the basis of a number of protected categories, including sexual orientation and gender identity.[24] Others, such as the Connecticut law against discrimination in public schools, guarantee all students the right to participate equally in school activities.[25] More recently, Iowa adopted a law broadly prohibiting bullying and harassment.[26]

In addition to the substantive differences in these laws, there are also a variety of enforcement mechanisms. Maryland schools are statutorily required to report incidents of harassment or intimidation on the basis of sexual orientation and gender identity, among other things, to the state department of education, which in turn is required to report to the legislature annually.[27] A number of other states, including New Jersey, Vermont, and Washington, have similar laws.[28]

In *L.W. v. Toms River Regional Schools Board of Education* (2007), the New Jersey Supreme Court decided that a school district may be liable for verbal and physical harassment on the basis of a student's perceived sexual orientation under the New Jersey antidiscrimination law.[29]

L.W.'s torment started in fourth grade and continued into middle school and high school; it began with name-calling and escalated into physical attacks. The state supreme court held that "because of the Act's plain language, its broad remedial goal, and the prevalent nature of peer sexual harassment, . . . the LAD permits a cause of action against a school district for student-on-student harassment based on an individual's perceived sexual orientation if the school district's failure to reasonably address that harassment has the effect of denying to that student any of a school's 'accommodations, advantages, facilities or privileges'" (547).

Unlike the U.S. Supreme Court, the New Jersey high court applied the more generous standard used in sexual harassment cases in the workplace to the educational setting rather than the narrower Title IX standard of deliberate indifference. Speaking for a unanimous court, Justice James Zazzali cited three factors that differentiate LAD from Title IX: first, unlike Title IX, LAD does not only apply to sex; second, LAD is not restricted to state-funded institutions but applies to all places of public accommodation; and, third, under LAD, plaintiffs are not required to prove an official's deliberate indifference but merely to show that the official knew (or should have known) of the harassment and failed to take reasonable actions to stop it. The court ordered the district to pay L.W. $50,000 and pay a $10,000 fine.

Although cases such as *Toms River* demonstrate the soundness of filing a state law claim for sexual harassment, most sexual harassment lawsuits are filed under Title IX (So 2002, 351).

Plaintiffs, however, have had to overcome a number of hurdles before the courts accepted these lawsuits.[30] Although many statutes explicitly authorize individual suits, others, such as Title IX, merely proscribe a type of conduct and leave enforcement to the federal government, typically by termination of federal aid. Arguing that terminating federal aid to the offending institution is ineffective, victims of discrimination turned to the courts, asking them to imply a private right of action under Title IX.[31] Most lower courts dismissed their cases, holding that the law does not permit private remedies.[32]

In *Cannon v. University of Chicago* (1979), the Supreme Court reversed a Seventh Circuit ruling, agreeing that although termination prevents the government from subsidizing discriminatory conduct, litigation is a more effective remedy for the victim of discrimination.

Cannon left open the question of whether successful plaintiffs were entitled to money damages or limited to injunctive relief.[33] In *Lieberman v. University of Chicago* (1981), the Seventh Circuit declined to expand the scope of Title IX to permit compensatory and punitive damages (see Pearlman 1982; Peterson 1983). Characterizing Title IX as a package of aid to higher education, the court ruled that Congress had not intended to subject the educational institution to suits for money damages. It granted that *Cannon* had enlarged the class of litigants but held that it had not expanded the recipient's financial liability. And because Title IX did not specify a damage remedy, the institution had no notice that it might be liable for financial losses in accepting federal aid.

The circuit court relied on *Pennhurst State School and Hospital v. Halderman* (1981) in which the Supreme Court held that by receiving federal aid, the state had entered into a contract with the federal government, agreeing to accept conditions in return for the funds. But Congress may not insert a financial obligation into an aid statute without adequate warning because a contract must clearly specify the terms of the agreement.

Judge Luther Swygert dissented in *Lieberman*, questioning the majority's logic in requiring Congress to specify money damages in a statute that had not expressly authorized a right to sue. He warned that barring a damage remedy will diminish the effectiveness of the law because well-qualified applicants, such as Lieberman, who are admitted to other schools will have no incentive to sue for discrimination, allowing the institution to escape liability.[34]

The ability to collect money damages in a lawsuit is an important factor in assessing the viability of litigation as a means of enforcement. In 1992,

the Supreme Court resolved the issue of the availability of money damages under Title IX.

The case arose when Christine Franklin, a Georgia high school student,
claimed that a teacher verbally and physically harassed her for more than
two years, including forcing her to have sexual intercourse with him three
times on school grounds.[35] According to Franklin, school officials knew
of the harassment but took no action to stop it and even discouraged her
from filing charges against him. Eventually, the school compelled his
resignation, agreeing to his condition that the matter be dropped and the
case considered closed.

Franklin's complaint to the federal government was dismissed because
the teacher had resigned and the school had instituted a grievance procedure. Her lawsuit was also dismissed because the court was unwilling to
allow money damages in a statute that did not explicitly authorize them.
In *Franklin v. Gwinnett County Public Schools* (1992), a unanimous decision announced by Justice Byron White, the Supreme Court noted that
the question of damages was "analytically distinct" from the question of
whether an implied right of action existed but cited a long-held presumption that federal courts have the authority to order appropriate relief,
absent a contrary indication from Congress.

Echoing Swygert's dissent in *Lieberman*, White said that it was not surprising to find that Congress had not indicated an intent to allow money
damages in Title IX since it had not explicitly authorized suit in the statute. In determining whether Congress intended to alter the presumption
of the availability of damage remedies, the Supreme Court cited two
laws enacted after *Cannon* was decided. First, the Civil Rights Remedies
Equalization Act of 1986 expanded the right to sue under Title IX, and
although it did not specify a right to damages, the Court was satisfied
that Congress had not intended to limit their availability.[36] Second, there
was no indication that the 1988 Civil Rights Restoration Act, which had
broadened the coverage of federal antidiscrimination statutes (including
Title IX), had intended to limit damage remedies under Title IX.

The most important part of the opinion addressed the propriety of
damage remedies in statutes enacted under Congress's spending clause
authority.[37] The school district, supported by the federal government,
cited *Pennhurst* and argued that damages should not be awarded in Title
IX suits because recipients had not been alerted to the possibility that
they would be liable for damages when accepting federal funding. But
although the Supreme Court agreed that they should not be held accountable for acts of unintentional discrimination because they lacked
notice of their liability, it believed that there was no bar against claims
of intentional discrimination. Title IX, White pointed out, put federally
funded school districts on notice that they must not discriminate on the

basis of sex. Because there is no other compensation available for victims of intentional sex discrimination, such as Christine Franklin, who have already graduated, White concluded that they were entitled to money damages. He reiterated the long-standing principle that federal courts are authorized to award appropriate relief in actions brought to enforce federally protected rights (see Wright 1992).

Franklin did not specify the standards for determining liability or the type of damages allowed, and by the late 1990s, the courts had still not settled the matter. The Office of Civil Rights (OCR) issued guidelines in March 1997 stating that Title IX encompasses claims by school employees, students, and even third parties and that schools must take the necessary actions to respond to complaints of harassment. The guidelines indicated that the conduct must be sufficiently severe and pervasive and adversely affect the student's educational experience or create a hostile environment (for a survey of lower court cases on the OCR Guidelines, see Collins 1998).

A year later, the Supreme Court resolved the debate over liability in *Gebser v. Lago Vista Independent School District* (1998), which arose over a fifteen-year-old's suit against a school for sexual harassment, seeking compensatory and punitive damages. She had not reported the sexual relationship with her teacher, with school authorities learning about it only when the two were discovered engaging in sex.

The teacher was subsequently arrested and fired, but the defendant, a Texas public high school, argued that it bore no liability because it had no direct knowledge of the harassment. Although there had been other complaints about this teacher, when he denied responsibility, the matter had been dropped. The school had no formal antiharassment policy or student grievance procedure.

Speaking for a Court that voted 5 to 4, Justice Sandra Day O'Connor narrowly framed the issue as one of how Congress would have handled the question of a Title IX defendant's liability had it expressly included a right to sue in Title IX. Because Title IX required the government to notify a school of a violation and give it an opportunity to comply with the law, the Court inferred that Congress did not intend to impose damage liability on a school that was unaware of its employees' actions.

O'Connor reasoned that Congress would not have wanted schools to be strictly liable for their employees' illegal acts. Citing *Pennhurst*, the Court reiterated the principle that recipients of federal funding must have notice of potential financial liability, so schools should be accountable only for conduct of which they are aware. O'Connor concluded that a school is liable for damages when it displays "deliberate indifference," that is, when the appropriate school official, that is, the official with responsibility to correct the behavior, knows of it and deliberately fails to act. By using this standard, the Court adopted an actual knowledge standard, rejecting the negligence standard in which the school would be liable if it knew or should have known of the harassment (see Underwood 1999).[38]

The courts were also asked to determine whether schools were liable for peer harassment, that is, when students create a hostile environment for other students. School personnel, who are typically inundated with complaints about varying degrees of inappropriate sexual behavior, often dismissed such incidents as childish teasing or name-calling, sexual banter, or harmless flirting; they contended that schools cannot be held legally responsible for the behavior of their students. There was a split among the circuits on the issue. In *Doe v. University of Illinois* (1998), the Seventh Circuit held that school districts could be held liable for peer harassment. But in *Rowinsky v. Bryan Independent School District* (1996), the Fifth Circuit dismissed the Title IX claim for peer harassment because the suit did not allege that the district itself was guilty of discrimination and there was no evidence that the school differentiated between harassment complaints brought by men and women.[39]

In *Franklin*, the Supreme Court had recognized that Title IX encompasses hostile environment harassment; in *Davis v. Monroe* (1999), it addressed the question of the school's liability for peer harassment. According to the complaint by the fifth grader at a Georgia elementary school, she was physically and verbally harassed for five months by the boy who sat next to her in class; he grabbed her breasts, rubbed against her, and made lewd comments. Although she and her mother complained to school officials numerous times, they were unresponsive. It was three months before a teacher finally allowed her to change her seat in the classroom. The district had no sexual harassment policy, nor had it trained school personnel in responding to complaints.

The child's grades began to suffer, and she threatened suicide. Eventually, the Davis family filed criminal charges against the boy, and he pleaded guilty to sexual battery in juvenile court. Their lawsuit against the school claimed that the harassment created a hostile, intimidating, and offensive environment and argued that the case was controlled by *Gebser* because, as in *Gebser*, a responsible school official knew of the behavior and was "deliberately indifferent" to it. They sought compensatory and punitive damages as well as injunctive relief, ordering the school to create a sexual harassment policy.

The lower courts dismissed her claim, ruling that schools are not liable for peer harassment. During oral argument before the Supreme Court, the justices expressed concern about the difficulty of distinguishing between ordinary teasing and the kind of harassment that was alleged here and the possible consequences if suits for student-on-student harassment were permitted. "Little boys tease little girls through their years in school," O'Connor commented during oral argument, asking "Is every incident going to lead to a lawsuit?" (*New York Times* January 13, 1999).

In her opinion for the Court that voted 5 to 4, O'Connor asked whether deliberate indifference to student harassment constitutes intentional discrimination under Title IX. The school board argued that the statute encompasses only actual grant recipients, not third parties such as students, over whom the recipients exercise little control. The Court appeared most troubled about the conditions under which a federally funded school district would be liable for damages, expressing concern that they have sufficient notice of their liability for the behavior of third parties when accepting the federal funds. But although it acknowledged the school's concern as legitimate, the Court nevertheless concluded that it could be liable under certain circumstances.

O'Connor cited federal law as well as state common law in addition to a publication released by the National School Board Association indicating that schools are aware that they are responsible for the acts of third parties, such as students, who are under their control. And when school authorities are aware of and deliberately indifferent to a student harassing another in the classroom, the school may be held liable under Title IX.

Spelling out the precise nature of the school's liability, O'Connor stated that "funding recipients are properly held liable in damages only where they are deliberately indifferent to sexual harassment, of which they have actual knowledge, that is so severe, pervasive, and objectively offensive that it can be said to deprive the victims of access to the educational opportunities or benefits provided by the school" (650). Responding to the dissent's charges that the ruling would require schools to "purge" all instances of peer harassment, she stressed that under Title IX, "the recipient must merely respond to known peer harassment in a manner that is not clearly unreasonable" (648–9).[40]

Acknowledging that children's behavior is often manifested in gender-specific name-calling and teasing, the majority reiterated that it was not subjecting schools to liability for every antisocial act that occurs there, including mere name-calling and teasing. Despite the restricted nature of the holding, the dissent by Justice Anthony Kennedy expressed concern about the implications of the majority's opinion, warning of federal control over the day-to-day disciplinary decisions in the nation's schools. Kennedy feared that the ruling would turn Title IX into a "Federal Student Civility Code" (684). Moreover, he questioned the Court's characterization of the child's inappropriate behavior as sex discrimination because, in his view, it was not necessarily sexual harassment, much less sex discrimination. Predicting that there would be a flood of litigation in the wake of the ruling, he cited the AAUW survey on the frequency of sexual harassment incidents in schools and warned that "the number of potential lawsuits against our schools is staggering" (680). Additionally, he cautioned, overzealous administrators whose main concern was to insulate themselves from liability would overreact to innocent acts, even extending to first and second graders who do not understand the consequences of their behavior.

"We can live with this standard," said the general counsel for the National School Board Association. "I think it will be the rare occasion when a school board is found liable in the future" (Savage 1999, 34). A number of school administrators echoed these views. "The days of boys will be boys and girls will be girls are long gone," another said. "The school needs to address all elements of the school environment . . . [and] there won't be liability if you are proactive and out there teaching kids about appropriate behavior" (*New York Times* May 25, 1999).

Many scholars believe that *Gebser* and *Davis* raised the bar too high for students; among other things, the Court placed the burden on them to come forward with complaints despite the absence of a school sexual harassment policy or a procedure for filing complaints (see Davies 2002; Safier 2000). McCarthy (2001) notes that most cases of peer harassment since *Davis* have failed and argues that the Court should have imposed a negligence standard in which an institution is liable if its officials knew or should have known of the harassment. However, others, such as Sponseller (2001), believe that the Court properly balanced the child's right under Title IX and the school's concern with liability.

Gebser and *Davis* provided little guidance to lower court judges on the appropriate standard for assessing "deliberate indifference."[41] Not surprisingly, there was variation in their interpretation of the degree to which schools should be held liable when plaintiffs charge that they took insufficient measures in responding to their sexual harassment complaints.

Vance v. Spencer County Public School District (2000) illustrates one of the paths the courts have taken. Alma McGowen complained of verbal and physical abuse to school officials, including the principal. Although her classmates called her "gay," it does not appear that she was harassed on the basis of her sexual orientation. Whatever the motivation, she and her mother reported numerous incidents—in which she was inappropriately touched, hit with books, stabbed with scissors, had her clothes pulled, and asked for sexual favors in public. Although the authorities spoke to various students involved, no real punishment followed despite her Title IX complaint. After being diagnosed with depression, she left school and later filed suit.

Kentucky District Court Judge Thomas Russell denied the district's motion for summary judgment and submitted the matter to the jury, which awarded her $220,000; the district appealed.[42] Speaking for a divided Sixth Circuit panel on appeal, Judge Damon Keith agreed that she had met her burden under Title IX by presenting evidence of severe and perversive harassment that deprived her of educational opportunity and providing notice to school officials. The "pivotal issue" he said was whether the school responded to the harassment "in a manner that is not clearly unreasonable" (260, quoting *Davis* 1999, 648–9). Agreeing that this gave school authorities wide latitude to avoid Title IX liability by responding to complaints in a variety of ways, he rejected the board's view that it is not liable as long as it "does something," including "merely investigating" without taking further action (*Vance* 2000, 260). Moreover, Keith held that the district acted unreasonably by continuing to use measures it knew were inadequate to stop the abuse. Despite the increasing severity of the incidents, the school's response of merely remonstrating with the students was unreasonable and displayed "deliberate indifference," he said.

Similarly, in *Murrell v. School District No. 1* (1999), the Tenth Circuit ruled against a school district that attempted to cover up a reported rape as well as failed to investigate the assault, discipline the offender, or inform law enforcement authorities. On the other hand, in *Soper v. Hoben* (1999) and *Kinman v. Omaha Public School District* (1999), the Sixth and Eighth Circuits held that the school districts acted properly by investigating the charges, informing the proper authorities, isolating the perpetrators, and providing additional security for the victim.

ANTI-GAY PEER HARASSMENT

Although *Davis* opened the door to Title IX suits for peer sexual harassment, it was not certain that the courts would extend the law to suits claiming peer harassment on the basis of sexual orientation (see Walker 1999).[43]

On January 19, 2001, the Department of Education Office of Civil Rights issued a document titled "Revised Sexual Harassment Guidance: Harassment of Students by School Employees, Other Students, or Third Parties Title IX" to address the issue of harassment based on sexual orientation for the first time. Its primary purpose was to advise public school systems of their responsibilities to students and the circumstances under which they would be liable in private suits for money damages. The document was issued in response to the Supreme Court's opinions in *Gebser* and *Davis*, replacing an earlier document titled "Sexual Harassment Guidance: Harassment of Students by School Employees, Other Students, or Third Parties," issued by the Office for Civil Rights on March 13, 1997. As the 1997 version had done, the 2001 guidance noted that it was intended to remind schools of their responsibilities to respond to sexual harassment complaints by students as a condition of federal funding. Under the 2001 guidance, schools are liable for harassment by teachers or other school employees regardless of notice, a position the Supreme Court has not adopted.[44]

The 2001 guidance differentiates between harassment of a "sexual nature" and "gender-based harassment." However, in response to public comments, the department noted that the document attempted to "clarif[y] that gender-based harassment, including that predicated on sex-stereotyping, is covered by Title IX if it is sufficiently serious to deny or limit a student's ability to participate in or benefit from the program." The guidance put schools on notice that they can be liable under the same standards (as in sexual harassment claims) if students are harassed because they fail to conform to stereotypical views of masculine and feminine behavior. This includes "conduct stemming from sexual desire as well as verbal or physical harassment 'based on sex or sex-stereotyping'" (U.S. Department of Education 2001).[45]

Although *Davis* appeared to pave the way for suits against schools for anti-gay harassment by their peers under Title IX, plaintiffs soon learned that the lower courts, analogizing Title IX to Title VII (of the 1964 Civil Rights Act), rejected their view that Title IX applies to suits for harassment based on sexual orientation. The issue appeared to be resolved when the Supreme Court decided in *Oncale v. Sundowner Services* (1998) that same-sex harassment was actionable under Title VII. The *Oncale* Court, however, did not equate same-sex harassment with anti-gay harassment, leaving open the question of the application of Title VII's prohibition against same-sex harassment to harassment based on sexual orientation (see Eisemann 2000). Nor, of course, did it address whether its interpretation of sexual harassment under Title VII in *Oncale* applies to Title IX.

Emphasizing that there is only a slight difference in the wording of the laws (Title VII bars discrimination in employment "because of sex," while Title IX forbids discrimination in educational institutions "on the basis of sex"), Mayes (2001, 651) argues that "when read in comparison, the two clauses are virtually identical [and] in fact any attempt to read 'because of' to include same-sex harassment while simultaneously reading 'on the basis of' to exclude same-sex harassment is both illogical and indefensible."[46] Nevertheless, a court that wishes to avoid treating discrimination based on sexual orientation the same as sex discrimination has merely to point to its obligation to adhere strictly to the text of the statute, in other words, to practice judicial restraint.

Ray v. Antioch Unified School District (2000) demonstrates the effect of *Oncale* on Title IX case law. Here, U.S. Magistrate Judge Maria-Elena James refused to accept the school district's argument that Title IX does not prohibit discrimination on the basis of sexual orientation. Applying the *Davis* standard, she held that the student had alleged sufficient facts to show that the harassment he was subjected to, based on a perception that he was gay, was "severe, pervasive, and objectively offensive" and that school authorities were deliberately indifferent to his repeated complaints.[47]

The ruling in *Montgomery v. Independent School District No. 709* (2000) was more nuanced, revealing the court's deliberations on the proper rules of statutory construction. Jesse Montgomery alleged that he was subjected to psychological and physical abuse from his classmates because of his perceived sexual orientation; the abuse continued for eleven years, beginning in kindergarten and persisting throughout junior high school and high school, and escalated over time. He filed suit under Title IX, the Fourteenth Amendment's due process and equal protection clauses, and the Minnesota Human Rights Act.[48] The school district moved to dismiss all but a portion of the state law claim.[49]

In ruling on his constitutional claim, Minnesota Federal Court Judge John Tunheim ruled that Montgomery had presented sufficient facts to show that he was treated differently because of his sexual orientation or perceived sexual orientation. However, he dismissed the Title IX claim, ruling that the law applied only to discrimination on the basis of sex and no other form of discrimination. Although he recognized that, since *Davis,* Title IX also applied to claims of peer sexual harassment, he was reluctant to expand the law to encompass same-sex harassment, in part, he said, because the harassment was based not on "sexual desire" but on hostility to his perceived homosexuality.[50]

Tunheim was, however, persuaded by Montgomery's argument that he was tormented not only because students thought that he was gay but also because they believed that he did not conform to their "stereotyped expectations of masculinity" (1090). Recognizing that this was an uncharted area of law, he took his cue from Title VII case law, observing that it offers a road map to interpreting Title IX. He noted that although *Oncale* had left open the question of whether the phrase "because of sex" in Title VII encompassed harassing behavior based on the plaintiff's failure to conform to expected stereotypical gender norms, a number of federal courts were interpreting Title VII more broadly to include harassment based on atypical gender behavior.

In the end, because there were unresolved factual disputes in the case—namely, whether the district officials were deliberately indifferent—Montgomery survived the district's motions for judgment on the pleadings and summary judgment.[51]

ANTI-GAY POLICIES

A number of school districts created programs, such as the Massachusetts Safe Schools Initiative, to curtail negative images of gay children and foster more inclusive attitudes toward gays. These included favorable (or at least neutral) references about gays in curricular and cocurricular programs and sponsorship of Gay Straight Alliances (GSAs).[52] In California, the attempt to pass such a law failed when, in September 2006, Schwarzenegger vetoed a bill that would have barred schools from presenting negative references of LGBT people by including sexual orientation within the list of characteristics, such as ethnicity, nationality, and gender, that cannot be portrayed negatively in the curriculum. It had passed in a vote of 47 to 31 in the assembly and 22 to 16 in the senate. The bill, Senate Bill 1437, already weakened from an earlier version that would have required schools to specify the contributions of LGBT people, was watered down after the governor threatened to veto it (*San Francisco Chronicle* September 7, 2006; *Baptist Press* September 7, 2006).

When school districts attempted to counter anti-gay activity, however, they met with resistance from anti-gay groups that, in turn, lobbied state legislatures to pass laws and policies intended to thwart the districts' efforts. A number of states enacted laws aimed at preventing gay and lesbian students from organizing and meeting at school. Others adopted legislation requiring written consent from parents before their children can participate in sexuality classes or allowing parents to remove them from such classes; they also prevent teachers from presenting positive images of "alternative sexual lifestyles" and discussing homosexuality without reference to AIDS or other sexually transmitted diseases (Cahill and Cianciotto 2004; Grattan 1999).

More recently, in Hillsborough County, Florida, County Commissioner Ronda Storms (elected to the state senate in November 2006) succeeded in restricting library displays during Gay and Lesbian Pride Month. The county commission voted to "adopt a policy that Hillsborough County government abstain from acknowledging, promoting or participating in gay pride recognition and events, little g, little p" (*St. Petersburg Times* June 9, 2005; June 16, 2005; December 16, 2007).[53]

Parents also resorted to litigation to restrain schools from fostering a more inclusive environment in schools. In *Parker v. Hurley* (2008), the First Circuit ruled against the plaintiffs, two sets of parents with children in a Lexington, Massachusetts, elementary school. They had asked the school to notify them when exposing their children to a curriculum containing positive messages about gays and gay families and to be allowed to remove them from the classroom. The parents argued that exposure to this material offended their religious beliefs and burdened their rights of free exercise and privacy to raise their children as well as their children's free exercise rights. Although Massachusetts law requires that parents be notified and allowed to remove their children when the lessons pertain to sexuality, the school chose not to apply that law to their situation because there was no sexuality involved in the literature. The court dismissed their claim, ruling that they had not shown that their rights were substantially burdened by merely hearing about or reading the antidiscriminatory messages in the books.[54]

ANTI-GAY MESSAGES

In addition to such laws and policies, individual students displayed their own anti-gay sentiments by wearing messages on their shirts or jackets. In seeking to curb such messages in an effort to forestall a hostile environment for gay students, school districts became vulnerable to First Amendment challenges for repressing speech on the basis of content (see Mostoller 2003).[55]

The courts addressed the constitutionality of these restraints on expression by weighing the school's interests in protecting gay youth and preserving order against the challenger's freedom of speech. In such cases, the courts struggled with the clash of conflicting rights, seeking to find answers in the high court's somewhat baffling position on students' free speech rights. Adjudicating these cases placed the court in the unenviable position of upholding the First Amendment in the face of countervailing pressures to protect the minority. However, unlike most circumstances when the First Amendment serves as a shield against minority oppression, in these cases it was used as a sword to enhance majority rights. Two rulings in the Third and Ninth Circuits illustrate opposing views on the constitutionality of school board policies to restrict anti-gay speech.

David Saxe and his sons sued the boys' school, arguing that the district's antiharassment policy abridged their freedom of speech. Seeking an injunction, they claimed that the policy was vague and overbroad and unconstitutional on its face. Federal District Court Judge James McClure Jr. upheld the policy, noting that it mirrored state and federal laws against harassment, including Title IX and the Pennsylvania Human Relations Act (*Saxe v. State College Area School District* 1999).

On appeal, in an opinion delivered by future Supreme Court Justice Samuel Alito, the Third Circuit panel reviewed the district's antiharassment policy and existing sexual harassment case law in the employment and education arenas.

The Saxes had alleged that "they believe, and their religion teaches, that homosexuality is a sin [and] . . . that they have a right to speak out about the sinful nature and harmful effects of homosexuality" (*Saxe* 2001, 203). Rejecting the school board's argument that antiharassment laws were protected by the First Amendment, Alito remarked on the existing tension between the two rights. Unlike federal law, however, that prohibited harassment based on race, sex, color, national origin, age, and disability, this policy included "other personal characteristics," such as appearance, clothing, and values. Emphasizing that the essence of the First Amendment requires freedom of discourse about values, the appeals court held that the policy's reach was too broad, striking at the heart of protected speech.

Alito noted that *Davis* had proscribed harassment that "has a systematic effect on educational programs and activities" (*Saxe*, 210, quoting *Davis* 1999, 633). The challenged policy was impermissible because it broadly punished speakers regardless of the effect of the harassment, thus bringing "simple acts of teasing and name-calling" within its purview (*Saxe*, 211).

Concluding that the district's policy exceeded the boundaries of federal antiharassment law, Alito assessed the extent to which the First Amendment permitted speech regulation in schools, beginning with the Court's landmark ruling in *Tinker v. Des Moines Independent Community School District* (1969).[56] He found that although the high court had narrowed students' right to speech in subsequent cases, it never retreated from its holding in *Tinker* that the school may proscribe only speech that significantly interferes with or disturbs school activities. In seeking to rid the education environment of offensive speech, the district policy exceeded the limits of *Tinker* and included protected speech within its prohibitions, thereby making the policy unconstitutionally overbroad as the Saxes had alleged.

Two years later, a Michigan federal court judge thoughtfully explained that freedom of expression requires schools to tolerate all manner of views. In *Hansen v. Ann Arbor Public Schools* (2003), Judge Gerald Rosen held that Pioneer High School in Ann Arbor, Michigan, violated the First Amendment by preventing a student member of "Pioneers for Christ" from expressing her views against homosexuality during the school's celebration of diversity in Diversity Week. Rosen held that the school engaged in unconstitutional viewpoint discrimination by not allowing opposing views on homosexuality to be heard. He pointed out that if schools were permitted to suppress critical views of homosexuality, nothing would preclude "school administrators in other districts . . . from holding a school forum on homosexuality and religion and refusing to permit a more gay-friendly message to be presented. . . . The point, of course," he concluded, "is that, no matter how well-intentioned the stated objective, once schools get into the business of actively promoting one political or religious viewpoint over another, there is no end to the mischief that can be done in the name of good intentions" (803).

The issue of anti-gay speech also arose in a California high school when a student, Tyler Chase Harper, challenged the school policy preventing him from wearing a shirt condemning homosexuality on the school's Day of Silence.[57] Harper's shirt had the phrase I WILL NOT ACCEPT WHAT GOD HAS CONDEMNED on the front and HOMOSEXUALITY IS SHAMEFUL ROMANS

1:27 on the back (*Harper v. Poway Unified School District* 2004, 1100). Because of the furor caused by the first Day of Silence in 2003, when Harper wore his shirt on the second Day of Silence, his teacher had asked him to remove it, saying that it violated the school's dress code and bordered on harassment. After lengthy discussions, the principal upheld the teacher, and Harper spent the remainder of the day in the office but was not disciplined in any other way.

A few weeks later, Harper filed a lawsuit against the district and sought a preliminary injunction, claiming that the school violated his freedom of expression and free exercise of religion as well as the establishment of religion and other federal rights. Federal District Court Judge John Houston denied the injunction and granted the district officials qualified immunity on Harper's damage claim.[58]

Speaking for a divided Ninth Circuit panel, Reinhardt agreed that Harper was not entitled to injunctive relief. Putting aside the issue of the dress code and the antiharassment policy, the court assessed the constitutionality of restrictions on speech under the *Tinker* standard. Reinhardt reiterated that schools may limit only nonobscene speech that would "impinge upon the rights of other students" or lead to "substantial disruption of or material interference with school activities" (*Harper* 2006, 1177, quoting *Tinker* 1969, 509, 514).[59]

Although the lower court had viewed the case within the framework of the "substantial disruption" doctrine, the appellate court cited another segment of the *Tinker* test: the so-called rights-of-students prong.[60] Stressing the vulnerability of gay high school students as an often-despised minority, the court had no difficulty in concluding that Harper's message was intimidating and painful to gay students—with a negative impact on their ability to learn—and that the school acted properly in refusing to allow him to wear it in school.[61]

Another case illustrating the problems schools encounter when trying to censor anti-gay expression occurred in Boyd County, Kentucky. The case arose from a lawsuit by the GSA against the school board for refusing to allow it to organize on campus, violating the First Amendment and the federal Equal Access Act (EAA). The court granted the group a preliminary injunction, ordering the school to treat the group on equal terms with other noncurricular organizations (*Boyd Country High School Gay/Straight Alliance v. Board of Education* 2003).

A few years later, Boyd High School again found itself in district court, this time as a defendant in a suit brought by a student, Timothy Morrison II. As a result of a consent decree with the GSA, the school was ordered to adopt written antiharassment policies and to require middle and high school students to attend diversity training. Concerned that these policies would inhibit their children's ability to oppose homosexuality, a group of parents sued the district on First and Fourteenth amendment grounds. After numerous discussions between the parents and the board, the policy was subsequently revised in August 2005 to allow students greater freedom to express themselves.

After noting that the parties' agreement that *Tinker* governed the constitutionality of the restrictions on student speech, Kentucky District Court Judge David Bunning declared his unwillingness to rule on an inoperative policy and granted the board's motion for summary judgment (*Morrison v. Board of Education* 2006).

Morrison, "a Christian . . . [who] believes that homosexuality is a sin," appealed, seeking nominal damages for the period of time (the 2004–2005 academic year) when the original antiharassment policy was in place; he claimed that his First Amendment rights were violated because the policy "chilled" his speech by preventing him from making negative comments on another student's sexual orientation (*Morrison* 2007, 497). Speaking for the Sixth Circuit panel, Judge Karen Nelson Moore reversed the district court, holding that the lower court inappropriately granted summary judgment because there were factual issues to resolve, namely, that the policy had a chilling effect on his constitutionally protected speech.

A year later in *Morrison* (2008), the same panel affirmed the district court; this time, however, the opinion was announced by Judge Deborah Cook, with Moore dissenting. The divided panel held that Morrison had not demonstrated that he was harmed by the policy because it was merely speculative that he would have been punished had he spoken out against homosexuality. The court pointed to the district's statement that its harassment policy "shall not be interpreted as applying to speech otherwise protected under the state or federal constitutions where the speech does not otherwise materially or substantially disrupt the educational process" (610). It ruled that Morrison therefore lacked standing to bring his claim.[62]

In 2007, Illinois District Court Judge William Hart attempted to balance the school's interest in protecting gay students from disturbing messages against its obligation to allow student speech under *Tinker*. The case began in March 2007 when two Naperville high school students sought a preliminary injunction against the school district for preventing them from wearing shirts with the slogan "Be Happy, Not Gay" (*Zamecnik v. Indian Prairie School District # 204 Board of Education* 2007a).[63] They argued that the school acted unconstitutionally in preventing them from expressing opposition to homosexuality and the annual Day of Silence. The students referred to themselves as "evangelical Christian[s]," proclaiming their belief that homosexuality "is immoral and contrary to biblical teachings" (at 3).[64]

The high school, built in 1997, with a diverse student body of more than 4,000 students, had a history of disturbances stemming from insulting messages, with gay students often the targets. Sensitive to the issue, school officials argued that they did not object to the plaintiffs' views on homosexuality but refused to allow them to display the message on shirts, buttons, or stickers because it denigrated gay students; they would, they said, permit a positive message, such as "Be Happy, Be Straight."

Hart began by acknowledging a conflict among the circuits, citing *Nixon v. Northern Local School District Board of Education* (2005), an Ohio federal court ruling that required the school to allow an eighth grader to wear a shirt saying "'Homosexuality is a sin! Islam is a lie! Abortion is murder!'" (*Zamecnik* 2007a, at 6). The *Nixon* court had held that the rights-of-others prong of the *Tinker* test merely meant that students had a right "to be secure and to be let alone" (*Zamecnik* 2007a, at 7, quoting *Nixon* 2005, 974, quoting *Tinker* 1969, 508) and found that gay students' rights were not affected by messages on clothing.

Hart found *Harper* more persuasive and more reflective of the Seventh Circuit's position on students' right of speech, rejecting *Nixon's* narrow view that *Tinker* protected only students' right to be left alone. Hart interpreted *Tinker* more broadly, as had the *Harper* court, finding that students also had the right to be protected from psychological attacks based on their minority group status. Although the Seventh Circuit had not directly ruled on this issue, Hart believed that it would approve of a high school in which shielding students from the disparaging speech contained in the plaintiffs' message was "a legitimate pedagogical concern" (*Zamecnik* 2007a, at 10).[65] On April 17, 2007, the day before the planned Day of Silence was to take place, Hart denied the motion for a preliminary injunction.[66]

On appeal, the Seventh Circuit proved Hart's prediction wrong. Writing for the three-judge panel, Judge Richard Posner's opinion seemed to raise as many questions as it resolved. Addressing himself first to the rule, he noted that although schools may not place a total ban on student speech, "the contribution kids can make to the marketplace in ideas and opinions is modest and a school's countervailing interest in protecting its students from offensive speech by their classmates is undeniable" (*Nuxoll* 2008, 671). However, after also acknowledging the harm caused by anti-gay comments, he believed that the school's interest in protecting them from exposure to such remarks did not outweigh the student's right to free expression. He would be more persuaded, he said, by the school's claim that the speech must be suppressed in the interests of order and discipline. Distinguishing *Tinker*, he characterized the Des Moines school district's regulation as unconstitutional viewpoint discrimination; in contrast, the Indian Prairie rule against derogatory comments was fair and "evenhanded," applying to numerous demographic identities.[67] Posner interpreted *Tinker* more narrowly, saying that he would grant a school wide latitude in restricting student speech, including for reasons such as "a decline in students' test scores, an upsurge in truancy, or other symptoms of a sick school" (*Nuxoll* 2008, 674).

Turning his attention to the shirt, Posner explained that its message is "a play on words" and that there might even be ambiguity about whether it is derogatory. Nevertheless, he acknowledged its negative connotations, especially for gay students, even agreeing that it was meant to be negative. Yet, in the end, he found it "only tepidly negative," adding that "'derogatory' or 'demeaning' seems too strong a characterization" (676).

The appeals court reversed the district court's ruling and directed it to order the school to allow students to wear T-shirts with the phrase "Be Happy, Not Gay" on the April 28, 2008, Day of Silence.

GSAs ON HIGH SCHOOL CAMPUSES

School districts were also faced with lawsuits from gay students who sought to organize and hold meetings and events on school property. Such challenges typically arose from gay rights student clubs, usually part of the GSA network. Ironically, in seeking access to school property for meetings and events, the gay student groups cited the EAA, enacted in 1984 to require schools to allow religious groups to meet in school if they allowed nonreligious groups to do so.[68] During debate over passage of the EAA, senators on both sides of the aisle indicated their understanding that the law would likely extend to student groups that advocated gay rights (Orman 2006; see Cahill and Cianciotto 2004).

In pursuing their right to organize, gay students contended that school officials violated their rights under the EAA as well as, in some cases, the First Amendment by denying them access to campus facilities. For the most part, the courts agreed that the schools must allow them to meet on campus.[69]

East High Gay/Straight Alliance v. Board of Education (1999), the first case to apply the EAA to gay high school students, addressed permissible restrictions on student groups under the EAA and the First Amendment.[70] In 1995, the East High GSA first sought the right to meet on campus as a noncurricular club, citing its right to do so under the EAA and the First Amendment. In response, the board took the extraordinary step of banning all extracurricular clubs.

In ruling on cross motions for summary judgment, Utah District Court Judge Bruce Jenkins succinctly stated the legal argument: "If, as defendants assert, the permissible subject matter is confined solely to 'curriculum-related' subjects within the meaning of the Equal Access Act, then they may exclude plaintiffs' explicitly non-curricular group from the limited forum under both the Act and the First Amendment." But, he continued, "if, as plaintiffs insist, the permissible subject matter embraces non-curricular subjects, and non-curricular student groups have been allowed access to the forum, then the exclusion of plaintiffs' non-curricular group from the forum may run afoul of both the Equal Access Act and the First Amendment" (1173). In the end, Jenkins denied the district's motion for summary judgment.

In response to the district's new policy of allowing a gay rights perspective in a curricular-related club, students formed the Prism Club (People Respecting Important Social Movements). After the school declined their application to meet on campus, the students again filed suit. In *East High School Prism Club v. Seidel* (2000), Federal District Judge Tena Campbell granted them a preliminary injunction because the school had deviated from its customary policy in judging the subject matter of curricular-related clubs (see Lambda Legal 2000).

Thus, five years after students at East High first petitioned to hold GSA meetings at school, the district settled the case after the Salt Lake City School Board voted to allow the gay students to meet on campus (Orman 2006, 234).

Caudillo v. Lubbock Independent School District (2004), resulting in a defeat for the GSA, represented a narrower interpretation of the EAA.

By allowing student groups to meet on campus, Lubbock High School created a limited open forum within the EAA and pledged to allow all student expression despite disagreement with the content of the speech. However, the school also followed an abstinence policy that proscribed all aspects of sex, including discussions of sexual activity by campus student groups.

In November 2002, gay students at Lubbock High School, calling themselves the Gay and Proud Youth Group (GAP Youth), sought permission to post fliers, access the public address system, and be recognized as a student group.[71] They petitioned the school's board of trustees and presented a letter describing their aims as educating and informing both heterosexuals and nonheterosexuals and attempting to better relationships between them.

School officials pointed to their abstinence-only policy and contended that they had a compelling interest in promoting the students' welfare by protecting them from the consequences of teen pregnancy, sexually transmitted diseases, and other harms arising from sexual activity. This interest, they claimed, was enhanced by the fact that Texas law prohibited same-sex partners from engaging in sex.[72] Additionally, they cited the group's website containing links to two websites (www.gay.com and www.youthresource.com) with sexually explicit material.

The students filed suit under the EAA and the First Amendment, claiming that school authorities based the decision against them on the content of their speech. In ruling on the summary judgment motion, Texas Federal Court Judge Sam Cummings observed that the issue was one of first impression in the circuit.[73] He easily distinguished the cases cited by the students, pointing out that those schools did not have an abstinence policy that prohibited all discussions of sexual matters on campus. And because of this ban, the school was not discriminating against the students' viewpoint.[74] The court also rejected the students' assertion that school officials singled out their website for examination, accepting as reasonable the school's explanation that it did so because the group's website address linked to indecent websites.

Cummings was also not persuaded by the students' argument that the school allowed groups with anti-gay views, such as the Fellowship of Christian Athletes, to meet on campus, ruling that there was no evidence that students in groups such as this ever discussed sexual matters of any kind at meetings. Thus, because the abstinence policy precluded all groups from discussing sex on campus, there was no favored or disfavored viewpoint and no First Amendment violation.

The judge acknowledged that because it established a "limited open forum," the school's public space was governed by the EAA; however, he relied on exceptions within the law that allowed schools to prohibit meetings that would "materially and substantially interfere" with school activities[75] and disrupt "order and discipline"[76] and "meetings that are otherwise unlawful."[77] Additionally, he accepted the school's contention that its compelling interest in protecting students extended to an affirmative duty to shield them from obscenities on the group's website.[78] Persuaded that all these exceptions were applicable, the court ruled that the school authorities had lawfully banned the GSA from the school premises.

Ironically, the district cited concern for the gay students' safety (there had been unsettling telephone calls) and argued that it had a duty under Title IX to protect them from harassment, which would make it liable for allowing them to meet. The court expressed sympathy with the district's position, agreeing that the school was "caught in a conundrum." If it permitted the GSA to meet, knowing that GSA members will be harassed, lawsuits will ensue from students as well as "outside groups." By preventing their meeting, the school subjects itself to suits such as this. Weighing these alternatives, the court found that the school opted for the more prudent measure, saying that "a school that chooses to prevent activities that invite harassment, safety problems, and lawsuits has chosen the wiser of the two possibilities" (569).

In the end, the court awarded the defendants summary judgment, applauding them for being steadfast in their efforts to protect the children in their care and for refusing to "surrender control of the public school system to students" (572).

STUDENT GROUPS ON UNIVERSITY CAMPUSES

The difficulties confronting GSAs on high school campuses were mirrored, to some extent, by gay rights groups at the college and university level. Because of the constraints imposed by the First Amendment and the limitations of the parens patriae argument, the courts generally supported the claims for recognition by gay rights groups at public universities.[79]

One of the first disputes over gay organizations on campus arose at Texas A&M University when the university denied recognition to a gay student club, Gay Student Services (GSS). Its members wishing to remain anonymous, the students had not even sought official university recognition but merely requested to be allowed to post notices and hold meetings on campus. The school refused to grant the students the limited permission they sought and denied recognition, citing the illegality of homosexual activity under Texas law and characterizing it as antithetical to the university's beliefs.

The federal district court had ruled in favor of the university, and a unanimous panel of the Fifth Circuit reversed, holding the district court's factual findings "clearly erroneous" (*Gay Student Services v. Texas A & M University* 1984).

The dispute was in part over whether the GSS was a political or social advocacy group or, as it claimed, a service-related group. At trial, a university witness testified that "in light of statistical evidence regarding homosexual behavior, 'it would be a shock really, if there were not homosexual acts engaged in at or immediately after' a meeting of a homosexual student organization" (1323).

Speaking for the Fifth Circuit panel, Judge John Brown cited *Healy v. James* (1972), a case involving recognition of Students for a Democratic Society at Central Connecticut State College in which the U.S. Supreme Court held that the First Amendment places a heavy burden on a university to justify its denial to recognize a student group. He noted that, as the Court had indicated in *Healy*, a mere fear of illegal activity is insufficient to justify infringing on the group's freedom of expression. Following *Healy*, Brown held that the university's purported justifications had not met this burden. He concluded by finding that the university had based its decision on the content of the group's message instead, an impermissible act under the principles of equal access articulated in *Widmar v. Vincent* (1981).[80]

In *Gay Students Organization of the University of New Hampshire v. Bonner* (1974), the First Circuit upheld a district court ruling against the university. The university had restricted the Gay Students Organization (GSO) from holding social functions after the university received unfavorable media attention following a GSO dance. The district court held, and the appeals court agreed, that the university had infringed on the GSO's associational rights even though the only interference was with the group's social activities. Delivering the opinion, Judge Frank Coffin went even further and found that the university had interfered with the group's right of expression as well. As in the other cases, the court rejected the university's assertion that its actions were justified to prevent illegal acts because there was no evidence that illegal acts were committed or even contemplated.

Shortly thereafter, in *Gay Alliance of Students v. Matthews* (1976), the Fourth Circuit reversed a lower court ruling in favor of Virginia Commonwealth University (VCU), which had refused to allow gay students to register as a student organization on the grounds that it "would tend to attract other homosexuals to the University and . . . [lead to] increased opportunities for homosexual contacts" (166–7). Judge Harrison Winter of the Fourth Circuit Court of Appeals ruled that the First Amendment protected the students' right to meet, even if the university's fear of incidences of homosexual contacts was borne out. Moreover, there was no evidence that the group intended to advocate illegal sexual activities, and by denying the GSA the right to register on the basis of the content of its message, VCU also infringed on the group's right to equal protection.

In *Gay Lib v. University of Missouri* (1977a), the Eighth Circuit reversed a lower court decision approving the university's denial of recognition to a student gay rights group. Citing medical evidence among its long list of particulars against homosexuality, the university had argued that recognizing the group would lead to increased incidences of acts of sodomy, a violation of Missouri law. Speaking for the divided panel of the appeals court, Judge Donald Lay found that the university had not met its burden of showing a "likelihood of imminent lawless action" to justify its use of prior restraint against the group (855).[81]

In addition, in *Gay and Lesbian Students Association v. Gohn* (1988), the Eighth Circuit reversed a district court ruling allowing the university to withhold funding from a gay rights group. Judge Richard Arnold held that the university was not obligated to fund all organizations at whatever amount they requested but that the First Amendment prohibited it from discriminating against groups on the basis of their message. Finally, in *Gay Lesbian Bisexual Alliance v. Sessions* (1996), Alabama District Court Judge Myron Thompson ruled that a law that "prohibited the payment of public university funds to any group that fostered or promoted a lifestyle or actions prohibited by the sodomy and sexual misconduct laws of the state" violated the First Amendment. He found the law unconstitutional because it committed viewpoint discrimination by withholding access to a university bank account from a University of South Alabama gay and lesbian student group.

These cases show that the gay rights groups in public universities and colleges largely succeeded in securing recognition because their claim was based on First Amendment rights. The courts were not as sympathetic to groups seeking recognition from private schools as the landmark ruling *Gay Rights Coalition of Georgetown University Law Center v. Georgetown University* (1987) illustrates. The case arose from a suit brought by two gay student groups against Georgetown University, a private Catholic school in Washington, D.C.

The groups began seeking university recognition and access to university services and facilities in 1978, citing the district's human rights ordinance, a version of Title IX that prohibited educational institutions from discriminating on the basis of sexual orientation. The university granted them the status of a student group, allowing them to organize and hold meetings on campus, but refused to confer "university recognition" on them, a classification that signifies that the university endorses the aims of the group. The students asked the university to reconsider, asking it to draw an explicit distinction between recognition and endorsement and thereby grant them the recognition they sought.

The lower court accepted the university's contention that the free exercise clause shielded it from endorsing student groups whose aims conflicted with the university's religious mission. The Court of Appeals of the District of Columbia, sitting en banc, avoided the constitutional issue and upheld the university's refusal to grant the student groups university recognition. Judge Julia Cooper Mack equated recognition with endorsement, holding that the law "does not require one private actor to 'endorse' the ideas and conduct of another" (17). She ruled, however, that the university must grant groups access to university facilities and services without regard to sexual orientation.[82]

SUMMARY

The litigation in the school setting was broadly divided into two types of claims: harassment and freedom of expression. With increasing instances of sexual and sexual orientation harassment in schools, children sought judicial intervention to compel school officials to take their complaints seriously and deal with the perpetrators effectively or risk hefty damages for failing to do so. The youngsters benefited from U.S. Supreme Court decisions that had expanded the school's liability for harassment by school employees as well as by their classmates. Ruling on the basis of constitutional law as well as state and federal statutes, the courts frequently agreed that the schools had not taken meaningful steps to end the harassment.

Another area of litigation stemmed from the efforts of anti–gay rights activists to express their disapproval of homosexuality. These anti-gay advocates challenged school district policies that attempted to portray positive images of gay culture and society; anti-gay children also sought to display messages disapproving of homosexuality, most frequently on their shirts and jackets. The litigation arose when schools attempted to intervene to shield gay youngsters from these anti-gay sentiments, fearful that they would harm them and also significantly interfere with order and discipline. Claiming the protection of the First Amendment, the anti-gay forces often succeeded in convincing the courts to rule in their favor. Although the judges were often sympathetic to the schools' attempts to protect a vulnerable minority, in the end, their adherence to First Amendment principles prevailed.

In a related category of freedom of expression claims, gay rights advocates contested high school and college policies that prevented gay student organizations from organizing and holding meetings on campus on an equal basis with other student groups. These cases were heard predominantly in the federal courts, and the plaintiffs prevailed in most of them by appealing to federal constitutional guarantees and the 1984 EAA, a Reagan administration law that was aimed at preventing discrimination on the basis of religion by allowing religious groups equal access to school facilities. As in the cases brought by anti-gay activists, the gay rights advocates in these cases benefited from the courts' commitment to principles of freedom of expression.

In adjudicating these disputes in the school setting, the courts were bound by well-established constitutional and statutory principles. Because they had less interpretive freedom in these cases, judges had little opportunity to choose between coordinate or subordinate policymaking roles.

NOTES

1. After surveying adolescents in grades 7 through 12, the National Longitudinal Study of Adolescent Health (known as "Add Health") estimated that 5 to 6 percent of American students are lesbian, gay, bisexual, or transgendered (see Lambda Legal 2002). The survey, the most comprehensive one at the time, was based on a representative sample of eighty high schools and fifty-two middle schools in the United States; it was conducted in two waves during 1994 and 1996 (Carolina Population Center 2003).

2. Basing its figures on the 1990 U.S. Census data of 45,249,989 children (between ages five and seventeen) in the United States, a Human Rights Watch (2001)

report titled *Hatred in the Hallways: Violence and Discrimination against Lesbian, Gay, Bisexual, and Transgender Students in U.S. Schools* claims that there are at least 2 million lesbian, gay, and bisexual youth. The report notes that there are no reliable data on the number of transgender people but cites the 1994 *Diagnostic and Statistical Manual of Mental Disorders* (4th ed.), which suggests that 1 per 30,000 adult males is male-to-female transsexual and that 1 per 100,000 adult females is female-to-male transsexual. See Frankowski (2004) for analysis of studies on sexual orientation and sexual conduct among teens.

3. The American Academy of Pediatrics warned that pediatricians must be prepared to address children's concerns and questions about their sexuality (see Frankowski 2004).

4. Cahill and Cianciotto (2004, 9) compiled the results of fifteen lawsuits by students against school districts and found that, from 1996 to 2002, known settlements or verdicts ranged from $40,000 to $962,000, not counting attorneys fees; for more recent information, see American Civil Liberties Union (2007) and Gay, Lesbian and Straight Education Network (2005a).

5. The courts are more constrained in First Amendment cases, as they are required to apply strict scrutiny to the challenged law or policy (regardless of which side is seeking the protection of the First Amendment). However, they have more flexibility in Fourteenth Amendment cases in applying heightened scrutiny to laws implicating sexual orientation.

6. In New York City, life became so problematic for gay youngsters that the city opened the Harvey Milk High School in July 2003. First operated as a private school in the 1980s, it was the nation's first public school to serve LGBT teens exclusively (Green 2004; Harris and Dyson 2004).

There is a debate over the wisdom and practicality of separate schooling for LGBT youngsters (see Harris and Dyson 2004). In 2008, a proposal to create the Social Justice High School-Pride Campus in Chicago was subject to criticism from conservatives who objected to providing public funding and public support for homosexuality as well as gay rights advocates who expressed concern about the potential damage from isolating gay students in a separate school (*Chicago Tribune* September 11, 2008). The proposal was eventually withdrawn.

7. A 2005 GLSEN survey was based on responses from 1,732 LGBT students between ages thirteen and twenty in secondary schools from fifty states and the District of Columbia (Harris Interactive and Gay, Lesbian, and Straight Education Network 2005; Kosciw and Diaz 2006). In the 2005 survey, 91 percent of teachers and 68 percent of students indicated awareness of their school's harassment policy. The survey found that 90 percent of LGBT students compared to 62 percent of non-LGBT students reported that they had been verbally or physically harassed or assaulted over the past year. Verbal harassment was the most common form of harassment for the LGBT students (66 percent reported being verbally harassed, 16 percent physically harassed, and 8 percent physically assaulted). Much of the harassment was prompted by appearance, primarily when they strayed from traditional images of masculinity and femininity. The report explained the connection this way: "one interpretation of this finding is sexual orientation, gender expression and appearance may be inextricably linked for many students and teachers. For example, a student, regardless of his or her sexual orientation, may

be harassed because of how masculine or feminine he or she acts or because of his or her physical appearance, which may lead them to be harassed because they are perceived to be gay or lesbian" (Harris Interactive and Gay, Lesbian and Straight Education Network 2005, 4).

8. The terminology is often confusing. The term "sex" denotes biological, that is, physical, differences between men and women; the term "gender" is socially constructed, indicating cultural characteristics and norms typically associated with a particular sex, such as "masculinity" and "femininity." Although most laws refer to sex rather than gender, most courts, including the U.S. Supreme Court, use the terms "sex" and "gender" interchangeably, using each incorrectly a good deal of the time (see Greenberg 1999).

9. Nabozny chose not to file suit under federal law because it was unclear whether it extended to suits for sexual harassment on the basis of sexual orientation. However, although constitutional equal protection principles apply to distinctions based on sexual orientation, the courts apply a higher level of scrutiny to claims of sex discrimination than to discrimination based on sexual orientation. The difference is illustrated in the high court's rulings in two 1996 cases: *United States v. Virginia* (1996) and *Romer*. In the former, although reluctant to adopt strict scrutiny, the Court applied heightened (that is, intermediate) scrutiny to the male-only admissions policy of Virginia Military Institute. In *Romer*, although it held that Colorado's Amendment 2 was unconstitutional, the Court applied only minimal scrutiny to the claim of discrimination based on sexual orientation.

10. Nabozny filed suit under 42 U.S.C. §1983, a statute that confers no substantive rights but provides access to the federal courts by allowing plaintiffs to sue state and local government officials who violate their federal constitutional or statutory rights. Section 1983, enacted as part of the Civil Rights Act of 1871, provides, "Every person who, under color of any statute, ordinance, regulation, custom, or usage, of any State . . . subjects, or causes to be subjected, any citizen of the United States . . . to the deprivation of any rights, privileges or immunities secured by the Constitution and laws, shall be liable to the party injured in an action at law, suit in equity, or other proper proceeding for redress."

11. The district court's discussion of the abuse to which gay students are subjected in *Gay-Straight Alliance Network v. Visalia Unified School District* (2001) indicates that Nabozny's experiences were not unique. In *Visilia*, the court held that a gay student's network had associational and direct standing to sue school authorities for discrimination against LGBT students—or those perceived to be—because the district's policies hampered the goals of the network to promote a nondiscriminatory and safe school environment.

12. Bedell (2003) argues that plaintiffs have a cause of action against school officials under §1983 for depriving them of their right to equal protection by not following district policy against gay harassment.

13. Plaintiffs alleging equal protection violations must show that the defendants committed acts of intentional discrimination (*Washington v. Davis* 1976).

14. Although the question of credibility is normally one for the finder of fact, since the motion for summary judgment was brought by the defendants, the court gave credence to the plaintiff's version of the facts.

15. The Supreme Court held in *Owen* (1980) that a municipality may not claim qualified immunity from liability in a §1983 action by asserting the good faith of the city officials. In *Monell v. New York City Department of Social Services* (1978), the Court overruled *Monroe v. Pape* (1961), which had held that local governments were wholly immune from suit under §1983 because they were not among the "persons" to whom the statute applies. *Monell* left open the question of whether cities were entitled to any kind of immunity at all; *Owen* decided that.

16. The question is whether the state has an affirmative obligation to protect him and, if so, whether the failure to do so constitutes a constitutional violation of the due process clause. If there is no affirmative duty to act, the state will not be liable for its inaction, even if it results in harm. In *DeShaney v. Winnebago County Department of Social Services* (1989), the Supreme Court held that absent a special relationship between the state and the individual, such as incarceration or institutionalization, the due process clause of the Fourteenth Amendment does not require the government to protect individuals from harm caused by private citizens.

The Seventh Circuit found that the compulsory attendance law did not create a "special relationship" that required the school to protect Nabozny from harm from other students. He had argued that he was denied due process because of the increased risk of harm to him and that the school should have acted to protect him. With no duty to act, the school was not responsible for the students' conduct.

17. The students originally alleged that the school violated their state and federal rights of equal protection (on the basis of sex and sexual orientation), due process, and privacy as well as Title IX and the California Education Code. The court granted the defendants summary judgment on all claims except the federal equal protection claim of discrimination on the basis of sexual orientation (*Flores v. Morgan Hill Unified* 1999).

18. The harassment took many forms, including pornography, threats, beatings, anti-gay comments, and name-calling. When a plaintiff showed one of the assistant principals a threatening note that was left in her locker and asked for a new locker, the official allegedly responded, "Yes, sure, sure, later. You need to go back to class. Don't bring me this trash anymore. This is disgusting" (*Flores v. Morgan Hill Unified School District* 2003, 1133).

19. The *Flores* litigation ended with a settlement in 2003 for $1.1 million (Gay, Lesbian and Straight Education Network 2005a). In *Henkle v. Gregory* (2001), Derek Henkle, a student at a Nevada high school, filed a §1983 action, complaining of violations under the First and Fourteenth Amendments and Title IX; he sought punitive damages against the individual defendants and the school district. Robert A. McQuaid Jr., a U.S. magistrate judge, dismissed his Title IX claim (because Title IX preempts §1983) and his equal protection claims (because they were based on the same facts as his Title IX claims). He held that Henkle alleged sufficient facts in his First Amendment claim to survive the defendant's motion to dismiss and rejected the defendant's claim of qualified immunity on the First Amendment and Title IX claims, allowing Henkle to seek punitive damages. The case eventually settled in 2001 for $451,000 (Gay, Lesbian and Straight Education Network 2005a; see this source as well for reports of other verdicts and settlement agreements).

20. 20 U.S.C.S. §1681(a), Title IX, provides, "No person in the United States shall, on the basis of sex, be excluded from participation in, be denied the benefits of, or be subjected to discrimination under any education program or activity receiving Federal financial assistance."

21. On June 17, 1997, Clinton issued a memorandum to commemorate the twenty-fifth anniversary of Title IX. In his remarks on signing the document, he charged federal agencies with enhancing Title IX enforcement to eliminate discrimination on the basis of sex (Clinton 1997). Several years later, on June 23, 2000, Clinton issued Executive Order 13160, explaining that it is intended to extend nondiscrimination principles in laws such as Title IX that are applied to private institutions and state and local governments receiving federal aid to "programs and activities conducted, operated, or undertaken by an executive department or agency" (Clinton 2000).

22. In March 2007, the Michigan House of Representatives considered legislation (House Bill 4162), known as "Matt's Safe School Law," that would have required schools to implement policies to prohibit bullying and harassment on the basis of "a pupil's actual or perceived religion, race, color, national origin, age, sex, sexual orientation, disability, height, weight, gender identity, socio-economic status, or any other distinguishing characteristic or is based on association with another person who has or is perceived to have any of these characteristics." The bill was referred to the Senate Committee on Education but was postponed indefinitely in November (Gay, Lesbian and Straight Education Network 2007e).

23. The following states have laws against discrimination and/or harassment on the basis of sexual orientation in schools: Connecticut, Massachusetts, Vermont, Washington, and Wisconsin.

The following states have laws against discrimination and/or harassment on the basis of sexual orientation and gender identity in schools: California, District of Columbia, Iowa, Maine, Minnesota, and New Jersey. The following states have generic laws against bullying in schools: Arizona, Arkansas, Colorado, Georgia, Illinois, Louisiana, Nevada, New Hampshire, Oklahoma, Oregon, Tennessee, Texas, Virginia, and West Virginia. The following states have regulations or policies prohibiting harassment and/or discrimination in schools: Maryland (on the basis of sexual orientation and gender identity), Pennsylvania, and Rhode Island. States with teachers' ethical codes prohibiting discrimination based on sexual orientation are Alaska, Colorado, Florida, Pennsylvania, and Utah (Gay, Lesbian and Straight Education Network 2005b; Human Rights Campaign 2007c).

24. Cal. Educ. Code §220 provides, "No person shall be subjected to discrimination on the basis of sex, ethnic group identification, race, national origin, religion, color, mental or physical disability, or any actual or perceived characteristic that is contained in the definition of hate crimes set forth in Section 422.55 of the Penal Code in any program or activity conducted by an educational institution that receives, or benefits from, state financial assistance or enrolls pupils who receive state student financial aid."

25. Conn. Gen. Stat. §10-15c(a) provides, "Each such child shall have . . . an equal opportunity to participate in the activities, programs and courses of study offered in such public schools . . . without discrimination on account of race, color, sex, religion, national origin or sexual orientation."

26. Iowa Code §280.28(1) provides, "It is the policy of the state of Iowa that school employees, volunteers, and students in Iowa schools shall not engage in harassing or bullying behavior . . . which is based on any actual or perceived trait or characteristic of the student and which creates an objectively hostile school environment."

27. Md. Educ. Code Ann. §7-424b(1) provides, "The Department shall require a county board to report incidents of harassment or intimidation against students attending a public school under the jurisdiction of the county board . . . [and] shall submit a report on or before March 31 each year to the Senate Education, Health, and Environmental Affairs Committee and the House Ways and Means Committee."

28. See N.J. Stat. Ann. §18A:37-15; Vt. Stat. Ann. tit. 16, §565; Rev. Code. Wash. §28A.600.480.

29. N.J. Stat. Ann. §10:5-4, the Law Against Discrimination, provides, "All persons shall have the opportunity to obtain . . . all the accommodations, advantages, facilities, and privileges of any place of public accommodation, publicly assisted housing accommodation, and other real property without discrimination because of race, creed, color, national origin, ancestry, age, marital status, affectional or sexual orientation, familial status, disability, nationality, sex, gender identity or expression or source of lawful income used for rental or mortgage payments, subject only to conditions and limitations applicable alike to all persons. This opportunity is recognized as and declared to be a civil right."

30. In one of the early Title IX cases, *Grove City College v. Bell* (1984), the U.S. Supreme Court held that there was no evidence that Congress intended to distinguish between direct and indirect aid and therefore that student aid, known as indirect aid, to an institution triggered Title IX coverage. The Court, however, accepted Grove City's argument that Congress did not intend Title IX to cover the entire institution, merely the program receiving the aid—in this case, the financial aid office. Grove City was a private, coeducational liberal arts college with approximately 2,200 students in western Pennsylvania. The college received federal financial aid indirectly through federal grants and loan programs to students. The case arose because Grove City College refused to file an assurance of compliance as required by the Title IX regulations and the government threatened to cut the funding. The issue was whether the financial assistance to the students meant that the school was "a program or activity" within Title IX. The civil rights community attacked the *Grove City* ruling in part because they feared its effect on other civil rights statutes with the same "program" or "activity" language as Title IX. In 1988, Congress passed the Civil Rights Restoration Act, reversing the Court's narrow interpretation of the program-specific language of the nation's federal civil rights laws.

31. In deciding whether to imply the cause of action, the Court seeks to determine if a private suit is compatible with the purpose of the statute by asking four questions: (1) Is the person bringing the suit someone for whose "especial benefit" the statute was designed? (2) Is there evidence that Congress intended to create or deny a private suit? (3) Is a private suit consistent with the legislative purpose of the statute? (4) Is it inappropriate to infer a cause of action because the suit is in an area that is traditionally within the bounds of state law (Mezey 1983).

32. See *Cannon v. University of Chicago* (1976), *Jones v. Oklahoma Secondary School Association* (1977), and *Cape v. Tennessee Secondary School Athletic Association* (1977).

33. Because the sex discrimination provisions received little attention during passage of Title IX, there is scant legislative history to guide the courts. Title IX is modeled after Title VI of the 1964 Civil Rights Act. Although Title VI has a broader reach—barring racial discrimination in all federally assisted programs or activities—to the extent that it was discussed, Congress intended the laws to be similarly interpreted.

34. In *Pfeiffer v. Marion Center Area School District* (1990), the Third Circuit held that the plaintiff would be entitled to money damages if she proved her claim of intentional discrimination. The court relied on the Supreme Court ruling in *Guardians Association v. Civil Service Commission of New York* (1983), in which a majority suggested that monetary compensation would be permissible under Title VI.

35. *Alexander v. Yale University* (1980) was the first case to allow sexual harassment claims under Title IX.

36. The act abrogated the state's Eleventh Amendment immunity in suits brought to enforce Title VI, Title IX, §504, of the 1973 Rehabilitation Act and the Age Discrimination in Employment Act.

37. To sue recipients of federal funds for violations of programs enacted under Congress's spending clause authority, it is necessary to show that the recipient is aware of the restrictions imposed by Congress.

38. Although the courts often borrow from Title VII law in deciding Title IX cases, they established different standards of liability under the two statutes, making it more difficult to hold Title IX defendants accountable for similar types of behavior (see Davies 2002).

39. Collins (1998, 800–18) shows the range of appellate and district court rulings in Title IX claims of peer harassment.

40. Davies (2002, 418), who believes that the "indifference" standard is "workable," acknowledges that lower courts have not agreed on the answers to several questions, such as what constitutes notice and, more important, the identity of the appropriate school official to whom notice must be given; that is, must it be a district officer, or does a principal or teacher suffice? Moreover, courts have had difficulty gauging the severity of the harassment that constitutes a denial of educational opportunity.

41. The Supreme Court also left the availability of punitive damages unclear in *Davis*, but in *Gregory* (2001), the district court ruled that if a school acted with "deliberate indifference," defined in the Ninth Circuit as "the conscious or reckless disregard of the consequences of ones [sic] acts or omissions," the plaintiff was entitled to punitive damages.

42. The court granted a directed verdict in the case of the original named plaintiff, Steven Vance, and he did not appeal. The actual defendant in the case is the Board of Education of Spencer County.

43. Eisemann (2000, 133) notes that such gay students have had a difficult time in Title IX actions; most of the scholarly analysis has urged the courts to interpret Title IX more broadly to include peer harassment on the basis of sexual orientation (see Mayes 2001).

44. But when enforcement is in the hands of the OCR, schools must have actual notice and be given an opportunity to take corrective action before the agency can terminate their funding.

45. The January 19, 2001, guidance indicated that Title IX would apply to peer same-sex harassment as long as such harassment is based on sex; it appeared, however, to set a higher bar for gay students, saying that "if students heckle another student with comments based on the student's sexual orientation (e.g., 'gay students are not welcome at this table in the cafeteria'), but [as] their actions do not involve conduct of a sexual nature, their actions would not be sexual harassment covered by Title IX" (U.S. Department of Education, 2001).

46. The Supreme Court adopted agency principles of liability in Title VII, and students are not considered agents of the school as employees are.

47. In *Doe v. Dallas Independent School District* (2000), the Fifth Circuit acknowledged that *Oncale* applied to Title IX actions of same-sex sexual harassment yet affirmed the lower court's award of summary judgment to the district, ruling that the school official had not been deliberately indifferent to complaints from male students about their male teacher's sexual misconduct.

48. Both sexes were guilty of the verbal abuse, but only boys committed the physical assaults and sexual acts.

49. In August 1993, the state amended its Human Rights Act to include sexual orientation as a prohibited basis of discrimination; the district argued that it was not liable for any acts of harassment before that date.

50. The U.S. Supreme Court specified in *Oncale* (1998, 79) that the harassment need not be "motivated by sexual desire" to violate Title VII.

51. The case was eventually settled for an undisclosed amount (Gay, Lesbian and Straight Education Network 2005a).

52. The Gay Straight Alliance, headquartered in San Francisco, is a nonprofit education and advocacy organization that promotes GSAs among high school students. GSAs are intended to foster understanding between gay and non-gay students and typically do not have an exclusively gay membership. As of September 2007, there were 3,612 GSAs in all states as well as Puerto Rico and Washington, D.C. According to GLSEN's interim director, Dr. Eliza Byard, the research shows an "enormous positive impact [that] Gay-Straight Alliances have on school climate. . . . First and foremost, all students are bullied and harassed less often based on actual or perceived sexual orientation when a school has a GSA. LGBT students also demonstrate a greater sense of safety and belonging in school and skip school less often" (Gay, Lesbian and Straight Education Network 2007c). Litigation over the formation of GSAs in public high schools is becoming increasingly common in various parts of the country (see Pratt 2007).

53. The reference to "little g, little p" meant the vote had the effect of banning all references to gay issues at all times from the public library.

54. Parents have also sued school districts that have provided counseling for their children who seek help in dealing with their sexual orientation, claiming that the schools violate their due process right to raise their children (see Henigan 1996).

55. Minnesota Federal District Court Judge Donovan Frank granted a preliminary injunction to a student who wished to wear a sweatshirt with the message

"Straight Pride." Although concerned about the nature of the message on the shirt and how it might affect the school atmosphere, the school could not prohibit him from wearing it absent a reasonable fear of disturbance (*Chambers v. Babbitt* 2001).

56. Although the lower courts generally hold that restrictions on anti-gay speech must be judged by the *Tinker* standard, they often differ on the degree to which anti-gay speech is constitutionally protected (see Mostoller 2003).

57. The National Day of Silence was begun in 1996 by students at the University of Virginia; GLSEN became a national sponsor in 2001. Designed to curb anti-LGBT bullying and harassment in schools, it is endorsed by GSAs on campuses around the nation. GLSEN reports that students from more than 7,500 middle and high schools signed up to participate in the Day of Silence in 2007 (Gay, Lesbian and Straight Education Network 2008).

58. The burden of proof is on the party seeking the injunction to show, among other things, that it is reasonably likely to succeed on the merits. In reviewing a lower court's grant or denial of a preliminary injunction, the appellate court must determine if the lower court abused its discretion, applied an incorrect legal standard, or made erroneous findings of fact.

59. The exceptions have overwhelmed the principle of free expression in schools, with the high court virtually limiting *Tinker* to its facts. In *Bethel School District No. 403 v. Fraser* (1986, 684–5), for example, it distinguished *Tinker* to allow the school to determine "the appropriate form of civil discourse and political expression" and punish a student for "his offensively lewd and indecent speech." And in *Hazelwood School District v. Kuhlmeier* (1988, 273), the Court held "that educators do not offend the First Amendment by exercising editorial control over the style and content of student speech in school-sponsored expressive activities so long as their actions are reasonably related to legitimate pedagogical concerns." More recently, in *Morse v. Frederick* (2007, 2640), the Court again distinguished *Tinker* and permitted schools to "take steps to safeguard those entrusted to their care from speech that can reasonably be regarded as encouraging illegal drug use." It agreed with the school principal that the banner "BONG HITS 4 JESUS" advocated "illegal drug use."

60. Reinhardt said that it was unnecessary to address the second *Tinker* test, as it based its ruling on the rights-of-others prong.

61. The Ninth Circuit also held that Harper was unlikely to prevail on his free exercise claim, as there was no evidence that his religious beliefs were burdened, and, in any event, the school had a compelling reason to prevent him from wearing the demeaning shirt; it dismissed the establishment clause issue as merely an echo of the free exercise claim. The Supreme Court granted certiorari in *Harper* (2007a), but because the district court had already entered final judgment against him, the high court vacated the judgment of the court of appeals and remanded the case to that court with instructions to dismiss his appeal as moot. As instructed, the circuit court dismissed Harper's appeal on April 23, 2007 (*Harper* 2007b).

62. The U.S. Supreme Court denied certiorari in *Morrison* (2009).

63. The anti–gay rights group, the Alliance Defense Fund (ADF), organized a Day of Truth to take place on April 19, 2007, to counter the Day of Silence. Its stated purpose was to express opposition to homosexuality from a Christian per-

spective. Although represented by the ADF in the lawsuit, the plaintiffs, Heidi Zamecnik and Alexander Nuxoll, claimed that they were independent of the ADF.

64. In 2006, Zamecnik had worn a shirt with the words "My Day of Silence, Straight Alliance" on the front and "Be Happy, Not Gay" on the back; school officials forced her to ink over "Not Gay." They believed that the expression "Be Happy, Not Gay" was offensive, just as "Be Happy, Not Christian," "Be Happy, Not Muslim," and "Be Happy, Not Jewish" would be (*Zamecnik* 2007a; *Nuxoll v. Indian Prairie School District #204* 2008).

65. According to Hart, the Seventh Circuit assesses the school's pedagogical interests in restricting the speech even if the speech is not school sponsored, thus giving the institution more regulatory power.

66. In an unpublished order issued on August 7, 2007, the Seventh Circuit dismissed the plaintiffs' appeal of the denial of the preliminary injunction as moot because the April 2007 Day of Silence had passed (*Zamecnik* 2007b). Then, in a later ruling on December 21, 2007, Hart allowed Nuxoll (the sole remaining plaintiff because Zamecnik graduated) to amend the complaint to seek a preliminary injunction to allow him to express his beliefs on homosexuality throughout the year (*Zamecnik* 2007c).

67. Judge Ilana Rovner's concurring opinion took Posner to task for erroneously depicting *Tinker* as a case about viewpoint discrimination and distinguishing it from this case. In her view, this case was *Tinker*, and under *Tinker*, the school was simply not justified in restricting Nuxoll's speech.

68. The Equal Access Act, 20 U.S.C. §4071(a), provides, "It shall be unlawful for any public school which receives Federal financial assistance and which has a limited open forum to deny equal access or a fair opportunity to, or discriminate against, any students who wish to conduct a meeting within that limited open forum on the basis of religious, political, philosophical, or other content of the speech at such meetings." Section 4071(b) specifies that a "limited open forum" exists when the school "grants an offering to or opportunity for one or more noncurriculum related student groups to meet on school premises during noninstructional time."

The law extended the Supreme Court's ruling in *Widmar* to high schools. *Widmar* held that public universities and colleges with limited open forums must permit religious groups to meet on campus. The high court upheld the EAA in *Board of Education v. Mergens* (1990) by ruling that because the school created a limited open forum, it must allow a student Christian club to meet on school premises for Bible study and prayer; it rejected the school's argument that permitting the group to meet would violate the establishment clause of the First Amendment.

On March 1, 2005, John Cornyn, Republican from Texas, introduced Senate Bill 483 to amend the EAA to extend it to elementary schools. The bill was referred to committee.

69. *Gay-Straight Alliance v. School Board of Okeechobee County* (2007) and *Colin v. Orange Unified School District* (2000). In *Franklin Central Gay/Straight Alliance v. Franklin Township Community School Corporation* (2002), the plaintiffs were awarded summary judgment, the court denying the defendant's motion to reconsider.

70. The "limited open forum" of the EAA differs from the "limited public forum" protected by the First Amendment.

71. During the course of the litigation, the group changed its name to the Lubbock Gay Straight Alliance.

72. Although the U.S. Supreme Court had struck the Texas antisodomy law in *Lawrence* before the students filed their suit in district court, the district pointed to Texas law, not at issue in *Lawrence*, that prohibited indecent acts with minors. As Orman (2006, 238 n79), points out, however, that statute was directed at sexual molestation, not consensual sexual activity.

73. The plaintiffs' motion for summary judgment was dismissed by the court on procedural grounds.

74. Under the First Amendment, schools may establish "limited public forums" in which they can reasonably limit the topics discussed but may not restrict expression on the basis of the viewpoint expressed.

75. 20 U.S.C. §4071(c)(4) provides, "Schools shall be deemed to offer a fair opportunity to students who wish to conduct a meeting within its limited open forum if such school uniformly provides that . . . the meeting does not materially and substantially interfere with the orderly conduct of educational activities within the school."

76. 20 U.S.C. §4071(f) provides, "Nothing in this title shall be construed to limit the authority of the school, its agents or employees, to maintain order and discipline on school premises."

77. 20 U.S.C. §4071(d)(5) provides, "Nothing in this title shall be construed to authorize the United States or any State or political subdivision thereof . . . to sanction meetings that are otherwise unlawful."

78. 20 U.S.C. §4071(f) provides, "Nothing in this title shall be construed to limit the authority of the school, its agents or employees . . . to protect the well-being of students."

79. See Rankin (2003) for the results of a survey on the degree to which colleges and universities accommodate the needs of LGBT students.

80. The U.S. Supreme Court denied certiorari in *Texas A&M University v. Gay Student Services* (1985). In *Wood v. Davison* (1972), the federal district court judge ordered the University of Georgia to allow the Committee on Gay Education to hold a dance. Citing *Healy*, the court found that the university's amorphous fear of illegal activities did not satisfy its "heavy burden" of justifying the infringement on the group's First Amendment rights of expression and association (*Wood* 1972, 547, quoting *Healy*, 193). The gay student group also triumphed in *Student Coalition for Gay Rights v. Austin Peay University* (1979).

81. The Supreme Court denied certiorari in *Gay Lib* (1977b).

82. Recent events indicated a change in the university's approach to gay students. Following a number of homophobic attacks at Georgetown University, on October 24, 2007, President John J. DeGioia stressed the need for "our community [to] work together on a more comprehensive initiative to strengthen Georgetown's approach to addressing the needs of LGBTQ students" (DeGioia 2007). To accomplish this task, he created three working groups that began their work on November 2, 2007. Shortly thereafter, at the end of January 2008, the groups submitted their reports, and on February 7, 2008, the president reported that the

administration would begin to implement their recommendations, among other things, by establishing a LGBTQ Resource Center for the fall 2008 semester. He announced that a national search for a director would begin immediately.

In May 2008, Georgetown's vice president for student affairs named Sivagami Subbaraman as the first director of the resource center (TheHoya.com August 29, 2008).

5

The Boy Scouts

An often-overlooked area of discrimination affecting gays revolves around their ability to engage in social interactions. The controversy is sharply illustrated by the refusal of the Boy Scouts of America (BSA) to admit gay boys and men into its ranks—as scouts, as leaders, and even, in some situations, as employees. In resolving disputes over the BSA's anti-gay policy, the courts were forced to reconcile conflicting constitutional and statutory claims at the state and federal levels, with each side arguing a rights-based discourse.

In *Boy Scouts of America v. Dale* (2000), the U.S. Supreme Court upheld the BSA's First Amendment right to exclude gay scouts despite the New Jersey law prohibiting discrimination in public accommodations on the basis of sexual orientation.[1] A federal district court judge correctly observed that "after *Dale*, it is clear that the Boy Scouts of America's strongly held private, discriminatory beliefs are at odds with values requiring tolerance and inclusion in the public realm, and lawsuits . . . are the predictable fallout from the Boy Scouts' victory before the Supreme Court" (*Barnes-Wallace v. Boy Scouts of America* 2003, 1263). Thus, instead of settling the matter, *Dale* led to a virtual free-for-all of litigation, with gays challenging the BSA's exclusionary policies and the Scouts suing when public officials attempted to withdraw their benefits following the negative publicity resulting from *Dale*.

THE BOY SCOUT ORGANIZATION

The BSA was incorporated on February 8, 1910, and chartered by Congress in 1916. As specified in the charter, the organization's purpose "is to provide an educational program for boys and young adults to build character, to train in the responsibilities of participating citizenship, and to develop personal fitness." Sponsored by churches, schools, corporations, and civic and community groups, the BSA benefits from their assistance in providing meeting space, funds, and a variety of programmatic needs. Local geographical units, called councils, are in turn chartered by the national organization, which exerts a great deal of control over scouting activities.

The national organization, headquartered in Irving, Texas, has hundreds of millions of dollars in assets but is heavily dependent on support from national charitable campaigns such as the United Way or by state and municipal charity campaigns.[2] Although its membership has declined recently, at the end of 2006 there were nearly 3 million youth members and more than 1 million adult members.[3] The Boy Scouts have a special relationship with the U.S. government; as a federally chartered organization, the BSA submits an annual report to Congress, and the president of the United States serves as its honorary head (Boy Scouts of America 2008a; Hughes and Moiseichik 2003).

PUBLIC ACCOMMODATION LAWS AND FREEDOM OF ASSOCIATION

The BSA has been the target of litigation since the 1970s as women, atheists, and, more recently, gays have sought admission into the ranks of scouts, claiming the organization violates state and local laws against discriminating in places of public accommodations.

A public accommodations law prohibits discrimination in privately owned places that are open to the public, such as stores, restaurants, hotels, and theaters. Such laws are frequently silent on whether private entities such as the Boy Scouts should be considered places of public accommodation or whether the defendant must be a physical structure.[4] In suits against the Boy Scouts, if plaintiffs succeed in overcoming this barrier, they also have to surmount the BSA's defense that its membership decisions are protected by the First Amendment's guarantee of freedom of association (see Goodman 1999).

In *United States Jaycees v. Roberts* (1984), the Supreme Court clarified the constitutional principle of freedom of association.[5] One manifestation of the right, intimate association, is "a fundamental element of personal liberty" that allows individuals to "enter into and maintain certain intimate human relationships" without "undue intrusion by the State." The size and character of an organization determine its ability to claim an intimate associational right. Expressive association, emanating from the First Amendment, affords individuals "a right to associate for the purpose of engaging in those activities protected by the First Amendment—speech, assembly, petition for the redress of grievances, and the exercise of religion. The Constitution guarantees freedom of association of this kind as an indispensable means of preserving other individual liberties" (617–8).

To prevail in an expressive association claim, an organization must demonstrate a relationship between its expressive pursuits and its exclusionary policies. Because the right of expressive association is fundamental but not absolute, the outcome of a case depends on balancing the group's First Amendment right against the state's interest in combating discrimination. The standard is a high one, permitting the state to limit a group's associational freedom only with "regulations adopted to serve compelling state interests, unrelated to the suppression of ideas, that cannot be achieved through means significantly less restrictive of associational freedoms" (623). In *Roberts*, the Court concluded that, at most, allowing women to become members of the Jaycees would result in only a slight invasion of the organization's associational rights, easily outweighed by the state's compelling interest against discrimination.

In *Board of Directors of Rotary International v. Rotary Club of Duarte* (1987) and *New York State Club Association, Inc. v. City of New York* (1988), the Court reached similar conclusions. These cases, together with *Roberts*, were known as the trilogy of private club cases and provided the framework for deciding *Dale*. However, the outcomes differed as the high court's ruling in *Dale* departed from the method of inquiry established in these three cases.

THE HISTORY OF LITIGATION AGAINST THE BSA

Prior to 1998, the prevailing view in the state and federal courts was that the Boy Scouts organization did not qualify as a place of public accommodation. In one of the first cases to challenge the BSA's exclusionary policy as a violation of a public accommodations law, *Schwenk v. Boy Scouts of America* (1976), the Oregon Supreme Court upheld the lower court's dismissal of a complaint by a nine-year-old girl who sought admission to the Cub Scouts. The court began by recognizing that the state public accommodations law guarantees access to public accommodations.[6] But, it added, the legislative history of the act showed that lawmakers did not intend to include the Scouts within the law, at least for the purposes of requiring it to accept girls as members.[7]

More than a decade later, two suits against the Boy Scouts met the same fate. In *Mankes v. Boy Scouts of America* (1991), an eight-year-old girl who was denied admission into the Scouts filed suit. Before dismissing her case on jurisdictional grounds, the federal court noted that the Scouts "did not, in creating its organization to help develop the moral character of young boys, intentionally set out to discriminate against girls" (411).[8]

In *Yeaw v. Boy Scouts of America* (1997a), a California appeals court reviewed a case brought by an eleven-year-old girl against the Scouts under the Unruh Civil Rights Act of 1959.[9] The court held that because the BSA was not a business establishment, the act did not apply, and the Scouts were free to exclude girls from membership.[10]

Since 1998, likely because of a shortage of male volunteers, women were allowed to be scoutmasters and assistant scoutmasters. By 2006, more than 400,000 women were registered as scouting volunteers at every leadership level, and the organization insists that there is no contradiction between excluding girls yet allowing their mothers to assist in "instilling values in boys" (Boy Scouts of America 2006).

In 1987, a woman challenged the policy of excluding women scoutmasters in *Quinnipiac Council, Boy Scouts of America v. Commission on Human Rights and Opportunities* (1987).

The case arose when the Connecticut Commission on Human Rights and Opportunities (CHRO) charged the BSA with violating the state public accommodations law by depriving Katherine Pollard of the opportunity to supply "goods and services" to the Scouts (360). The Connecticut Supreme Court held that the law does not protect an individual's right to provide "goods and services," only to receive them, and concluded that, although arguably a public accommodation, the Scouts did not violate the law by refusing to allow her to serve as a scoutmaster.[11]

The bulk of the BSA litigation was brought not on gender grounds but on grounds of religious discrimination. Characterizing itself as nonsectarian, the BSA excludes atheists and agnostics as scouts and leaders and requires its members to affirm their belief in God.[12] In challenging these conditions of membership, plaintiffs often cited the First Amendment's Establishment Clause as well as state laws against promoting religion.

In *Sherman v. Community Consolidated School District 21 of Wheeling Township* (1993a), the district court dismissed a suit against the Wheeling Township School District, rejecting the family's (a father and a son) claim that the district violated the establishment clause by allowing the Cub Scouts to meet in school in the evening and permitting school personnel to assist with recruitment during school hours.[13] Similarly, in *Powell v. Bunn* (2002), an Oregon court of appeals affirmed the lower court's ruling against a woman who had sued the school district on First Amendment grounds for allowing the Scouts to recruit at her son's school.[14]

More recently, in *Scalise v. Boy Scouts of America, Lake Huron Area Council # 265* (2005), a Michigan court was also reluctant to evict the Scouts from the local school premises. Here, a father and son, who objected to the BSA's "declaration of religious principle" (858), filed suit against the local Scout council and the school district. Citing the scouting presence in the school, they claimed that the defendants violated the state constitution's establishment clause and civil rights law by discriminating on the basis of religion.[15] The trial court judge granted the defendants' motion for summary judgment, and the appellate court affirmed.[16] The plaintiffs even acknowledged that the BSA was a private organization with a First Amendment right to associate but argued that it should be considered a public accommodation because it carried out its practices in the public school, which is a place of public accommodation. The court disagreed.

In the federal courts, the Seventh Circuit also found in favor of the Scouts by ruling that Title II—the public accommodations section of the 1964 Civil Rights Act—does not apply to the Boy Scouts (*Welsh v. Boy Scouts of America* 1993a). Comparing the Scouts to the public accommodations specified in the law, the court held that Congress intended to restrict Title II to membership organizations that were closely connected to a physical facility.[17]

Acknowledging the difficulty of balancing a public accommodations law with associational freedom, Bigham (1994) argues that the court interpreted "place of public accommodation" in Title II too narrowly. In his view, because Title II is remedial, the court should have privileged the equality principle in the law over the BSA's associational rights.

The litigation against the BSA continued throughout the decade. In *Seabourn v. Coronado Area Council, Boy Scouts of America* (1995), the Kansas Supreme Court held that the BSA was neither a "public accommodation" nor "a place of public accommodations" within the state public accommodations law.[18]

In one of the most widely publicized lawsuits against the BSA, the California Supreme Court ruled on whether the organization was within the reach of the state public accommodations law, the Unruh Act. These two cases arose when Timothy Curran and Michael Randall sued the organization for discrimination on the basis of sexual orientation (Curran) and religion (Randall). Curran was a former Eagle Scout, like Dale. When the Boy Scouts rejected his application for assistant scoutmaster, he sued, claiming that the BSA discriminated against him by refusing to accept him because of his sexual orientation. The trial judge held that the BSA was covered by the state civil rights act, but she also accepted the organization's claim that its right of expressive association permitted it to exclude gays and therefore reject Curran. A divided appellate court reversed, holding that the BSA was not a "business establishment" as defined by the Unruh Act, and affirmed the lower court's ruling for the BSA on the expressive association claim (*Curran v. Mount Diablo Council of the Boy Scouts of America* 1994).

In the companion case (*Randall v. Orange County Council* 1994), the Cub Scouts had tried to expel eleven-year-old twins William and Michael Randall for protesting the religious achievement requirement.[19] A superior court ruling in their favor was affirmed by the appellate court. Citing the appellate court's decision in *Curran* (1994) that the BSA was governed by the Unruh Act, the judge found the Scouts guilty of discrimination on the basis of religion.

On March 23, 1998, the state supreme court settled the matter with a consolidated ruling in favor of the Boy Scouts in both cases, holding that the BSA was not a "business establishment" as defined by the act (*Curran* 1998). However, the chief justice indicated that although the Unruh Act was inapplicable, the government was not without resources. Citing *Bob Jones University v. United States* (1983), he seemed to imply that the BSA's discriminatory policies might jeopardize its tax-exempt status.[20]

THE *DALE* LITIGATION

Thus, the courts held that the Scouts were excused from complying with the antidiscrimination provisions of state and federal public accommodations laws. In *Boy Scouts of America v. Dale* (1999), the New Jersey Supreme Court departed from the majority view.

The case began in 1990 when the BSA expelled James Dale after learning that he was gay.[21] Dale became a scout at eight, an adult member at eighteen, and a volunteer assistant scoutmaster three years later.[22] A model scout, he earned an Eagle Scout badge as well as numerous honors and awards. When he was featured in a local newspaper story about gay college students and identified as copresident of the Rutgers University Lesbian/Gay Alliance, the BSA rescinded his registration on the grounds that he had "demonstrated his failure to live by the Scout Oath and Law by publicly avowing that he was a homosexual" (*Dale v. Boy Scouts of America* 1998, 275).[23] Dale stressed that he never tried to discuss his views on homosexuality, adding that the Scouts allowed heterosexual scout leaders to advocate gay rights. He filed suit, arguing, among other things, that the BSA had violated the New Jersey antidiscrimination law.

A Monmouth County Superior Court awarded summary judgment to the Scouts, ruling that LAD did not apply because the BSA was not a public accommodation. Arguably, even if it were, the judge ruled, as a "distinctly private" group, it was exempted from the law.[24] He further held that the BSA's First Amendment right of expressive association justified Dale's expulsion, finding that the Scouts "had consistently excluded from youth and adult membership any self-declared homosexual and that the BSA considered homosexual conduct neither 'morally straight' under the

Scout Oath nor 'clean' under the Scout law" (*Dale v. Boy Scouts of America* 1998, 277, citing *Dale v. Boy Scouts of America* 1995).

In *Dale v. Boy Scouts of America* (1998), the state appellate court reversed, with Judge James Havey ruling that the Boy Scouts organization is a place of public accommodation under state law, which the BSA violated by excluding Dale. Acknowledging the Seventh Circuit's contrary position in *Welsh* (1993a) as well as several opposing state court rulings, Havey refused to construe "place of public accommodation" as a physical location only. As remedial legislation, he stressed, LAD is meant to reach discriminatory behavior regardless of where it takes place.

Havey took his cue from *National Organization for Women v. Little League Baseball, Inc.* (1974a), in which a New Jersey appellate court held that the Little League, with its open invitation to the community, was a public accommodation within LAD's ambit and must permit girls to participate.[25] He further cited the BSA's advertising and recruitment materials to negate the claim that its selective membership policy exempted it from LAD. Finally, after reviewing the trilogy of private club cases in which the U.S. Supreme Court interpreted the parameters of the right of expressive association, the court ruled that applying LAD to the Boy Scouts did not infringe on its freedom of expressive association and ordered the BSA to restore Dale's membership.

On appeal, the New Jersey Supreme Court unanimously affirmed the appellate court (*Boy Scouts of America v. Dale* 1999). Writing for the court, Chief Justice Deborah Poritz ruled that the BSA is a public accommodation and declared that courts must interpret remedial statutes such as LAD broadly. She also rejected the BSA's other argument that it was a "distinctly private" organization and therefore exempt from LAD. Except for age and sex, she noted, the BSA's admissions policy was virtually open to all and, therefore, it was not private.

Assessing the BSA's claim that its First Amendment right of expressive association outweighed LAD, Poritz also found that Dale's membership in the Boy Scouts did not invade its right of expressive association. Dale would not, she declared, "significantly" affect the organization's position on homosexuality because "Boy Scout members do not associate for the purpose of disseminating the belief that homosexuality is immoral" (*Boy Scouts of America v. Dale* 1999, 1223).

Poritz distinguished the U.S. Supreme Court's opinion in *Hurley v. Irish-American Gay, Lesbian and Bisexual Group of Boston* (1995).[26] She observed that unlike the group that sought to march in Boston's St. Patrick's Day Parade with its name on a banner, Dale did not display his sexual orientation in any way at meetings. Moreover, *Hurley* was not dispositive, she said, because it was a free speech case, decided on the basis of the First Amendment's "compelled speech" doctrine, not expressive association.

And although the BSA had argued that *Hurley* controlled in *Dale*, the state high court disagreed, noting that the *Hurley* Court had not followed the *Roberts'* expressive association analysis. Rather, it had obliquely indicated that it would have reached the same result had it followed the *Roberts* approach.[27]

The BSA presented a number of documents, including a 1978 internal memorandum, to show that the words "morally straight" and "clean" in the Scout Oath and Law signified a long-standing belief that homosexuality was immoral.[28] The court disagreed, saying that these writings failed to prove their case, as they either had not been widely distributed throughout the membership or had been promulgated only in 1991 and 1993—after Dale's removal.[29] Instead, the court focused on the Scout Oath and Law in deciding the validity of the BSA's expressive association claim and held that the command to be "morally straight" and "clean" were irrelevant to the membership's shared views on the immorality of homosexuality.

Nor did the court accept the BSA's contention that it expelled Dale on moral grounds; rather, the court believed that, as suggested by the letter to him, the organization was motivated by anti-gay prejudice. The court concluded that the state's compelling interest in eliminating discrimination on the basis of sexual orientation outweighed the BSA's claim of expressive association, prohibiting the Scouts from excluding gays.

The Scouts appealed. The U.S. Supreme Court opinion, announced by Chief Justice William Rehnquist for O'Connor, Scalia, Kennedy, and Clarence Thomas, centered on the BSA's claim that LAD conflicted with its First Amendment right of expressive association (*Boy Scouts of America v. Dale* 2000). Speaking for the majority, Rehnquist outlined three issues in the case: "whether the group engages in expressive association" (648), "whether the forced inclusion of Dale as an assistant scoutmaster would significantly affect the Boy Scouts' ability to advocate public or private viewpoints" (650), and "whether the application of New Jersey's public accommodations law to require that the Boy Scouts accept Dale as an assistant scoutmaster runs afoul of the Scouts' freedom of expressive association" (656).

In answering the first question, Rehnquist explained that the First Amendment allows private organizations that engage in expressive activity to exclude members who advocate opposing views. Reviewing the mission statement as well as the Scout Oath and Law, Rehnquist concluded that the BSA is entitled to First Amendment protection because it instills values and beliefs, including patriotism, reverence, and morality—in other words, expressive activity.

As the state court had done, the Court inquired into the BSA's assertion that Dale's membership would hinder it from expressing its disapproval of homosexuality. However, Rehnquist departed from the precedent set in the trilogy of private club cases in failing to assess the validity of the BSA's assertion and readily accepted its declaration that homosexuality is antithetical to being "morally straight" and "clean." He simply stated he was satisfied that the BSA's documents, including the 1978 internal memorandum and the 1991 and 1993 position statements, substantiated its claim. Thus, in answering the second question, he ruled that courts must defer to the BSA's judgment that "Dale's presence in the Boy Scouts would . . . send a message, both to its youth members and to the world, that the Boy Scouts accepts homosexual conduct as a legitimate form of behavior" (653).

Although the Court had not decided *Hurley* on the basis of freedom of association, Rehnquist cited it for support, declaring that if Dale were an assistant scoutmaster, he would clearly "interfere with the Boy Scouts' choice not to propound a point of view contrary to its beliefs" (*Boy Scouts of America v. Dale* 2000, 654).

The Court never explicitly decided whether the BSA was a public accommodation, but although Rehnquist acknowledged that such laws are not limited to physical locations, he noted that the New Jersey Supreme Court overreached by applying LAD to a private organization with no connection to a physical site. He stressed that the state court's interpretation inevitably leads, as it has done in this case, to a conflict between principles of equality and First Amendment rights of expression.

Rehnquist conceded that the Court had held that a state's compelling interest in eradicating discrimination against women justified enforcing a public accommodations law. But, he emphasized, in those cases, requiring men-only clubs to admit women did not significantly "burden" their First Amendment right of expressive association, and there was no need to balance the state's interests against the club's First Amendment freedoms (*Boy Scouts of America v. Dale* 2000, 658). In this case, Dale's presence as a scout leader would significantly burden the BSA's right of expressive association.

Writing in dissent for Souter, Ruth Bader Ginsburg, and Stephen Breyer, Stevens criticized the Court for departing from precedent by merely accepting the BSA's claim of expressive association to excuse its exclusionary membership policy.[30] Conceding that the BSA had a right to expressive association, he rejected its assertion that a gay scout (or scoutmaster) interfered with it. He argued that the majority had merely accepted the BSA's claims about its views on homosexuality at face value without probing into the truth of its pronouncements and that the phrases "morally straight" and "clean" had never been remotely related to or taken as a position on gays as members.

The BSA documents were ambiguous, Stevens said. In any event, the 1991 and 1993 statements appeared after Dale's expulsion and should be accorded no weight. Indeed, he stressed that although it had ample opportunity to do so prior to expelling Dale, "the BSA never took any clear and unequivocal position on homosexuality" and disseminated no public documents expressing its opposition to homosexuality before expelling Dale on the basis of its alleged policy (676).[31] He noted that it had ample opportunity to do so since at least 1984, when it had submitted amici briefs in *Roberts* and *Duarte*. The BSA was thus clearly aware that courts were scrutinizing the restrictive admission policies of private organizations and balancing their right to expressive association against the dictates of state public accommodation laws. Indeed, he pointed out, because the BSA had been forced to defend itself in discrimination cases in state court, it was aware that it would need to substantiate its claims of expressive association.

The Court's private club cases make it clear, Stevens emphasized, that simply engaging in some expressive activity and loosely connecting an exclusionary policy to that activity does not insulate a group from the reach of a public accommodations law. Quoting from earlier cases, he reiterated that "the relevant question is whether the mere inclusion of the person at issue would 'impose any serious burden,' 'affect in any significant way,' or be 'a substantial restraint upon' the organization's 'shared goals,' 'basic goals,' or 'collective effort to foster beliefs'" (*Boy Scouts of America v. Dale* 2000, 683). In his view, the BSA attempted to justify Dale's expulsion by evoking a latter-day rationalization of its principles, and he was astonished that the majority simply accepted its "litigating posture" (686). He concluded by warning of the danger of subverting the antidiscrimination principles of public accommodations laws by giving credence to assertions of obliquely stated expressions of belief.

Pleased with the ruling, a BSA spokesperson said, "This decision affirms our standing as a private association with the right to set its own standards for membership and leadership" (*Boy Scouts of America News Release* June 28, 2000). Confirming the organization's intent to maintain its exclusionary policy, another official proclaimed, "We believe an avowed homosexual is not a role model for the values espoused in the Scout Oath and Law. We respect other people's right to hold differing opinions and ask that they respect ours" (*Houston Chronicle* June 29, 2000).[32]

Although the Scouts applauded the decision, critics charged that the Court had erred by simply accepting the BSA's assertion that Dale's homosexuality would impair its ability to deliver its expressive message and minimizing the state's interest in combating discrimination on the basis of sexual orientation (Chermerinsky and Fisk 2001; Kelly 2002).[33]

The Supreme Court's imprimatur on the BSA's exclusionary admissions policy led to continued concerns about the effectiveness of state and local laws against discrimination in public accommodations.[34] It also led to speculation that *Dale* would encourage private employers and landlords to evade such laws by arguing that hiring or renting to openly gay persons would send a message of approval of homosexuality (see Lim 2003; Troum 2002).[35] More broadly, there was concern that because of the BSA's status as a state and federally tax-exempt entity and recipient of public benefits, taxpayer dollars were subsidizing its discriminatory practices (see Brennen 2001; Upton 2001).

DALE AND THE LOWER COURTS

Within the next two years, the lower courts revealed a split over how to interpret the U.S. Supreme Court's ruling in *Dale*, in part because the Court was vague on the parameters of the BSA's right of expressive association. Noting the disarray among the lower courts after *Dale*, Griffith (2006, 10) argues that the high court failed to clarify whether the BSA was justified in expelling Dale because of his role "as a gay activist, a gay scout leader, or merely [his] self-identification as being gay." In his view, *Dale* should apply only to adults because the state's interest in preventing discrimination against gay children overrides the BSA's right to exclude them.

Koppelman also believes that *Dale* left some important questions unanswered and created an enigma for the lower courts attempting to comply with it. Prior to *Dale*, he says, the courts applied a "message-based approach," essentially the *Roberts* balancing test, in which organizations were required to defend their exclusionary policies. But some, in his words, "neolibertarians," have argued that *Dale* must be interpreted to require the courts to adopt a complete hands-off policy for all membership decisions by "noncommercial private associations" (Koppelman 2004, 27; see Reuveni 2006). In his view, this approach could render antidiscrimination laws like LAD inoperative when challenged by private organizations. Although Koppelman regards *Dale* as "a mess" and a "muddled" opinion, he is comforted by the fact that at least it retained the *Roberts* "message-based approach," and, considering how the lower courts might have interpreted it, he believes that confusion may be the best possible outcome.

Another unanswered question in the wake of *Dale* is its effect on gay scouts. Much of the opinion focused on Dale's role as a scout leader and the BSA's characterization of him as an inappropriate role model; it did not specifically address its applicability to boys who are not in leadership positions. According to the BSA's lawyer, however, although the question of sexual orientation is largely irrelevant for scouts within the age range of six to fourteen years, "in the unlikely event a 17-year-old would decide to hold himself out as gay, then that person would not be able to be a role model for the scouting principles for younger Scouts" (*Austin*

American-Statesman July 3, 2000). Other courts also interpreted *Dale* to allow the Scouts to restrict gays from serving as members or in leadership positions (see, for example, *Boy Scouts of America, South Florida Council v. Till* 2001).

Two cases illustrate the ambiguity surrounding *Dale* and the extent to which it affected the future of gays in the Scouts. The first case arose when G. Keith Richardson filed an employment discrimination complaint against the Chicago local BSA council in 1992. The complaint, filed with the Chicago Commission on Human Rights, charged the council with violating the city's human rights law by discriminating against him on the basis of his sexual orientation.[36]

In 1996, the commission agreed and imposed a $100 fine, ordering the council to refrain from considering an applicant's sexual orientation; it also awarded Richardson $500 in damages as well as attorney fees and costs of almost $350,000. Declaring that the BSA's "opposition to homosexuality was not a significant, expressive goal," the commission rejected the council's argument that its policy was protected by the First Amendment (765).

The Scouts filed suit in an Illinois trial court, which vacated the award of fees and costs. The court held that Richardson did not have standing in the case because he was not genuinely seeking a job but was merely testing the council's willingness to hire a gay.[37]

On appeal, the appellate court reversed the trial court, holding that the commission had the authority to act despite Richardson's lack of standing (*Chicago Area Council of Boy Scouts of America v. City of Chicago Commission on Human Relations* 2001a). However, it also determined that the commission's injunction not to consider sexual orientation in hiring was too broad in light of *Dale*. Richardson had argued that unlike Dale, who held an important leadership position, he would merely be an employee whose status would not send any messages about homosexuality and thereby would not impair the council's right of expressive association. The appellate court remanded the case to allow the commission to determine whether the position that Richardson sought was expressive or nonexpressive. If the latter, a narrower injunction could be issued because he would not burden the BSA's message by working in that capacity. The court remanded the case to the commission for further fact-finding.[38]

A year later, in *Boy Scouts of America v. District of Columbia Commission on Human Rights* (2002), the District of Columbia Court of Appeals resolved another issue left open in *Dale* when it reversed the finding of the Commission on Human Rights that the BSA and its local council, the National Capital Area Council, violated the district's Human Rights Act.[39] The commission had ordered the BSA to reinstate two dismissed adult leaders and pay them each $50,000 in damages (*Houston Chronicle* June 24, 2001).

The appellate court did not decide whether the act applied to the BSA but held that even if it did, the BSA was not required to accept gays in leadership positions. It dismissed the men's argument that opposition to homosexuality was not an integral part of the BSA's viewpoint, saying that *Dale* had settled that issue. And although the commission had found that the men differed from James Dale because they were not activists, the D.C. Court instead focused on the similarities among them and concluded that there was no discernible difference in the degree to which their presence in the Scouts would burden the BSA's right of expressive association. Thus, although the court implied that activism was an important consideration in *Dale*, in equating any gays who openly acknowledged their sexual orientation with Dale's activism, it seemed to make the point moot.[40]

CONGRESSIONAL REACTION TO *DALE*

On July 19, 2000, less than a month after *Dale* was announced, Representative Lynn Woolsey, a Democrat from California, sponsored a bill called the "Scouting for All Act" (House Resolution [HR] 4892) that attempted to repeal the BSA's federal charter.[41] The relevant portions of section 2 of the bill stated that the BSA "sets an example of intolerance through its discriminatory policy regarding sexual orientation [and] federal support for the Boy Scouts of America supports the organization's policy to exclude homosexuals, [therefore] a policy of excluding homosexuals is contradictory to the Federal Government's support for diversity and tolerance and should not be condoned as patriotic, charitable, or educational."

Introducing the bill, Woolsey indicated that although the Supreme Court had decided that the "Boy Scouts have the right to establish anti-gay policy," the real issue is "whether the Boy Scouts' anti-gay policy is right." She and the other bill sponsors believed that Congress must express its disapproval of the policy and make it clear "that the Federal Government . . . does not support intolerance" (*Congressional Record* 2000, H6565). Woolsey compared the BSA's policy with the Daughters of the American Revolution (DAR) action in 1939 that refused to permit opera star Marian Anderson to sing at DAR-operated Constitutional Hall because she was African American; the DAR was also a federally chartered organization (*Congressional Record* 2000, H7448).[42]

Most members of Congress opposed Woolsey's proposed bill, criticizing it for attempting to interfere with the BSA's admission policies.[43] During debate on the floor of the House, Representative Steve Buyer, a Republican from Indiana, called it an "extremist measure" that "promotes intolerance." He praised the Supreme Court decision for "allow[ing] the

Scouts to continue developing young men of strong moral character without imposing the mores on them that they find abhorrent" (*Congressional Record* 2000, H7006).

Representative Greg Walden, a Republican from Oregon, placed a statement in the *Congressional Record* that called Woolsey's measure a "misguided attempt to bully one of the finest youth organizations in America [and] represents an incredibly arrogant attempt to impose the beliefs of a small minority on a private institution." He believed it "absurd that Congress is targeting an institution as wholesome as the Boy Scouts" and "urge[d] his colleagues to reject this offensive legislation and send a clear message to the nation's Scouts that they have both the support and admiration of the United States Congress" (*Congressional Record* 2000, E1525).

Although it was referred to the Judiciary Committee, no hearings were held on the bill. Later, against Woolsey's wishes (and without her knowledge), Republicans brought the bill to the floor of the House under a suspension of the rules, barring members from asking questions or offering amendments. Much of the debate on the House floor on September 12, 2000, was over this procedure, with Democrats accusing Republicans of preventing them from holding hearings and giving adequate consideration to the bill and Republicans countering that the Democrats should be pleased that they were permitted to vote on it (*Congressional Record* 2000, H7448). A day later, on September 13, 2000, the measure was soundly rejected in a vote of 362 to 12 (*Congressional Record* 2000, H7521).[44]

Although it never reached the Senate, the day after it was rejected in the House, it was decried in the Senate as well. Without explicitly referring to the subject matter of the bill, Senator Strom Thurmond, a Republican from South Carolina, called it "absurd" and declared that although he "recognize[d] that traditional values and institutions which uphold those values are under attack and considered out of date by some elements of our society," he found it "disappointing that at a time when the United States is in critical need of organizations to teach our youth character and integrity, some would choose to attack the Boy Scouts of America" (*Congressional Record* 2000, S8565).

Woolsey's voice was a solitary one. Most members of Congress reacted to *Dale* with legislation and resolutions supporting the Scouts. A more typical reaction to *Dale* was Colorado Republican Thomas Tancredo's proposed bill. Titled the "Scouts Honor Act," it precluded the use of federal funds "to discriminate against . . . or deny or withdraw access to public property" for the BSA's exercise of its associational rights or to require the BSA to "accept as a member or volunteer an individual whose sexual orientation, sexual behavior, religious beliefs, or absence of religious beliefs . . . is inconsistent with the organization's policies, programs, morals, or mission." Although it did not pass, it reflected the views of the majority of Congress.

THE BOY SCOUTS COME UNDER ATTACK

The Boy Scouts, coming under a barrage of criticism when its policies became known after *Dale*, became the target of attacks from hundreds of public bodies across the nation. School and park districts, police and fire departments, and state and local government agencies withdrew support from the BSA, most often by ending their sponsorship, to express their disapproval of its anti-gay stance. Almost 350 school districts in ten states withdrew their sponsorship or disassociated themselves in other ways. The Scouts lost millions of dollars when corporate sponsors, such as Chase Manhattan Bank, Wells Fargo, and Levi Strauss, ceased their donations, contributing to a decline in the BSA's financial health. The Pew Charitable Trust suspended a $100,000 grant to the Cradle of Liberty Council in Philadelphia (*San Francisco Chronicle* December 23, 2001; *Boston Globe* September 14, 2003). Criticism also came from prominent individuals; producer Steven Spielberg, a member of the BSA's national advisory board for ten years, resigned, saying that he "could no longer serve a group that practices 'intolerance and discrimination'" (France 2001).

Even more significant was the reaction by United Way chapters around the country. As reported by Lambda Legal (2003), United Way charitable campaigns had been substantial sources of funding for the national organization, topping $83 million a year. Following *Dale*, more than fifty United Way chapters in cities such as San Francisco, Miami, Seattle, and Philadelphia discontinued their support, citing the United Way's non-discrimination policy. The magnitude of the United Way reaction was sharply illustrated in August 2001, when the United Way of Central New Jersey announced that it would continue its financial assistance to the Central New Jersey Council because the council agreed not to discriminate against gays despite the national organization's exclusionary policy. The agreement came about after a group of Central New Jersey United Way board members had raised questions about continuing the council's funding after *Dale*. The amount involved was $81,350. Such action was replicated across the nation (*New York Times* August 31, 2001).

The American Medical Association, although without explicitly mentioning the Boy Scouts, urged organizations "to reconsider exclusionary policies that are based on sexual orientation," linking such policies to high incidences of gay teen depression and suicide (France 2001; *Houston Chronicle* June 24, 2001). And although the Roman Catholic and Mormon churches, the largest sponsors of scouting nationwide, supported *Dale*, the United Church of Christ and the Union of American Hebrew Congregations, as well as some Baptist and Episcopal congregations, expressed opposition to it (France 2001).[45]

Within the organization, local councils in New York, Chicago, Providence, and Los Angeles, to mention a few, unsuccessfully attempted to persuade the national organization to abandon its anti-gay policy (*New York Times* February 27, 2001). In 2004, the Philadelphia-area Cradle of Liberty Council went further by formulating a nondiscrimination policy, independent of the national BSA's position; it was forced to rescind the policy in response to threats from the national organization. Local charters in New York City; Stamford, Connecticut; and Oak Park, Illinois, lost their charters from the BSA when their sponsors objected to the anti-gay policy (*New York Times* January 28, 2001; July 1, 2001).

Council leaders across the nation, from cities such as Los Angeles, San Francisco, Minneapolis, Chicago, New York, and Boston, asked the national organization to allow them autonomy in determining policy toward gays as troop leaders; it refused (*New York Times* July 3, 2003). In New York, chancellor Harold Levy ordered that public schools cease sponsoring most activities of Boy Scout groups and prevented the Scouts from recruiting members during school hours (*New York Times* June 17, 2001).

A year after the decision, a representative of the Scouts conceded that the reactions to *Dale* had created financial problems and public relations concerns for the BSA, but hastened to add that the reactions were not all negative. According to him, the Boy Scouts had received "cards, letters, donations, volunteers . . . [and] remains strong. We're reaching more young people than we did a year ago," he insisted; "we're financially healthy and we're looking forward to continuing our mission of helping build the character of America's young people." Moreover, he noted, the decrease in United Way contributions was overshadowed by an increase in donations from other sources (*Houston Chronicle* June 24, 2001).

SCHOOL FACILITIES

Although nationally few schools took steps to bar scouts from meeting on school premises (*New York Times* June 17, 2001), the Broward County, Florida, school district was an exception. Prior to *Dale*, the board had made its school facilities readily available to numerous groups, including the Scouts. Additionally, the school board and the local Scout council had an arrangement in which school administrators assisted in recruitment efforts; the agreement between them included a nondiscrimination provision.

Following *Dale*, the school superintendent questioned the council about the nondiscrimination clause, asking whether it intended to honor it. A council official responded that the clause was not relevant to its membership decisions and threatened to sue if the district attempted to dislocate the Scouts, citing viewpoint discrimination. Despite the threat, the school district sent the requisite thirty-day notice to the council board to terminate the relationship as well as to deny them the use of school facilities. In discussions, school board members stressed their obligation to take a stand against discrimination, but they had made no attempt to sever relationships with other groups, including those that had membership restrictions based on gender, age, national origin, race, and religion. When the board refused to allow the Scouts to continue to use the school building and buses, the council sued, claiming viewpoint discrimination and infringement on its rights of expressive association and equal protection. It sought an injunction to restrain the board from denying it space to hold meetings (*Till* 2001).[46]

Both sides to the dispute claimed the moral high ground, with the Scouts citing their First Amendment guarantees and the school authorities pointing to their antidiscrimination policies. The legal issue to be resolved was whether the schools were guilty of illegal viewpoint discrimination by denying the Scouts access to public facilities because of their anti-gay message.

Analysis of viewpoint discrimination begins with *Cornelius v. NAACP Legal Defense & Educational Fund, Inc.* (1985), in which the federal government attempted to exclude certain advocacy groups from its charitable campaign. Because the high court ruled in *Cornelius* that the charitable campaign was a nonpublic forum, it determined that the government could limit access to it only if the restrictions were "reasonable" and unrelated to "the speaker's view" (800).

Cornelius was part of a long line of cases spelling out types of forums and the varying degrees of First Amendment protection accorded speakers in each.[47] The first is the "traditional public forum," such as a street or park, which has long been open to the public for meeting and debating. The state may impose neutral time, place, and manner restrictions on speech in a traditional public forum, but it must have a compelling interest to restrict the content of the speech, and the restriction must be narrowly tailored to attain that interest. The second type is a limited, or designated, public forum in which, based on the purpose of the forum, the government may reasonably restrict the groups involved and the subjects for discussion, but it may not restrict speech on the basis of the viewpoint expressed. The Supreme Court includes "metaphysical" space within the definition of a forum; in *Rosenberger v. Rector and Visitors of University of Virginia* (1995, 830), it depicted the university's program of subsidizing student clubs as a limited public forum. The third type of forum, the nonpublic forum, is controlled by the government and may be made available for some types of expression. As in the limited public forum, the government may impose reasonable time, place, and manner restrictions but may not exercise viewpoint discrimination in restricting the speech (for further discussion of access to forums, see Fast 2002; Reuveni 2006).

In ruling on the motion for a preliminary injunction, Florida Federal District Court Judge Donald Middlebrooks began by acknowledging the inevitable conflict between the board's antidiscrimination policy and its obligation to allow speech in the forum. However, he explained, because it had established a limited public forum, the board may not unreasonably exclude speech or discriminate on the basis of the viewpoint contained in the speech. Middlebrooks relied on a Fifth Circuit opinion in *Knights of the Ku Klux Klan v. East Baton Rouge Parish School Board* (1978), in which the court held that the First Amendment required the school board to allow the Klan access to after-hours school facilities. Doing so, it ruled, would not identify it with the Klan's message.

The Broward County Board attempted to distinguish *Knights of the Ku Klux Klan*, arguing that it would be painful for any children and teachers who were excluded from scouting events. Perhaps so, the judge said, but that was an inevitable price to pay for the First Amendment, adding that if parents withdrew their children from scouting, the Scouts might be persuaded to change the policy. Finally, the judge noted that the board's action was not narrowly tailored enough to serve its purpose; indeed, he found that it would have no effect on the group's discriminatory policies. Thus, the court held that the BSA met the standard for a preliminary injunction and enjoined the school board from preventing the Scouts from using its facilities and buses.

Notwithstanding the BSA's victory in *Till*, members of Congress expressed concern that other school districts would follow Broward County's lead and attempt to bar the Scouts from meeting in their schools. They seized the opportunity to act during the consideration of the Bush administration's signature piece of education legislation, the law known as the No Child Left Behind Act.[48] Senator Jesse Helms, a Republican from North Carolina, and Representative Van Hilleary, Republican of Tennessee, each sponsored amendments to ensure the Boy Scouts equal access to public school facilities. Speaking on the floor of the House, Hilleary explained that his amendment was necessary because

all over the country the Boy Scouts are under attack and being thrown out of public facilities that are open to other similarly situated groups. From Florida to California, the Boy Scouts are being removed, not because they support an illegal right, but as retribution for the Supreme Court's ruling in the *Boy Scouts of America versus Dale*. The Boy Scouts won this case but they have repeatedly once again defended this right in court. Thus far, the courts upheld the Boy Scouts' first amendment rights in assembly and speech and overturn their removal from public meetings areas such as schools. However, more and more schools continue to act, and the Scouts repeatedly have to get an injunction in court. This amendment is designed to stop this wasteful cycle in litigation and harassment. If one allows for an open forum for other groups to meet, it is only fair to allow equal access to the Boy Scouts. (*Congressional Record* 2001, H2618)

About a month later, Helms and several others echoed these views in the Senate. He began by explaining that in *Dale*, the Court "found it essential to uphold constitutional rights of Boy Scouts of America, oddly enough, to abide by and practice the Boy Scout moral guidelines for membership and leadership, including no obligation to accept homosexuals as Boy Scout members or leaders." But, now, he said, "radical militants . . . are pressuring school districts across the country to exclude the Boy Scouts of America from federally funded public school facilities . . . because the Boy Scouts would not agree to surrender their first amendment rights and because they would not accept the agenda of the radical left" (*Congressional Record* 2001, S6249). Senate Majority Leader Trent Lott, Republican from Mississippi, added, "I don't know quite how to react to the fact that in America even the Boy Scouts seem to be under attack. Is motherhood and apple pie next? Is there nothing sacred anymore?" (*Congressional Record* 2001, S6250).

Opposing the Helms amendment, Patty Murray, a Democrat from Washington, pointed out that federal law already guarantees equal access to all groups and that the bill would extend "special, unequal access for just one group" and force local school boards to always offer their facilities or face the loss of federal aid (*Congressional Record* 2001, S6251).

Senator Richard Durbin, a Democrat from Illinois, warned that the Helms amendment "raises some serious problems" for school districts with antidiscrimination policies. "What this amendment is trying to do is, frankly, create an environment which is antithetical, antagonistic to the beliefs of many school districts which have basically said: We will not sponsor organizations that discriminate" (*Congressional Record* 2001, S6254).

The Hilleary amendment won approval by a voice vote in the House on May 23, 2001; on June 14, 2001, the Helms amendment, initially limited to the Boy Scouts, was adopted in a vote of 51 to 49; it was subsequently amended by the Senate in a voice vote to include other youth groups, and the Senate and House approved the Conference Report in December 2001 (*CQ Almanac* 2001).[49]

CHARITABLE CAMPAIGN

Although Congress preserved the BSA's access to public school facilities, other public entities attempted to take action against the BSA and its local councils over the next several years. In May 2000, the Connecticut State Employee Campaign Committee excluded the Connecticut Rivers Council and three other councils from participating in the state's workplace charitable contribution campaign.

After the New Jersey Supreme Court had declared that the BSA policy of excluding gays violated state law, the executive director of the Connecticut Commission on Human Rights and Opportunities (CHRO) wrote to the campaign committee, expressing her view that to permit the BSA to participate would make the state a party to discrimination and therefore violate the state's guarantee against discrimination on the basis of sexual orientation.[50]

Given the apparent contradiction between the BSA's declaration of its nondiscrimination policy (when initially applying to be in the campaign), the CHRO asked for an explanation, asking it to reconcile the affirmation of nondiscrimination with its policy of excluding gays. The BSA responded with a letter outlining its exclusionary policy, and the CHRO voted to bar it from participating in the campaign.

On June 7, 2000, the BSA, which had benefited from the campaign for thirty years, sued. It charged the state with violating its First Amendment right of expressive association by excluding it from the charitable campaign on the basis of its viewpoint as well as violating provisions of state law.[51] After the U.S. Supreme Court announced *Dale*, the campaign committee sought the CHRO's advice on the effect of the ruling. The CHRO reaffirmed its view that the BSA should be excluded from the charitable campaign because of its discriminatory policy.

Connecticut District Court Judge Warren Eginton awarded the state summary judgment in *Boy Scouts of America v. Wyman* (2002). The Scouts appealed, citing the U.S. Supreme Court's ruling in *Dale*.

Speaking for a unanimous panel of the Second Circuit, Judge Guido Calabresi treated the charitable campaign as a nonpublic forum, asking whether the committee's decision to remove the BSA from the campaign was reasonable and viewpoint neutral or whether it was based on the BSA's exclusionary policy toward gays (*Wyman* 2003). He began by determining whether *Dale* allowed the BSA to exclude only gay activists from leadership positions or whether it permitted the organization to exclude all gays: leaders and members, activist or not. But he sidestepped that issue, holding that, at a minimum, *Dale* protected the BSA's constitutionally protected right to bar gay activists. However, because the matter had come to the appellate court on the appeal of the district court's award of summary judgment, there was insufficient evidence in the record to determine the basis of the committee's decision.

Calabresi agreed that the committee's action implicated the BSA's right of expressive association.[52] However, he distinguished the facts in *Wyman* from the facts in *Dale*. In the latter, the state law directly infringed on the BSA's right of expressive association by requiring the Scouts to put Dale in a leadership role; in *Wyman*, however, the BSA's First Amendment right was only indirectly affected by the committee.[53]

In inquiring whether the state's action was consistent with the First Amendment, Calabresi emphasized that he must look to the purpose of the law to determine whether it was reasonable and viewpoint neutral. And because the legislature had intended it to end discrimination against gays, not to curb expressive association, he found the Connecticut law viewpoint neutral on its face and rejected the BSA's charge that it had been targeted because of its anti-gay position. He concluded that the BSA had not been subject to viewpoint discrimination because it had not shown that it was treated differently from comparable groups; in other words, the law affected all groups that discriminated on the basis of sexual orientation equally.

Citing *Cornelius* to illustrate the permissible limits of government regulation of nonpublic forums, the court held that the committee's action to exclude the BSA was a reasonable means to advance the state's "legitimate interest in preventing conduct that discriminates on the basis of sexual orientation" (*Wyman* 2003, 98).[54] Thus, ruling that the state's actions were reasonable and viewpoint neutral and had not infringed on the BSA's right of expressive association, the appeals court affirmed the lower court, permitting the state to exclude the BSA from its charitable campaign.[55]

MARINA FACILITIES

In 1998, a group of fourteen Berkeley Sea Scouts sued the city, claiming, among other things, that it violated their right to freedom of association under the First Amendment and the Unruh Act and breached its contractual obligations.

The Berkeley Scouts, an ethnically diverse group open to boys and girls, was affiliated with the BSA and the Mount Diablo Regional Council. Beginning in the 1930s, it was granted free space at the city's boat facilities. In 1997, the city adopted a nondiscrimination policy that prohibited private groups that discriminated on the basis of sex, religion, or sexual orientation, among other characteristics, from using city funds or property at the marina.[56] The next year, the city informed the Scouts that they would no longer have free access to the marina unless they provided a written guarantee that they had ended their policy of discriminating against gays and atheists. The Scouts attempted to placate the city, arguing that they had never discriminated on the basis of sexual orientation; they said that they would comply with antidiscrimination laws but that they would lose their BSA charter if they actually adopted a nondiscrimination policy.[57] Because of this response, the city began to charge the group rent for space at the marina.

A California superior court judge dismissed the action, and the appeals court affirmed. Speaking for the appellate court, Judge Lawrence Stevens ruled that the city had not deprived the Sea Scouts of freedom of speech and association under the First Amendment and the Unruh Act because it had not "attempted to muzzle anyone's speech" or to penalize it for its association with the BSA (*Evans v. City of Berkeley* 2002, 703). Nor, he said, had it ordered the Sea Scouts to end the discriminatory policy or give up its associations; rather, it had merely taken away a benefit. The court emphasized the government's well-established authority to condition a subsidy on the cessation of a discriminatory policy.

The California Supreme Court unanimously affirmed the lower courts, dismissing the claim by the Sea Scouts that the city was punishing them for the BSA policy of discrimination (*Evans* 2006a). The Sea Scouts had claimed they were victims of "guilt by association," for there was no evidence that they had discriminated or intended to discriminate (399). Indeed, they argued, they had agreed not to discriminate. The court agreed with the city that the verbal assurances of the Sea Scouts were insufficient and that it was justified in securing a written guarantee of nondiscrimination before providing a subsidy. Moreover, it declared, because of the relationship of the Sea Scouts with the BSA, it was reasonable for the city to believe that the Sea Scouts would be unable to provide such assurances.

To dispel the charge of viewpoint discrimination, the court cited a long line of cases in which the courts permitted the government to condition funding on a recipient's conduct. In its view, refusing to subsidize a group does not equate to censoring its viewpoint or infringing on freedom of association; it simply requires the recipient to make a choice. Nor, it held, did the city force the Sea Scouts to terminate its relationship with the national organization; the threat to terminate came from the BSA. It ended by saying that it found "no authority for the extraordinary proposition that government infringes on associational rights by offering one group a financial benefit that, if accepted, could lead another group to sever its association with the recipient" (405).[58]

Commenting happily on the victory in the supreme court, the Berkeley city attorney said, "We believe now it is crystal clear that taxpayers have no constitutional duty to fund discriminatory clubs" (*Inside Bay Area* October 17, 2006).

PUBLIC LANDS

A few months after the high court decided *Dale*, two couples (one lesbian and the other agnostic) and their sons contested the arrangement between San Diego and the BSA in which the Scouts held leases on public parklands. The city had entered into long-term lease arrangements at little or no cost with the Desert-Pacific Council for the highly desirable properties in Balboa and Mission Bay parks. Each lease contained a clause prohibiting discrimination on the basis of sexual orientation and religion as well as other characteristics, but the parties agreed that the clause had no effect on the organization's membership decisions. The plaintiffs claimed that the city violated the federal and state constitutional prohibitions against establishment of and aid to religion. A few months after the lawsuit was initiated, the parties entered into a new lease in which the Scouts were required to pay $2,500 a year in fees (*San Diego Union-Tribune* December 22, 2006).

Although the city settled privately with the two couples in January 2004, the Boy Scouts insisted on taking the matter to trial. The outcome of the ruling in *Barnes-Wallace v. Boy Scouts of America* (2003) seemed likely when the district court judge began by characterizing the high court's opinion in *Dale* as allowing the BSA to hold "long-held discriminatory anti-homosexual, anti-agnostic, and anti-atheist" views (1263).

Ruling on the parties' cross motions for summary judgment, California Federal District Court Judge Napoleon Jones Jr. engaged in a lengthy analysis of the Supreme Court's establishment clause decision making and identified the crucial question in the case as "whether government aid has the effect of advancing religion because the leases either result in governmental indoctrination or define their recipient by reference to a religion" (1269).

Offering innumerable examples of the BSA's entanglement with religion, he depicted the BSA as a religious organization and delved into its relationship with the government to determine if the leases were part of a "religion-neutral" program (1273). Jones rejected the council's contention that the city granted hundreds of similar leases to nonprofit agencies, finding that the records showed that the Balboa Park lease was not part of the normal leasing process but came about as a result of a special arrangement with the city that was unavailable to others. Accepting the plaintiffs' argument that the city's actions in leasing the Balboa Park land was unconstitutional, he concluded that "a reasonable observer would most naturally view the exclusive negotiations and effective preclusion of secular groups as the City's endorsement of the BSA-DPC because of its inherently religious program and practices" (1276).

Jones granted the plaintiffs summary judgment and held that the Balboa Park land leases also contravened the "no preference" and "no aid" clauses of the state constitution and awarded the plaintiffs summary judgment on those claims as well.[59]

In a few brief paragraphs at the end of the opinion, he addressed the council's assertion that terminating the leases infringed on its freedom of association and constituted unconstitutional viewpoint discrimination. The plaintiffs are not asking the court to interfere with its discriminatory policies, he said, nor does the defendant's right of expressive association equate to a right to government support. He rejected the defendant's argument that he should follow *Rosenberger's* analysis of viewpoint discrimination. Unlike the University of Virginia's neutral program of support for disparate student groups, San Diego does not have a "religion-neutral" leasing program that includes the BSA as well as other beneficiaries. Moreover, there is no illegal viewpoint discrimination when the government decides which organizations are appropriate beneficiaries of its aid. Citing *Cornelius* and *Wyman* (2003), Jones held that the city would not be guilty of illegal viewpoint discrimination even if it were motivated by the BSA's discriminatory policy because its purpose would be to combat discrimination, not to retaliate against the BSA for discriminating.

On appeal, in *Barnes-Wallace v. City of San Diego* (2006), the Ninth Circuit certified several questions to the California Supreme Court, asking it to adjudicate the state constitutional issues. The circuit court stayed Jones's ruling pending a response from the state high court.[60]

CONGRESS (AGAIN) INTERVENES FOR THE BOY SCOUTS

Another lawsuit, initiated in 2000, again sparked congressional intervention in favor of the Boy Scouts. Although the BSA was not a defendant in the case and the issue did not revolve around gay rights, it seemed clear that *Dale* had made members of Congress, especially Republicans, sensitive to all attacks on the Scouts. It spurred them to action, and in defending the Scouts against the charge of religious discrimination, members of Congress frequently criticized gay rights activism against the Scouts.

Winkler v. Chicago School Reform Board (2000) began when five plaintiffs (two clergymen, two community leaders, and an Eagle Scout) filed suit against the Chicago School Board and the U.S. Transportation Command. Suing as taxpayers, they charged the defendants with violating the First Amendment by sponsoring scouting programs in which adherence to God plays an important role.[61] Although gay rights advocates were not parties to the litigation, there were numerous veiled (and not-so-veiled) references from BSA supporters to the Scouts being under siege from a coalition of liberal, secular, and gay rights groups.

District Court Judge Blanche Manning granted the federal agency's motion to dismiss, ruling that the plaintiffs lacked standing to sue as federal taxpayers. However, because the rules of standing are not as strict for state taxpayers, she denied the board's motion to dismiss.[62]

The plaintiffs returned to court, again naming the Chicago School Board and adding the Department of Defense (DOD) and the Department of Housing and Urban Development (HUD) and their heads as defendants. They charged the agencies with acting under Congress's direction and spending federal tax money on scouting programs, thus violating the First Amendment's establishment clause. Specifically, they cited federal laws governing the DOD's sponsorship of BSA activities at military installations and its support for international and national Boy Scout jamborees. They pointed to DOD's and the National Guard's support in providing supplies, transportation, equipment, and facilities for several organizations, including the Boy Scouts. Similarly, they claimed that HUD's expenditures under the Community Development Block Grant (CDBG) program and the Public Housing Drug Elimination Program were unconstitutional. Although Manning dismissed the actions against HUD and DOD, she found that the plaintiffs' allegations satisfied the requirements for federal taxpayer standing in their suits against the secretaries of these agencies in their official capacities, at least as far as the "motion to dismiss" stage of the litigation (*Winkler v. Chicago School Reform Board* 2001).[63]

On March 16, 2005, Manning ruled once again on the parties' cross motions for summary judgment. In a complex decision, she granted the plaintiffs' motion for summary judgment on the statute relating to the jamboree and HUD's motion for summary judgment on the CDBG program (*Winkler v. Chicago School Reform Board* 2005a).[64]

Three months later, Manning permanently enjoined DOD from providing aid to future Boy Scout jamborees (*Winkler v. Chicago School Reform Board* 2005b). At the plaintiffs' request, her injunction did not take effect until after the upcoming jamboree planned for the week of July 25 through August 3, 2005 (*Chicago Daily Law Bulletin* April 4, 2006).

On March 16, 2005, the same day Manning's decision was announced, the "Support Our Scouts Act of 2005" was introduced in both houses of the 109th Congress. In a lengthy statement to support her bill, HR 1337, Jo Ann Davis, a Republican from Virginia, said,

> There are some who believe that this simple acknowledgment of God by young men is reason to sever a nearly 100-year-old relationship between the Boy Scouts and the Federal Government. This amendment will ensure that the Boy Scouts are treated fairly by guaranteeing their right to equal access to public facilities, forums and programs, and will clarify Federal law

so that the Boy Scouts of America will receive the same amount of support from the Department of Defense as any other non-profit organization in this country, including the right to continue the Boy Scout Jamboree at Fort A.P. Hill in Caroline County, Virginia, in my district. The Department of Defense has every right to support the activities of the Boy Scouts of America, and this amendment will protect this important relationship. This relationship between the Scouts and DOD should not be manipulated or infringed upon. The national jamboree is an incomparable opportunity for training our military, and it would be a detriment to our armed services and to the Boy Scouts to jeopardize it by frivolous lawsuits. (*Congressional Record* 2005, H4006-7)

An identical bill, Senate Bill 642, was introduced in the Senate by Majority Leader Frist. The bill, offered as an amendment to the Defense Authorization Bill, would reverse *Winkler* and allow the Defense Department to continue its support of the jamboree by preventing federal agencies from refusing to allow scouts to hold meetings or camping events on federal property.[65] Section 2 would reverse the Second Circuit's ruling in *Wyman* (2003) by amending section 109 of the 1974 Housing and Community Development Act to bar state or local government recipients of funds under the act from forbidding youth organizations equal access to a public or nonpublic forum.[66]

Speaking on the Senate floor on July 21, 2005, Frist reminded his colleagues that he was "offering the legislation [because] since the Supreme Court decided *Boy Scouts of America v. Dale,* Boy Scouts of America's relationships with government at all levels have been the target of multiple lawsuits." Aside from linking the legislation to *Dale* (to reinforce the reference to gays), he also portrayed the image of the Boy Scouts under siege from the American Civil Liberties Union (ACLU), emphasizing that "the Federal Government has been defending a lawsuit brought by the ACLU aimed at severing the ties between Boy Scouts and the Departments of Defense and HUD."[67] Referring to the *Winkler* litigation, he noted that "the ACLU of Illinois claims that Defense Department sponsorship violates the first amendment because the Scouts are a religious organization. This is a red herring," he charged. The real problem is that "the Scouts are a youth organization that is committed to developing qualities, such as patriotism, integrity, loyalty, honesty, and other values, in our Nation's boys and young men. Part of that development is asking them to acknowledge a higher authority regardless of denomination. . . . Such acknowledgment and respect" he stressed, "is an integral part of our culture, our values, and our traditions" (*Congressional Record* 2005, S8602).

During debate over the measure, James Inhofe, a Republican from Oklahoma, stressed the "need to reaffirm our support for the vital work they [the Scouts] have done and continue to do." Also citing the lower court ruling in *Winkler* (with an implicit reference to gay rights advocacy groups), Inhofe insisted that the bill was necessary "because the Boy Scouts have come under attack from aggressive liberal groups blatantly pushing their own agenda" (*Congressional Record* 2005, S3271).

To celebrate the upcoming passage of the bill, Frist recalled the BSA's victimization. "Over the last few years," he proclaimed, "the Boy Scouts have been subjected to repeated attempts to exclude them from public facilities. The attacks have mounted so quickly that exclusion from Government forums has become the greatest legal challenge for the existence of the Boy Scouts" (*Congressional Record* 2005, S13976). He released a statement when the Senate approved the conference report on December 21, 2005, saying that the bill "preserves the longstanding relationship between the Defense Department and the Scouts, ensures that the Scouts have access to public facilities across the United States, and expresses strong Congressional support for the Boy Scouts of America." He added, "I sincerely hope the clear voice of Congress on this issue will quell the senseless legal and political attacks on the Boy Scouts especially at a time when our nation needs the organization's emphasis on strong character and community service more than ever" (*State News Service* December 21, 2005).

On January 6, 2006, the president signed the Save Our Scouts Act of 2005 into law as §1058 of the National Defense Authorization Act for Fiscal Year 2006.[68]

The government appealed Manning's decision, supported by an amicus brief from the BSA.[69] Two days before oral argument in the Seventh Circuit, an ACLU staff attorney explained that the "appeal is not about equal access by the Boy Scouts to government aid"; rather, he said, "it's about special access" (*Chicago Daily Law Bulletin* April 4, 2006). The case had reached the Seventh Circuit after the president signed the Support Our Scouts Act of 2005 into law. In a decision announced on April 4, 2007, the court of appeals reversed Manning and dismissed the action—on the grounds that the plaintiffs lacked standing to sue (*Winkler v. Gates* 2007).[70]

THE PHILADELPHIA STORY

When it seemed as if BSA litigation had finally run its course, on May 23, 2008, the Cradle of Liberty Council (CLC) of the BSA, covering the area of Delaware and southeastern Pennsylvania, filed a federal lawsuit against the City of Philadelphia (*Cradle of Liberty Council v. City of Philadelphia* 2008a).[71] The conflict between the two sides had been brewing for almost a decade—ever since *Dale* was decided—with the CLC persisting in its exclusionary policies and city officials intent on enforcing the antidiscrimination ordinance.

Among myriad state and federal charges, the CLC contended that the city retaliated against it for exercising its First Amendment right of expressive association. Additionally, it charged that by singling it out among other groups and organizations with restrictive membership policies and denying it access to a government-created forum, the city was guilty of viewpoint discrimination as well as equal protection violations.[72]

The litigation arose in 2003 when Philadelphia Mayor John Street's legal department determined that the CLC's anti-gay leadership policies violated the 1982 Fair Practices Ordinance, which prohibits taxpayer support for any group that discriminates on the basis of religion, race, color, and sexual orientation, among others characteristics. The city announced that the CLC would be asked to vacate its building headquarters on 22nd and Winter streets in Center City.

In part to cement its relationship with the local United Way chapter, the CLC—the third largest in the nation, serving more than 80,000 young men—attempted to depart from the national organization's discriminatory policy by unanimously voting to end discrimination against gays. It rescinded the policy a month later when the national organization threatened to revoke its charter and replace its board (*Philadelphia Inquirer* December 21, 2003; September 17, 2003).

Amid the CLC's promise that it would conform to the city's antidiscrimination law and its assertion that it was trying to engineer a compromise that would satisfy the city and the national BSA, it expelled an eighteen-year-old Philadelphia Life Scout who had disclosed that he was gay at the National BSA Convention. Defending the expulsion, a CLC official explained that the decision was made after a news conference in which the scout announced he was gay. "Our staff knew he was gay and never made a big deal about it. He decided to make a big deal about it. The 'don't ask, don't tell policy' is pretty clear" (*Pittsburgh Post-Gazette* June 13, 2003). There had been no public mention of a "don't ask, don't tell" policy before this.

Over the next two years, no action was taken by either side, but CLC leadership seemed to be moving toward a statement against discrimination modeled after the one adopted by several Greater New York councils in 2002. In June 2005, the CLC adopted a policy that "prejudice, intolerance and unlawful discrimination in any form are unacceptable" (*Philadelphia Inquirer* July 27, 2006). The city complained, however, that the policy was ambiguous, never mentioning sexual orientation explicitly, and the CLC never clarified it, despite requests to do so. Then, on July 20, 2006, a new city solicitor wrote the CLC, informing it that the policy statement was insufficient and that the Fair Practices Act prevented the city from subsidizing the CLC's use of its headquarters building. It ordered the CLC to revoke its membership restrictions or begin to pay the city a "fair market" rent.[73] If it failed to do either, the letter stated, it would be evicted.

Immediately after the letter, the Fairmont Park Commission, which owned the property, voted to end the CLC's use of the building. And, on May 31, 2007, the Philadelphia City Council voted 16 to 1 to order the CLC to vacate the building by May 31, 2008 (*New York Times* December 6, 2007).[74]

On May 23, 2008, the CLC filed suit against the city on First Amendment grounds and in doing so stayed the eviction proceedings (*Cradle of Liberty Council* 2008a). On September 26, 2008, Federal District Court Judge Ronald Buckwalter declined to dismiss the case, holding that the CLC had presented sufficient evidence to show that its First Amendment rights may have been violated (*Cradle of Liberty Council* 2008b).

SUMMARY

The Boy Scouts have long maintained the right to exclude certain classes of individuals, such as women, atheists, and gays, from membership. Not surprisingly, numerous plaintiffs turned to the courts to challenge the BSA's exclusionary policies, relying chiefly on subnational public accommodations laws that sprang up around the nation during the 1970s and 1980s. The gay rights cases likely received the most media attention over the past several years, with litigants on both sides of the controversy adopting a rights-based discourse, appealing to broader principles of freedom of expression and equality.

The first barrier the plaintiffs had to overcome was to persuade the courts that the BSA was a "place of public accommodation" within the meaning of state and local public accommodations laws. Most courts rejected their arguments, as they construed the laws narrowly with a literal interpretation of the term "place of public accommodations."

However, in 1998, gay rights advocates succeeded in surmounting this hurdle and successfully argued that the BSA's discriminatory membership policy violated the state law against discrimination. In defending itself against the gay rights litigants, the BSA asserted that its First Amendment right of freedom of association permitted it to determine qualifications for membership and override the antidiscrimination principles of the state law. On appeal, notwithstanding contrary rulings in men-only club membership cases, the U.S. Supreme Court accepted the BSA's claim that the First Amendment protected its right to exclude gay scouts and scout leaders because they would vitiate its message of disapproval of homosexuality.

Congress reacted to the Supreme Court decision with a resolution praising the BSA and supporting the organization's right to reject members that it believed contravened its principles and ideals. Despite the endorsement by Congress, the Boy Scouts received negative publicity and harsh criticism for the exclusionary membership policy from various private individuals and organizations as well as public entities. And when a number of public agencies attempted to restrict the organization's access to public facilities, it was the BSA's turn to seek refuge in the courts, claiming that it was being subjected to unlawful discrimination because of its lawful policy of excluding gay members.

Although the first case resulted in a victory for the BSA in federal court, Congress intervened again with legislation to ensure the organization's access to public school facilities. However, the litigation continued as other types of public entities took action against the BSA and local councils. Over the next several years, state and federal court judges around the nation were asked to balance competing claims of freedom of expression and equality. Ironically, in some of these cases, local councils argued that they did not want to discriminate but were forced to maintain the BSA's exclusionary policy at the risk of losing their charters. There have been no clear winners in the BSA litigation, as the unhappy saga of the Philadelphia council clearly demonstrates.

As in the cases in the school setting, most judges had little opportunity to select between a subordinate or coordinate policymaking role on the gay rights issue. The outcome of these disputes was determined largely by each court's view of the protections offered by the First Amendment rather than by its perception of its role as a policymaker or its position on the gay rights claim.

NOTES

1. As of 2007, thirteen states (California, Connecticut, Hawaii, Illinois, Iowa, Maine, Maryland, Massachusetts, Minnesota, New Hampshire, New Jersey, Oregon, and Vermont) and the District of Columbia included lesbians and gays within the ambit of their public accommodations laws; the laws also often applied to housing and employment discrimination (Infanti 2007, 27). As a result of laws such as these, almost half the gay, lesbian, and bisexual adults in the United States reside in states where such discrimination is illegal. Additionally, a number of cities, such as Atlanta, Dallas, Miami, Houston, and Philadelphia, independently of their state governments, prohibit discrimination on the basis of sexual orientation in employment, housing, and public accommodations (Lambda Legal 2007b). The absence of a national public accommodations law means that enforcement of equal access is spotty.

2. United Way supports tax-exempt, nonprofit community-based organizations run by volunteers; among other things, sponsored organizations must have nondiscrimination policies. Each United Way chapter determines its funding recipients, and, conversely, some contributors to United Way conditioned their

funding on guarantees that no money would go to the BSA (Hughes and Moiseichik 2003).

3. There was a 2.7 percent decline in membership between 2002 and 2003 (*Christian Science Monitor* January 26, 2004).

4. The Little League and the National Football League presented similar arguments when characterized in lawsuits as places of public accommodation.

5. *NAACP v. Alabama* (1958) was the first case in which the high court articulated a constitutional right of expressive association, derived from First Amendment principles of free speech and assembly.

6. Or. Rev. Stat §659A.403(1) provides, "All persons within the jurisdiction of this state are entitled to the full and equal accommodations, advantages, facilities and privileges of any place of public accommodation, without any distinction, discrimination or restriction on account of race, religion, sex, marital status, color, national origin or age if the individual is 18 years of age or older."

7. The court declined to rule on whether the Boy Scouts was exempt from the law as a private organization, simply holding that, like the YMCA and YWCA, the legislature did not intend the law to apply to its membership decisions.

8. The plaintiff failed to meet the diversity of citizenship and amount in controversy requirements for federal court litigation.

9. Cal. Civ. Code §51(b), the Unruh Civil Rights Act, provides, "All persons within the jurisdiction of this state are free and equal, and no matter what their sex, race, color, religion, ancestry, national origin, disability, medical condition, marital status, or sexual orientation are entitled to the full and equal accommodations, advantages, facilities, privileges, or services in all business establishments of every kind whatsoever." The act was passed in 1959 and has been amended since then.

10. The state supreme court granted review in *Yeaw* (1997b) but withheld a ruling pending its subsequent decision in *Curran* (1998). In *Curran*, the California high court held that the Unruh Act did not apply to the Boy Scouts and remanded Yeaw's case to the lower court, which subsequently dismissed it.

11. Conn. Gen. Stat. §46a-64(a) provides, "It shall be a discriminatory practice in violation of this section: (1) To deny any person within the jurisdiction of this state full and equal accommodations in any place of public accommodation, resort or amusement because of race, creed, color, national origin, ancestry, sex, marital status, age, lawful source of income, mental retardation, mental disability or physical disability, including, but not limited to, blindness or deafness of the applicant, subject only to the conditions and limitations established by law and applicable alike to all persons."

12. As its website explains, "the Scout Oath 'duty to God' reminds everyone that a Scout is reverent, and Scout leaders are expected to be a positive religious influence. The BSA believes that, to be the best kind of citizen as possible, a Scout must recognize his obligation to God" (Boy Scouts of America 2008b).

13. The Seventh Circuit affirmed in *Sherman* (1993b) and the Supreme Court denied certiorari in *Sherman* (1994).

14. The state supreme court denied review (*Powell* 2003).

15. Mich. Comp. Laws 37 §.2302(a), the Elliott-Larsen Civil Rights Act, provides, "A person shall not: deny an individual the full and equal enjoyment of the

goods, services, facilities, privileges, advantages, or accommodations of a place of public accommodation or public service because of religion, race, color, national origin, age, sex, or marital status."

16. The Michigan Supreme Court denied leave to appeal in *Scalise v. Boy Scouts of America* (2005), and the U.S. Supreme Court denied certiorari in *Scalise v. Boy Scouts of America* (2006).

17. The Supreme Court denied certiorari in *Welsh* (1993b). More recently, in *Vargas-Santana v. Boy Scouts of America* (2007), the district court cited *Welsh* and granted the BSA's motion to dismiss, flatly ruling that Title II does not apply to the organization.

18. Kan. Stat. Ann. §44-1001, the Act Against Discrimination, provides, "It is . . . declared to be the policy of this state . . . to assure equal opportunities to all persons within this state to full and equal public accommodations . . . without distinction on account of race, religion, color, sex, disability, familial status, national origin or ancestry."

19. The twins remained in scouting until they were sixteen and about to receive Eagle Scout badges when they decided to quit (*Houston Chronicle* March 24, 1998).

20. In *Bob Jones University v. United States* (1983), the Supreme Court ruled that the government's compelling interest against racial discrimination justified the revocation by the Internal Revenue Service of the university's tax-exempt status.

21. See Mezey (2007, ch. 2).

22. Young men may become assistant scoutmasters at eighteen and scoutmasters at twenty-one.

23. He was later told that the BSA had a policy against homosexuals as evidenced by a 1978 policy statement that "an individual who openly declares himself to be a homosexual [may not] be a volunteer scout leader [or] . . . a registered unit member." The statement was never disseminated, and similar statements, appearing in 1991 and 1993, were written after litigation had begun in other states (*Dale v. Boy Scouts of America* 1999, 1205).

24. LAD exempts "any institution, bona fide club, or place of accommodation, which is in its nature distinctly private" (N.J. Stat. Ann §10:5-5[1]).

25. The New Jersey Supreme Court summarily affirmed the appellate court's ruling in *National Organization for Women* (1974b).

26. In *Hurley* (1995), the U.S. Supreme Court had ruled that the Massachusetts public accommodations law did not require the organizers of the annual St. Patrick's Day Parade to include the gay marchers. The parade organizers claimed that they objected not to individual gays but to the group as an entity with its own banner in the parade because it would interfere with their freedom of speech. Under the "compelled speech" doctrine, the high court agreed that the First Amendment protects an organization's autonomy to determine the content of its speech, that is, to exclude unwelcome messages.

27. Scholars argue that the Court's one-paragraph discussion of freedom of association in *Hurley* was not part of the ruling and thus mere dicta (see, for example, Goodman 1999).

28. The 1978 document, an internal memorandum indicating that gays were inappropriate leaders, emanated from the head of the Scouts to the executive

council; it was never publicly disseminated. In 1983, another document from the BSA legal counsel continued in this vein (Goodman 1999, 853–4).

29. The 1991 and 1993 position statements were prepared by the BSA after Timothy Curran initiated his suit in the California courts (Goodman 1999).

30. Souter dissented separately, for himself, Breyer, and Ginsburg.

31. Discussing the veracity of the BSA's assertion of an official anti-gay policy, Upton (2001, 794 n3) reports that in a search of the BSA's website in 2001, the word "gay" was used only as part of a last name and "homosexual" only in a reference to an article about the increase in prejudice among American youth and "the need for the BSA's ethical teachings" to combat it. Indeed, a search conducted by me in June 2008 failed to reveal any references to "homosexual," and a single reference to "gay" referred to a scouting official's last name.

32. Ironically, on June 27, 2000, one day before *Dale* was decided, Executive Order 13160, banning discrimination on the basis of sexual orientation in federally conducted programs and activities, was published in the *Federal Register*.

33. The Court claimed that it was not indifferent to such discrimination.

34. One report indicates that at the time *Dale* was decided in 2000, there were thirteen states and 244 local jurisdictions with anti-gay discrimination laws and policies in place (France 2001).

35. Most employment cases involving gay teachers arise in the public school setting; see *National Gay Task Force v. Board of Education of Oklahoma City* (1984) and *Weaver v. Nebo School District* (1998).

36. Section 2-160-030 of the Chicago Municipal Code provides, "No person shall directly or indirectly discriminate against any individual in hiring, classification, grading, discharge, discipline, compensation or other term or condition of employment because of the individual's race, color, sex, gender identity, age, religion, disability, national origin, ancestry, sexual orientation, marital status, parental status, military discharge status or source of income."

37. A former Eagle Scout, Richardson answered an advertisement for ex-scouts from an organization called Forgotten Scouts, which wanted to challenge the BSA's anti-gay employment policies. The BSA hires professional "Scouters" to assist the volunteers; they are governed by the same rules as the volunteer leaders.

38. The Illinois Supreme Court denied the petition for leave to appeal (*Chicago Area Council of Boy Scouts of America* 2001b).

39. D.C. Code Ann. §2-1401 provides, "It is the intent of the Council of the District of Columbia . . . to secure an end in the District of Columbia to discrimination for any reason other than that of individual merit, including, but not limited to, discrimination by reason of race, color, religion, national origin, sex, age, marital status, personal appearance, sexual orientation, gender identity or expression, familial status, family responsibilities, matriculation, political affiliation, genetic information, disability, source of income, status as a victim of an intrafamily offense, and place of residence or business."

40. In September 2001, following the commission ruling, the U.S. House of Representatives approved HR 2390 with a substantial margin of 262 to 152. Introduced by Representative John Hostettler, a Republican from Indiana, it amended the Fiscal Year 2002 District of Columbia Appropriations Act to bar the use of

funds to implement or enforce any order that would force the Boy Scouts to have
gay employees or volunteers as troop leaders (*CQ Almanac* 2001).

41. Even before *Dale* was decided, a group of California scouts and ex-scouts
founded the organization Scouting for All to confront the BSA's anti-gay policy.
The members demonstrated at BSA offices following *Dale*.

42. Eleanor Roosevelt reacted to the discrimination by resigning her membership in the DAR and arranging for Anderson to sing at the Lincoln Memorial. The
DAR eventually changed its policy.

43. A week after Woolsey introduced her bill, Representative Steve Buyer introduced a concurrent resolution in the House (H. Con. Res. 384) "recognizing the
Boy Scouts of America for the public service it performs through its contributions
to the lives of the Nation's boys and young men." The measure was referred to
the House Judiciary Committee, but no action was taken on it. Over the next several years, other concurrent resolutions to support the Scouts in a variety of ways
were introduced. For example, H. Con. Res. 522 and S. Con. Res. 147 (introduced
in the second session of the 108th Congress on November 18, 2004) expressed
Congress's view that the Department of Defense should maintain its support of
the Scouts, especially with respect to the quadrennial jamborees.

44. The twelve affirmative votes included eleven Democrats and one Republican; fifty-one Democrats, who might have been expected to vote for the bill, voted
"present" instead, in essence abstaining from taking a position on the measure.

45. The Catholic Church and the Church of Jesus Christ of Latter-Day Saints
(Mormons) charter 60 percent of scouting groups (*Christian Science Monitor* January 26, 2004).

46. The Broward County action sparked a furor, as, in the midst of debate over
passage of the No Child Left Behind Act, members of Congress strove to protect the
Boy Scouts from attack. But although a number of senators cited the findings of a
Congressional Research Service report to support their position that the Boy Scouts
were under siege from school boards around the nation, the truth was that, other
than Broward County, no other school district had expressly barred scouts from
holding meetings on school property. The report cited reactions from governing
bodies in Seattle; New York City; Los Angeles; Minneapolis; Madison, Wisconsin;
and Chapel Hill, North Carolina, variously criticizing the BSA's discriminatory policy, threatening to withhold sponsorships, and promising to review contracts and
end special privileges giving the Scouts access to the classroom to recruit members.
But although ending their sponsorship would require the Scouts to pay a fee like
other nonprofit or private groups, denying access to school property for meetings
was quite different from failing to sponsor; there was no constitutional obligation
for public schools to sponsor a group or organization and give it special access to its
property (*Congressional Record* 2001, S4867; *New York Times* June 17, 2001).

47. See *Perry Education Association v. Perry Local Educators' Association* (1983);
Cornelius (1985); *Lamb's Chapel v. Center Moriches Union Free School District* (1993);
Rosenberger (1995); *Capitol Square Review and Advisory Board v. Pinette* (1995); and
Good News Club v. Milford Central School (2001).

48. Approved by the House in May 2001 and by the Senate a month later, the
education bill was signed by the president on January 8, 2002 and enacted as
Public Law 107-110.

49. 20 U.S.C. §7905, the Boy Scouts of America Equal Access Act, provides, "No public elementary school, public secondary school, local educational agency, or State educational agency that has a designated open forum or a limited public forum and that receives funds made available through the Department shall deny equal access or a fair opportunity to meet to, or discriminate against, any group officially affiliated with the Boy Scouts of America, or any other youth group listed in title 36 of the United States Code (as a patriotic society), that wishes to conduct a meeting within that designated open forum or limited public forum, including denying such access or opportunity or discriminating for reasons based on the membership or leadership criteria or oath of allegiance to God and country of the Boy Scouts of America or of the youth group listed in title 36 of the United States Code (as a patriotic society)." Among the patriotic organization serving youngsters listed in Title 36 are the Boy Scouts, the Boys & Girls Clubs of America, Little League Baseball, Future Farmers of America, Big Brothers/Big Sisters, and the Girl Scouts of the United States of America.

50. Conn. Gen. Stat.§§46a-81a-r, known as "Connecticut's Gay Rights Law," was adopted in 2000 to ban discrimination on the basis of employment, housing, public accommodations, and credit in the public and private sectors.

51. The Supreme Court has not been very clear on the difference between content-based discrimination and viewpoint-based discrimination. Although the former is constitutionally acceptable in nonpublic and limited public forums, regulations based on the speaker's viewpoint are almost always unacceptable. *RAV v. St. Paul* (1992) and the examples in Scalia's majority opinion attempt to make this distinction clearer (see Fast 2002).

52. Summary judgment is appropriate if the court documents "show that there is no genuine issue as to any material fact and that the moving party is entitled to judgment as a matter of law" (*Federal Rules of Civil Procedure* §56[c]).

53. Calabresi also identified a First Amendment doctrine that prevents the government from conditioning the disbursement of government benefits on the recipients abandoning their constitutional rights. As in the nonpublic forum cases, this doctrine permits some regulation of speech and associational rights; see *Regan v. Taxation with Representation of Washington* (1983) and *NEA v. Finley* (1998). Because the analysis is the same under both doctrines, he decided that the court did not have to select between them.

54. The U.S. Supreme Court denied certiorari in *Wyman* (2004).

55. Assessing the range of judicial responses to the BSA cases after *Dale*, some observers were most troubled by *Wyman*, arguing that the Scouts were singled out for exclusion from the charity donation campaign, because the state disapproved of the BSA's anti-gay message (Fast 2002; Reuveni 2006).

56. In addition to the Marina policy, §13.28.060A of the Berkeley Municipal Code provides, "It shall be an unlawful service practice for any person to deny any individual the full and equal enjoyment of, or to place different terms and conditions on the availability of, the use of any City facility on the basis of such individual's sexual orientation [or] . . . to deny any individual the full and actual enjoyment of, or to impose different terms or conditions on the availability of, any City service on the basis of such individual's sexual orientation [or] . . . to deny any individual the full and equal enjoyment of, or to impose different terms and

conditions upon the availability of, any service, program or facility wholly or partially funded or otherwise supported by the City on the basis of such individual's sexual orientation."

57. The Scouts attempted to negotiate with the BSA, but counsel for the Scouts admitted during oral argument that the BSA had barred them from saying that they do not discriminate on the basis of sexual orientation. Thus, the Scouts admitted that despite a promise not to discriminate, if a gay person attempted to join them, they would have to follow BSA policy and refuse admission.

58. The U.S. Supreme Court denied certiorari in *Evans* (2006b). The BSA filed an amicus brief but was not a direct party in the case.

59. Because the parties had presented insufficient information to determine the origins of the Mission Bay Park lease, the court declined to rule on it.

60. A series of complex legal actions followed. In ruling on motions for rehearings, the circuit court's certification order of December 18, 2006, was withdrawn on June 11, 2008 (*Barnes-Wallace v. City of San Diego* 2008a). At the same time, the appeals court certified new questions to the state supreme court. On December 31, 2008, the circuit court clerk was instructed to transmit those questions to the court (*Barnes-Wallace v. City of San Diego* 2008b). There is no record of a subsequent action in the case.

61. The arrangement between the BSA and numerous groups (known as "chartered organizations"), such as community organizations, government bodies, and business, civic, and educational groups, allows such groups to avail themselves of BSA scouting programs. In doing so, these organizations enter into agreements with the BSA in which they supply adult leaders, meeting places, and other support and are bound by BSA rules and procedures.

62. It is unclear what happened to the Chicago defendant.

63. The primary issue in the case was whether the statutes cited by the plaintiffs were enacted as part of Congress's taxing and spending authority; the defendants argued that all the statutes were enacted under other areas of congressional authority.

64. In 1972, Congress enacted 10 U.S.C. §2554 (Public Law 92-249) to authorize the military to donate equipment and services to assist the National Scout Jamboree. Since 1981, the jamboree has taken place on federal land, Fort A. P. Hill, near Fredericksburg, Virginia. The cost to the government for the last two jamborees was $6 million and $8 million, respectively (*Winkler v. Chicago School Reform Board* 2005a).

65. 5 U.S.C. §301 provides, "No Federal law . . . shall be construed to limit any Federal agency from providing any form of support for a youth organization (including the Boy Scouts of America . . .) that would result in that Federal agency providing less support to that youth organization . . . than was provided during the preceding fiscal year to that youth organization."

66. 42 U.S.C. §5309(e)(2) provides, "No State or unit of general local government that has a designated open forum, limited public forum, or nonpublic forum and that is a recipient of assistance under this chapter shall deny equal access or a fair opportunity to meet to, or discriminate against, any youth organization, including the Boy Scouts of America . . . , that wishes to conduct a meeting or otherwise participate in that designated open forum, limited public forum, or nonpublic forum."

67. Attorneys for the ACLU and private law firms were listed as counsel for the plaintiffs.

68. Public Law 109-148.

69. The Pacific Legal Foundation, the Foundation for Moral Law, the Commonwealth of Virginia, and six members of Congress, including Republican John Warner of Virginia, filed briefs on behalf of the government. Americans United for Separation of Church and State and other individuals and groups led by the Unitarian Universalist Association of Congregations supported the plaintiffs (*Chicago Daily Law Bulletin* April 4, 2006).

70. Although the circuit court's ruling was based on standing, the court also stressed that the jamboree was open to the public and not restricted only to BSA members. However, as one of the lawyers for the plaintiffs pointed out, "The general public is allowed to visit the Jamboree, but all they can do is watch the Scouts participate in various activities" (*Chicago Daily Law Bulletin* April 4, 2006). This was confirmed by a scout official, the chair of the jamboree fishing program. Despite the federal government's role in stocking a trout pond for the jamboree at a cost of hundreds of thousands of dollars, he declared that the activity at the pond is "not open to the public" (France 2001).

71. In 1996, the Philadelphia and Valley Forge councils merged into the CLC. In accordance with a 1928 ordinance, a half acre of city-owned land was provided for the Philadelphia Council building; the building and the land were city property but would be made available to the council for its exclusive use, and the council would be responsible for their upkeep (*Cradle of Liberty Council* 2008a).

72. The CLC claimed that the city had created a forum by allowing numerous organizations access to its property.

73. The rent would increase from $1 a year to $200,000. Other city tenants were required to include nondiscriminatory language in their leases, but because the council never had a lease, it had escaped this requirement (*New York Times* December 6, 2007).

74. Robert Bork, national spokesman for the BSA, pointed out that the city risked losing more than $60 million in federal funding from HUD for violating the 2005 Support Our Scouts Act (*Philadelphia Inquirer* July 25, 2006).

✝

Conclusion

Most studies of earlier civil rights movements concluded that litigation played a critical role in helping achieve the movement's goals. Following the tradition of these civil rights struggles, the gay rights movement also relied on litigation as an important weapon in its battle for social and legal reform. In an effort to assess the role of litigation in securing equal rights for members of the lesbian, gay, bisexual, and transgender (LGBT) community, this study examined published and unpublished state and federal court rulings in four policy areas affecting children and families (parenting, marriage, schools, and membership in private social organizations, specifically the Boy Scouts). Its primary aim was to determine the extent to which the courts furthered the policy goals of gay rights advocates. Although the outcome of a single case is insufficient to gauge the effectiveness of litigation in expanding equal rights and opportunities, quantifying the accumulated successes and failures of the litigation over time offers an opportunity to assess its role in advancing the objectives of the LGBT community.[1]

In analyzing these rulings, the study focused on three variables often used to explain the judicial decision-making process: the type of case, the type of court, and the judge's role as policymaker.

TYPE OF CASE

Because it appeared that courts would be more likely to favor litigants requesting narrow forms of relief rather than those who asked for broad-based declarations of constitutional rights, it was expected that the gay rights claim would be more successful when plaintiffs sought political and civil rights (such as freedom from harassment and freedom of expression) and less successful when they sought to expand social rights (such as in cases involving adoption, marriage, and membership in private organizations).

At first glance, it appears that the expectation about this variable was confirmed when the rate of success in each type of case was compared: the plaintiffs in the marriage cases were the least successful, while the plaintiffs in the gender harassment cases had the highest success rate. However, a closer look at the outcome of the litigation reveals that this analysis is too simplistic.

From 1990 to 2007, there were twenty-four decisions in joint and second-parent adoption cases in eighteen states representing all regions of the nation; in each case, gays were the plaintiffs, and the state or local government was the defendant. The gay rights claim prevailed in seventeen of the twenty-three decisions resulting in final judgments with unambiguous outcomes (that is, a decisive victory for either side), for a success rate of 74 percent. (One case was remanded to await a decision by another court.)

There were thirty-six rulings in cases challenging restrictions on same-sex marriage from 1971 to 2009; the cases arose in twenty-six states from every part of the country. With two exceptions, all suits were brought by or on behalf of gays seeking to strike a restrictive marriage law or policy on state or federal constitutional grounds. For the most part, these suits arose when a government official denied a gay couple's application for a marriage license. The state, or more often, the county, was the defendant in most of these cases; some suits named both the state and federal governments as defendants and, in a few cases, the litigants sued the federal government alone. In contrast to their impressive success rate in the adoption cases, the gay rights claims prevailed in only eleven cases, or 31 percent of the rulings with final judgments and unambiguous outcomes. (The California Supreme Court's Prop 8 decision is not included in these figures because it resulted in a partial victory for each side.)

The variety of claims in the school setting from 1996 to 2008 reflects the diverse experiences of gay youngsters and the degree to which sexual orientation plays a role in the nation's schools. These lawsuits were brought to expand students' political and civil rights. Within the broad category of cases in the school setting, there were thirty-one cases revolving around federal and state statutes as well as federal constitutional guarantees; the suits were brought in twenty-two states, ranging from California to New Hampshire, with every region of the country represented. Twenty-two defendants were public school districts, eight were public colleges and universities, and one was a private university. Unlike the adoption cases, all of which were brought to advance gay rights claims, these suits were brought by litigants on both sides of the gay rights debate. Overall, the gay rights claims prevailed in twenty-four cases, or 77 percent of the rulings involving a school setting.

Breaking down the school cases into the four types that made up the broader category of school litigation, the seven plaintiffs who charged schools with failing to respond to harassment against them had the highest success rate, a perfect score of winning 100 percent of their lawsuits. The next most successful group, those challenging restrictions on gay student groups at the college and university level, prevailed in 89 percent of the cases; the gay rights claim was defeated only in the suit against the private university. At the high school level, students who sought to organize gay clubs or gay–straight alliances were almost as successful, winning 86 percent of their claims. Finally, plaintiffs who complained of restrictions on their anti-gay expression in public schools prevailed in 62 percent of the cases.

The nine cases making up the Boy Scouts of American (BSA) litigation, with the Scouts as plaintiffs in five cases and defendants in four, included a mix of statutory claims based chiefly on subnational antidiscrimination laws as well as federal constitutional guarantees. There were nine rulings in these cases over a ten-year period from 1998 to 2008, with suits brought in seven states. The gay rights claim prevailed in only three rulings with final judgments and unambiguous outcomes, for a success rate of 38 percent. (One case had no final outcome, as the lower federal court decision against the BSA was stayed by the circuit court of appeals awaiting certification to the state supreme court.)

The results show that although there was some variation in the outcome of the litigation by the type of case, overall, there was no clear distinction between the plaintiffs who sought civil and political rights and those who demanded greater social equality. The plaintiffs who attempted to achieve marriage equality were the least successful of the litigants in the analysis (prevailing in only 31 percent of the rulings), but, unexpectedly, those who litigated to attain another form of social equality in the second-parent and joint adoption cases were among the most successful. And although the gay rights claimants in the cases involving schools did well in the courts, the anti-gay opposition scored significant victories as well. Moreover, the courts did not rule in favor of the gay rights claim in most of the cases in which the BSA was the opposing party.

Thus, although the type of case provided some information about the outcome of the litigation, the expectation that the courts would distinguish between the broad categories of social and civil rights and would prefer the latter proved wrong; this was not the deciding factor in the cases.

TYPE OF COURT

The type of court in which the case was heard also proved somewhat disappointing in explaining the outcome of the cases. There were fifty-six cases with final judgments and unambiguous results decided in the state courts and forty-one decided by the federal courts. The gay rights claims were somewhat more successful in the federal courts, prevailing at a rate of 60 percent, but the claims in the state courts had an only slightly lower success rate of 53 percent. These differences are easily explained by the fact that the marriage cases, with their lower success rates, were decided predominantly by the state courts and that the majority of cases in the school setting, with their high success rates, were almost all decided in the federal courts.

Because there was almost no variation in the type of case decided by each court, there was no opportunity to compare the outcome of each type of case within each type of court. The marriage and adoption cases were overwhelmingly decided in the state courts; the school cases were decided predominantly by the federal courts; the only cases that were split between the two types of courts were the Boy Scout cases.

More precisely, twenty-two of the adoption cases were decided in the state courts and only two in the federal courts. Similarly, the bulk of the marriage cases—twenty-nine of the thirty-six —were decided in the state courts, with only a few, chiefly those challenging DOMA, heard in the federal courts. And with the exception of three state court rulings, the other twenty-eight cases in the school setting were decided in the federal courts. Although the eight Boy Scout cases were evenly divided between the state and the federal courts, there was no pattern in the outcome of these cases either; the gay rights claims won twice and lost twice in each type of court.

Thus, although there were some differences between the state and federal courts as a whole, with the federal courts slightly more favorably disposed to the gay rights claims, when the analysis focused on the type of court within each area of law, there were no appreciable differences.

ROLE OF THE COURT

All individuals seeking to adopt a child must go through a lengthy and complex investigation period and ultimately require court approval of their adoption petitions. In most cases, this inquiry revolves around the fitness of the parents and a determination of whether the prospective adoptive parents will further the best interests of the child. In second-parent or joint adoption situations, when the prospective adoptive parent or parents are gay, a different analysis takes place. In such cases, the most common scenario is when the child's legal parent (either biological or adoptive) and his or her partner seek to establish a legal relationship with the child. However, in following the prescribed procedure in most states, the existing parent must renounce his or her parental rights unless the court waives this termination requirement. All states permit waiver in the case of stepparent adoptions but in almost no other situations. Refusing to extend the stepparent exception to the gay couple leads to the logical absurdity of depriving the child of any parent for the length of time it takes the adoption to be finalized (and taking the risk that the child will have no legal parent if it is not). Gays therefore argue that the courts should simply extend the stepparent exception to them, notwithstanding the contrary indication in the adoption laws.

With the practice of adoption unknown at common law, the rights and obligations of the parties involved depend entirely on state legislatures in crafting laws to govern the procedures. In interpreting such laws, judges are especially constrained to follow traditional norms of judicial restraint and adhere closely to the statutory text. Thus, the crucial factor in the outcome of most of the adoption cases involving one or two gay parents was the court's philosophy of judicial decision making and the extent to which it was willing to go beyond the confines of the text. In deciding these cases, judges were forced to balance conflicting principles of legislative deference and their responsibility to effectuate the child's best interests and approve the adoption. In other words, the outcomes of the cases were dependent largely on the degree to which the judges acted as subordinate or coordinate policymakers.

The choice of deferring to legislative policymaking or effectuating the purpose of the adoption laws was especially evident in the Florida and California litigation. In Florida, the federal courts emphasized their obligation to follow precedent and use minimal scrutiny in upholding the state law. Thus, they subordinated their policymaking role to that of the legislature by ratifying the discriminatory state policy preventing gays from adopting based on rather flimsy evidence of the reasonableness of the legislative design. In California, by contrast, the courts took on the role as coordinate policymakers, liberally construing the state adoption laws to bypass the termination requirement and expand the ability of gays to secure second-parent adoptions.

Of all the cases in the analysis, the marriage cases most clearly tested the limits of the usefulness of the movement's strategy of litigating for social reform. In denying their constitutional due process and equal protection claims, the courts manifested their unwillingness to interfere with the legislative prerogative to determine marriage policies and, for the most part, refused to require states to grant same-sex and opposite-sex couples equal access to civil marriage.

The determining factor in most of these cases was the level of scrutiny the courts used to decide the claims. In refusing to apply heightened scrutiny to the challenged laws, the courts accepted almost any rationale offered by the states for barring same-sex couples from marrying. This pattern persisted in the face of testimony and evidence that although the state's goals might have been reasonable, the ties between the goals and the classification were tenuous at best. By applying a higher form of scrutiny, as occurred in a few state supreme courts, the courts would have quickly come to the conclusion that the restrictions on marriage equality stemmed from bias and stereotypical thinking. Similarly, in deciding challenges to state and federal DOMAs, the courts denied standing to same-sex couples, refusing to even hear their arguments against the inequality of the laws.

After considering the laws and policies restricting marriage to opposite-sex couples, most judges concluded that it was outside their purview to interfere with the legislative design in marriage laws or override the people's will by permitting gay couples to marry. In opting for this role of subordinate policymaker, the courts rejected the gay rights advocates' appeals to marriage equality. Conversely, when the courts granted relief to the gay rights litigants, they did so largely by applying a higher level of scrutiny to the challenged law, thus acting as coordinate policymakers and supplanting the judgments of other policymakers.

The final outcome of the California marriage equality litigation exemplifies judicial restraint in the name of democratic decision making. By upholding the validity of Prop 8, the supreme court chose not to exercise the role of coordinate policymaker; ironically, the same court had acted as a coordinate policymaker less than a year earlier.

Although there is no way of knowing to what extent the courts are influenced by the political environment of the same-sex marriage debate, they are quickly reminded of it whenever they step out of their subordinate roles. In the instances when judges side with the gay rights litigants, they are subject to widespread criticism and accused of violating norms of judicial restraint. In some cases, threats of impeachment or recall have even followed gay rights victories in the marriage cases.

The courts were confronted with several different issues in the school cases. One set of plaintiffs charged that the school districts failed to respond—or responded inadequately—to their complaints of victimization on the basis of their sexual orientation or, in some instances, on the basis of their perceived sexual orientation. The treatment they received—which had usually continued for many years, often escalating as they grew older—ranged from persistent hostile teasing to vicious physical attacks. And when they reported these incidents to the school authorities, the officials seemed to respond with halfhearted attempts at disciplining the culprits.

The students' success in these cases was attributable to two factors. First, the plaintiffs captured the courts' sympathies; judges appeared genuinely outraged at the severity of the harassment and the extent to which school authorities seemed to ignore the children's suffering and allowed the behavior to continue. Second, the plaintiffs were able to take advantage of evolving case law in Title IX, the federal law barring sex discrimination in publicly funded educational institutions. Supreme Court rulings had established the principle that, under certain conditions, Title IX allowed monetary damages for victims of sexual harassment by school employees; shortly thereafter, the Court ruled that schools could also be held liable for sexual harassment by schoolmates. Some lower courts followed suit and extended these principles to suits involving claims of gender harassment by school employees or other children.

Another group of litigants, gay college students, typically filed their suits when their universities rejected their applications for funding, meeting space, or simply recognition as a student group. Most litigants arguing the gay rights position were successful because they benefited from case law in which the U.S. Supreme Court placed a heavy burden on public universities that sought to deny student groups the freedom to express themselves. Similarly, the courts were very sympathetic to the claims of high school students who were denied permission to organize into clubs or organizations by school officials who perceived their message as supportive of gay rights. Based on more than a decade of Supreme Court rulings interpreting free speech rights in public forums, the high school students were also able to persuade the courts that they had been deprived of their First Amendment rights. Ironically, they were able to take advantage of a 1984 law intended to ease the way for religious organizations to meet on campus.

The cases brought by children protesting disciplinary actions for displaying anti-gay messages on signs or clothing represented the other side of the gay rights litigation. Most of these anti-gay litigants also succeeded in convincing the courts that the First Amendment protected their right to express negative views of homosexuality. For the most part, they based their claims on *Tinker*, the 1969 landmark First Amendment school speech case that set the standard for determining when a school may silence speech in the interests of order and discipline. In interpreting First Amendment principles broadly, the courts were inclined to order the schools to refrain from censoring student speech—notwithstanding the anti-gay nature of the messages. The judges in these cases were unwilling to restrict First Amendment freedoms on the basis of such anti-gay expressions as "Be Happy, Not Gay" and "Straight Pride." And although he recognized that they offended gay students, at least one judge allowed the display of such messages because he viewed them as relatively mild statements of disapproval.

Both gay and anti-gay litigants benefited from their First Amendment stance in the litigation arising in the school setting. With the exception of the harassment cases, the dispositive factor in the outcome of these cases was the extent to which the litigants on either side were able to convince the courts that their First Amendment rights were being threatened. Thus, the success of the litigation was explained largely by the court's adherence to precedent in applying strict scrutiny to laws and policies restricting First Amendment freedoms.

The BSA's policy of restricting membership on the basis of sex, religion, and sexual orientation was a target of litigation for more than two decades, with the courts granting it near complete autonomy to determine its membership. The gay rights litigants had hoped that they would benefit from a series of U.S. Supreme Court rulings restricting men-only private clubs from excluding women members on the basis of subnational public accommodations laws, laws patterned after the historic effort by Congress to expand minority civil rights in the 1964 Civil Rights Act. However, both state and federal courts interpreted such laws narrowly, and by confining them to their text, they uniformly rejected the litigants' efforts to expand their civil rights by challenging the BSA's membership policies.

This state of affairs appeared to change when, in *Dale*, the New Jersey Supreme Court held that the state law against discrimination was intended to deter private organizations from imposing discriminatory admissions requirements. However, the U.S. Supreme Court decision in *Dale* did not turn on the validity of the state public accommodations law; rather, it turned on the Court's interpretation of the BSA's right of expressive association. The high court was persuaded that the BSA's objection to gays was a bedrock principle and that forcing the organization to admit gays in any capacity would infringe on its right to expressive association, as guaranteed by the First Amendment.

Ironically, *Dale* proved to be somewhat of a pyrrhic victory for the Scouts, setting off a torrent of negative publicity for the organization and subjecting its policies to an intense glare of (mostly) hostile public opinion. A significant number of corporate and public sponsors disassociated themselves from the Scouts, donations dwindled, and public entities revoked their rent-free arrangements in public facilities, such as marinas, schools, and parks, as well as participation in charitable campaigns.

The BSA and its local affiliates retaliated with lawsuits of their own, claiming that by excluding scouting from public facilities because of their constitutionally protected membership policies, the government was not only infringing on their right of expressive association but also engaging in illegal viewpoint discrimination, each a First Amendment violation. Most courts agreed with the BSA and held that public entities were constitutionally barred from treating the Scouts differently from other groups. A minority of courts took the opposite position and pointed to the state and local antidiscrimination laws to justify withholding benefits from the BSA and the local councils.

The outcome of the cases involving the Boy Scouts showed that, as in the school cases, the ruling depended mostly on the extent to which the litigants were able to ground their arguments in First Amendment principles; for the most part, the BSA proved more successful at this than the gay rights advocates. Therefore, just as in the school cases, the court's approach to First Amendment case law was the most important determinant of the result of the litigation. Following precedent by applying strict scrutiny to laws and policies restricting First Amendment guarantees, most courts upheld the litigants' claims of freedom of expression.

FINAL THOUGHTS

The aim of this inquiry was to determine the extent to which litigation helped accomplish the gay rights movement's goals of furthering equality by removing constraints on opportunities for members of gay families over the past several decades. It revealed that, as with other social movements, the litigation succeeded in achieving some of these goals. The overall success rate of the gay rights litigation discussed in this study was 57 percent. Of course, quantifying the results of the lawsuits does not indicate whether the courts satisfied the LGBT community's *most important* goals. But to the extent that it helped minimize or eliminate the role of sexual orientation in structuring the rights and opportunities of gay youth and gay adults, the litigation served a useful purpose. Moreover, it is possible that their litigation successes established a marker for equality of rights and helped spur more egalitarian treatment of gay families in unknown and unaccountable ways.

In the end, this study has provided support for the gay community's beliefs in litigation as a strategy for achieving social and political reform. And as expected, the court's perception of its role as a subordinate or coordinate policymaker proved to be the pivotal factor in accomplishing these goals. The cases showed that the litigation was more successful when, as in the adoption cases, the courts were more willing to perform in a coordinate policymaking role and less inclined to defer to majoritarian decision making. It was less successful when, as in the marriage cases, the courts acted as subordinate policymakers and allowed decisions made in other policymaking arenas to stand.

NOTE

1. The quantitative analysis is based on all gay rights cases discussed in these chapters that resulted in final judgments with unambiguous outcomes. The unit of analysis is the case (that is, the lawsuit) and the designation of the prevailing party is based on the final judgment by the highest level of court or, in one instance, on a subsequent ruling in which the trial court judge determined the final outcome of the case on remand. The success rate for the type of case is calculated by dividing the rulings in favor of the gay rights claim by the total number of cases resulting in a final judgment with a decisive victory for either side. Because the legal issues in the cases arising in the school setting differ, after computing the success rate for these cases as a whole, there are separate calculations for each of the four types of cases within the category. For purposes of this analysis, courts are divided into state and federal only, with Washington, D.C., treated as a state, and its courts considered as state courts.

References

Alaska Judicial Appointment Process. 2008. Available at http://www.state.ak.us/courts/ctinfo.htm#appointment

American Association of University Women. 1993. *Hostile Hallways: The AAUW Survey on Sexual Harassment in America's Schools.* Washington, D.C.: AAUW Education Foundation Research.

———. 2001. *Hostile Hallways: Bullying, Teasing, and Sexual Harassment in School.* Washington, D.C.: AAUW Education Foundation Research.

American Bar Association Section Family Law Working Group on Same Sex Marriages and Non-Marital Unions. 2004. *A White Paper: An Analysis of the Law Regarding Same-Sex Marriage, Civil Unions, and Domestic Partnerships.* Chicago: American Bar Association. Available at http://www.abanet.org/family/whitepaper/fullreport.pdf

American Civil Liberties Union. 2007. *The Cost of Harassment: A Fact Sheet for Lesbian, Gay, Bisexual and Transgender High School Students.* Available at http://www.aclu.org/lgbt/youth/11898res20070209.html

Ancar, Katina. 2003. "California Supreme Court Protects Legal Rights of Children Adopted by Same-Sex Couples." *Youth Law News*, October–December. Available at http://www.youthlaw.org/fileadmin/ncyl/youthlaw/publications/yln/2003/issue_4/03_yln_4_ancar_couples.pdf

Andersen, Ellen Ann. 2005. *Out of the Closets and into the Courts: Legal Opportunity Structure and Gay Rights Litigation.* Ann Arbor: University of Michigan Press.

Answer Brief in Response to Petition for Extraordinary Relief, *Tyler v. California*, December 19, 2008.

ArkansasVotersGuide.com. 2008. *Ballot Issues.* Available at http://www.arkansasvotersguide.com/ballotissues.asp?issueid=5

Armstrong, Rachael L. 2004. "Eleventh Circuit Update: Homosexual Adoption: Not a Fundamental Right: *Lofton v. Sec'y of Dep't of Children and Family Servs*, 358 F.3d 804 (11th Cir. 2004)." *Florida Coastal Law Review* 6: 217–26.

Backer, Megan. 2006. "Giving *Lawrence* Its Due: How the Eleventh Circuit Underestimated the Due Process Implications of *Lawrence v. Texas* in *Lofton v. Secretary of the Department of Children & Family Services.*" *Minnesota Law Review* 90: 745–79.

Ball, Carlos A. 2003. "Lesbian and Gay Families: Gender Nonconformity and the Implications of Difference." *Capital University Law Review* 31: 691–749.

———. 2007. "The Immorality of Statutory Restrictions on Adoption by Lesbians and Gay Men." *Loyola University Chicago Law Journal* 38: 379–97.

Bartlett, Katherine. 1984. "Rethinking Parenthood as an Exclusive Status: The Need for Legal Alternatives when the Premise of the Nuclear Family Has Failed." *Virginia Law Review* 70: 879–963.

Bedell, Jeffrey I. 2003. "Personal Liability of School Officials under § 1983 Who Ignore Peer Harassment of Gay Students." *University of Illinois Law Review* 2003: 829–62.

Benkov, Laura. 1994. *Reinventing the Family: The Emerging Story of Lesbian and Gay Parents.* New York: Crown Publishers.

Berman, Jessica, and Kenneth Leichter. 2005. "Adoption and Foster Care." *Georgetown Journal of Gender and the Law* 6: 667–89.

Bigham, Edward. 1994. "Seventh Circuit Permits Boy Scouts of America to Exclude Atheist—*Welsh v. Boy Scouts of America*, 993 F.2d 1267 (7th Cir.), cert. denied, 114 S. Ct. 602 (1993)." *Temple Law Review* 67: 1333–56.

Black, Stefan H. 2006. "A Step Forward: Lesbian Parentage after *Elisa B. v. Superior Court.*" *George Mason University Civil Rights Law Journal* 17: 237–66.

Black's Law Dictionary. 2004. 8th edition.

Bossin, Phyllis. 2005. "Same Sex Unions: The New Civil Rights Struggle or an Assault on Traditional Marriage?" *Tulsa Law Review* 40: 381–420.

Boy Scouts of America. 2006. *Boy Scouts of America National Council Legal Issues Website and Blawg.* Available at http://www.bsalegal.org/faqs-195.asp

———. 2008a. *BSA at a Glance.* Available at http://www.scouting.org/Media/FactSheets/02-501.aspx

———. 2008b. *Rank Advancement.* Available at http://www.scouting.org/BoyScouts/GuideforMeritBadgeCounselors/RankAdvanceFAQ.aspx

Bradley, Richard R. 2007. "Making a Mountain Out of a Molehill: A Law and Economics Defense of Same-Sex Foster Care Adoptions." *Family Court Review* 45: 133–43.

Brennan, William J., Jr. 1986. "The Bill of Rights and the States: The Revival of State Constitutions as Guardians of Individual Rights." *New York University Law Review* 61: 535–53.

Brennen, David A. 2001. "Tax Expenditures, Social Justice, and Civil Rights: Expanding the Scope of Civil Rights Laws to Apply to Tax-Exempt Charities." *Brigham Young University Law Review* 167–228.

Brewer, Sarah, E., David Kaib, and Karen O'Connor. 2000. "Sex and the Supreme Court: Gays, Lesbians, and Justice." In *The Politics of Gay Rights*, edited by Craig A. Rimmerman, Kenneth D. Wald, and Clyde Wilcox, 377–408. Chicago: University of Chicago Press.

Broz, Alycia. 1998. "*Nabozny v. Podlesny*: A Teenager's Struggle to End Anti-Gay Violence in Public Schools." *Northwestern University Law Review* 92: 750–78.

Bush, George, W. 2004a. "Address before a Joint Session of the Congress on the State of the Union." *Weekly Compilation of Presidential Documents*, January 20, 2004. Available at http://frwebgate1.access.gpo.gov/cgi-bin/waisgate.cgi?WA ISdocID=968832313441+10+0+0&WAISaction=retrieve

———. 2004b. "Remarks Calling for a Constitutional Amendment Defining and Protecting Marriage." *Weekly Compilation of Presidential Documents*, February 24, 2004. Available at http://frwebgate1.access.gpo.gov/cgi-bin/waisgate .cgi?WAISdocID=968832313441+0+0+0&WAISaction=retrieve

———. 2004c. "Statement Calling for a Constitutional Amendment Defining and Protecting Marriage." *Weekly Compilation of Presidential Documents*, May 17, 2004. Available at http://frwebgate1.access.gpo.gov/cgi-bin/waisgate .cgi?WAISdocID=968832313441+5+0+0&WAISaction=retrieve

———. 2004d. "Statement on the Decision of the Massachusetts Supreme Judicial Court on Same-Sex Marriage." *Weekly Compilation of Presidential Documents*, February 4, 2004. Available at http://frwebgate4.access.gpo.gov/cgi-bin/wais gate.cgi?WAISdocID=9714327489+6+0+0&WAISaction=retrieve

———. 2006a. "President's Radio Address," June 3, 2006. Available at http:// www.whitehouse.gov/news/releases/2006/06/20060603.html

———. 2006b. "Remarks by the President on the Marriage Protection Amendment," June 5, 2006. Available at http://www.whitehouse.gov/news/ releases/2006/06/20060605-2.html

Button, James W., Barbara A. Rienzo, and Kenneth D. Wald. 1997. *Private Lives, Public Conflicts: Battles over Gay Rights in American Communities*. Washington, D.C.: Congressional Quarterly Press.

Cahill, Sean, and Jason Cianciotto. 2004. "U.S. Policy Interventions That Can Make Schools Safer." *Journal of Gay and Lesbian Studies in Education* 2: 3–17.

Cain, Patricia A. 2000. *Rainbow Rights: The Role of Lawyers and Courts in the Lesbian and Gay Civil Rights Movement*. Boulder, Colo.: Westview Press.

Carbone, June. 2005. "The Legal Definition of Parenthood: Uncertainty at the Core of Family Identity." *Louisiana Law Review* 65: 1295–344.

Carolina Population Center. 2003. Available at http://www.cpc.unc.edu/projects/ addhealth

Chen, Lisa S. 2005. "Second-Parent Adoptions: Are They Entitled to Full Faith and Credit?" *Santa Clara Law Review* 46: 171–204.

Chermerinsky, Erwin. 2004. "In Defense of Judicial Review: A Reply to Professor Kramer." *California Law Review* 92: 1013–25.

Chermerinsky, Erwin, and Catherine Fisk. 2001. "Perspectives on Constitutional Exemptions to Civil Rights Laws: *Boy Scouts of America v. Dale*: The Expressive Interest of Associations." *William and Mary Bill of Rights Journal* 9: 595–617.

Choper, Jesse H. 2009. "Should Proposition 8 Be Held to Be Retroactive?" *California Journal of Politics and Policy*. Available at http://www.bepress.com/cjpp/ vol1/iss1/12

Clinton, Bill. 1997. "Remarks on Signing a Memorandum Strengthening Enforcement of Title IX." *Weekly Compilation of Presidential Documents* (June 17, 1997). Available at http://frwebgate1.access.gpo.gov/cgi-bin/TEXTgate.cgi?WAISdo cID=175497237357+0+1+0&WAISaction=retrieve

———. 2000. "Executive Order 13160—Nondiscrimination on the Basis of Race, Sex, Color, National Origin, Disability, Religion, Age, Sexual Orientation, and Status as a Parent in Federally Conducted Education and Training Programs." *Weekly Compilation of Presidential Documents* (June 27, 2000). Available at http://frwebgate3.access.gpo.gov/cgi-bin/TEXTgate.cgi?WAISdocID=17713014877+0+1+0&WAISaction=retrieve

CNN.com. 2008. *Local Ballot Measures—Election Center 2008.* Available at http://www.cnn.com/ELECTION/2008/results/ballot.measures

Cohen, Talia. 2003. "Protecting or Dismantling the Family: A Look at Foster Families and Homosexual Parents after *Lofton v. Kearney.*" *Temple Political and Civil Rights Law Review* 13: 227–50.

Collins, Kathy Lee. 1998. "Student-to-Student Sexual Harassment under Title IX: The Legal and Practical Issues." *Drake Law Review* 46: 789–834.

Colorado, Christopher. 2005. "Tying the Braid of Second-Parent Adoptions—Where Due Process Meets Equal Protection." *Fordham Law Review* 74: 1425–73.

Congressional Record. 104th Cong., 2d sess., vol. 142 (1996).

Congressional Record. 106th Cong., 2d sess., vol. 146 (2000).

Congressional Record. 107th Cong., 1st sess., vol. 147 (2001).

Congressional Record. 109th Cong., 1st sess., vol. 151 (2005).

Connecticut Attorney General. 2004. *Opinion on Same Sex Marriage.* Available at http://www.ct.gov/AG/cwp/view.asp?A=1770&Q=282004&pp=12&n=1

Connolly, Catherine. 1996. "An Analysis of Judicial Opinions in Same-Sex Visitation and Adoption Cases." *Behavioral Sciences and the Law* 14: 187–203.

———. 2001. The Description of Gay and Lesbian Families in Second-Parent Adoption Cases. In *The Gay and Lesbian Marriage and Family Reader,* edited by Jennifer M. Lehmann, 109–25. New York: Gordian Knot Books.

———. 2002. "The Voice of the Petitioner: The Experiences of Gay and Lesbian Parents in Successful Second-Parent Adoption Proceedings." *Law and Society Review* 36: 325–46.

Coolidge, David Orgon. 1998. "Playing the *Loving* Card: Same-Sex Marriage and the Politics of Analogy." *Brigham Young University Journal of Public Law* 12: 201–38.

Cooper, Leslie, and Paul Cates. 2006. *Too High a Price: The Case against Restricting Gay Parenting.* 2d ed. New York: American Civil Liberties Union Foundation. Available at http://www.aclu.org/images/asset_upload_file480_27496.pdf

Crane, Jonah M. A. 2003–2004. "Legislative and Constitutional Responses to *Goodridge v. Department of Public Health.*" *New York University Journal of Legislation and Public Policy* 7: 465–85.

Croteau, Alona R. 2004. "Voices in the Dark: Second Parent Adoptions When the Law Is Silent." *Loyola Law Review* 50: 675–709.

Crowley, Timothy P. F. 2002. "*Lofton v. Kearney:* The United States District Court for the Southern District of Florida Holds Florida's Statutory Ban on Gay Adoption Is Not Offensive to the Constitution." *Law and Sexuality: A Review of Lesbian, Gay, Bisexual, and Transgender Legal Issues* 11: 253–65.

Dahl, Robert, A. 1957. "Decision-Making in a Democracy: The Supreme Court as a National Policymaker." *Journal of Public Law* 6: 279–95.

Davies, Julie. 2002. "Assessing Institutional Responsibility for Sexual Harassment in Education." *Tulane Law Review* 77: 387–442.

DeGioia, John J. 2007. *Remarks as Delivered at Open Meeting on LGBTQ Student Resources.* Available at http://president.georgetown.edu/speeches/jjd10242007 .html

Delaney, Elizabeth A. 1991. "Statutory Protection of the Other Mother: Legally Recognizing the Relationship between the Nonbiological Lesbian Parent and Her Child." *Hastings Law Journal* 43: 177–216.

Duncan, William C. 2003. "In Whose Best Interests: Sexual Orientation and Adoption Law." *Capital University Law Review* 31: 787–802.

———. 2004. "The Litigation to Redefine Marriage: Equality and Social Meaning." *Brigham Young Journal of Public Law* 18: 623–63.

———. 2005. "The Role of Litigation in Gay Rights: The Marriage Experience." *St. Louis Law Review* 24: 113–27.

Duran-Aydintug, Candan, and Kelly A. Causey. 2001. "Child Custody Determination: Implications for Lesbian Mothers." In *The Gay and Lesbian Marriage and Family Reader,* edited by Jennifer M. Lehmann, 47–64. New York: Gordian Knot Books.

Egan, Patrick, Nathaniel Persily, and Kevin Wallsten. 2006. "Gay Marriage, Public Opinion and the Courts." Prepared for delivery at the annual meeting of the Midwest Political Science Association, April 20–23, Chicago.

Eisemann, Vanessa. 2000. "Protecting the Kids in the Hall: Using Title IX to Stop Student-on-Student Anti-Gay Harassment." *Berkeley Women's Law Journal* 15: 125–60.

Eisold, Barbara K. 2001. "Recreating Mother: The Consolidation of 'Heterosexual' Gender Identification in the Young Son of Homosexual Men." In *The Gay and Lesbian Marriage and Family Reader,* edited by Jennifer M. Lehmann, 221–38. New York: Gordian Knot Books.

Erera, Pauline I., and Karen Fredriksen. 2001. "Lesbian Stepfamilies: A Unique Family Structure." In *The Gay and Lesbian Marriage and Family Reader,* edited by Jennifer M. Lehmann, 80–94. New York: Gordian Knot Books.

Eskridge, William. 2002. *Equality Practice: Civil Unions and the Future of Gay Rights.* New York: Routledge.

Evan B. Donaldson Adoption Institute. 2008. *Expanding Resources for Waiting Children II: Eliminating Legal and Practice Barriers to Gay and Lesbian Adoption from Foster Care.* Available at http://www.adoptioninstitute.org/publications/2008 _09_Expanding_Resources_Legal.pdf

Evans, Carrie. 2004. *Equality from State to State: Gay, Lesbian, Bisexual and Transgender Americans and State Legislation.* Washington, D.C.: Human Rights Campaign Foundation. Available at http://www.hrc.org/Template .cfm?Section=About_HRC&Template=/ContentManagement/ContentDisplay. cfm&ContentID=24538

Fairchild, Betty, and Nancy Hayward. 1998. *Now That You Know: A Parents' Guide to Understanding Their Gay and Lesbian Children.* Orlando, FL: Harcourt.

Family Research Institute. 2008. *Our Mission.* Available at http://www.family researchinst.org/Home/tabid/36/Default.aspx

Fast, Carolyn. 2002. "Scouting Out Discrimination against the Discriminating Boy Scouts: Does Connecticut's Exclusion of the Boy Scouts from Its State Employee

Charitable Campaign Violate First Amendment Rights?" *Columbia Journal of Law and Social Problems* 35: 255–74.

Feiock, Katie. 2002. "The State to the Rescue: Using State Statutes to Protect Children from Peer Harassment in School." *Columbia Journal of Law and Social Problems* 35: 317–44.

Feldblum, Chai R. 1997. "The Moral Rhetoric of Legislation." *New York University Law Review* 72: 992–1008.

Fishel, Andrew, and Janice Pottker. 1977. *National Politics and Sex Discrimination in Education.* Lexington, Mass.: Lexington Books, 1977.

Fitzpatrick, Robert K. 2004. "Neither Icarus nor Ostrich: State Constitutions as an Independent Source of Individual Rights." *New York University Law Review* 79: 1833–72.

France, David. 2001. "Scouts Divided." *Newsweek*, August 6.

Frankowski, Barbara L. 2004. "Sexual Orientation and Adolescents." *Pediatrics* 113: 1827–32.

Friedman, Barry. 1998. "The History of the Countermajoritarian Difficulty, Part One: The Road to Judicial Supremacy." *New York University Law Review* 73: 333–433.

Gallup News Service. 2007. *Tolerance for Gay Rights at Highwater Mark.* Available by subscription only at http://www.galluppoll.com/content/?ci=27694

Gardner, Martin R. 2004. "Adoption by Homosexuals in the Wake of *Lawrence v. Texas.*" *Journal of Law and Family Studies* 6: 19–58.

Gates, G., L. M. V. Badgett, J. E. Macomber, and K. Chambers. 2007. *Adoption and Foster Care by Lesbian and Gay Parents in the United States.* Available at http://www.urban.org/publications/411437.html

Gavin, Meghan M. 2004. "The Domestic Partners Rights and Responsibilities Act of 2003: California Extends Significant Protections to Registered Domestic Partners and Their Families." *McGeorge Law Review* 35: 482–95.

Gay and Lesbian Advocates and Defenders. 2009. *Challenging Federal Marriage Discrimination.* Available at http://www. glad.org/doma/lawsuit

Gay, Lesbian and Straight Education Network. 2005a. *Fifteen Expensive Reasons Why Safe Schools Legislation Is in Your State's Best Interest.* Available at http://www.glsen.org/cgi-bin/iowa/all/library/record/1859.html

———. 2005b. *2004 State of the States Report: The First Objective Analysis of Statewide Safe Schools Policies.* Available at http://www.glsen.org/cgi-bin/iowa/all/library/record/1687.html

———. 2007a. *Colorado Attack Illustrates Need for Schools to Address Anti-LGBT Bias, Behavior.* Available at http://www.glsen.org/cgi-bin/iowa/all/library/record/2058.html

———. 2007b. *GLSEN Hails Signing of Comprehensive Safe Schools Bill in Iowa.* Available at http://www.glsen.org/cgi-bin/iowa/all/news/record/2042.html

———. 2007c. *GLSEN Releases Research Brief Showing Benefits of Gay-Straight Alliances.* Available at http://www.glsen.org/cgi-bin/iowa/all/news/record/2216.html

———. 2007d. *Rep. Sanchez Introduces Federal Bill to Protect Students from Bullying.* Available at http://www.glsen.org/cgi-bin/iowa/all/news/record/2175.html

———. 2007e. *Student Testifies before Michigan House Committee about Matt's Law.* Available at http://www.glsen.org/cgi-bin/iowa/all/library/record/2046.html

———. 2008. *Day of Silence 04.25.08, 2008.* Available at http://www.glsen.org/cgi-bin/iowa/all/news/record/2291.html

Gerstmann, Evan. 2003. *The Constitutional Underclass: Gays, Lesbians, and the Failure of Class-Based Equal Protection.* Chicago: University of Chicago Press.

Gesing, Erica. 2004. "The Fight to Be a Parent: How Courts Have Restricted the Constitutionally-Based Challenges Available to Homosexuals." *New England Law Review* 38: 841–96.

Glidden, Melissa A. 2004. "Recent Development: Federal Marriage Amendment." *Harvard Journal on Legislation* 41: 483–99.

Goodman, Marissa L. 1999. "A Scout Is Morally Straight, Brave, Clean, Trustworthy . . . and Heterosexual? Gays in the Boy Scouts of America." *Hofstra Law Review* 27: 825–90.

Grattan, Regina M. 1999. "It's Not Just for Religion Anymore: Expanding the Protections of the Equal Access Act to Gay, Lesbian, and Bisexual High School Students." *George Washington Law Review* 67: 577–99.

Green, Boaz. I. 2004. "Discussion and Expression of Gender and Sexuality in Schools." *Georgetown Journal of Gender and the Law* 5: 329–41.

Greenberg, Julie A. 1999. "Defining Male and Female: Intersexuality and the Collision between Law and Biology." *Arizona Law Review* 41: 265–328.

Griffith, Sean. 2006. "Leave Those Kids Alone: Why the First Amendment Does Not Protect the Boy Scouts of America in Its Discrimination against Gay Youth Members." *American University Modern American* 2: 8–11.

Grodin, Joseph H. 2009. "On Amending and Revising the Constitution: The Issues behind the Challenge to Proposition 8." *California Journal of Politics and Policy.* Available at http://www.bepress.com/cjpp/vol1/iss1/13

Gunther, Gerald. 1972. "The Supreme Court, 1971 Term—Foreword: In Search of Evolving Doctrine on a Changing Court: A Model for a Newer Equal Protection." *Harvard Law Review* 86: 1–48.

Harris Interactive and Gay, Lesbian, and Straight Education Network. 2005. *From Teasing to Torment: School Climate in America, a Survey of Students and Teachers.* Available at http://www.glsen.org/binary-data/GLSEN_ATTACHMENTS/file/499-1.pdf

Harris, Nicolyn, and Maurice R. Dyson. 2004. "Safe Rules or Gays' Schools? The Dilemma of Sexual Orientation Segregation in Public Education." *University of Pennsylvania Journal of Constitutional Law* 7: 183–214.

Harvard Law Review Association. 2003. "Developments in the Law: IV. Changing Realities of Parenthood: The Law's Response to the Evolving American Family and Emerging Reproductive Technologies." *Harvard Law Review* 116: 2052–74.

Hawaii State Judiciary. 2008. Available at http://www.courts.state.hi.us/page_server/Courts/Supreme/Justices/5FCA912B84259E92EBD80CFEF5.html

Henigan, Patrick. 1996. "Is Parental Authority Absolute? Public High Schools Which Provide Gay and Lesbian Youth Services Do Not Violate the Constitutional Childrearing Right of Parents." *Brooklyn Law Review* 62: 1261–91.

Hillygus, D. Sunshine, and Todd G. Shields. 2005. "Moral Issues and Voter Decision Making in the 2004 Presidential Election." *PS: Political Science and Politics* 38: 201–9.

Holland, Maurice J. 1998. "The Modest Usefulness of DOMA Section 2." *Creighton Law Review* 32: 395–408.

Holtzman, Mellisa. 2006. "Definitions of the Family as an Impetus for Legal Change in Custody Decision Making: Suggestions from an Empirical Case Study." *Law and Social Inquiry* 31: 1–31.

Hong, Kari E. 2003. "Parens Patriarchy: Adoption, Eugenics, and Same-Sex Couples." *California Western Law Review* 40: 1–77.

Hughes, Jean, and Merry Moiseichik. 2003. "Expressive Association: The Right of a Congressionally Chartered Membership Organization to Discriminate." *Journal of Legal Aspects of Sport* 13: 305–18.

Human Rights Campaign. 2006. *Custody and Visitation Laws: State by State.* Available at http://www.hrc.org/PrinterTemplate.cfm?Section=Custody_Visitation&CONTENTID=20488&TEMPLATE=/TaggedPage/TaggedPageDisplay.cfm&TPLID=66

———. 2007a. *Parenting Laws: Joint Adoption.* Available at http://www.hrc.org/Template.cfm?Section=Get_Informed3&Template=/ContentManagement/ContentDisplay.cfm&ContentID=16302

———. 2007b. *Parenting Laws: Second-Parent Adoption.* Available at http://www.hrc.org/Template.cfm?Section=Get_Informed3&Template=/ContentManagement/ContentDisplay.cfm&ContentID=16302

———. 2007c. *Statewide Laws or Policies Affecting Schools & Educational Institutions.* Available at http://www.hrc.org/documents/schoollaws20060928(1).pdf

———. 2008a. *Proposed State Constitutional Amendments.* Available at http://www.hrc.org/documents/amendments_pending.pdf

———. 2008b. *Relationship Recognition in the U.S.* Available at http://www.hrc.org/documents/Relationship_Recognition_Laws_Map.pdf

———. 2008c. *Statewide Marriage Prohibitions.* Available at http://www.hrc.org/documents/marriage_prohibitions.pdf

———. 2009a. *About Us.* Available at http://www.hrc.org/about_us/index.htm

———. 2009b. *California Supreme Court Takes Step Back from Equality.* Available at http://www.hrc.org/12755.htm

Human Rights Watch. 2001. *Hatred in the Hallways: Violence and Discrimination against Lesbian, Gay, Bisexual, and Transgender Students in U.S. Schools.* Available at http://www.hrw.org/reports/pdfs/c/crd/usalbg01.pdf

Hutchinson, Darren Lenard. 2005. "The Majoritarian Difficulty: Affirmative Action, Sodomy, and Supreme Court Politics." *Law and Inequality* 23: 1–93.

Infanti, Anthony C. 2007. *Everyday Law for Gays and Lesbians.* Boulder, Colo.: Paradigm Publishers.

Jozwiak, Christopher D. 2005. "*Lofton v. Secretary of the Department of Children & Family Services*: Florida's Gay Adoption Ban under Irrational Equal Protection Analysis." *Law and Inequality* 23: 407–28.

Judicial Council of California. 2008. *News Release: California Supreme Court Takes Action on Proposition 8.* Available at http://www.courtinfo.ca.gov/presscenter/newsreleases/NR66-08.PDF

———. 2009. *News Release: Supreme Court to Hear Oral Arguments in Prop 8 Cases on March 5, 2009.* Available at http://www.courtinfo.ca.gov/presscenter/newsreleases/NR08-09.PDF

Keck, Thomas M. 2009. "Beyond Backlash: Assessing the Impact of Judicial Decisions on LGBT Rights." *Law and Society Review* 43: 151–86.

Kelly, Scott. 2002. "Scouts' (Dis)Honor: The Supreme Court Allows the Boy Scouts of America to Discriminate against Homosexuals in *Boy Scouts of America v. Dale*." *Houston Law Review* 39: 243–74.

Klarman, Michael J. 2005. "*Brown and Lawrence (and Goodridge)*." *Michigan Law Review* 104: 431–89.

Koppelman, Andrew. 1996. "Same-Sex Marriage and Public Policy: The Miscegenation Precedents." *Quinnipiac Law Review* 16: 105–34.

———. 2004. "Case Studies in Conservative and Progressive Legal Orders: Should Noncommercial Associations Have an Absolute Right to Discriminate?" *Law and Contemporary Problems* 67: 27–57.

———. 2005. "Recognition and Enforcement of Same-Sex Marriage: Interstate Recognition of Same-Sex Marriages and Civil Unions: A Handbook for Judges." *University of Pennsylvania Law Review* 153: 2143–94.

Kosciw, Joseph G., and Elizabeth M. Diaz. 2006. *The 2005 National School Climate Survey: The Experiences of Lesbian, Gay, Bisexual and Transgender Youth in Our Nation's Schools*. Available at http://www.glsen.org/binary-data/GLSEN_ATTACHMENTS/file/585-1.pdf

Kosciw, Joseph G., Elizabeth M. Diaz, and Emily A. Greytak. 2008. *The 2007 National School Climate Survey: The Experiences of Lesbian, Gay, Bisexual and Transgender Youth in Our Nation's Schools*. Available at http://www.glsen.org/binary-data/GLSEN_ATTACHMENTS/file/000/001/1290-1.pdf

Kramer, Larry D. 2004. "Popular Constitutionalism, circa 2004." *California Law Review* 92: 959–1011.

Krasnoo, Ethan M. 2006. "Foster Care and Adoption." *Georgetown Journal of Gender and the Law* 7: 999–1016.

Kubasek, Nancy K., Alex Frondorf, and Kevin J. Minnick. 2004. "Civil Union Statutes: A Shortcut to Legal Equality for Same-Sex Partners in a Landscape Littered with Defense of Marriage Acts." *Florida Journal of Law and Public Policy* 25: 229–59.

Lambda Legal. 2000. *Students and Salt Lake City School Board End Feud over Gay-Supportive Clubs*. Available at http://www.lambdalegal.org/news/pr/students-and-salt-lake-city.html

———. 2002. *Facts: Gay and Lesbian Youth in Schools*. Available at http://www.lambdalegal.org/our-work/publications/facts-backgrounds/page.jsp?itemID=31991643

———. 2003. *The Impact of the Boy Scouts of America Anti-Gay Discrimination*. Available at http://www.lambdalegal.org/our-work/publications/facts-backgrounds/page.jsp?itemID=31989419

———. 2005. *Proposed Antigay Texas Law Is Unconstitutional and Harmful to Children in Foster Care, Lambda Legal Says*. Available at http://www.lambdalegal.org/news/pr/proposed-antigay-texas-law-is.html

———. 2007a. *Adoption and Parenting*. Available at http://www.lambdalegal.org/our-work/issues/marriage-relationships-family/parenting

———. 2007b. *Celebrating Recent LGBT Legislative Advances*. Available at http://www.lambdalegal.org/our-work/publications/facts-backgrounds/recent-lgbt-advances.html

———. 2008. *California Will Continue to Honor Marriages of Same-Sex Couples Who Married before the Possible Passage of Prop 8.* Available at http://www.lambdalegal.org/news/pr/california-will-continue.html

Larsen, Matt. 2004. "*Lawrence v. Texas* and Family Law: Gay Parents' Constitutional Rights in Child Custody Proceedings." *New York University Annual Survey of American Law* 60: 53–96.

Lauretta, Diana. 2003. "Protecting the Child's Best Interest: Defending Second-Parent Adoptions Granted Prior to the 2002 Enactment of California Assembly Bill 25." *Golden Gate University Law Review* 33: 173–205.

LeBlanc, Jeff. 2006. "My Two Moms: An Analysis of the Status of Homosexual Adoption and the Challenges to Its Acceptance." *Journal of Juvenile Law* 2006: 96–107.

Lee, Eugene C. 1991. "The Revision of California's Constitution." *CPS Brief: A Publication of the California Policy Seminar.* Available at http://www.ucop.edu/cprc/documents/caconst.pdf

Letter Supporting Review. 2002. *Southern California Review of Law and Women's Studies* 11: 449–59.

Levchuk, Karen. 2008. "Civil Unions—Considerations for New Hampshire Employers as the Rights of Marriage Are Extended to Civil Union Partners and Their Dependents." *New Hampshire Bar Journal* 49: 10–16.

Lewis, Gregory B., and Jonathan Edelson. 2000. "DOMA and ENDA: Congress Votes on Gay Rights." In *The Politics of Gay Rights,* edited by Craig A. Rimmerman, Kenneth D. Wald, and Clyde Wilcox, 193–216. Chicago: University of Chicago Press.

Lewis, Gregory L. 2005. "Same Sex Marriage and the 2004 Presidential Election." *PS: Political Science and Politics* 38: 195–99.

Lim, Karen. 2003. "Freedom to Exclude after *Boy Scouts of America v. Dale*: Do Private Schools Have a Right to Discriminate against Homosexual Teachers?" *Fordham Law Review* 71: 2599–642.

Lovell, Amy. 1998. "Other Students Always Used to Say, 'Look at the Dykes': Protecting Students from Peer Sexual Orientation Harassment." *California Law Review* 86: 617–51.

Lynch, John. 2009. *Statement Regarding Same-Sex Marriage Legislation.* Available at http://www.governor.nh.gov/news/2009/051409same.html

Mallon, Gerald P. 2006. *Lesbian and Gay Foster and Adoptive Parents: Recruiting, Assessing, and Supporting an Untapped Resource for Children and Youth.* Washington, D.C.: Child Welfare League of America.

Manternach, Maggie. 2005. "Where Is My Other Mommy?: Applying the Presumed Father Provision of the Uniform Parentage Act to Recognize the Rights of Lesbian Mothers and Their Children." *Journal of Gender, Race, and Justice* 9: 385–417.

Massachusetts Court System. 2006. Available at http://www.mass.gov/courts/courtsandjudges/courts/supremejudicialcourt/about.html

Maurer, Elizabeth L. 2006. "Errors That Won't Happen Twice: A Constitutional Glance at a Proposed Texas Statute That Will Ban Homosexuals from Foster Parent Eligibility." *Appalachian Journal of Law* 5: 171–93.

Maxwell, Nancy G., and Richard Donner. 2006. "The Psychological Consequences of Judicially Imposed Closets in Child Custody and Visitation Disputes Involving Gay or Lesbian Parents." *William and Mary Journal of Women and Law* 13: 305–48.

Mayes, Thomas A. 2001. "Confronting Same-Sex, Student-to-Student Sexual Harassment: Recommendations for Educators and Policy Makers." *Fordham Law Review* 29: 641–82.

McCarthy, Martha. 2001. "Students as Targets and Perpetrators of Sexual Harassment: Title IX and Beyond." *Hastings Women's Law Journal* 12: 177–214.

Meezan, William, and Jonathan Rauch. 2005. "Gay Marriage, Same-Sex Parenting, and America's Children." *The Future of Children* 15: 97–115.

Menand, Louis. 2004. "Permanent Fatal Errors: Did the Voters Send a Message?" *New Yorker*, December 6.

Meyer, David D. 2004. "Domesticating *Lawrence*." *University of Chicago Legal Forum* 2004: 453–93.

Mezey, Susan Gluck. 1983. "Judicial Interpretation of Legislative Intent: The Role of the Supreme Court in the Implication of Private Rights of Action." *Rutgers Law Review* 36: 53–89.

———. 2007. *Queers in Court: Gay Rights Law and Public Policy.* Lanham, Md.: Rowman & Littlefield.

Miller, Kenneth P. 2005. "Anatomy of a Backlash: The Response to *Goodridge v. Dept. Of Public Health.*" Paper presented at the annual meeting of the American Political Science Association, September 1–4, Washington, D.C.

Miller, Mark C. 2006. "Conflicts between the Massachusetts Supreme Judicial Court and the Legislature: Campaign Finance and Same-Sex Marriage." *Pierce Law Review* 4: 279–316.

Milligan, Heather L. 2002. "The Influence of Religion and Morality Legislation on the Interpretation of Second-Parent Adoption Statutes: Are the California Courts Establishing a Religion?" *California Western Law Review* 39: 137–62.

Mishler, William, and Reginald S. Sheehan. 1993. "The Supreme Court as a Countermajoritarian Institution? The Impact of Public Opinion on Supreme Court Decisions." *American Political Science Review* 87: 87–101.

Mucciaroni, Gary. 2008. *Same Sex Different Politics: Success and Failure in the Struggles over Gay Rights.* Chicago: University of Chicago Press.

Moss, Susan M. 2005. "*McGriff v. McGriff*: Consideration of a Parent's Sexual Orientation in Child Custody Disputes." *Idaho Law Review* 41: 593–644.

Mostoller, Lynn. 2003. "Freedom of Speech and Freedom from Student-on-Student Sexual Harassment in Public Schools: The Nexus between *Tinker v. Des Moines Independent Community School District* and *Davis v. Monroe County Board of Education.*" *New Mexico Law Review* 33: 533–63.

National Center for Lesbian Rights. 2000. *Fact Sheet: Custody Cases.* Available at http://nclrights.org/publications/custody.htm

———. 2003. *Second Parent Adoptions: A Snapshot of Current Law.* Available at http://www.nclrights.org/publications/pubs/2pa0803.pdf

———. 2004. *Adoption by Lesbian, Gay and Bisexual Parents: An Overview of Current Law.* Available at http://nclrights.org/publications/adptn0204.htm

———. 2006. *State by State List of Custody Cases Involving Same-Sex Partners.* Available at http://nclrights.org/publications/states_custodycases.htm

National Conference of State Legislatures. 2008. *Timeline—Same Sex Marriage.* Available at http://www.ncsl.org/programs/cyf/samesextime.htm

National Gay and Lesbian Task Force. 2007. *Second-Parent Adoptions Laws in the U.S.* Available at http://www.thetaskforce.org/downloads/reports/issue _maps/2nd_parent_adoption_5_07_color.pdf

Nelson, Christine. 2008. *Civil Unions and Domestic Partnership Statutes.* Available at http://www.ncsl.org/programs/cyf/civilunions_domesticpartnership _statutes.htm

New Jersey Court System. 2008. Available at http://www.judiciary.state.nj.us/ process.htm#three

Newman, Bernie Sue, and Peter Gerard Muzzonigro. 2001. "The Effects of Traditional Family Values on the Coming Out Process of Gay Male Adolescents." In *The Gay and Lesbian Marriage and Family Reader*, edited by Jennifer M. Lehmann, 65–79. New York: Gordian Knot Books.

Niemczyk, Brian N. 2005. "*Baker v. Nelson* Revisited: Is Same-Sex Marriage Coming to Minnesota?" *Hamline Law Review* 28: 425–64.

Nolan, Laurence C. 1998. "The Meaning of *Loving*: Marriage, Due Process and Equal Protection (1967–1990) as Equality and Marriage, from *Loving* to *Zablocki*." *Howard Law Journal* 41: 245–70.

Office of the Attorney General. 2008. *Attorney General Brown Urges California Supreme Court to Invalidate Proposition 8.* Available at http://ag.ca.gov/news alerts/release.php?id=1642

Orman, Sarah. 2006. "'Being Gay in Lubbock': The Equal Access Act in *Caudillo*." *Hastings Women's Law Journal* 17: 227–48.

Oswald, Ramona Faith. 2001. "Family and Friendship Relationships after Young Women Come Out as Bisexual or Lesbian." In *The Gay and Lesbian Marriage and Family Reader*, edited by Jennifer M. Lehmann, 149–70. New York: Gordian Knot Books.

Patterson, Charlotte J. 1995. "Adoption of Minor Children by Lesbian and Gay Adults: A Social Science Perspective." *Duke Journal of Gender Law and Policy* 2: 191–205.

Pearlman, Elyse. 1982. "*Lieberman v. University of Chicago*: Implying Remedies for Implied Causes of Action." *John Marshall Law Review* 16: 153–63.

Pearson, Jennifer, Chandra Muller, and Lindsey Wilkinson. 2006. "Adolescent Same-Sex Attraction and Academic Outcomes: The Role of School Attachment and Engagement." *Social Problems* 54: 523–42.

Perrin, Ellen C. 2002. "Technical Report: Coparent or Second-Parent Adoption by Same-Sex Parents." *Pediatrics* 109: 341–44.

Peterson, Kavan. 2004. *50-State Rundown on Gay Marriage Laws.* Available at http://www.stateline.org/live/ViewPage.action?siteNodeId=137&languageId =1&contentId=15576

Peterson, Nancy. 1983. "*Lieberman v. University of Chicago*: Refusal to Imply a Damages Remedy under Title IX of the Education Amendments of 1972." *Wisconsin Law Review* 1983: 181–210.

Pew Research Center for the People and the Press. 2006. *Less Opposition to Gay Marriage, Adoption and Military Service.* Available at http://people-press.org/ reports/print.php3?PageID=1043

Pierceson, Jason. 2005. *Courts, Liberalism, and Rights: Gay Law and Politics in the United States and Canada.* Philadelphia: Temple University Press.

Pinello, Daniel R. 2003. *Gay Rights and American Law.* Cambridge: Cambridge University Press.

Polikoff, Nancy. 1990. "This Child Does Have Two Mothers: Redefining Parenthood to Meet the Needs of Children in Lesbian-Mother and Other Nontraditional Families." *Georgetown Law Journal* 78: 459–575.

———. 1997. "Resisting 'Don't Ask Don't Tell' in the Licensing of Lesbian and Gay Foster Parents: Why Openness Will Benefit Lesbian and Gay Youth." *Hastings Law Journal* 48: 1183–93.

———. 2001. "The Impact of *Troxel v. Granville* on Lesbian and Gay Parents." *Rutgers Law Journal* 32: 825–55.

Pollack, Sandra, and Jeanne Vaughn. 1987. *Politics of the Heart: A Lesbian Parenting Anthology.* Ithaca, N.Y.: Firebrand Books.

PollingReport.com. 2008. *Law and Civil Rights.* Available at http://www.pollingreport.com/civil.htm

Popkin, William D. 1999. *Statutes in Court: The History and Theory of Statutory Interpretation.* Durham, N.C.: Duke University Press.

Pratt, Carolyn. 2007. "Protecting the Marketplace of Ideas in the Classroom: Why the Equal Access Act and the First Amendment Require the Recognition of Gay/Straight Alliances in America's Public Schools." *First Amendment Law Review* 5: 370–99.

Quinnipiac University Polling Institute. 2009. *April 30, 2009—Gays in the Military Should Be Allowed to Come Out, U.S. Voters Tell Quinnipiac University National Poll: Key Is Belief That Being Gay Is by Choice or by Birth.* Available at http://www.quinnipiac.edu/x1295.xml?ReleaseID=1292

Rankin, Susan R. 2003. *Campus Climate for Gay, Lesbian, Bisexual, and Transgender People: A National Perspective.* New York: National Gay and Lesbian Task Force Policy Institute.

Reding, Ann M. 2003. "*Lofton v. Kearney*: Equal Protection Mandates Equal Adoption Rights." *U.C. Davis Law Review* 36: 1285–312.

Reuveni, Erez. 2006. "On Boy Scouts and Anti-Discrimination Law: The Associational Rights of Quasi-Religious Organizations." *Boston University Law Review* 86: 109–71.

Richmond, Diana. 2005. "Parentage by Intention for Same-Sex Partners." *Journal of the Center for Families, Children, and the Courts* 6: 125–35.

Rimmerman, Craig A. 2000. "Beyond Political Mainstreaming: Reflections on Lesbian and Gay Organizations and the Grassroots." In *The Politics of Gay Rights,* edited by Craig A. Rimmerman, Kenneth D. Wald, and Clyde Wilcox, 54–78. Chicago: University of Chicago Press.

Robson, Ruthann. 2001. "Our Children: Kids of Queer Parents and Kids Who Are Queer: Looking at Sexual Minority Rights from a Different Perspective." *Albany Law Review* 64: 915–48.

Roper Center for Public Opinion Research. 2009. *Third Way Marriage Equality Survey.* Available by subscription only at http://www.ropercenter.uconn.edu/ipoll.html

Rosato, Jennifer L. 2006. "Children of Same-Sex Parents Deserve the Security Blanket of the Parentage Presumption." *Family Court Review* 44: 74–82.

Rosenberg, Gerald N. 2008. *The Hollow Hope: Can Courts Bring About Social Change?* Rev. ed. Chicago: University of Chicago Press.

Safier, Kristen. 2000. "A Request for Congressional Action: Deconstructing the Supreme Court's (In)activism in *Gebser v. Lago Vista Independent School District*, 118 S. Ct. 1989 (1998) and *Davis v. Monroe County Board of Education*, 119 S. Ct. 1661 (1999)." *University of Cincinnati Law Review* 68: 1309–29.

Savage, David. 1999. "Look the Other Way and Pay: Schools Are Liable for 'Deliberate Indifference' to Student-on-Student Sexual Harassment." *American Bar Association Journal* 85: 34.

Scaparotti, Linda M. 2002. "Fighting to Be a Family: Lesbian and Gay Adoption Issues in California." *San Francisco Attorney* 34–38.

Schacter, Jane S. 2000. "Constructing Families in a Democracy: Courts, Legislatures and Second-Parent Adoption." *Chicago-Kent Law Review* 75: 933–50.

Sedgwick, Eve Kosofsky. 1993. "How to Bring Your Kids Up Gay." In *Fear of a Queer Planet: Queer Politics and Social Theory*, edited by Michael Warner, 69–79. Minneapolis: University of Minnesota Press.

Shapiro, Julie. 1999. "A Lesbian-Centered Critique of Second-Parent Adoptions." *Berkeley Women's Law Journal* 14: 17–39.

Skidmore, Kif. 2000–2001. "A Family Affair: Constitutional and Prudential Interests Implicated When Homosexuals Seek to Preserve or Create Parent-Child Relationships." *Kentucky Law Journal* 89: 1227–64.

So, Suyin. 2002. "Sexual Harassment in Education." *Georgetown Journal of Gender and the Law* 4: 351–68.

Spector, Robert G. 2005. "The Unconstitutionality of Oklahoma's Statute Denying Recognition to Adoptions by Same-Sex Couples from Other States." *Tulsa Law Review* 40: 467–80.

Sponseller, Carrie Urrutia. 2001. "Peer Sexual Harassment in Light of *Davis v. Monroe County Board of Education*: A Successful Balance or Tipping the Scales?" *University of Toledo Law Review* 32: 271–91.

Stacey, Judith, and Timothy J. Biblarz. 2001. "(How) Does the Sexual Orientation of Parents Matter?" *American Sociological Review* 66: 159–83.

Starr, Karla J. 1998. "Adoption by Homosexuals: A Look at Differing State Court Opinions." *Arizona Law Review* 40: 1497–513.

State of Connecticut. 2006. *Judicial Branch*. Available at http://www.jud.state .ct.us/Publications/es201.pdf

Stauss, David M. 2004. "The End or Just the Beginning for Gay Rights under the New Jersey Constitution? The New Jersey Domestic Partnership Act, *Lewis v. Harris*, and the Future of Gay Rights in New Jersey." *Rutgers Law Journal* 36: 289–348.

Steely, Victoria. 2007. "The Parent/Child Relationship: . . . But a Child Can Have Two Mothers." *Journal of Contemporary Legal Issues* 16: 35–42.

Stoddard, Tom. 1997. "Bleeding Heart: Reflections on Using the Law to Make Social Change." *New York University Law Review* 72: 967–91.

Storrow, Richard F. 2006. "Rescuing Children from the Marriage Movement: The Case against Marital Status Discrimination in Adoption and Assisted Reproduction." *U.C. Davis Law Review* 39: 305–70.

Strasser, Mark. 2004. "Adoption and the Best Interests of the Child: On the Use and Abuse of Studies." *New England Law Review* 38: 629–42.

———. 2005. "The Legislative Backlash to Advances in Rights for Same-Sex

Couples: Rebellion in the Eleventh Circuit: On *Lawrence, Lofton,* and the Best Interests of Children." *Tulsa Law Review* 40: 421–42.

Sungalia, Mary-Christine. 2002. "On the Cutting Edge: As Pending Supreme Court Cases concerning Contraceptive Coverage and Second-Parent Adoption Show, California Continues to Be at the Forefront of the Law." *Southern California Review of Law and Women's Studies* 11: 399–405.

Supreme Court of California. 2007. Available at http://www.courtinfo.ca.gov/courts/supreme/about.htm

———. 2008. *Supreme Court Orders: S168047/S168066/S168078.* Available at http://www.courtinfo.ca.gov/courts/supreme/highprofile/documents/S168047_S168066_S168078-11-19-08_ORDER.pdf

———. 2009. *Supreme Court Orders: S168047/S168066/S168078.* Available at http://www.courtinfo.ca.gov/courts/supreme/highprofile/documents/feb_order.pdf

Susoeff, Steve. 1985. "Assessing Children's Best Interests When a Parent Is Gay or Lesbian: Toward a Rational Custody Standard." *UCLA Law Review* 32: 852–923.

Swisher, Peter Nash, and Nancy Douglas Cook. 2001. "*Bottoms v. Bottoms*: In Whose Best Interest? Analysis of a Lesbian Mother Child Custody Dispute." In *The Gay and Lesbian Marriage and Family Reader,* edited by Jennifer M. Lehmann, 251–99. New York: Gordian Knot Books.

The Voice. 2009. *Gay Activists File Suit Want Judge to Overturn Marriage Act.* Available at http://www.thevoicemagazine.com/headline-news/479-gay-activists-file-suit-want-judge-to-overturn-marriage-act.html

Troum, Neal. 2002. "Expressive Association and the Right to Exclude: Reading between the Lines in *Boy Scouts of America v. Dale*." *Creighton Law Review* 35: 641–91.

Turbe, Laura A. 2003. "Florida's Inconsistent Use of the Best Interests of the Child Standard." *Stetson Law Review* 33: 369–99.

Tushnet, Mark. 1999. *Taking the Constitution Away from the Courts.* Princeton, N.J.: Princeton University Press.

Underwood, Montre. 1999. "*Gebser v. Lago Vista Independent School District*: The Supreme Court Adopts Actual Knowledge Standard as Basis for School District's Liability under Title IX." *Tulane Law Review* 73: 2181–93.

U.S. Bureau of the Census. 2003. *Married-Couple and Unmarried-Partner Households: 2000.* Available at http://www.census.gov/prod/2003pubs/censr-5.pdf

U.S. Department of Education, Office for Civil Rights. 2001. *Revised Sexual Harassment Guidance: Harassment of Students by School Employees, Other Students, or Third Parties Title IX.* Available at http://www.ed.gov/about/offices/list/ocr/docs/shguide.html

Upton, Russell J. 2001. "Bob Jonesing, Baden-Powell: Fighting the Boy Scouts of America's Discriminatory Practices by Revoking Its State-level Tax-Exempt Status." *American University Law Review* 50: 793–858.

Vaid, Urvashi. 1995. *Virtual Equality: The Mainstreaming of Gay and Lesbian Liberation.* New York: Anchor Books.

Vermont Supreme Court. 2008. Available at http://www.vermontjudiciary.org/courts/supreme/SupremeBrochure.htm

Wald, Jenny. 2005. "Legitimate Parents: Construing California's Uniform Parentage Act to Protect Children Born into Nontraditional Families." *Journal of the Center for Families, Children, and the Courts* 6: 139–57.

Wald, Kenneth D. 2000. "The Context of Gay Politics." In *The Politics of Gay Rights*, edited by Craig A. Rimmerman, Kenneth D. Wald, and Clyde Wilcox, 1–28. Chicago: University of Chicago Press.

Walker, Becky S. 1999. "Practice Tips: *Davis* Puts Schools on Notice about Student-On-Student Harassment." *Los Angeles Lawyer* 22: 15–43.

Wardle, Lynn D. 1998. "*Loving v. Virginia* and The Constitutional Right to Marry." *Howard Law Journal* 41: 289–347.

———. 2003. "Preference for Marital Couple Adoption—Constitutional and Policy Reflections." *Journal of Law and Family Studies* 5: 345–88.

———. 2004. "Considering the Impacts on Children and Society of 'Lesbigay' Parenting." *Quinnipiac Law Review* 23: 541–75.

———. 2005. "The 'Inner Lives' of Children in Lesbigay Adoption: Narratives and Other Concerns." *St. Thomas Law Review* 18: 511–42.

Wright, Susan. 1992. "*Franklin v. Gwinnett County Public Schools*: The Supreme Court Implies a Damage Remedy for Title IX Sex Discrimination." *Vanderbilt Law Review* 45: 1367–86.

Cases

Cases

✛

Index

About the Author

Susan Gluck Mezey is professor of political science and department chair at Loyola University Chicago. She publishes in the area of the courts and social reform policymaking; her recent publications include *Queers in Court: Gay Rights Law and Public Policy* (2007), *Disabling Interpretations: Judicial Implementation of the Americans with Disabilities Act* (2005), *Elusive Equality: Women's Rights, Public Policy, and the Law* (2003), and *Pitiful Plaintiffs: Child Welfare Litigation and the Federal Courts* (2000). She has a J.D. from DePaul University and a Ph.D. from Syracuse University and teaches courses on constitutional law and public policy.

03/10